Contents

Part Four   Insurance

Part Five   Final Facts

Preface

Today, modern science and technology make it possible for Americans to live longer, healthier lives. The good news is that at retirement, the average person can now expect to live another twenty to thirty years. The bad news is that for those extra years, you will need additional money. Those extra years also mean that inflation, taxes, and health care will have more time to erode your resources. Your goal in retirement planning, therefore, should be to make certain that your assets last as long as you do. This is a complex task and few are armed for it.

To plan properly requires knowledge of financial planning, the very heart of successful retirement. In addition, successful planning involves some knowledge of pensions and Social Security, of life and health insurance, of basic legal considerations, and of housing options. Finally, we all need to know how to plan realistically to make it easier to cope with life's inevitable losses.

Over the years, while serving as an officer of a welfare fund, I had the opportunity to observe individuals approaching retirement. In most cases, they are unaware of the basic considerations relating to retirement until the reality is upon them. These people seldom recognize

that thinking and planning ahead can make the difference between a successful retirement and one marred by faulty decisions. This is true even for those who consider themselves knowledgeable in the field.

Many books currently on the market attempt to supply necessary information, but a review of these works indicates that many of them fail to grapple with the central issues. In some, the coverage is cursory; in others, encyclopedic. Some completely omit important components of a practical retirement plan or are out of date. Many have no index, depriving the reader of a convenient way to locate specific information. To overcome these weaknesses, I have sought to cover the major areas in sufficient depth to provide the reader with a clear understanding of the issues.

Various chapters in *Retiring Right* delve into specific retirement concerns: the roles of work and leisure in retirement; budgeting; sources of income such as Social Security, pensions, savings, investments, life insurance, and annuities. Medical concerns—Medicare, Medicaid, and health insurance—as well as housing options and legal affairs (property ownership, second and late marriages, and choosing and using a lawyer) are also explained. Rounding out the coverage are chapters on estate planning, nursing homes, and funeral arrangements. In addition, technical words and terms are defined in a glossary at the end of each chapter. Most important, *Retiring Right* offers you, the reader, the opportunity to personalize the material through self-study. Each chapter provides self-study sections and worksheets that enable you to develop an individual retirement program. Such interaction between book and reader is also provided in Appendix A, which will help you to set up an inventory of personal and financial data. Further opportunity for personalization is provided by Appendix B, a list of resources, and Appendix C, a selected bibliography.

Thinking and planning ahead can make a significant difference in your future. To enjoy the good life after retirement, it is essential that you plan for it. What follows will help you to achieve that goal.

Introduction

Why plan for retirement? If you are under 55, you probably have not given much thought to retirement. You see getting old as something that happens to other people. You tell yourself that you will plan for retirement when the time comes, that there is no need to think about it now.

This is wrong thinking! If you want the so-called golden years of your life to be truly golden, you must prepare for them now. The sooner you get started and the more you investigate and understand your situation, the better your retirement will be. Planning for your retirement will enable you to reach the following goals:

■ *Eliminate fear and uncertainty, and achieve a sense of security.* Many people approach retirement with fear and trepidation. This is quite natural because most people fear the unknown. Thinking about the future and planning for it will allow you to reach the retirement stage of your life with knowledge and preparation. The unknown will become known, and the fear and uncertainty of retirement will be replaced with a sense of security.

■ *Prepare for the unexpected.* As you move along in life, problems constantly present themselves. Without a plan that looks into the future, you tackle each crisis in a purely haphazard manner. If you plan ahead, however, you will not be thrown by an unexpected problem such as an illness in the family or a downturn in the economy that affects your savings or investments. You will be better able to cope with the difficulty and make the necessary adjustments.

■ *Gain flexibility.* By starting your planning early, you will have enough lead time to prepare for the things that you want to do when you retire. You will have time to prepare for a second career, if you want one, or to learn a new hobby or sport. If you change your mind about your choice, you will have enough time to modify your plan and try something else.

■ *Make the right decisions.* If you plan for retirement, you will not have to make hasty, ill-considered decisions. For example, housing plays a large role in shaping retirement. By investigating numerous housing locations and living arrangements during your pre-retirement years, you will be able to base your retirement housing decision on a seasoned judgment.

Each of us approaches retirement with different needs, interests, and attitudes. The goal of all of us, however, is successful retirement. That means a sound financial plan, psychological and social stability, and stimulating and satisfying activities that provide a sense of accomplishment and a feeling of usefulness. The purpose of this book is to help you develop a total, individualized retirement plan that will generate maximum satisfaction, security, and fulfillment.

First Facts About Retirement and Planning

What is retirement? Retirement can be defined as a withdrawal from one's office, service, or business that brings with it a lifestyle that is less structured and offers more free time. If we assume that the life cycle consists of four stages—childhood, the teen years, the mature years, and the retirement years—then the retirement years are the culmination of the mature years, which are also the working years. At this stage of the life cycle, an individual can reach the highest level of development, when he or she can harvest and enjoy the fruits of a lifetime of labor. Or this period can plunge a person into boredom, restlessness, depression, or even despair.

WHO ARE THE RETIREES?

Our youth-oriented society generates many misconceptions about the 65-and-older population, which is usually retired. These myths are so pervasive that many older people accept them as truisms. Popular myths include the following: Most older people live in old-age homes, nursing homes, or mental hospitals. As a group, older people are lonely, socially isolated, bored, and no longer able to enjoy life. If they have jobs, the jobs are unproductive. The elderly cannot learn new things. And, in terms of economic status, they are the most poverty-stricken group in the country. Are these allegations true? Not at all, as you will see by the following description of Americans age 65 and over.

Numbers

The total population of the United States was estimated to be 261 million in 1994. Based on the Census Bureau's latest projections, it will grow to about 268 million by the year 2000. In 1994, the 65-and-older population was about 12.7 percent of the total, or about 33 million. As the population born during the post-World War II baby boom ages and joins the ranks of the elderly, the 65-and-older group may reach 35 million by the year 2000.

Life Expectancy

Babies born in the year 1900 could not anticipate very long lives—only 46 years for males and 48 years for females. Babies born in 1995, however, have life expectancies of 72 years for males and 78 years for females, or life spans of about 25 years more than those of their great-grandparents.

Income

The majority of people 65 or older have incomes well above the official poverty level, which a recent Census Bureau report estimates at about $8,740 for a couple. This same Census Bureau report shows that only 12.9 percent of people 65 or older are classified as poor or living below the poverty line. The percentage would probably be even lower if noncash benefits for the poor, such as food stamps, Medicare, and Medicaid, were counted as income. Nevertheless, there are elderly Americans living below the poverty level, struggling to feed and house themselves.

The majority of the elderly are living comfortably. Social Security benefits are indexed to keep pace with inflation and are for the most part tax-free. At the same time, children are grown and on their own, mortgages generally are paid off, and work-related expenses no longer are straining the budget.

Employment

The labor force was 134 million in 1995. The trend to retire before the age of 65 appears to be slowing down in the final decade of the twentieth century. Federal law states that it is illegal for an employee to be fired, denied a job or a promotion, or demoted because of age.

As for the myth that elderly workers are unproductive, studies of the labor force reveal that the elderly perform as well as or better than younger workers, even though a decline in perception and reaction speed has been noted. While it may take an elderly employee a little longer to learn something new, older workers can learn new things as well as younger workers can.

Housing

Housing surveys show that the elderly live in homes that are older than those occupied by the rest of the population. However, this generally is because they purchased their homes about thirty or forty years before retiring. The overwhelming majority of the elderly live in safe, standard housing. At the same time, though, many elderly below the poverty line do not live in proper housing. Some live in shabby hotels, in broken-down tenements, or, worse yet, on the streets. A significant percentage of the homeless in America are over 65. It has been estimated that 30 to 40 percent of the elderly living in nursing homes are there because they cannot care for themselves and have nowhere else to go. The Census Bureau reports that less than 5 percent of the elderly live in old-age or nursing homes.

Physical Health

The health of 80 percent of the 65-and-older group is excellent, good, or fair. Among the healthy elderly, a significant decline in activities and interests occurs only among those who are 85 or older, a population that in 1994 numbered 3.5 million, or about 10 percent of the elderly. The overwhelming majority of elderly people are well and living normal lives. However, as retired people know, health care becomes a much more important cost item after age 65. Health care for the elderly is estimated to cost three to four times what it costs younger Americans.

Mental Health

Although as many as one-third of the elderly

experience stress or have an occasional bout of depression, the proportion is not substantially different from that of the younger population. It is significant to note that not more than 10 percent of the elderly suffer from senility. Perhaps another small percentage suffers from defective memory, but about 80 to 85 percent of the elderly enjoy good to excellent mental health.

Social Activity

While almost one-third of the elderly live alone, the majority have friends and relatives, and actively participate in various functions sponsored by religious congregations or other voluntary organizations. They are neither socially isolated nor lonely. Studies show that most older people prefer some degree of separation from their children, even if their family ties are close. The elderly are generally happy, have high morale, and enjoy living. The most comfortable among them probably spent time planning for retirement.

MAJOR CATEGORIES OF RETIREMENT PLANNING

Retirement planning involves the projection of individual needs and goals into the future in an effort to adequately and properly prepare for the retirement years. It can be divided into six major categories.

1. **Financial planning.** Financial planning is concerned with income and expenses during the retirement years. The major sources of retirement income include Social Security, pensions, savings, investments, life insurance, and annuities, which usually form the basis of the retirement budget. Useful activities in planning a budget are calculating net worth, using credit, coping with inflation, applying tax benefits for older citizens, and using tax shelters.

2. **Estate planning.** This area of planning involves designing a program for the effective management or disposition of assets at death at the least possible tax cost. Tools to use include wills and trusts.

3. **Legal affairs.** Some of the legal concerns of retirement planning involve the various forms of property ownership, a late or second marriage, bankruptcy, setting up a new business, and choosing and using a lawyer.

4. **Physical and mental health.** This category entails the maintenance of good health. An important related aspect is interpreting Medicare—how it works and what you need to supplement it. You should also be familiar with other forms of health insurance, such as health maintenance organizations and Blue Cross-Blue Shield. Mental or psychological health includes the adjustments that need to be made as part of the transition from work to retirement. It also involves alcoholism and drug abuse, and mental illness.

5. **Housing.** This area requires an assessment of housing needs—deciding whether to stay where you are or to move elsewhere; considering whether to buy or to rent; evaluating condominiums, cooperatives, mobile homes, and other housing alternatives; and taking into account all the financial aspects of the housing decision.

6. **The retirement lifestyle.** This category deals with work options and challenges at or after retirement, such as second careers, full- or part-time work, volunteer work, and job hunting. It also covers the entire area of leisure planning.

STEPS IN THE PLANNING PROCESS

The four steps involved in the retirement planning process are presented below.

1. **Analyze the present.** Analyze your present situation by assembling all the relevant facts and information for each of the major categories of retirement planning. This will give you a starting point from which you can project into the future.

2. **Expand your research efforts.** Broaden your sources of information. Talk to retirees you know to learn about the problems they faced when making the transition to retirement. Talk to counselors who are trained to offer guidance and assistance. Visit your local library, whose senior-citizen collection of books and articles may be quite extensive.

3. **Set retirement goals.** Write down some of the goals you would like to achieve in retirement.

4. **Update your plan periodically.** Review your plan from time to time and update it as the need arises. Obviously, if your present situation changes, you must make adjustments that reflect the changes.

A TIMETABLE FOR RETIREMENT PLANNING

When should you start to plan for your retirement? Actually, you took your first steps in the retirement planning process when you got your first full-time job—you began making contributions to Social Security, and you joined your employer's pension plan. Through these, you set into motion the accumulation of your nest egg. But during this early period of employment, most people are immersed in job and family responsibilities, and retirement is just too far off in the future to think about seriously.

So a realistic time to start the retirement planning process is *at least ten years before* your estimated retirement date. Ten years of lead time

will enable you to make corrections and adjustments in the major planning areas. In your financial plan, for example, you can check your annual net-worth analysis against your financial goals. If you find that your income is inadequate, you have enough time to change jobs, to earn more money in a second job, to save more, or to change your investment portfolio. These options are generally foreclosed to individuals already in their 60s. In addition, by thinking ahead and planning ahead, you may be able to avoid the trauma of *retirement shock*, a psychological condition resulting from being totally unprepared for the new retirement lifestyle.

But all is not lost if you do not start ten years in advance. You can start five years, or even one year, in advance and still benefit. In fact, the guidelines here will be helpful to you even if you are already retired. But remember, the earlier you start, the more flexibility you will have.

MAKING THE RETIREMENT DECISION

Unless you are forced to retire, you will probably reach a time in your working life when you must make the decision whether to retire or to remain on the job. Aside from health concerns, the most important factor affecting the decision will most likely be economic, revolving around the question, "Will my retirement income be sufficient to enable my spouse and me to live reasonably well?" A significant related question is, "Will my retirement income be adequate five years from now? Ten years from now?"

Because they are concerned with inflation and general economic uncertainties, some older Americans put off retirement. Others retire and then return to work. A recent Congressional study indicates that 65 is no longer the standard retirement age. The median age at which workers start drawing pensions is 62, with almost 60 percent receiving pensions before age 65.

Whether this trend will continue is not presently clear.

Reasons for Retiring

There are many incentives to retire. The anticipation of a reasonably sufficient retirement income is the strongest incentive. Up until the mid-1970s, this fact was reflected in the official statistics on the number of people working. Between the early 1950s and mid-1970s, half the work force retired by around age 65. Inflation during that period was not a problem, and the economy was enjoying continued prosperity. Related to the preceding are three additional factors that may prompt retirement.

The first factor is that the Social Security program encourages older workers to retire by providing a full pension at age 65 or a pension with actuarially reduced benefits at age 62, 63, or 64. Early retirement between the ages of 62 and 64 began for women in 1956 and for men in 1961. The number of people opting for early retirement increased significantly when these changes in the Social Security law were approved.

A second factor encouraging retirement is the knowledge that Social Security benefits will increase as the cost of living increases. Known as the *cost-of-living adjustment (COLA)*, this periodic adjustment in benefits enables Social Security income to keep up with inflation.

A third factor that encourages older workers to leave the job market is the growth of private pensions. Over the last thirty or forty years, private businesses have initiated a variety of retirement benefit programs for their employees. Most beneficiaries find that these private pensions, supplemented by Social Security, provide a comfortable retirement income.

A variety of other reasons for retirement are worth noting:

■ Some retirements are prompted by poor health or by unsatisfactory working conditions.

■ Some people are encouraged to retire by their employers because of their age, even though federal law no longer mandates retirement at age 70.

■ Some people retire in order to realize and expand their talents more fully; to engage in new interests or develop new or existing skills; to pursue new knowledge; or to begin a second career.

■ Some people want to have leisure time to develop closer relationships with their children, other family members, or friends.

Reasons for Continuing to Work

For a long time, the retirement age was considered to be 65. Then it was changed to 70. The government was supportive, but it has changed its policy once again. Under the Federal Age Discrimination in Employment Act Amendments of 1986, mandatory retirement at any age has been eliminated. The thinking behind the law is that individual ability to do a job should be the basis for continued employment, and most people agree.

The 1979 amendment to the Social Security law also offers encouragement for retiring at a later age. Under this amendment, potential retirees can receive an increase in benefits for each year beyond age 65 that they continue to work and postpone retirement.

The threat of inflation is another reason for continuing to work. Many older workers think that their dreams of retirement are unaffordable. They worry about their economic future. Even though Social Security's cost-of-living clause offsets the impact of inflation, most private pensions are not raised automatically as prices rise.

A final reason for remaining at work is that

many jobs which used to be strenuous and physically draining are easier to perform with the aid of newly developed machines. Similarly, boring and repetitive types of work are being eliminated by automated robots on assembly lines. These changes are encouraging older workers to stay on the job.

Self-Study
Record Your Retirement Goals

Record your preliminary retirement goals. Of course, all of these will begin as approximations and be subject to change as you progress in the retirement planning process. (This list omits the financial, estate planning, and legal areas. Self-study sections are found in chapters dealing with those topics.)

1. **Physical and Mental Health**

a. **Physical.** What is your plan for a program of physical activity—a sport; an exercise program; another physical activity (such as walking, dancing, or gardening)?

_____

_____

_____

_____

b. **Social.** How do you plan to make new friends—through political, cultural, or social activities; volunteer work; senior centers?

_____

_____

_____

_____

c. **Religious.** What is your plan, if any, for becoming active or more active in religious activities?

_____

_____

_____

_____

2. **Retirement Lifestyle**
a. **Housing.** What is your retirement housing plan—stay where you are or relocate; be an owner or a renter; live in a single-family home, a two-family home, or a multi-family home; a condominium or a cooperative; or in a retirement village?

_____

_____

b. **Leisure.** What is your leisure plan—engage in hobbies, travel, do volunteer work?

_____

_____

c. **Employment.** What is your employment plan after retirement—no work at all, full-time or part-time work, same type of work or a different occupation? What training or retraining, if any, is required?

_____

_____

d. **Educational.** What is your plan for continuing your education—take individual courses of interest; participate in a structured program leading to an undergraduate, graduate, or professional degree?

_____

_____

e. **Cultural.** What is your plan for developing a greater interest and involvement in the arts and letters—attending theater productions, listening to concerts, visiting the library, viewing museum exhibits?

_____

_____

f. **Artistic.** If you have artistic or musical talent, how do you propose to develop these abilities?

_____

_____

Glossary

Cost-of-Living Adjustment. A periodic adjustment in Social Security benefits to enable Social Security income to keep up with inflation.

Estate planning. The process of designing a program for the effective management, enjoyment, and disposition of assets at the least possible tax cost.

Financial planning. The process of analyzing your net worth (assets minus liabilities), setting financial goals for the future, and deciding what you must do to achieve your goals.

Life cycle. The four stages of development—childhood, the teen years, the mature years, and the retirement years.

Retirement planning. The process of predicting needs and goals of the future and devising a plan to meet them, including a sound financial plan, a plan for the management or disposition of assets at death, a plan covering the legal implications of retirement, a plan for staying physically healthy and making the necessary psychological adjustments, a housing plan, and plans for work and leisure.

Retirement shock. A psychological condition resulting from being totally unprepared for retirement.

PART ONE
Lifestyles

1

Working in Retirement

At some point in your life, perhaps when you are in your 50s or 60s, you will retire from your job and begin a new lifestyle. You may retire by choice—because you have had enough of the work routine—or by the force of circumstance—because of ill health, because your firm goes out of business or changes management, or because your job is no longer necessary. Whatever the reason, you leave the labor force and become a retiree. Suddenly, you have at least fifty extra hours a week to spend however you choose. Some people enjoy this added leisure time and find retirement to be the most rewarding period of their lives. Others are unable to cope with all the free time and quickly become bored and restless.

THE ROLE OF WORK IN YOUR LIFE

Some research evidence indicates that if retirees had a choice, most would opt for some kind of work because work contributes something to life that cannot easily be replaced. Some of the satisfactions offered by work include:

■ A feeling of self-worth stemming from the contribution you are making.

■ A sense of fulfillment because you enjoy your work and others appreciate and recognize your ability.

■ A sense of belonging through the social contacts and friendships you make at work.

■ A structure to your life that gives order to your day and makes time pass quickly.

These satisfactions or goals do not disappear at retirement. Whether you are actively employed or retired, these needs remain the same because they are basic human needs.

You can satisfy these needs at or after retirement through the following four options:

1. Working full-time at the same job or in a new career.

2. Working part-time for the same employer or for a different employer.

3. Doing volunteer work in the community.

4. Establishing and operating a small business.

A discussion of each of these options follows.

Option 1—Continue Full-Time Work

If you wish to work beyond age 65 or 70 as a full-time, paid employee, you might want to approach your employer to discuss the possibility. With your lifetime experience in your job, you may very well qualify to serve as a consultant on a full-time basis, acting as a company troubleshooter wherever problems arise; as a trainer for younger staff members, who often need guidance and advice; or as an ombudsman to handle the gripes of individual employees. A recent Social Security Administration poll reveals that 80 percent of white-collar workers, who generally do office or professional work, and 60 percent of blue-collar workers, who generally do manual labor, get new jobs in their fields after they retire.

If you remain at the same company beyond your retirement date, several work arrangements are possible. The following five are the most common:

1. **Job reassignment.** You can accept less money to do a less-demanding job.

2. **Job redesign.** You can have your job specifications, or job description, changed to eliminate functions that cause you physical or mental stress.

3. **Compressed work week.** You can work fewer days by doing your week's work in, for example, four 10-hour shifts instead of five 8-hour shifts.

4. **Flexible location.** You can spend part of your week working on the company's premises and the other part working at home.

5. **Flextime.** You can arrange a flexible work schedule to fit a new set of job specifications. For instance, you can come in earlier and leave earlier, or start later and leave later.

Arrangements such as these can yield benefits for both your employer and you.

You may instead decide to work full-time at a new career. This can be a job that you have always wanted to do but for one reason or another could not undertake. Retirement gives you the opportunity to make a fresh start. You may wish to enter a field that requires more traveling, or less. You may want to work with your hands after having spent your first career at a desk. You may enjoy cooking professionally or spending your time at a college or university teaching in your area of expertise. Retirement is the time to take advantage of these options while at the same time continuing to earn an income.

Option 2—Shift to Part-Time Work

Most people who are retired would like to have a not-too-demanding part-time job that provides income and keeps them in the mainstream. For many people who have been out of the job market for years, part-time work offers a chance to return gradually. Some people feel that temporary positions in their own fields are preferable to jobs that are regular but out of their fields. If such thinking is part of your retirement plan, you should approach the quest with the same care and lead time you used when seeking a new full-time job while still in the labor market. Some occupations have better part-time prospects than others do. A retired lawyer can continue in his or her profession by serving a reduced number of established clients. A teacher can become an adjunct at a college or a tutor. An office worker or factory worker can fill in for people who are ill or on vacation.

Businesses are hiring more part-timers because this arrangement fits their needs, too. Fast-food shops, for example, hire many workers only for peak hours. Doctors, lawyers, and accountants working in partnerships sometimes discover that they prefer shorter working hours to larger incomes. In some places, the demand for computer specialists is so great that companies are offering part-time positions to attract skilled workers, even though they might prefer full-time employees.

Many companies hire part-time workers because the practice saves money. Part-time and temporary workers do not have the costly fringe benefits of full-time workers. The company does not need to make pension contributions, offer participation in a profit-sharing plan, or pay for Blue Cross, Blue Shield, or any other health benefits program. This is a significant advantage for employers, while at the same time helps people who choose or need to work fewer hours, particularly retirees seeking to ward off boredom.

Part-time workers (people who work fewer than 35 hours a week) are continuing to grow in number and currently total about 20 percent of the nonfarm work force. In industry, a new concept known as *phased retirement* has been developed and appears to be adding more part-time workers to the labor force.

Phased Retirement

Phased retirement helps older employees retire gradually by reducing their present work time without reducing their ultimate pension benefits. In this program, as you reduce your work time, you also reduce your take-home pay, which helps you to adjust to living on less money. In addition to helping you make a financial adjustment, phased retirement increases your free time, thus enabling you to slowly increase your leisure-time activities. A positive financial advantage to the employer in phased retirement is the gradual reduction in salaries. At the same time, the company derives the benefit of utilizing

a veteran employee's job knowledge to train new workers and of keeping job functions operative. Variations of the phased retirement program include:

■ Varied part-time schedules such as mornings only, afternoons only, alternating mornings and afternoons, or reduced daily hours.

■ Alternation of regular daily work hours and extended vacation time, such as two months work followed by a one-month vacation.

Job Sharing

In job sharing, two workers divide the hours and responsibilities of a single full-time job. For example, one person may work from 8:30 A.M. to 1 P.M., and the other person may work from 11:30 A.M. to 4 P.M. For many people, this is the perfect answer. Some job-sharing arrangements are family affairs in which neither party wants to work full-time. For example, a mother and a daughter may operate a small business. One works on Mondays and Wednesdays, the other on Tuesdays and Thursdays, and both on Fridays, one in the morning and one in the afternoon.

If any of these variations of reduced work hours is of interest to you, discuss it with your company management or with your union.

Option 3—Do Volunteer Work

If you wish to participate in a volunteer activity after you retire, retirement planning gives you the opportunity to try out various volunteer jobs in your spare time. This may enable you to find out what type of volunteer work you like to do. By sampling several different organizations before you retire, you can make a more intelligent decision as to which gives you the most fulfillment. If you make up your mind a sufficient amount of time ahead of your actual retirement, you will have the opportunity to gain a great deal of experience, possibly even enough to qualify for a volunteer executive position after you retire.

A variety of groups and organizations utilize volunteers on the local level. They include:

■ *Hospitals.* Hospitals generally rely heavily on the work of volunteers. All types of jobs are available, but basically, you must be capable of working closely with people who need help on the road to recovery. A smile and a helping hand brighten the day for the sick or infirm. If you are interested, contact your nearest hospital.

■ *Cultural institutions.* Many cultural institutions, such as museums and public television stations, offer opportunities for volunteers. Typical jobs include guiding tours, raising funds, and stuffing envelopes.

■ *Schools.* School volunteers assist teachers in the classroom or tutor students in basic skills. Contact your local school.

■ *Community service organizations.* Churches and synagogues offer a variety of volunteer jobs. In addition, charitable organizations, neighborhood groups, and YMCAs, YWCAs, and YMHAs are always seeking the assistance of volunteers.

Option 4—Own a Business

You may be interested in starting your own business after you retire. Such a venture offers you the opportunity to be your own boss, to be financially independent, and to work in a field that you enjoy. The idea is enticing to many people who are contemplating work options after retirement. Many small businesses succeed and generate high incomes for their entrepre-

neurs. However, most do not survive for very long. According to the Small Business Administration (SBA), which studies mortality rates of small businesses, about 20 percent close in the first year, 20 percent in the second, and another 10 percent in the third year.

The reasons for small-business failure are varied. They include poor location, poor management, insufficient capital, ineffective purchasing, and unsuccessful marketing. Each of these areas should be thoroughly studied prior to undertaking a small business. Some of the knowledge required in these areas can be learned by working for a few years in the type of business you are thinking of running or by supplementing your personal experience with formal education or training. The probability of failure is high for the inexperienced and untrained. However, there are many resources available, including free ones such as the Small Business Administration. You might also consult various books such as *Starting and Operating a Business After You Retire* by Bess Ritter May (see page 357).

JOB HUNTING

Job hunting is a difficult and frustrating experience for most people. The rejections appear to pile up all too quickly. But always in the back of your mind you know that your goal is the single acceptance that is out there someplace. The methods used in job hunting include the following:

■ *Visit personnel departments.* Experts estimate that about 27 percent of job-seekers are hired directly by the personnel officers of companies through whose doors they walk. The *personnel officer* is the company staffer in charge of hiring and firing employees. So choose a company for which you would like to work and visit the personnel department. If a vacancy exists and if you meet the requirements, you may have a job. It is always wise to draw up a plan of company visits and to know precisely what type of work you are seeking.

■ *Read classified help-wanted advertisements.* Read the employment ads in the classified sections of all your local publications and check off the ones that describe jobs for which you may be particularly well qualified. Answering an ad may require a personal visit, a letter, or a phone call.

■ *Visit employment agencies.* Two kinds of employment agencies are available—state employment services, which are tax-supported agencies, and private employment agencies, which charge either the employer or the employee a fee for filling or finding a job. Since private agencies generally specialize in certain fields or types of jobs, select an agency in your area of expertise. In your job hunt, apply at both public and private agencies.

■ *Network for job leads.* When you are in the job market, networking may prove helpful. Networking involves talking to personnel officers as well as to friends and relatives. In the course of a conversation, a job lead may be offered. Follow up on all these leads; leave no stone unturned.

The Resume

One of the most important tools in job hunting is the resumé. While you cannot rely on a resumé alone to get the job you want, you can use it to open the door. Essentially, a resumé is a summary of your work experience, your education, and your training. If properly prepared, it can indicate to a potential employer that you do, indeed, have something positive to offer. It should be easy to read, well organized, and preferably no longer than one page. The following information should be included:

■ Name, address, and telephone number.

■ Job objective.

■ Work history.

■ Education and special training.

■ Awards and activities.

■ A note that references will be supplied upon request.

If you mail your resumé to a prospective employer, include a cover letter along with it. Here are a few points that should be included:

■ Identify the positon for which you are applying and indicate how you learned about the firm and the position.

■ Indicate why you are applying for this particular position.

■ Describe your main qualifications.

■ Refer the reader to the enclosed resumé.

■ Request the next step in the employment process—a personal interview and an answer to your letter.

■ Be sure to sign the letter.

The Interview

When you are called in for an interview, you have an opportunity to sell yourself and your specialized experience and training to a prospective employer. The two key elements during interviews are personal appearance and attitude. Be prepared to answer a variety of questions about your work experience, your education, and your beliefs and personality. Highlight the special benefits of mature workers. Remember, you cannot be denied a job because of age. Prepare in advance the answers to possible questions, turning weak points into strengths that may benefit the employer.

The Thank-You Letter

After an interview, send a thank-you letter as a follow-up. Later, you can write additional letters or telephone periodically to determine if any jobs have opened up. You have made a contact, and if you continue to display an interest in working for that particular employer, you may eventually land a job.

Where to Look

The job market changes almost daily. Because of this, mature individuals re-entering the job market in the 1990s may require some retraining or upgrading of skills to help them find employment on their own terms. For example, an experienced typist, stenographer, or bookkeeper is still in demand, but an experienced typist/stenographer with word-processing skills will have no difficulty locating a position. Similarly, with the growth of computer technology, the demand for computer operators is constantly increasing. Mature individuals can learn how to operate a computer without needing to learn how a computer functions.

With the 65-and-over group expanding more rapidly than the population as a whole, the need for retirement counselors and pension-planning consultants is growing. The health care field will also be offering enormous opportunities over the next decade since more and more people will be needed to provide health care for the aged. In addition, the health-insurance field is expanding because even younger Americans are becoming increasingly concerned about their health and are purchasing more insurance than ever before.

The field of retail sales has always offered opportunities to older individuals. Salesperson and clerk positions in retail stores account for millions of jobs, with hundreds of thousands becoming available each year. A growing company may suddenly need to increase its staff, causing a whole network of positions to open up.

The greatest number of part-time jobs are found in the service industries, including schools, libraries, restaurants, cafeterias, and day-care centers. Many part-time jobs are also available in businesses that have evening hours. About one-third of Americans over age 65 have part-time jobs, which are more plentiful than full-time jobs. One of the advantages of part-time employment for individuals collecting Social Security is that it enables them to earn up to the maximum allowed by Social Security without losing their benefits.

In the 1990s, opportunities have been growing in financial services such as banks and brokerage houses. Nurses and medical technicians are in heavy demand. Hotels and spas are offering all types of job opportunities, both full-time and part-time. Teachers are in great demand in the sciences, mathematics, and computer technology.

Holding down some kind of job contributes to physical and emotional health, in addition to providing a financial return. Working at least part-time during the retirement years is definitely worthwhile. Older workers need the same sense of usefulness and accomplishment as do younger workers. A work affiliation offers these benefits.

Self-Study
Rate Yourself for Postretirement Work

1. What are your long-range plans for work after retirement? Check the appropriate box or boxes.

Work Options After Retirement	Full-time	Part-time
Continue in present job	❏	❏
Seek a new position in pre-retirement field	❏	❏
Seek a position in a new field	❏	❏
Do volunteer work	❏	❏
Start a business	❏	❏
Stop working, enjoy leisure	❏	❏

2. Personnel officers as well as owners and managers of large and small businesses have pinpointed the characteristics of employees that they feel are the most important to the success of their enterprises. How would you rate yourself on each of the following characteristics? Check the appropriate boxes. If most of your ratings are above average, your employability index is high. Your first step is to find a vacancy.

Characteristic	Average	Above Average	Below Average
Appearance	❏	❏	❏
Work habits (punctuality, absenteeism)	❏	❏	❏
Writing, spelling, and mathematical skills	❏	❏	❏
Ability to accept supervision	❏	❏	❏
Attitude (minimum irritability or anger)	❏	❏	❏
Pride in work	❏	❏	❏
Thoroughness	❏	❏	❏
Ability to complete assignments	❏	❏	❏
Knowledge and skills	❏	❏	❏
Personality	❏	❏	❏
Productivity	❏	❏	❏

Characteristic	Average	Above Average	Below Average
Company loyalty	❑	❑	❑
Motivation	❑	❑	❑
Enthusiasm	❑	❑	❑
Flexibility	❑	❑	❑

3. The following are characteristics of people who have successfully run their own small businesses. How do you rate? Check the appropriate boxes.

❑ Willingness to work long hours
❑ High energy level
❑ High initiative
❑ Ability to persevere
❑ Pleasant attitude
❑ High sincerity level
❑ Good leadership skills
❑ Ability to make good decisions

❑ Ability to organize
❑ Industriousness
❑ Willingness to take responsibility
❑ Financial reserves to keep you afloat in case of setbacks
❑ Emotional strength to cushion possible failure

Self-Study
Compose Your Resumé

An attractive, well-organized resumé highlighting your most important qualifications can provide an introduction for you to a company or organization for which you would like to work. It also remains after the interview, leaving an impression of you that is independent of the opinions or impressions of the interviewer. To prepare your personal resumé, follow the guideline below.

SAMPLE RESUMÉ

Name _____

Address_____

City_____State_____Zip _____

Telephone number _____
                    (Area code)

Job objective _____

_____

_____

Work History (List current or most recent employment first)

Dates From To	Job title and duties in brief	Name and title of supervisor Employer name and address
__ __	_____	_____
__ __	_____	_____
__ __	_____	_____
__ __	_____	_____
__ __	_____	_____

Education

Dates From To	Diploma/ Name and address of school	Degree	Major
— —	_____ (High school)	_____	_____
— —	_____ (College)	_____	_____
— —	_____ (Graduate school)	_____	_____

Special Training
(Company training courses, armed forces schools,
adult education courses, home study, correspondence courses)

Dates From To	Type of training, sponsor's name and address
— —	_____
— —	_____
— —	_____
— —	_____

References are available upon request.

Self-Study
Prepare for Job Interviews

A job interview gives you an opportunity to present yourself and your qualifications to a representative of a company or organization for which you want to work. Following are questions that often come up during interviews. To prepare for an interview, you can practice your responses in advance.

Work

What type of job are you seeking? _____

What did you enjoy doing most in your last job? _____

What did you not enjoy doing? _____

How would your supervisor have described you as a person? _____

For what did he/she criticize you? _____

For what did he/she praise you? _____

Education

How would you describe your educational accomplishments? _____

How did you come to choose the kind of work you did? _____

Has not having a college degree (or graduate degree) hindered you

in your vocational progress? _____

Personal

How would you describe yourself? _____

How do you spend your leisure time? _____

What are your major strengths? _____

What are your weaknesses? _____

Why do you want to work for us? _____

What salary are you seeking? _____

Are you seeking full-time or part-time employment? _____

Glossary

Blue-collar worker. A person whose employment requires manual labor and who wears work clothes or other specialized clothing on the job.

Classified help-wanted advertisements. Listings of job opportunities published in newspapers and magazines.

Compressed work week. A rearrangement of time so that more hours are worked on some days and no hours on other days. For example, five 8-hour days are compressed into four 10-hour days.

Employment agency. An organization that helps people find jobs. The services of a public agency are free; private agencies charge a fee. Also known as a *personnel agency.*

Flexible location. A work arrangement under which part of the time is spent working on the company's premises and the rest of the time is spent working at home.

Flextime. A work schedule in which the starting and stopping times are arranged to satisfy the special needs of the employee.

Interview. A meeting between an employer or employer representative and a job-seeker to determine suitability for a job.

Job reassignment. The shifting of an employee from one job to another job with a different set of job specifications.

Job redesign. A change in job specifications that eliminates unwanted functions and adds desired functions.

Job sharing. The splitting of the hours and responsibilities of a single full-time job between two workers.

Job specifications. A detailed description of the functions that must be performed in a particular job.

Networking. Talking to personnel officials, relatives, and friends regarding job opportunities.

Personnel department. The department of a business firm that interviews applicants for jobs and handles employee problems.

Personnel officer. An employee who handles personnel decisions and problems.

Phased retirement. A program that helps older employees to ease into retirement by gradually reducing their work time but without reducing their ultimate pension benefits.

Productivity. A measurement of the output of workers in relation to input of resources.

Resumé. A summary of a person's work experience, education, and training. It is one of the most important tools used in job hunting.

Small Business Administration (SBA). A United States government agency created in 1953 to aid small business concerns by providing financial, technical, and managerial assistance.

White-collar worker. A person whose job does not involve manual labor; generally a salaried or professional worker.

2

Playing in Retirement

The proper use of leisure time in retirement is the basic determinant of whether your retirement will be happy and fulfilling or boring and restless. The transition from full-time work to retiree status adds at least 50 additional hours a week with which you can do as you please. You must begin early to plan to use this extra time so that your feeling of usefulness and contribution to society will continue. Managing your time effectively should be given primary consideration.

Some people turn to *hobbies* to provide the satisfaction of creativity and recognition that had previously come from work. Library shelves are filled with books on hobbies and on how to select one or more for fulfillment in retirement. Retirees also turn to the world of *education and learning*. Throughout the nation, older adults are studying to achieve never-completed degrees or simply pursuing new academic interests and enjoying the excitement and sense of purpose generated by the world of academia. Still others turn to *travel* in retirement. You definitely will have the time and probably also the money. Add a little imagination and you can satisfy the wanderlust. Some retirees become involved in *volunteer work* to preserve the sense of identity,

self-worth, and usefulness that are derived from work. A carefully selected volunteer job will give you all the job satisfaction you need.

Your leisure plan should include one or more of the leisure activities noted above. The choice or choices you make must be based upon your desire for personal satisfaction and happiness. Do what pleases you.

HOBBIES

Hobbies are important to retirees. Those who enjoy a hobby appear to be happier and better adjusted to the retirement lifestyle than those who do not.

During their working years, many people discover various hobbies that help them unwind, relax, and enjoy whatever spare time they manage to find. Others become so absorbed in work and everyday essentials that they have little time for extra activity. Retirement provides an excellent opportunity to continue and expand those hobbies that might have been on-going for years, or to develop new interests that can become gratifying and fulfilling.

The variety of hobbies is unlimited. Some are thousands of years old, others are being developed daily. Some are indoors and sedentary, others are outdoors and ambulatory. Some excerise the mind, others exercise the body. For example, collections of almost anything you can name have recently become popular. Some collect buttons, bottles, small banks, butterflies, baseball cards, beads—and that's only the beginning of the alphabet for collectibles. The list is endless. In short, there are as many hobbies as there are people to create them.

Most hobbies are inexpensive but some require an outlay of cash for clothing and equipment. Golf requires clubs, a golf bag, special shoes, and, of course, fees to play the game. Painting requires brushes, paint, canvas, sketch pads. Before investing money, it is wise to borrow or rent what you may need until you are certain that the hobby is really something you'll enjoy. It might also be helpful to take an adult education course, or to read up on the activity before making any commitment, financial or otherwise.

Hobbies may be classified according to four general classes: doing things, collecting things, making things, and studying and learning about things.

An excellent "doing" hobby is being an amateur radio operator. Thousands of people, including retirees, enjoy the useful and interesting hobby of amateur radio. These radio amateurs or *hams* send messages on their home radio stations to new friends on the next block or halfway around the world. Messages can be sent by voice (talking) or by Morse code.

The governments of most countries encourage radio amateurs because trained radio opertors are needed in emergencies. Hams provide emergency communications during floods, fires, tornadoes, hurricanes, and earthquakes. The Federal Communications Commission (FCC) has often praised hams for their voluntary work in emergencies.

Amateur radio is the only hobby regulated by international treaty. Transmitting channels, agreed upon by most nations, are sandwiched in among the short-wave radio frequencies assigned to ships, aircraft, international broadcasting stations, armed forces, police, and others. To operate an amateur station in the United States, an amateur must first obtain a license from the FCC. Information about obtaining a license can be gotten from the American Radio Relay League (ARRL), 225 Main Street, Newington, CT 06111.

If you want a hobby that combines travel and learning, consider the Elderhostel program. A nonprofit educational organization, Elderhostel offers inexpensive, short-term academic programs hosted by educational institutions in the United States, Canada, and forty-five other countries. Participants live on college and university campuses, in conference centers, or other places and enjoy the cultural and recreational resources of the area. In 1994, almost one-quarter million people enrolled in Elderhostel.

For as little as $275 plus travel costs, a participant can enjoy a one-week stay on a college campus in the United States during the academic year or during the summer. The fee includes a dorm room, cafeteria meals, three college-credit courses, and extracurricular activities. The program requires no homework, no grades, and no prior knowledge of the subject.

For more information, contact Elderhostel, 75 Federal Street, Boston, MA 02110, or call (617) 426-8056 for a free catalog.

Self-Study
New Directions of Activity

Review the following examples of hobbies and check those that may interest you.

A. *Doing Things*: This group of hobbies is probably the most common.

❑ Amateur radio operation   ❑ Photography

❑ Card games   ❑ Ping-pong

❑ Chess and checkers   ❑ Playing a musical instrument

❑ Computer activities   ❑ Raising pets

   (games, bulletin boards)   ❑ Sports (tennis, swimming, softball)

❑ Dancing   ❑ Storytelling

❑ Gardening   ❑ Yachting

❑ Hunting   ❑ Other

B. *Collecting things*: The desire to own things is one of man's strongest instincts.

❑ Antiques   ❑ Match books

❑ Art   ❑ Rare books

❑ Butterflies   ❑ Shells

❑ Buttons   ❑ Stamps

❑ Coins   ❑ Other

C. *Making things*: Many people prefer to make things rather than to collect them.

❑ Bookbinding   ❑ Sculpturing

❑ Building model train layouts   ❑ Sewing

❑ Furniture building   ❑ Weaving

❑ Knitting   ❑ Writing stories, poems, essays

❑ Model building (ships, planes, cars)   ❑ Other

D. *Learning*: Some people make a hobby of studying a particular subject or of investigating many different fields.

- ❑ American sign language
- ❑ Computer operation and programming
- ❑ Culinary arts
- ❑ Drama
- ❑ Foreign language(s)
- ❑ Home repair
- ❑ Interior decorating
- ❑ Literature
- ❑ Managing and investing money
- ❑ Meditation
- ❑ Personal development
- ❑ Philosophy
- ❑ Public speaking
- ❑ Voice and diction
- ❑ Other

VOLUNTEER WORK

Volunteer work during retirement years can bring you a whole new slant on life. Perhaps you were one of those people who go to work every day just waiting for pay day. Now is your opportunity to become one of the scores of people who are "paid" by the smiles, thanks, and comfort of those they help.

Volunteers visit the elderly and shut-ins, help school children learn their lessons, teach adults to read, distribute magazines in hospitals, serve as guides in museums, and do office work for fund-raising organizations. Contact your local school, hospital, library, or museum for information about volunteer programs at those institutions. Call your favorite philanthropic or civic organization and offer your assistance. You can also call Volunteers of America (1-800-899-0089) or Literacy Volunteers of America (1-315-445-8000) for information about programs in your area. ACTION, a federal agency, also administers programs in which older volunteers may participate (see page 355). For additional suggestions, see pages 355–356.

CONSIDERATIONS WHEN PLANNING LEISURE TIME ACTIVITIES

The following are suggested guidelines for you to use in planning your leisure:

■ *Variety.* Try to develop a reasonable mix of activities. Variety will keep you interested *and* interesting. Select some activities that are within your physical ability, some that are intellectual, and some that are creative. Take into account the issue of physical ability, which often declines in later years.

■ *Interaction.* Choose some activities that will enable you to enjoy social contact with other people. Socialization and communication are basic to sound psychological adjustment. At the same time, each person needs private time for reading, listening to music, watching television, or contemplating things.

■ *Overextension.* In the early enthusiasm of retirement, many individuals tend to overextend themselves, trying to do too much. Develop your involvement in your leisure activities slowly, adding or subtracting time as your interest increases or diminishes. Do not take on more than you can handle, and keep your leisure plan flexible.

■ *Fulfillment.* There is much to be said for lightening the burdens of others. To maintain your feeling of self-worth, choose one activity that gives you the opportunity to spend time helping others who may be less fortunate than you. This is the whole area of volunteer work.

Enormous satisfaction can be derived by contributing to the welfare of people in need: spending time with them, providing simple needs, and engaging in conversation.

■ *Pre-retirement Experimentation.* Try out a few new activities before you retire. See how well you enjoy the activity before making a commitment.

Self-Study
Your Plan for Leisure Activities

1. To develop a retirement plan for leisure, you must first determine the number of hours a week to be considered. Counting time at work and the time consumed getting to and from work, how many additional free hours per week will you have after you retire? _____

2. Which of your *present activities* would you like to continue after you retire? How much of your additional free time would you like to devote to each?

| | Hours per week for each activity | |
Present activities	Now	After retirement
_____	_____	_____
_____	_____	_____
_____	_____	_____

3. What *new activities* would you like to pursue after retirement? Are you taking classes or receiving training for these activities?

New activities	Current preparation for these activities
_____	_____
_____	_____
_____	_____

4. Courses and classes in any subject might open new horizons for you.
   A. List schools and colleges in your area that offer classes in various academic areas.

_____

_____

_____

B. List subject matter areas in which you have an interest.

_____

_____

_____

5. Seniors in particular enjoy meeting new people and making friends with others who have similar interests. List senior clubs and groups in your area that encourage new members to join, such as religious groups, community groups, libraries, senior centers.

_____

_____

_____

6. Often, individuals seek others to join them in making new contacts. List friends and neighbors who may be willing to join you in broadening your circle of acquaintances.

_____

_____

_____

3

Retirement Housing

Food, clothing, and shelter are the basic ingredients of any budget. The retirement budget, detailed on page 174, distributes expenses of these three elements as 22 percent, 5 percent, and 30 percent, respectively, a total of 57 percent. Shelter, the largest budgetary component, can be obtained in a variety of ways.

Census statistics indicate that about three out of four households are headed by individuals 65 years of age or older, about 85 percent of whom have paid off their mortgages. The other 25 percent of households are renters.

Planning for housing in retirement raises many issues: where to live after retirement—stay where you are or move elsewhere; own or rent; same size, larger, or smaller dwelling. These are urgent issues that require thorough research and study. This chapter provides the information that will help you in making these important decisions.

The most difficult decision to make, after you have decided to retire, is where to live after retirement. Over 90 percent of retirees choose to remain in the area in which they have been living, either in their own home or in a rented apartment. The rest move to a new location; a few move hundreds of miles away.

Should you stay where you are or move elsewhere? What type of residence should you choose? On what should you base your choice? Among the considerations in choosing a new residence are the following: type of ownership, size of residence, degree of privacy, and types of conveniences desired.

These issues must be resolved because the housing decision is at the heart of any financial retirement plan. The ensuing discussion may help you to decide where you want to live after retirement.

YOUR HOUSING REQUIREMENTS

Before deciding on the type of retirement housing you desire and need, you should first review the specific characteristics you are seeking.

Size. How many bedrooms do you need? If you have children or other family members who visit you periodically and stay for one or more days, you may require a second or third bedroom. Extra bedrooms generally require extra bathrooms. Also, do you need a dining room? Do you periodically entertain family or friends in a formal setting?

Layout. Should you seek a housing unit that is all on one floor, thus avoiding the need for walking up and down stairs? Do you or your spouse have any leg or back ailments that require your living on one level? Generally, a single-level home is more desirable for retirees who are 65 or older.

Extras. Do you favor a large kitchen with a great deal of counter space or would you settle for a smaller kitchen? Is a garage or fireplace essential to your lifestyle?

Climate. Northern states generally have very cold winters and heavy snows. People approaching retirement dream of sun belt areas such as Florida, southern California, or southwestern states. Southern Florida and states bordering on the Gulf Coast have very hot summers with extremely high humidity. Try living for a while in the state of your dreams before making your housing decision.

YOUR SOCIAL NEEDS

The dwelling in which you are now living has given you roots in a community that developed over many years. Your home or apartment may be close to your children and grandchildren as well as to your relatives, friends, and neighbors. Sickness or bereavement can highlight the importance of these associations. Moving more than 25 miles away from your present home will result in some loss of these close associations. Moving further away can completely sever these relationships. These *personal associations* represent a significant component of your non-housing requirements, and will have to be redeveloped in a long-distance move. Some other nonhousing requirements that should be considered include those discussed below.

Professional Services. Over the years you have probably developed an association with a family physician, a family dentist, an attorney, an accountant, a stock broker and/or a banker. If you move, new relationships will have to be made with one or more of these professionals. This may be of particular concern if you have a physical ailment that requires a particular type of medical treatment.

Recreational Facilities. A neighborhood religious institution may offer recreational activities in addition to religious services. Such a center of activities may offer lectures, concerts, sports activities. Local libraries offer many intellectual activities. Are such facilities available in the new community? Do you participate in civic, social, or political groups in your present community?

SHOULD YOU MOVE OR STAY IN YOUR PRESENT HOUSING SITUATION?

At the point of retirement, chances are that your children are on their own and the house or apartment that provided for everyone's needs is now too big. You and your spouse are probably overburdened with maintenance chores. On the other hand, you may like the community, have many friends and neighbors, and be accustomed to the comforts that your dwelling provides. Take a close look at both your reasons for remaining in your present housing and the reasons for moving.

Reasons for Staying in Your Present Housing

If you are a homeowner or renter:

■ You enjoy the space and have room for visits from children, grandchildren, and friends who can stay overnight.

■ You get along well with your neighbors and are participating in community activities.

■ The neighborhood is still very nice since many of your friends and neighbors remain.

■ Shopping and medical facilities are conveniently located.

■ Your home or apartment is exactly the way you want it. The furniture fits in just right, and you can avoid the trauma of a move.

■ The happy events you enjoyed make for pleasant memories.

A homeowner has additional considerations:

■ You have probably paid off the mortgage and can afford to maintain your home on your anticipated fixed income.

■ If you ever need money, you can borrow against the equity in your home.

Reasons for Moving

If you are a homeowner or renter:

■ Your house or apartment is too big and is hard to keep clean.

■ The neighborhood is changing—many of your friends and neighbors have moved.

■ Your children have moved to distant states and visit infrequently.

■ You live far from shopping and medical facilities.

A homeowner has additional considerations:

■ Maintenance is a problem. Cutting the grass in the summer and snow removal in the winter are becoming harder, and hired help is expensive.

■ Taxes, cost of utilities, and repairs keep rising every year. These and other costs may become more than you can afford.

■ Stairs are becoming a problem.

■ If you sell, you can enjoy a one-time $125,000 exclusion from income taxes. In other words, $125,000 of the gain from the sale of the house is not subject to income tax. (Details on excluding $125,000 of the gain can be found in the IRS publication *Tax Information for Older Americans*, Publication Number 554. To order a copy, call the IRS toll-free at 1-800-829-1040.)

SHOULD YOU OWN OR RENT?

If you stay in your present housing or move elsewhere, the next basic question to consider is owning versus renting. A mortgage-free home is cheaper than paying rent in most parts of the country. Against this, you have to consider the gain of the interest or dividends that you would earn if you sold your home and invested the proceeds.

The Advantages of Owning

The advantages of owning your own home are the following:

■ You are not subject to the terms of a lease and are free to do as you wish.

■ Home ownership is a sound investment.

■ You enjoy pride in ownership.

■ Your living situation is more permanent.

■ Interest paid on your mortgage loan is tax deductible.

■ Property taxes paid are tax deductible.

The Disadvantages of Owning

The disadvantages of owning your own home are the following:

■ You have the responsibility for maintenance.

■ Capital that is tied up in your home can earn a greater return elsewhere.

■ Owning a home is a long-term commitment.

■ You always face the potential deterioration of your neighborhood.

If you're a renter, you always have the freedom to change your residence. Moreover, you know the monthly rent, and know whether you can handle it without too much difficulty. At the same time, you should be aware that rents can be raised to meet inflationary pressures. And there is always the threat that your structure may be converted to a cooperative or a condominium. (In some instances, senior citizens may continue to rent after a coop conversion.)

The Advantages of Renting

Among the advantages of renting are the following:

■ The landlord or owner is responsible for maintenance.

■ Exterior chores, such as cutting the grass and snow removal, are handled by paid staff.

■ You face no unexpected repair costs.

■ You have freedom to move or travel.

The Disadvantages of Renting

The disadvantages of renting are the following:

■ You build up no equity.

■ There is no possibility of long-term capital gain.

■ A lease limits your freedom of action.

■ Your lease may not be renewed by the landlord.

Self-Study
Prioritizing Your Housing Needs

1. Check the characteristics of your retirement housing that you consider most important:

    Number of bedrooms: _____

    Number of bathrooms: _____

    Characteristics:

    ❑ Dining room   ❑ Modern appearance
    ❑ Living room   ❑ Terrace
    ❑ Den   ❑ Garage
    ❑ Eat-in kitchen   ❑ Single-level
    ❑ Fireplace   ❑ Hot climate
    ❑ Gardens and grounds   ❑ Cold climate

2. Check nonhousing requirements you consider important:

    ❑ Near a medical building   ❑ Steam room and sauna
       (doctors and dentists)   ❑ Library
    ❑ Near a general hospital   ❑ Churches and synagogues
    ❑ Recreational facilities   ❑ Commuting convenience
    ❑ Cultural facilities   ❑ Large complex
    ❑ Swimming pool   ❑ Younger families

3. Make the housing decision: Move or stay in present home.

    _____

4. List the factors you have considered in making your decision:

a. _____

b. _____

c. _____

d. _____

e. _____

IF YOU STAY
IN YOUR PRESENT HOUSING

If you are a homeowner, it probably makes sense to keep your home during retirement years. Your home, lived in for so many years, is an important part of your life and reflects your style of living. If your present home fully satisfies your housing and social requirements, and you have decided to remain there during your retirement years, you should do some advance planning to prepare your home for this time of your life.

Useful Changes in Your Present Home

If you stay where you are, you must evaluate your present home in terms of future needs. Does it provide the facilities you will need to do all that you plan for your retirement? For example, does it provide individual space for you and your spouse in which to relax or study and to pursue separate hobbies and interests?

Some useful changes in your home include the following:

■ *Remodeling.* You may wish to add a bathroom on the main floor to eliminate the need for using stairs. Or you may wish to make a major room addition, such as an extra bedroom or den that may be used as a study or hobby room. Such changes can be expensive, but moving costs and refurnishing costs are also high. Savings can result by replacing a bed with a sofa-sleeper, thus converting a spare room into a study or some other type of room.

■ *Safety Improvements.* Older individuals are particularly prone to disabling accidents in the home. Many of these accidents can be avoided if proper precautions are taken. For example, add non-slip surfaces to walkways, driveways, bathrooms; provide handgrips in bathrooms and bathtubs; install adequate lighting in hallways and stairwells; add non-skid rubber underliners beneath rugs and carpets.

■ *Convenience Improvements.* Some improvements can eliminate many maintenance burdens. Making these improvements before you retire will eventually provide you more time to do things you prefer, save you money when your income is fixed and/or limited, and free you from tasks for which you may not be physically able. For example, aluminum or vinyl siding on your exterior walls will eliminate the need for periodic painting; paneling some interior walls will save on painting; tiling or other floor coverings will make for easier care; rearrangement of utilities in the kitchen and laundry room will save steps. Adding a deck or patio will cut down or eliminate the need for lawn-mowing.

■ *An Additional Source of Income.* Adding a small kitchen and bathroom to a basement or spare room in your home can produce a rental unit that can provide a source of income. Rental income can at least pay for monthly maintenance costs, help meet mortgage payments, or finance other improvements. A renter may offer companionship, or perhaps serve as a housesitter when you're away. Such a change in your home will require approval of your local zoning authority. (In some locales, adding a "kitchen" that does not have a stove removes the two-family label that requires getting zoning approval.)

There are a number of ways in which you can finance these changes. Chief among these is tapping your home equity.

TAPPING YOUR HOME EQUITY

Many retired homeowners find themselves in a cash bind each month. The value of their homes has grown, but inflation has reduced the buying power of their pensions. To compound the problem, many retirees cannot sell their houses because affordable alternative housing is not available. For such individuals, a number of options are available that make it possible to get monthly income from property.

A Home Equity Loan

You can tap the equity in your home by signing up for a home equity loan that, when approved by your bank, enables you to borrow money as you need it by writing a check or using a credit card. Such a loan should be used only for special needs, such as home improvements, financing a child's education, or medical bills, and not for buying an auto or paying for a vacation. Failure to make payments on a home equity loan can result in the loss of your home, the collateral that enabled you to make the loan.

If you do decide to apply for a home equity loan, consider the following tips:

■ *Compare loan offers.* Obtain at least three equity loan offers. Carefully compare the details of each loan offer before choosing a lender.

■ *Evaluate the list of charges.* The interest charge is the largest, but lenders usually include a number of other charges such as an application fee, points, and closing costs. Some lenders levy an up-front processing fee of up to $2,000. Ask each potential lender for a list of all charges.

■ *Interest tied to an accepted index.* In an adjustable rate loan, be sure that interest rate adjustments over time are pegged to one of the accepted common indexes, such as one-year, three-year, or five-year United States Treasury issues. Avoid lenders who peg interest rates to their own internal prime rate.

■ *Require fixed contract terms.* Contract terms regarding issues other than interest should be

fixed and unchangeable. Be sure that the lender does not have the power to change the contract at his own discretion.

■ *Look for an interest rate cap.* Interest levels on adjustable rate loans can rise to over 15 percent. Seek a home equity loan contract that specifies an interest cap or maximum. Also be sure that there is no "floor," a specification as to how low the interest rate can drop.

■ *Consider a fixed rate loan.* While many lenders favor adjustable rate loans, others offer fixed-rate loans, which means that the interest rate cannot rise or fall over the term of the loan. Depending on fluctuations in interest rates, the fixed rate loan may be more cost effective over the long run.

■ *Be sure the loan can be amortized.* Avoid a home equity loan on which you are required to repay interest-only with no amortization of principal. Under these terms, after a certain period, a large lump sum or balloon payment, is required. In some cases, a balloon payment can be advantageous. This kind of mortgage permits older people to buy an apartment and make the relatively low interest payments during their lifetime. The heirs then pay the large lump sum after the sale of the apartment. Many prefer loans that can be repaid on a regular periodic basis, usually monthly.

■ *Check affordability of loan payments.* Be sure you can afford to repay the monthly interest and amortization specified in the contract. The monthly repayment for all your outstanding loans should not exceed 35 percent of your gross income.

■ *Seek professional review of the contract.* Before signing a home equity loan contract, have it checked by your accountant or tax attorney. While interest payments on home equity loans may be fully tax deductible, you should consult with a professional before signing on the dotted line.

■ *Limit withdrawals.* Withdraw from your line of credit only what you need for major, necessary expenditures, such as home improvements, college education, or medical bills. Avoid using your loan for buying food, clothing, or vacations.

Reverse Mortgage

Assume that the market value of a home is $150,000, that the retirees, a couple, are in their 70s, and that they need additional income. They approach a savings and loan bank. They present the case, and the bank offers to lend them up to 80 percent of the home's current value, or up to $120,000. The bank then will use the money to purchase an annuity that, for this couple, will pay about $14,000 a year. The bank subtracts the interest charge from this amount, and pays the remainder to the couple in monthly checks. These checks will continue to be paid as long as either of the retirees lives. After both have passed away, the home will be sold. Out of the proceeds, the loan from the bank is repaid and the balance goes to the estate of the deceased. The concept of the *reverse mortgage* is relatively new. It was approved by the Federal Home Loan Bank Board in December 1978.

Sale Leaseback

Under the *sale leaseback* arrangement, the homeowner sells his house in exchange for life-time tenancy and a guaranteed monthly income. An investor buys the home at a discount that can range from 20 percent to 35 percent under the market value. A 73-year-old man might sell his $150,000 house for $112,500, a 25-percent or $37,500-discount. The investor pays the home-owner a cash downpayment of 10 percent of the purchase price (in this case, $11,250). The homeowner and the investor reach agreement as to a reasonable rent to be paid by the home-owner; for example, $550 a month. The investor pays all taxes, insurance, and maintenance costs, as well as regular monthly payments to the homeowner; for example, $875 a month, over a period of 10 or 15 years. The investor must also purchase a lifetime annuity to take over when his liability ends, that is, when he has completed his payments for the home.

The homeowner is taken care of by the downpayment of $11,250; by the investor's continuing $875 monthly payments; and, ultimately, by the lifelong annuity payments. Moreover, this retiree has a monthly net income of $325 ($875 minus $550). The retiree can continue to live in the home for life at the established rent. The benefits to the investor are notable too. He has purchased a home at a 25-percent discount; he has a regular monthly rental income; and he will probably realize a significant capital gain after the seller has passed away or decided to move.

Charitable Remainder Trust

In this case, the property is donated to a worthwhile institution in exchange for a lifetime annuity and the privilege of remaining in the home for life. (For further details, see page 300.)

Self-Study
Financial Data for Making Changes in Current Housing

1. If you are planning to stay in your present home at retirement, evaluate the home in terms of future needs. List the changes you would like to make and indicate the estimated cost for each change.

Change	**Estimated Cost**
a. _____	_____
b. _____	_____
c. _____	_____
d. _____	_____
e. _____	_____
f. _____	_____

2. Have you considered tapping your home equity? ❑ Yes ❑ No

   If yes, which option do you favor?

   ❑ Reverse mortgage

   ❑ Sale leaseback

   ❑ Charitable remainder trust

   ❑ Home equity loan

   Your choice should be discussed with your lawyer and/or accountant.

IF YOU DECIDE TO MOVE

If you decide to make a change, it makes good sense to analyze and evaluate the advantages and disadvantages of the alternative types of housing available. You should also compare housing costs and the suitability of the new location before you sever your ties with your present location.

Buying or selling a home, leasing an apartment or a house, or entering into a contract for a care facility all have both legal and economic implications. You should consult a lawyer before signing any documents relating to any of these major transactions. An accountant and/or investment adviser should be consulted prior to undertaking negotiations involving a large sum of money.

Selling Your Present Home

A home can be sold through a licensed real estate agent, a professional who deals in real estate, or by yourself. At some stage you will need a lawyer for the closing, particularly if you are working with an agent. If you decide to sell your house on your own, you need a lawyer at the outset. As a seller, you have certain legal obligations and financial liabilities. No standard printed sales contract fits every situation. Every property sale is unique and requires a contract that is drawn to suit the particular situation.

If you select a real estate agent to sell your house, you can offer an *exclusive listing*—an agreement that gives one real estate agent the right to sell a property for a specified period of time but does not restrict the right of the owner to sell the property on his or her own without payment of a commission. An agent can also have an exclusive right-to-sell listing, a written agreement that gives a real estate agent the exclusive right to sell and entitles him or her to a commission regardless of who sells the property

during the period of the agreement, or you can use the brokers' *central listing service*. In the central listing service, all the realtors in your area are advised by the listing realtor that your house is on the market, and the realtor who sells the property must give a percentage of the commission to the listing realtor.

Selling property involves a number of legal documents, agreements, and tax liabilities. A qualified lawyer can help you avoid mistakes and realize the maximum return.

Economic Considerations

The market is not always advantageous for selling or for buying. The ups and downs of the economy bring with it inflation on one hand and recession and unemployment on the other. Record-high mortgage rates in 1979–1983 made buying and selling difficult. Yet the real estate industry did make adjustments. In some of the new types of mortgages, interest rates rise and fall with changes in the money market.

Tax Implications

Effective July 20, 1981, the Federal Economic Recovery Tax Act of 1981 makes it possible to sell your house, make up to $125,000 in profit on the sale, and not pay any federal taxes on the gain. A married couple filing separate income tax returns can each claim $62,500 in profit on the sale. You must be 55 years or older and the home must have been your principal residence for at least 3 of the last 5 years to avail yourself of this right.

For homes sold before July 27, 1978, the owner had to be at least 65 years of age before the sale date and was permitted to exclude up to $35,000 of the gain from the adjusted sales price, provided that he or she owned and lived in the home for 5 of the 8 years preceding the sale date.

There are also tax implications when you move to another state. Some retirees choose to relocate to Sunbelt states, such as Arizona, Florida, Nevada, or Texas, to enjoy warm winter temperatures and possibly lower taxes. If you are considering a move to one of these states or any other state, you should be aware of the tax implications. If you do not plan carefully, you may find that you owe taxes in two states at the same time. This involves the concept of *domicile,* which refers to the state in which you have established permanent (legal) residence and intend to remain.

Most state laws specify the number of days you must live in the state in order to be a legal resident. In New York and New Jersey, for example, you are considered a legal resident if you maintain residence in the state and spend more than 183 days a year there. As a resident, you are responsible for paying the state's taxes, including the personal income tax. If your new state has a personal income tax, you must file a tax return there even though you may be eligible for a credit from one of the two states.

Any out-of-state real estate and personal property you own, such as a home, jewelry, or works of art, are generally subject to estate and/or inheritance taxes in the state in which the property is located. If you maintain residences in two states, then your estate must pay estate and/or inheritance taxes in both states because you are a legal resident in both.

Tips for Relocating

If you plan to relocate, the following tips may prove helpful:

■ *File a declaration of nondomicile*. To make sure your former state knows you are relocating, file a *declaration of nondomicile* with your last state income tax return. If such a form is not available in your former state, attach a statement announcing your move when you file your tax return.

■ *Establish domicile in your new state.* To become a legal resident in your new state, file a statement of domicile with the clerk of the circuit court in your new county. You should also change your auto registration, driver's license, bank accounts, and voter registration. It is important also to draw up a new will not only to conform with the community property rules of many Sunbelt states, but also to declare that you are a legal resident of the new state.

■ *Sell your old home*. If you are certain that you will remain in the new state and do not wish to maintain two homes, it would be wise to sell your old home, thus confirming your decision to establish a legal residence in your new state.

■ *Maintain careful records if you retain two homes*. If you retain your old home and establish domicile in another state, you must keep careful records showing that you do not spend more days in your old home than specified by your former state's laws on legal residency. If you become subject to an income tax audit, the burden of proof as to where you legally reside is yours.

■ *Roll over capital gains within two years.* If you sell your principal residence in your former state, you have two years to roll over any capital gains into a new primary home, or you must pay income taxes on the capital gain.

■ *Profit from the one-time $125,000 exclusion from federal tax.* As indicated previously, if you wish to obtain the $125,000 one-time exclusion from the federal income tax, you must be 55 or older and have lived in your old home for three of the last five years before you sold it. You cannot rent in your new location for more than two years, or you will lose the $125,000 exclusion.

Buying a Smaller Home

Prior to their retirement, many people buy a relatively small home that they use for their vacations. Generally, such a second home is located in the country, possibly near a lake. While working, the people pay off the mortgage, and at the time of retirement, the smaller home is available as a primary residence. The people like the smaller home, are familiar with the area, and over the years have developed good relationships with their neighbors. When they retire, they can rent their old house rather than sell it, and use the rental income to supplement their pension and Social Security income.

This may be ideal for some people, but others want to live closer to the central city with more people around and with urban cultural and recreational activities readily available.

In any case, if your present home is too large, a smaller home offers many *advantages*:

■ A smaller home costs less than your present home.

■ Surplus capital from the sale of your larger house can be invested.

■ A bank will grant a mortgage loan if you need one.

■ Cleaning chores are reduced.

■ Lawn cutting and snow shoveling are reduced.

■ You retain the privacy and comfort of owning your own home.

■ Home ownership is a good investment.

■ You can choose your ideal location.

The *disadvantages* of a smaller house are the following:

■ It still requires cleaning and upkeep.

■ It requires exterior and interior maintenance.

■ The house ties up a portion of your investment capital.

■ Appreciation in value may be less rapid than you anticipated.

■ Living quarters may be more cramped than you had expected.

Legal Considerations

Buying a home or condominium involves several transactions, each of which requires an agreement in writing. If your interests are not properly protected, you may suffer significant financial loss and frustration.

First, an offer to buy is usually made in writing and includes a deposit or binder. This sales agreement indicates under what conditions the deposit will be returned if the purchase is not consummated; the purchase price; a legal description of the property; and fees and taxes to be paid. Second, the purchase may involve a mortgage in which the inclusion or omission of a few significant clauses can cost you a large sum of money before you pay it off. For example, is the interest rate fixed or is it flexible to reflect the changing cost of mortgage funds? Is there a penalty for prepayment? These and other contract terms involve thousands of dollars. Third, taking title to your home is more than the mere transfer of ownership. The type of property ownership, as detailed in Chapter 5, could have a significant impact on estate planning. This stage of the transaction also requires a title search, that is, checking conditions that may affect your ownership, as well as other legal details, such as a title insurance. And, finally, a purchaser of property may also be party to an escrow agreement, which sets forth the conditions that must be fulfilled before any money, held by a third party, can be paid. It is important that the interests of the buyer be protected.

Renting an Apartment

Renting an apartment is another alternative. By living in a rented apartment, you can enjoy a relatively carefree lifestyle. This is especially desirable for people who enjoy traveling and do not wish to be burdened with the responsibilities of housing maintenance.

The federal government sponsors subsidized or public housing projects for older people. Rents in these developments are set on a sliding scale based on income. People 62 or older and handicapped people can qualify for a federal rent subsidy in nonprofit housing projects built under this program.

People planning to retire whose incomes are moderate but too high for public housing should consider rental housing for people over 62 sponsored by nonprofit groups and financed with low-interest government mortgages.

The *advantages* of apartment renting are the following:

■ Monthly rent is fixed for the duration of the lease.

■ Maintenance cost is included in the rent.

■ Lawn care and snow removal services are provided.

■ You can enjoy the freedom to move or to travel.

■ Renting requires a minimal financial investment, permitting more favorable investments of your capital.

■ The trouble and expense of selling are eliminated.

■ Renting may include recreational facilities at no additional cost.

The *disadvantages* of apartment renting are the following:

■ Renting generally provides less space than owning.

■ The landlord has the right to evict a tenant under certain conditions.

■ The landlord may not renew a lease if he wishes to convert to cooperatives or condominiums.

■ The tenant builds up no equity and merely collects rent receipts.

■ The tenant enjoys no income tax savings.

■ A portion of the rent includes vacancy costs and landlord profit.

■ The lease usually restricts tentant activities, such as ownership of pets.

■ The monthly rent may include extra charges for garage space or air conditioning units.

Legal Considerations

Many leases are written in archaic legalese and say things in two or three ways. However, the average person can read a lease and understand it. If you do not understand something, ask the landlord or property manager to explain it. If you still have doubts, you should ask a lawyer to go over the lease with you. The fee will be small.

The simplest kind of lease is an oral agreement. You rent by the month, and either you or the landlord can terminate the contract by giving thirty days' notice. To be safe, put your notification in writing. Most leases, however, are written contracts.

For any lease, whether oral or written, you should check the following points:

■ *Term of the lease.* Leases usually run for a year or more.

■ *Expiration clause*. You may be able to remain on a month-to-month basis. Or the lease can be automatically renewed for another term.

■ *Move-out notice*. The number of days you must give as notice before moving out is specified. The landlord may be subject to a similar requirement.

■ *Legal notice of rent increase, change in lease terms, or eviction*. Do not waive your right requiring legal notification of rent increase, change in lease terms, or eviction.

■ *Children and/or pets*. Lease terms state whether you may have children and/or pets in the unit.

Other clauses in a lease that may restrict you include such points as the following: a cost-escalator clause (as maintenance costs and taxes rise, the rent can be increased), penalty for late rent payment, subletting your quarters, maintenance of appliances, and a schedule of repainting. Make sure that the lease you sign contains provisions you can accept.

Buying a Condominium

"Condominium" was a strange-sounding word twenty years ago, raising questions as to its meaning. Today, the concept has spread into every aspect of real estate. What is a condominium? A *condominium* is a legal plan of ownership in which you buy and own your house or apartment. You can purchase this home by making a down payment and borrowing the rest of the cost from a lending institution in the form of a mortgage. You own your housing unit plus a proportional interest in common facilities, such as grounds, hallways, elevators, and recreational areas, paying a monthly maintenance fee for their care.

Increasingly, people are choosing to live in condominiums rather than in one-family detached homes or rentals. The United States League of Savings Institutions estimated that there were about 85,000 condos in the United States in 1970. Today, there are approximately four million condos in the United States.

One of the most significant attractions for the individual or couple contemplating retirement housing is the cost-saving potential. The price for a condominium unit is generally less than for a single-family home. Large scale construction of a condominium complex with shared roofs, walls, and heating facilities reduces unit costs. Condominium units, therefore, sell for 8 to 10 percent less than equivalent single-family homes. For this reason, condominiums account for about 25 percent of all homes purchased, up from only 11 percent in 1979, according to the United States League of Savings Institutions.

Owning a condominium has both advantages and disadvantages. The *advantages* of condominium living are the following:

■ It is a safe investment against inflation.

■ Monthly mortgage payments build up equity.

■ Condominium ownership provides income tax savings: Mortgage interest and real estate taxes are income tax deductions.

■ You enjoy the freedom to change your property as you wish.

■ Exterior property maintenance is provided.

■ Monthly costs are not related to a landlord's overhead and profit.

■ Policies are set by the owners' association, in which you have a vote.

The *disadvantages* of condominium living are the following:

■ Buying a condominium requires a significant downpayment with the potential loss of income from more favorable investment alternatives.

■ The collective judgment of the owners may not yield the wisest operating decisions.

■ The monthly maintenance fee is usually increased to keep pace with inflation and/or poor management.

■ The time and costs involved in selling are the same as those associated with home ownership.

■ The structure or complex may be overcrowded, with a consequent loss of privacy.

■ The different lifestyles and interests of your immediate neighbors may be displeasing.

Legal Considerations

As with the purchase of a house, your interests should be properly protected to avoid financial loss and frustration. The transactions involved in buying a condominium are the same as those for buying a house. Please see page 46 for specific information.

Buying a Cooperative

A *cooperative* is a legal plan of ownership in which the purchaser buys shares in the corporation that owns the land and the entire structure or complex. You do not own your living space, but you own shares in the corporation that owns the land and the entire structure or complex. The purchaser cannot get a mortgage but may get a loan to purchase the shares. This obviously differs from a condominium. If you leave the cooperative, you sell your shares, either to the corporation or directly to the new shareholder, as required by the bylaws. The corporation is composed of the inhabitants of the building, who together share the responsibility of overall management. The amount of your monthly mainte-

nance fee depends on the size of your dwelling, which may be an apartment, a row house, or an individual home.

The bylaws of a cooperative may give the board of directors the authority to approve or disapprove the buyer of a particular share or dwelling unit. Cooperatives exist almost exclusively in urban areas.

The *advantages* of cooperative living are the following:

■ Co-ops are usually located in the best areas of cities.

■ Co-op membership motivates pride of ownership.

■ Shareholders have a vote in setting management policies.

■ Co-ops offer an opportunity for capital gain.

The *disadvantages* of cooperative living are the following:

■ Some co-ops are overcrowded, resulting in loss of privacy.

■ The bylaws of some co-ops, set by members of the association, do not allow children or pets.

■ Decisions on interior and exterior painting are controlled by the board of directors, resulting in loss of control by a co-op shareholder.

■ Inept management can result in rising monthly maintenance costs.

Buying a Mobile Home

A *mobile home* is a factory-manufactured housing unit. The unit is transported on wheels from the factory where it was built to a site where the wheels are removed and the unit is set upon a permanent foundation of concrete blocks or poured concrete. Mobile homes are reasonably priced. On a per-square-foot basis, the highest quality mobile home costs about half the price of a traditional home. This includes only the cost of the house. After buying the house, you have to locate a mobile home park where a vacancy exists and then either buy or rent a site. A mobile home park contains dozens of units that share a certain look-alike appearance.

A mobile home offers a unique opportunity for a retired couple to own a low-cost housing unit and settle in a community with other retired people who have chosen a similar lifestyle. Residents often have access to a recreation building containing a swimming pool, sauna, gymnasium, music room, club rooms, and an auditorium.

The *advantages* of a mobile home are the following:

■ The cost of a mobile home on a per-square foot basis is half-or-less than the cost of a traditional home (excluding the land, which is a costly component if purchased).

■ A mobile home is frequently taxed as personal property, a low tax, whereas a regular home is taxed as real property.

■ Mobile home parks offer outstanding social and recreational opportunities.

■ Occupants are usually of similar age and financial position.

■ Maintenance costs are low.

■ Occupants have the opportunity to live in resort areas without making a large investment.

The *disadvantages* of a mobile home are the following:

■ The opportunity for appreciation in land value is less in a mobile home park where the land is usually rented.

■ As a mobile home becomes older, the costs of repair and maintenance increase.

■ The value of the mobile home itself tends to fluctuate. Some homes have depreciated in value.

■ While monthly rents in a mobile home park are cheaper than renting a traditional home, rents do go up, and often quite rapidly.

■ After a few years, some owners no longer enjoy the lifestyle but find it too costly to make a change.

■ It is costly to move a mobile home.

■ Mortgage institutions may not be willing to offer a loan for the purchase of a used mobile home.

Other Housing Arrangements

Individuals planning for retirement have a number of other options. Many retirees now live in retirement communities, and the number of people choosing this option is growing. An individual or a couple who is beginning to encounter health problems that require professional help may choose a care facility. Other options include moving in with others or asking someone to live with you.

Retirement Community

Retirement communities, retirement villages, or life-care centers are springing up all across the country, particularly in areas that provide a warm climate, intellectual stimulation and/or excellent recreational facilities. Constructed exclusively for retired people, *a retirement community* often includes apartments for independent living, assisted-living units, and a skilled nursing center for those who may require it.

Planned exclusively for retired people to free them from the noise and commotion of living among young families, retirement communities provide excellent recreational facilities, including golf courses, tennis courts, and swimming pools, as well as libraries, club rooms, and auditoriums. The physical arrangements and types of services provided vary widely. Some offer a shopping center and hospital on the grounds with full-time doctors and nursing staff.

Types of housing available include single-family detached homes, duplexes, town houses, and high-rise buildings, ranging in size from one to three bedrooms. Units may be rented or purchased. Some retirement villages are sponsored by nonprofit organizations, such as churches, unions, fraternal societies, veterans' organizations, civic associations, and teachers' organizations. Others are sponsored by business corporations as investments.

For those living independently, a retirement community provides the usual recreational facilities, a shopping center, and transportation services. The *assisted-living units* provide maid service and a central dining room for meals, even though your apartment may contain a fully equipped kitchen. And the *skilled nursing facility* is actually a hospital on the grounds with full-time doctors and nursing staff.

Costs vary depending on the option. Unit prices range from $100,000 to $300,000; monthly maintenance fees range from $1,000 to $2,500, including health care and one or two meals in the central dining room. In case of death or departure, some communities rebate 90 percent of the purchase price. A retirement community is likely to be at least 40 to 80 miles away from a large city, at which distance land costs drop sharply. Property taxes are lower because the communities do not have the large educational expense of areas with many children.

The *advantages* of a retirement community or village are the following:

■ It is a self-contained community that meets all your needs.

■ Recreational and social facilities are excellent.

■ Planned activities for the residents keep active seniors busy at all times.

■ Monthly maintenance costs are low.

■ Security guards protect entrances and grounds.

■ Good medical attention is readily available.

The *disadvantages* of a retirement community or village are the following:

■ The initial entrance cost is high.

■ The monthly maintenance fee keeps rising.

■ Social contacts limited to a group of retirees may become boring.

■ The lifestyle requires close living with neighbors.

■ The location is usually isolated.

■ You may miss the noise and bustle of a big city.

Care Facilities

As you grow older, you may find it increasingly difficult to maintain independent living. A *care facility* is designed for the individual or couple beginning to encounter some health problems that require professional help. Care facilities provide three different levels of service. Details about these facilities are provided in Chapter 4.

Moving In With Others

How times have changed! When America was a rural economy, it was very common to find three generations of a family living together under one roof. Each member of the family had specific chores to perform to keep the farm functioning. The farm house was spacious, and as parents became older, the chores they performed changed, but living space was always available for them.

Today, in our urbanized economy and with the mobility that characterizes our society, young couples buy a house, live in it for a while, find jobs in other places, sell the house, and buy another. If generations lived together, it would restrict both mobility and easy turnover of housing. Today, older parents, for the most part, are on their own. The children grow up and make their own lives, leaving an empty nest. Sometimes, an older parent who is alone may decide to move in with children or relatives, mainly for companionship. Both generations may benefit from such a relationship.

Other older adults may decide to share a household, thus pooling their financial resources. In this economical arrangement, each adult may have his or her own bedroom, sharing the kitchen and other common space. Each individual should carefully evaluate whether this option is best since it is not a suitable arrangement for everyone. You may wish to move in together on a trial basis before making a final decision.

The *advantages* of moving in with others are the following:

■ Both parties in the relationship enjoy companionship.

■ Living with others offers a degree of security.

■ The arrangement is less expensive than owning a home or renting an apartment.

■ House maintenance chores are shared.

■ You are free to take periodic vacations without having to close the house.

■ It is convenient and reassuring to have someone nearby in case of illness.

The *disadvantages* of moving in with others are the following:

■ You give up your personal privacy.

■ Living with another individual or family may bring differences to the forefront.

■ The feeling of independence is lost in such a relationship.

■ A disruption in lifestyle may occur because of a feeling of responsibility for another individual.

Asking Someone to Live With You

At some time, you may wish to ask a friend or relative to live with you so as to provide companionship and/or assistance with day-to-day chores. A formal agreement in writing that sets forth specific financial arrangements should be considered. The agreement should be prepared by a lawyer. In exchange, you may wish to leave such an individual or individuals some portion of your estate in appreciation. If a bequest is to be made, it should be included in your will.

In many cases, the individual involved may be a son or a daughter, making it inappropriate to discuss financial arrangements. Such a situation, however, may create many subsequent problems when an estate is divided up among survivors. For example, the offspring who assumed the responsibilities associated with living with an elderly parent may feel that he or she is entitled to a larger share of the estate. If you ask someone to live with you, you should address the issue of the disposition of individual and/or joint assets in case of death.

Self-Study
Comparative Housing Costs
Present Housing vs. Retirement Housing

1. Before making a decision on retirement housing, it is wise to compare the costs of your present accommodations with the costs of a prospective new location. To assist you in making this analysis, a comparative housing cost worksheet is provided below. The worksheet is also useful in that it suggests ways of cutting costs in your present home.

| | Average monthly expenses | | |
| | Present housing | Retirement housing | |
Cost item		Alternative A	Alternative B
Mortgage payment or rent	$ _____	$ _____	$ _____
Property taxes[1,2]	_____	_____	_____
Insurance on house[1,3]	_____	_____	_____
Fuel[1,4]	_____	_____	_____
Electricity[1]	_____	_____	_____
Gas[1]	_____	_____	_____
Water[1]	_____	_____	_____
Furnace maintenance[5]	_____	_____	_____
Repairs[6]	_____	_____	_____
Services[7]	_____	_____	_____
Painting	_____	_____	_____
Total	_____	_____	_____

[1] Total your annual expenses using your bills or check stubs, and divide the year's total by 12 to get your average monthly cost.

[2] If your county or town grants a property tax reduction for homeowners over 65, use your senior citizen tax rate to compare with retirement housing costs.

[3] Check to determine whether your home insurance premium can be reduced by switching to a different company, taking a policy for a longer period, combining coverages in a homeowner policy, or taking a larger deductible.

[4] Can you reduce fuel costs with more adequate insulation; storm doors and windows; weatherstripping of doors and windows; or a more efficient burner?

[5] Includes repairs, cleaning, and burner insurance.

[6] Includes repairs on roofing, gutters, and leaders, plumbing, electrical, and windows.

[7] Includes cost of lawn service (seeding, fertilizing, pest control), lawn cutting, shrubs, lawn and shrubbery supplies, tools, and snow removal.

2. In addition to comparing alternative costs for retirement housing, you must also consider two related factors: furnishings and security.
    Furnishings: Will your present furniture and furnishings fit into your retirement home?
    ☐ Yes   ☐ No
    If no, estimate the cost for new furniture, new draperies, and carpeting in your retirement housing, using the following worksheet:

| | Retirement housing | |
Furnishings	**Alternative A**	**Alternative B**
Furniture	_____	_____
Draperies	_____	_____
Carpeting	_____	_____
Total	_____	_____

Security: The issue of personal security and safety must be taken into account in planning for retirement housing. Will the alternatives you are considering offer you the security you want, both in your housing unit and in the public areas outside your unit?
    ☐ Yes   ☐ No

3. If you are planning to sell your home, list the names, addresses, and telephone numbers of three real estate firms in your community who can serve as your agent:

    a. _____

    b. _____

    c. _____

4. List the locations you are considering for retirement housing and evaluate each in terms of advantages and disadvantages.

Location		**Location**	
Advantages	**Disadvantages**	**Advantages**	**Disadvantages**
_____	_____	_____	_____
_____	_____	_____	_____
_____	_____	_____	_____
_____	_____	_____	_____

5. To arrange for your retirement housing, will you be involved in buying or selling a home, leasing an apartment or a house, or entering a care facility? ☐ Yes ☐ No

If yes, have you discussed your plans with your lawyer? _____

OF SPECIAL INTEREST TO WOMEN

Wives and husbands must sit down together in their retirement planning to decide where to live after retirement and what type of housing accommodation best suits their needs. That's a good starting point. But, then, women must project beyond the immediate decision. Remember that about 50 percent of all women 65 or older in the United States are widows, and in general about 85 percent of women die as singles.

If the husband dies and the widow lives in the family home alone, the housing issue arises again. At age 55 or older, $125,000 of profit from the sale of a home is tax-free. If the property has appreciated in value, the sale of the home prior to the husband's death would have a large taxable gain as compared with the original price (the tax basis). But, when a husband dies, a new tax basis on the home is established—the current market value. If the widow sells after the husband dies, she will have no taxable gain and can keep all the profit.

A divorced woman, however, according to current provisions of the Internal Revenue Code, does not get a new tax basis. The divorcee can sell the house, but will owe a large income tax unless she buys another house whose value is the same or more than her current house. This may not be the best choice if the divorcee wishes to live in smaller accommodations. Another alternative is to rent the house, but then you have the responsibilities of a landlord.

RETIREMENT HAVENS ABROAD

Individuals at all income levels may think about retiring to a country outside of the United States but may not consider it seriously. However, individuals who retire with limited incomes may be surprised to discover that some retirement havens abroad offer gracious living in beautiful surroundings on a meager budget, while retirees with higher incomes can live regally in some of these retirement Edens. The decision to start a new life in another part of the world should not be made hastily but should be based on careful research and planning. The Self-Study: Evaluating a Retirement Haven Abroad lists the wide range of factors you should consider in order to make a sound decision.

No place in the world is perfect in every respect: The Garden of Eden was lost early in human history. But some locations offer natural beauty, a climate that is comfortable year-round, and most important, a significantly higher level of living than a limited income can buy in the United States. Retirement Edens at bargain prices can be found in the following countries, to name but a few: Costa Rica, Greece, Ireland, Italy, Mexico, Portugal, and Spain. Each of these countries offers distinctive characteristics that make it unique. Retirees with limited incomes may find a retirement paradise within the borders of these countries.

In Mexico, for example, $400 a month will provide a couple with a two-bedroom house, ample and delicious food, and full-time help.

Any money left over from this $400 can be used for travel and entertainment, including trips back to the United States for visits with family and friends. An annual income of about $5,000 a year can provide a comfortable life. In Spain, there are about 6,400 retired Americans; about half of them reside in Costa Del Sol (Sun Coast) overlooking the blue Mediterranean. It has been estimated that a couple can live well at this location on about $12,000 a year, or about $1,000 a month, which includes the cost of domestic help.

If the possibility of retirement abroad interests you, contact the embassy of the country you're interested in, and you will receive a wealth of information. Hundreds of thousands of Americans have taken advantage of this option. The Social Security Administration mails about 350,000 monthly checks to retirees living outside the United States.

The *advantages* of retirement abroad are the following:

■ You can enjoy a fuller lifestyle on a limited budget in some foreign countries.

■ You can experience amenities of life not available to you in the United States because of cost.

■ Some of the low-cost-of-living countries offer an ideal year-round climate in beautiful surroundings.

■ You may fulfill a wish to return to your family's roots.

The *disadvantages* of retirement abroad are the following:

■ Medicare coverage ends if you live outside the United States.

■ You may lose contact with your family and friends.

■ A wrong choice of location can be an expensive and time-consuming mistake.

■ You may not have access to the same level of medical competence as in the United States.

TIPS FOR RETIRING ABROAD

If you plan to retire abroad, the tips given below may prove helpful.

■ Before you make a final decision to move to a foreign retirement haven, spend a couple of vacations there or perhaps a winter or summer season as a visitor.

■ Don't burn your bridges. Try the new living arrangements for a year or two before you abandon your ties to your old neighborhood. You can rent your present home for the time you're away.

■ Consider carefully the state of your health and your need for specialized medical and/or hospital services.

■ Carefully evaluate all the features and characteristics of a retirement haven using the following Self-Study as a guide.

■ If you've made the move and find you've made a mistake, remember that the decision is not irrevocable. Retrace your steps.

Self-Study
Evaluating a Retirement Haven Abroad

Economic Considerations

1. What is the cost of living as compared with the United States?
2. What are the tax consequences of living in this foreign country?
3. Does the haven offer economic freedom to invest, buy and sell property, or set up a business?
4. What are the job opportunities in that country if you should decide to re-enter the labor force?
5. What types of housing are available and what are their costs?

Physical Aspects

1. What is the climate?
2. Do sanitation and water quality present problems?
3. Is the potential location accessible to an international airport?
4. What is the quantity and quality of roads, trains, and buses? Telephone and mail services?

Political Structure

1. Is the government stable, or is it subject to revolutionary upheavals?
2. What will be your legal status as a long-term resident?
3. Is your potential location subject to crime and violence?
4. As a foreign resident, can you enjoy personal and property safety?
5. Do the people there enjoy the freedoms of speech, press, religion, and assembly?

Amenities

1. What is the quantity and quality of the following facilities?
   a. Educational: schools and colleges
   b. Cultural and religious: museums, libraries, and houses of worship
   c. Entertainment: theaters and movies
   d. Recreational: sports stadium, television, radio, and nightclubs
   e. Shopping: specialty stores and department stores
2. What are the food and travel facilities like in this country, including restaurants, bars, and hotels?
3. Is there any language barrier?
4. Is the native population friendly?

Health Facilities

1. What is the level of medical, hospital, and dental services in terms of quality and cost? *Please note that Medicare benefits are not payable outside the United States.*
2. Are health facilities accessible to your potential location?
3. Are medical insurance policies available, and what are their costs?

Glossary

Adjustable rate mortgage. At specified intervals, such as every six months, or thirty months, or three years, the interest rate may be moved up or down by the lender. (*See* Conventional Mortgage, Graduated Payment Mortgage, Negative Amortization.)

Amortization. A method of liquidating a debt by making periodic payments of the principal and interest over a fixed period of time.

Binder. A deposit requested by a seller to hold a piece of property for an interested buyer until a set date.

Care facility. A form of housing for the individual or couple beginning to encounter some health problems requiring professional help.

Central listing service. Information on dwelling units for sale or rent is disseminated to all member real estate brokers in a given area. Even though the property may have been listed with one of them, each has the right to sell or rent, splitting the commission with the broker who obtained the listing. Also known as *Multiple Listing Service.* (*See* Exclusive Listing, Exclusive Right to Sell Listing.)

Charitable remainder trust. An arrangement with a charity under which a property is donated to the charity in exchange for a lifetime annuity and the right to remain in the home for life. (*See* Reverse Mortgage, Sale Leaseback.)

Closing costs. Costs resulting from the financing and transfer of property ownership in a real estate sale.

Condominium. A legal plan of ownership in which a home or an apartment is bought with a down payment with the rest borrowed from a lending institution in the form of a mortgage. The purchaser of a condominium owns the space he or she occupies with the right to dispose of this space as he or she wishes.

Conventional mortgage. A home loan available to good credit risks, with fixed monthly payments covering interest and amortization for the life of the loan, and usually not insured by the Federal Housing Administration or guaranteed by the Veterans Administration. Also known as a *fixed rate mortgage.* (*See* Adjustable Rate Mortgage, Graduated Payment Mortgage, Negative Amortization.)

Cooperative. A legal plan of ownership in which the purchaser buys shares in the corporation that owns the land and the entire structure or complex. The purchaser cannot get a mortgage but may get a loan to purchase the shares. If the occupant wishes to sell his or her shares, permission must be obtained from the board of directors of the cooperative.

Cost-escalator clause. A statement in a lease, stipulating that as maintenance costs and taxes rise, the rent can be increased.

Deed. A written instrument that conveys *title* to real property. (*See* Title.)

Domicile. The state in which a person has a permanent (legal) residence and intends to remain.

Down payment. The cash a borrower puts toward a purchase, with the remainder of the purchase cost borrowed from a creditor.

Equity. The dollar value of a property owned by an individual or individuals beyond any mortgage on it; the difference between fair market value and current indebtedness.

Escrow. The deposit of money and documents in the custody of a neutral third party until the terms and conditions of an agreement or contract are fulfilled.

Exclusive listing. A written agreement that gives one real estate agent the right to sell a property for a specified period of time but does not restrict the right of the owner to sell the property on his or her own without payment of a commission. (*See* Exclusive Right to Sell Listing, Central Listing Service.)

Exclusive right-to-sell listing. A written agreement that gives a real estate agent the exclusive right to sell and entitles him or her to a commission regardless of who sells the property during the period of the agreement. (*See* Exclusive Listing, Central Listing Service.)

Federal Housing Administration. A United States government agency that insures mortgages of qualified buyers against loss due to default, thus encouraging lenders to make mortgage loans on favorable terms.

Lease. A contract that gives a tenant possession and use of a property under the conditions and terms stated. (*See* Rental Apartment.)

Mobile home. A factory-manufactured housing unit that is transported on wheels to a site where the wheels are removed and the unit is set up on a permanent foundation of concrete blocks or poured concrete.

Mortgagee. A borrower or owner in a mortgage transaction who pledges property as security for a debt.

Mortgagor. A lender in a transaction involving a mortgage instrument.

Multiple listing service. *See* Central Listing Service.

Prepayment penalty. A charge levied by a lender when a mortgage is paid off in part or in full prior to maturity.

Rental apartment. A dwelling unit that is leased from an owner and for which the occupant pays rent in accordance with the terms of a *lease*. (*See* Lease.)

Retirement community. A self-contained community offering homes or apartments set in carefully maintained grounds, providing excellent recreational facilities and possibly a shopping center and fully-staffed hospital. Also known as a *retirement village*.

Reverse mortgage. A monthly payment to a homeowner by a mortgage lender, using the home equity as collateral, where the monthly payment amounts are accumulated as a mortgage against the house, to be repaid when the homeowner(s) dies and the house is sold. (*See* Sale Leaseback, Charitable Remainder Trust.)

Sale leaseback. Sale by a homeowner of his or her home in exchange for lifetime tenancy and a guaranteed monthly income. (*See* Charitable Remainder Trust, Reverse Mortgage.)

Sales contract. An agreement between two or more parties, containing the terms and conditions of the sale. The contract must be written and signed by both parties.

Title. A document indicating the legal right by the owner of record to the possession of some real property. *Title* may be acquired through purchase, inheritance, gift, or foreclosure of a mortgage.

Title insurance. Designed to protect owners and lenders against loss from defects in the *title*.

Title search. The examination of all public records to disclose all facts pertinent to the *title* of the property.

Town houses. Dwelling units that have their own front and back but common side walls.

4

Care Facilities

For some, aging brings with it infirmities that make living alone impractical. The couple or individual who are finding it increasingly difficult to handle daily tasks might consider a care facility. Care facilities provide three different levels of service.

RESIDENTIAL CARE FACILITIES

As the nomenclature suggests, *residential care facilities* provide secure and healthful accommodations to individuals who are capable of meeting their own basic needs. The emphasis is on the social requirements of the resident, rather than on the medical needs. Residential care facilities give particular attention to the social, recreational, and spiritual requirements of the residents. They also relieve the resident of anxiety and frustration by providing housekeeping services including meals, and medical assistance as required.

These facilities are usually apartment complexes in which tenants occupy their own apartments and have access to cafeteria facilities for meal service when desired. Twenty-four-hour-nursing service is available if medical treatment is required. This arrangement offers the lowest level of care, since it is designed for the individual who has a greater degree of independence.

INTERMEDIATE CARE FACILITIES

Second-level or *intermediate care facilities*, often referred to as ICFs, are designed for those who do not require intensive care. Nevertheless, for those who are not capable of independent living, the ICFs provide room and board along with medical, nursing, social, and rehabilitative services on a regular basis.

Tenants live two or three to a single room, without kitchen facilities. All meals are supplied by the care facility and the people living here must be well enough to care for themselves physically. The facility provides around-the-clock nursing to insure that tenants take medications when necessary and that nurses are available for emergencies. This type of facility is eligible to participate in both Medicare and Medicaid programs. (For information about insurance coverage for ICFs, see Chapter 17.)

NURSING HOMES

The third or highest level of care facility is a

convalescent hospital or *nursing home* for people who require nursing care. Some people who go to nursing homes may be partially paralyzed as a result of strokes, some may have no bowel or bladder control. Others require special care such as medication or the changing of dressings. The occupants are referred to as patients. Registered nurses are on duty and the patients are in hospital beds or wheelchairs. The patients in a convalescent hospital or nursing home do not require intensive medical care. They are stable, merely requiring personal maintenance. Those requiring surgery or care for acute illness go to medical hospitals.

It is estimated that almost half of all Americans turning 65 this year will be confined to a nursing home at some point in their remaining lifetime. And it is worse for women. A recent study indicates that it is 300 percent more likely for a woman to require nursing home care than for a man. Of those requiring five or more years of nursing home care, 80 percent will be female.

Some nursing homes are *skilled nursing facilities*, often referred to as SNFs. These provide registered nurses, licensed practical nurses, and nurse's aides to carry out the instructions of the patient's physician. Physical, occupational, and other therapies are provided to help restore the patient's health. Service is on a twenty-four-hour basis. This type of facility is eligible to participate in both Medicare and Medicaid programs, but many skilled nursing facilities are not certified by Medicare. Remember, most nursing homes in the United States are *not* skilled nursing facilities.

Anyone who has ever given the subject any thought probably has a preconceived notion about a nursing home. The stereotype, usually negative, pictures a place to locate the elderly when the family can no longer respond to the individual's needs, and the individual is unable to care for his or her own person. Surprisingly, a nursing home is not what most people envision. A nursing home is actually meant for people of all ages who are convalescents, some of whom will recover completely and quickly, as well as for people of any age who are in need of long-term care. For convalescents, the goal of the nursing home is to help the patient recover and return to routine life and to his or her community as soon as possible.

Types of Services Offered

Nursing homes provide a variety of services to patients requiring care, whether they are elderly or not. These include nursing care, personal care, and residential service.

■ *Nursing care* requires the professional skill of a registered nurse or a licensed practical nurse. The nurse follows the instructions of the attending physician and may be called upon to administer medications and injections. Additionally, the nursing home provides physical therapy, occupational therapy, dental services, dietary consultation, and X-ray services for post-hospital care of stroke, heart, or orthopedic cases. Also, a pharmaceutical dispensary is usually available in a nursing home.

■ *Personal care* implies that in a nursing home a patient will receive help getting in and out of bed, bathing, dressing, eating, and walking. Attention will also be given to special diets that are prescribed by the physician.

■ *Residential service* means that a nursing home offers a secure environment in which the patient is comfortable, as well as a program to meet the social and recreational needs of the individual. In some cases, religious services are also offered.

ADVANTAGES AND DISADVANTAGES

The *advantages* of a care facility are the following:

■ It provides housing as well as facilities for personal and medical care at various levels of need.

■ An individual or couple requiring personal and medical services can choose a care facility most suitable to his or her needs.

■ Many of these facilities are subsidized by the government.

The *disadvantages* of a care facility are the following:

■ Costs of living in a care facility are generally high.

■ It is difficult to locate the best possible facility.

■ Usually a choice has to be made with haste and in a time of stress.

■ The various kinds of alternative care facilities may not all be available in your community.

■ License regulations and administrative procedures vary from state to state.

■ Abuses in care facilities occur from time to time.

SELECTING A SUITABLE FACILITY

Locating a suitable nursing home is a time-consuming and painstaking task. You can obtain some guidance by referring to the *Directory of Nursing Homes*, published annually by HCIA, Inc., and available in libraries. The 1994 update includes detailed information for more than 16,000 nursing facilities in the United States. It is the most comprehensive national listing of nursing facilities currently available. Informa-

tion was compiled by means of questionnaires sent to all facilities.

The nursing facilities are arranged alphabetically by state and then by city. Within each city, facilities are arranged in alphabetical order and each entry includes the name, address, and telephone number of the facility. The administrator, medical director, director of nursing, and number and type of staff (full-time, part-time, and consulting) may also be listed. An index sorted by facility name is included for easy access to information.

Listings may include any or all of the following: facility type; number of beds listed by total and by number of each type; payer mix; state license information; owner type; name of owner, management company, and chain company; programs and services offered; admission requirements including age, sex restrictions, and referral requirements; detailed lists of special facilities and activities at each; affiliations (religious, fraternal, professional society, or other); and languages spoken.

Make a list of the nursing homes you think meet the needs of the person you have in mind. Arrange to visit each of the facilities on your list. Ask for a tour of the premises as well as an opportunity to talk to the administrator. Evaluate each nursing home, and then narrow your list to those that are most suitable. What you uncover in your search will enable you to decide practically and intelligently what is most appropriate for the person you have in mind.

If you or your spouse needs a nursing home, it is important that you personally inspect the facility to make sure that it is the right choice for your specific needs.

Costs

The average cost of a nursing home in the United States is $30,000 per year. Medicare covers 100 days in a skilled nursing facility. Medicare pays all costs for all covered services for the first 20 days. Since 1995, people have had to pay $89.50 in coinsurance each day for the 21st day through the 100th day of continuous confinement. After 100 days, individuals must pay all the costs of their care. Medicaid coverage for skilled nursing facilities varies from state to state, and is only for the indigent. (For information on the various types of insurance coverage available, see Chapter 17.)

LEGAL CONSIDERATIONS

If you are contracting for a care facility, it is essential that you understand clearly what services you will receive, what the costs will be, and what the rules and regulations of the establishment are. The fine print of many of these contracts is designed to protect the owners rather than the residents.

Among the specific details that should be incorporated into the contract are the following: a description of the premises to be occupied; the services that will be provided and their cost; the procedure for escalation of fees to reflect increased costs; safeguards against overcharges; the forms of recreation available and costs, if any; the rules and regulations that limit, for example, visitation privileges, hours for watching television, freedom to have a pet, and the resident's right to sell or bequeath his or her property.

Before you invest your savings in a care facility, it is wise to consult a lawyer to assist you in interpreting the fine points. The fee involved is well worth it.

As with any legal document, nursing home contracts must be read before they are signed. Some experts recommend that a contract, which may be twenty to thirty pages long, be reviewed by a lawyer.

Whether or not your lawyer reads the contract, you should be aware that it is against federal law for the home to require a co-signer as a term of admission. A family member cannot be held responsible for payment.

Rights of Patients in Nursing Homes

The Omnibus Budget Reconciliation Act of 1987, signed into law by President Reagan on December 22, 1987, imposes dozens of rules for nursing homes that protect the rights of patients. The law also provides rules for home health agencies and guarantees home care patients many of the same rights as nursing home residents, such as the right to be informed in advance of any treatment, to help plan their own care, and to voice grievances. Some of the most important new requirements are the following:

■ *Quality.* Nursing homes must maintain or enhance "the quality of life of each resident."

■ *Evaluation.* At least once a year, nursing homes must conduct a comprehensive assessment of each patient's ability to perform such everyday activities as bathing, dressing, eating, and walking. Results of such assessments will be used to prepare a written plan of care, describing how the person's medical, psychological, and social needs will be met.

■ *Screening.* A nursing home must not admit any patient who is mentally retarded unless a state agency first certifies that the person requires the type of care provided in a nursing home. The state agency must also determine whether the person needs "active treatment" for either mental illness or retardation.

■ *Nurses.* A nursing home must have licensed nurses on duty around the clock and must have a registered nurse on duty for at least eight hours a day, seven days a week. State officials may grant an exemption if the nursing home can show that it was unable to recruit the necessary personnel and that the exemption will not endanger the health or safety of patients.

■ *Training.* Every nurse's aide must receive at least seventy-five hours of training in nursing skills and residents' rights. Nursing homes are responsible for making sure that nurse's aides are competent to perform the tasks they are assigned.

■ *Registry.* Each state must maintain a registry of people who have completed the training course for nurse's aides. If an aide is accused of neglecting or abusing patients or stealing their property, the state must investigate. If the charge is verified, the finding will be recorded in the registry. Nursing homes must check the registry before hiring nurse's aides.

■ *Staff.* Any nursing home with more than 120 beds must have at least one full-time social worker with at least a bachelor's degree in social work or sufficient years of service to qualify for being "grandfathered" into the profession.

■ *Transfers.* Nursing homes must ordinarily give thirty days' notice before discharging or transferring a patient. The patient may challenge such decisions by filing an appeal under procedures established by each state.

■ *Access.* Residents of nursing homes must be granted the right to see family or officials if they so desire. Nursing homes must permit "immediate access" to any resident by relatives and by federal and state officials, including specially designated ombudsmen. Every state has an ombudsman to investigate complaints about long-term care facilities. Patients, their relatives, and their lawyers may file complaints.

■ *Penalties.* If a nursing home fails to meet federal standards, the government may deny payment under Medicaid and Medicare and may appoint new managers to operate the facility. Payment must be withheld if the home is found to be substandard in three consecutive annual surveys.

The law protects more than 1.3 million people in 16,000 nursing homes that participate in Medicaid or Medicare. In addition, the law protects 1.7 million people who receive care each year from 6,000 health agencies that provide care in the home paid by Medicare or Medicaid. The costs of compliance are shared by nursing homes, federal and state governments, and some patients. The overall purpose of the law is to help residents of nursing homes attain the highest level of physical, mental, psychological, and social well-being.

Self-Study
How to Evaluate a Nursing Facility

If the occasion should arise when you need a skilled nursing care facility, use the following checklist to compare the facilities that are available. The importance of personal inspection cannot be overemphasized.

Evaluation of a Nursing Facility

Item	Yes	No
1. Is the facility tidy?	❏	❏
2. Does it have a clean smell?	❏	❏
3. Are the food menus acceptable?	❏	❏
4. Does it have cheerful day rooms?	❏	❏
5. Do the patients appear well-cared-for?	❏	❏
6. Is the building fireproof?	❏	❏
7. Are handrails and other safety aids in evidence?	❏	❏
8. Are the physical and occupational programs satisfactory?	❏	❏
9. Is your own physician on ready-call?	❏	❏
10. Are house physicians on ready-call?	❏	❏
11. Is the nursing staff adequate?	❏	❏
12. Have you studied the facility's operating certificate to confirm the services offered?	❏	❏
13. Have you seen the Department of Health inspection report?	❏	❏
14. Is the general atmosphere of the facility pleasant?	❏	❏
15. Have you spoken to a few patients?	❏	❏

Glossary

Intermediate care facility. Designed for patients or residents who do not require the type of intensive care provided by a *skilled nursing facility* but who need room and board along with medical, nursing, social, and rehabilitative services. (*See* Residential Care Facility, Skilled Nursing Facility.)

Residential care facility. Provides secure and healthful accommodations to individuals who are capable of meeting their own basic needs, paying special attention to the social, recreational, *and* spiritual requirements of the residents. (*See* Intermediate Care Facility, Skilled Nursing Facility.)

Skilled nursing facility. A specially qualified facility that has the staff and equipment to provide skilled nursing care or rehabilitation services and other related health services. (*See* Intermediate Care Facility, Residential Care Facility.)

5

Legal Affairs

Although you may consider yourself a free and independent spirit, you belong to a society that is directed by law. In fact, law directs an extraordinary amount of your activities. From the filing of birth, marriage, and death certificates to enrollment in school at a set age and attendance for a specified number of years, from the payment of taxes to the signing of documents to purchase an automobile, from the possession of a passport while traveling in a foreign country to the meeting of certain health requirements, you are affected by laws every day. And every day, new laws are being considered for future implementation. Your life would not be the same without laws. Indeed, civilized society could not exist without them.

In this chapter, the law will be reviewed in relation to retirement planning. Legal questions that may affect you as a retiree involve property ownership, premarital planning, age discrimination, paid companions, new business setup, personal bankruptcy, and contracts. A lawyer can play an essential role in many of these and in quite a few other areas as well. For example, laws regarding Social Security and pensions are complex and frequently require legal interpretation. Likewise, protection of your savings and investments may on occasion call for legal intervention. In estate planning, a lawyer is important in helping you draw up a will to assure that your bequests are executed according to your wishes. Clearly, the law plays just as important a role in retirement planning as it does in every other aspect of your life.

FORMS OF PROPERTY OWNERSHIP

The word *property* is a general term for things that people own. The two basic types of property are real property and personal property. *Real property*, also known as *real estate*, is land and the buildings on it. *Personal property* can be tangible or intangible. *Tangible personal property* consists of items that you can touch, such as a car, boat, clothing, or stamp collection. *Intangible personal property* consists of things such as a right or an interest that is protected by law. Examples are an invention, musical composition, stock certificate, or savings account.

Items of both real and personal property can be owned or possessed to control or enjoy their private use. Items can also be possessed without being owned. For example, the tenant in an apartment or the driver of a rented car possesses the item without owning it. Conversely, items can be owned without being possessed. The owner of an apartment building is not in possession of the rented-out apartments. The car rental agency owns the cars but is not in possession of them while they are rented out.

Property can be owned by an individual, a group, or a state. When one individual owns a piece of property, he or she has *sole ownership.* When more than one person own the same piece of property at the same time, they have *concurrent ownership,* which is also called *plural ownership.*

Sole Ownership

The basic form of property ownership is sole ownership. In *sole ownership,* one person owns and controls a piece of property and has the right to leave it to whichever heirs he or she chooses. The owner has title to the property. *Title* is evidence of the right of a person to possess or enjoy property to the exclusion of all others and to dispose of the property. Title to any type of property—real or personal—exists once the property is owned by anyone. A seashell, for example, belongs to no one while it is lying on the beach, but once you pick it up for your collection, you have greater rights to it than anyone else does. Disposing of property is accomplished by transferring the title.

In many situations, even those involving married couples, sole ownership may be the wisest choice. For example, the husband can be the sole owner of a couple's securities and automobile, and the wife can be the sole owner of the couple's real estate. In this way, each can pass $600,000 to their heirs, tax-free. The assignment of ownership to a husband and wife is a complicated matter and is treated differently in the various states. In forty-two states, the *separate-property system* is followed. Under this system,

each spouse has sole ownership of property in his or her name but owns all real estate jointly. The remaining eight states follow the *community-property system* under which property acquired after marriage is owned equally by both partners. (For a discussion of community property, see page 72.)

Concurrent Ownership

Concurrent ownership exists when two or more people have ownership rights to the same piece of property at the same time. The types of concurrent ownership are joint tenancy with right of survivorship, tenancy in common, tenancy by the entirety, and community property. Each type is treated differently upon the death of an owner.

Joint Tenancy With Right of Survivorship

Joint tenancy with right of survivorship (JTWROS) is a traditional way for husbands and wives to hold property—each owns 50 percent of the property and when one of the owners dies, the property goes to the surviving owner free from the claims of the heirs or creditors of the deceased owner.

If there are three joint tenants, each owns one-third of the property. When one of the three owners dies, the surviving co-owners each own one-half of the property. When a second of the original three co-owners dies, the remaining one becomes the recipient and owner of all the property.

Since property held as JTWROS passes to the surviving owners, it bypasses the directives of a person's will, thus eliminating probate proceedings. This is one of the principal reasons many people opt for this type of ownership. Nevertheless, it is wise to indicate in the will to whom the property should pass just in case both owners die simultaneously in an accident or within a short time of each other. Designating an ultimate beneficiary in a will is a prudent clarification of the owners' wishes.

Bank accounts are usually opened as JTWROS. If you are considering this type of ownership, it is important that both you and your spouse or other partner understand that either owner of the account can withdraw all the funds at any time.

All in all, there are many advantages to JTWROS. Among them are the following:

■ *A sense of togetherness.* JTWROS indicates that the marriage is a joint relationship in which the two individuals involved share everything. It provides a feeling of unity, harmony, and security.

■ *Protection for a wife.* If a wife has no wealth of her own, JTWROS offers her protection because neither owner can sell the property or borrow against it without permission from the other.

■ *Automatic transfer to the survivors.* When one owner dies, the property automatically passes to the survivors outside of the will and without probate.

■ *Protection from claims after death.* In many states, certain jointly owned property is not subject to claims made by creditors or to damage-injury claims made against the deceased owner.

■ *Avoidance of publicity.* Prompt transfer of ownership can be completed without the publicity that might accompany the probate of a will.

■ *Reduction of estate administration costs.* Since ownership of JTWROS property passes automatically to the survivors, administration expenses of probate are not applicable to that part of the estate.

■ *Tax consideration.* If the joint tenants are spouses, at the death of one, one-half of the value of the property is included in the estate of the deceased for federal estate tax purposes.

Among the disadvantages of joint tenancy with right of survivorship are:

■ *Loss of the right to dispose of the property at death.* A person who places property in joint ownership usually gives up the right to dispose of it using a will. This applies even though the person states in the will that the property is to go to someone other than the co-owner.

■ *Need for complete agreement.* Decisions concerning how jointly held property is to be used, managed, and invested must be made harmoniously. Such unanimity may be difficult to achieve, especially in cases of separation, divorce, or intrafamily dispute.

■ *Need to protect children of first marriage.* If you have children from a first marriage, marry a second time, place your property into JTWROS, and die before your second spouse, your second spouse will inherit all your property. This individual may not be concerned with the welfare of your children from the first marriage.

■ *Loss of control.* In most cases, joint tenancy reduces a person's legal control over property. If you have a joint bank account and become ill, the other joint tenant can withdraw sums of money from the account without your knowledge or consent. If your marriage is bad, you may find one day that your spouse has withdrawn all your money and left town.

■ *Freezing of a joint bank account.* A joint bank account may be frozen in some states when one spouse dies so that the state can make sure all required taxes and claims have been settled. It may take some time for the funds to be released. Each spouse, therefore, should have some money in an individual account.

Tenancy in Common

Tenancy in common is a form of joint ownership with no right of survivorship and no automatic transfer at death. If two people co-own property, each can own 50 percent or any other percentage of the total. If four people invest in property as tenants in common, one can own 35 percent, another 25 percent, and the last two 20 percent each. The portion owned by each partner can be sold, given away, used as collateral, or passed on by a will.

In most cases, a deceased tenant in common's share of property is passed on by means of a will. If a co-owner dies without a will, his or her share of the property is disposed of according to applicable state laws. Ownership under tenancy in common is convenient for two or more friends or relatives who wish to co-own a piece of property but also want to preserve their freedom to dispose of their individual shares as they like.

To inherit property held under tenancy in common, a survivor must depend upon a will.

Tenancy by the Entirety

Tenancy by the entirety is a form of joint ownership in which a husband and wife own property (usually real estate) jointly because each spouse in his or her own right owns the *entire* property. Under this arrangement, the property passes to the surviving spouse in the same way it does under JTWROS. Tenancy by the entirety is usually applicable only to real property, and the owners must be husband and wife. Some states do not recognize this type of holding.

Community Property

In certain states, the laws provide that property acquired after marriage is community property. *Community property* is property that is owned equally—50 percent each—by both spouses no matter who contributes the money to pay for its purchase or upkeep. Nine states have community-property laws—Arizona, California, Idaho, Louisiana, Nevada, New Mexico, Texas, Washington, and Wisconsin. The remaining states determine property rights according to *common law*, which is law based on court decisions and customs rather than on written codes. Common law states follow one of two rules concerning property acquired after marriage. The first rule is that property acquired after marriage is owned solely by the husband even if the wife contributed money toward the purchase. The other rule is that each spouse owns the property derived from his or her earnings.

In both common law and community property states, property owned by either spouse before marriage is the sole property of the original owner. Furthermore, the income or capital gain produced by premarital property is separate property. In addition, also excluded from community property rules in community property states is property acquired after marriage by gift or inheritance.

Community property does not carry the right of survivorship. When one spouse dies, the other does not automatically assume full ownership of the property. The deceased partner's half is disposed of by will or, if there is no will, by the state's interstate laws. Only the deceased partner's half of the property is included as part of the estate for tax purposes. If, however, the property is willed to the spouse, then it qualifies for the unlimited marital deduction. Community property laws usually permit couples to set up other types of ownership, either separate or joint, but the laws in each of the nine community property states differ. If you move from a common law state to a community property state, or vice versa, be sure to have your will checked.

WHICH TYPE OF OWNERSHIP IS BEST?

An estate attorney is the best advisor concerning the way various types of property should be held. Some forms of property should be in your own name because this gives you maximum flexibility in handling the property. You can sell the property, use it as collateral, give it away, or pass it on to your heirs through your will. The following are examples of property for which individual ownership is suggested:

■ *Life insurance.* A life insurance policy can be written in the name of the insured or in the name of the insured's spouse, with the same beneficiaries. Many people put their policy in their spouses' names to keep the proceeds of the policy out of their estate if they should die, but this is no longer necessary because of the unlimited marital deduction. In addition, the proceeds of a life insurance policy pass to beneficiaries outside of the will, avoiding probate.

■ *Stocks and bonds.* Individual ownership makes sense for stocks and bonds. Since only one signature is needed, sole ownership allows flexibility in the purchase and sale of these instruments. The couple can agree privately to split ownership of them, each holding about 50 percent.

■ *Car.* Individual ownership is suggested for a car. In case of a lawsuit for damages, only the assets of the owner are threatened. With joint ownership, the assets of both owners are vulnerable.

Some forms of property that would benefit from joint ownership are the following:

■ *House.* Joint ownership with the right of survivorship is the usual method of ownership of a house. Home ownership is considered a joint effort. Furthermore, when one spouse passes away, the surviving spouse and children are guaranteed a roof over their heads. A jointly owned house passes to the survivors outside the will. However, when an estate exceeds $600,000, ownership of a house should be changed to tenancy in common in order to save on estate taxes.

■ *Savings and checking accounts.* Joint accounts are convenient because both spouses have access to them. In some states, however, savings and/or checking accounts can be frozen by the bank when one of the account holders dies. Occasionally, an alert survivor who is aware of this possibility withdraws money immediately. Instead of counting on being quick enough, however, it is better for each spouse to maintain an individual account of a few thousand dollars so that each has readily available cash if the joint accounts are frozen.

■ *Safe deposit box.* Most couples keep a safe deposit box in joint ownership so that each has equal access. When one spouse dies, the surviving spouse should empty the box immediately because the bank may seal it until the tax authorities can inventory its contents and collect whatever taxes are due. To avoid the problem of a sealed box, a married couple can store the husband's will and valuables in a box rented in the wife's name, and her will and valuables in a box rented in his name. It is also possible to name a deputy (an adult child, relative, or friend) who has access to the box.

ASPECTS OF RETIREMENT WITH LEGAL IMPLICATIONS

Situations may arise during the retirement years that require legal assistance. In the case of a second marriage or late first marriage, a legal agreement should be made to protect the property rights of one or both partners or their children. Legal guidance may also be helpful if you ask someone to care for you or to handle your financial affairs during an illness. This also applies if you are asked to provide the care. Knowledge of the law is additionally invaluable when you run into problems associated with age discrimination, bankruptcy, new business setup, or contracts.

Late or Second Marriage

If you marry late in life for the first time or for a second time, you should be aware of potential legal problems, especially in relation to property. Take the case of a second marriage in which each spouse has children from a first marriage. On the death of one spouse, the second spouse inherits all the property. The surviving spouse can then draw up a will leaving all the property to his or her children, with nothing going to the children of the deceased.

A lawyer should be consulted to determine whether a *premarital* or *prenuptial agreement* would help to protect the property rights of children, if any, from a previous marriage. The lawyer can help you draw up a premarital or *antenuptial agreement*, which is entered into *before* marriage. It is a contract between a man and a woman in which the property rights and interests of either the prospective husband or wife or both are determined or in which property is guaranteed to one or both or to their children.

An antenuptial agreement can be supplemented with a *trust agreement*. By leaving all of his or her assets in a trust, the first spouse to die can guarantee that the surviving spouse will enjoy an income from the trust for life but that upon the surviving spouse's death, part of the remainder will go to the first spouse's children. Or the arrangements can be that all of the remainder of the trust fund go to the first spouse's children or that any part of it go to anyone else desired. This type of agreement gives you con-

trol in the ultimate distribution of your assets. A lawyer can advise you and your future spouse of potential financial and/or legal problems that may arise unless valid agreements are made before marriage.

Individuals who live together unmarried should be aware that in case of death, all property of the deceased goes to the family of the deceased and not to the live-in partner unless a will spells out the desired distribution of property. Hire an attorney to draw up a written living-together agreement to spell out specifics in case the relationship ends due to death or a decision to separate.

For married couples, if the marriage terminates by divorce, it is essential for you to consult with an attorney in order to avoid the many pitfalls that may occur. Know your legal rights to insure fair handling of all the major financial transactions involved. The attorney you select should be an independent and not involved in any of your husband or wife's business affairs so that you have total commitment.

If your spouse dies, advise your attorney immediately so that probate proceedings and the filing of the will can be initiated.

Legal and professional fees you pay are deductible if your miscellaneous deductions exceed two percent of your Adjusted Gross Income (AGI).

Someone to Care for You

At retirement, most people are in good health and fully capable of handling all sorts of activities, such as managing an investment portfolio, depositing monthly Social Security and pension checks, paying bills, taking care of household chores, and walking the dog. Suddenly, however, you may suffer a mild stroke, necessitating time in the hospital and then several months at home or in a nursing facility to recuperate. Who will take care of your myriad daily activities? You can plan ahead so that everything will be handled the way you want until you are once again able to take over.

Informally, you can arrange with your spouse or a relative or friend who knows your ,economic affairs to step in if such a crisis should arise. Or you can make more formal arrangements, granting power of attorney to a person of integrity to take care of your affairs while you are incapacitated.

A *power of attorney* is a legal document by which the principal (you, the signer) designates another person (such as your lawyer, a relative, or a friend) to act for you in financial transactions. The laws of all states permit you to give someone a power of attorney. However, in the case of an ordinary power of attorney, if you become *incompetent*—unable to manage personal affairs such as handling mail, making bank transactions, and paying bills—the power may automatically be revoked. State law provides that a power of attorney may contain appropriate language so that even if you become incompetent, the designated holder of the power can continue to act in your behalf. A power of attorney that contains this language is known as a *durable power of attorney* (see page 284 for a full discussion). The holder of the power can deposit and withdraw money from your bank accounts, buy and sell property and securities on your behalf, and negotiate contracts for you.

Your lawyer should prepare the power of attorney. Do not buy a printed form and fill it in yourself. A properly executed power of attorney not only protects you but also your agent and those with whom he or she deals.

Caring for Someone Else

Many people have an elderly parent or other relative who is unable to handle his or her affairs because of illness or senility. If this is your situation, it may become necessary for you to petition a court to appoint you or another relative as the person's *conservator*. For a conservator to be appointed, the *ward* must first be proven incompetent.

The functions of a conservator include responsibility for all the ward's monies as well as real and personal property; maintenance of an accurate record of income and expenditures; and meeting of housing, medical, food, and clothing needs. To have an individual declared incompetent requires the services of an attorney, since so many legal responsibilities are involved.

Age Discrimination

Almost all Americans are covered by the Federal Age Discrimination in Employment Act (ADEA) of 1968, as amended in 1978. ADEA makes it illegal for employers to practice *age discrimination*, that is, to refuse to hire, promote, or reward an individual because of age if that person is above 40. It applies to private employers of twenty or more people in industries affecting commerce. Most federal, state, and local government employees are covered, as are employment agencies serving covered employers and labor unions representing twenty-five or more members or functioning as hiring halls.

ADEA, as amended in 1986, also prohibits mandatory retirement at any age for employees protected by the law. In general, the act also prohibits discrimination in job retention, promotions, compensation, and other terms and conditions of employment. People who believe that their rights have been violated under the act can file a charge with the Equal Employment Opportunity Commission.

The federal ADEA and its amendments do

not preempt state age discrimination laws if the state laws are more liberal. Therefore, employers located in states having age discrimination laws are subject to both the federal and state laws, and must generally comply with the more liberal provisions of each. For example, if a state law does not permit the tenured employee exemption, then the state law applies.

The Age Discrimination Act (ADA) of 1975 is different from ADEA. ADA's prohibition against age discrimination affects Americans of every age and forbids most age discrimination in programs and activities receiving federal financial assistance. ADA's effects are widespread, as many institutions receive federal money in some form.

Complaints under ADA can be filed with any or all agencies that provide money for the program or activity in question. All complaints within the jurisdiction of the act will be referred to the Federal Mediation and Conciliation Service, which will try to reach a solution satisfactory to both parties.

Bankruptcy

Occasionally, individuals become mired in debt. Whatever the reasons for this unfortunate situation, these people may have no alternative but to declare *bankruptcy*, that is, to declare in a bankruptcy court that they cannot pay their accumulated debts. Legally, bankruptcy is a constitutionally guaranteed right of Americans.

Under federal bankruptcy law as revised in 1978, bankruptcy can take one of two forms for an individual. These are straight bankruptcy (Chapter 7 of the Bankruptcy Act) and the wage earner's plan (Chapter 13 of the Bankruptcy Act). Under *straight bankruptcy*, the court appoints a trustee to list all your debts, to determine whether it is possible for you to repay the debts, and, if it is not possible,

to sell your assets to repay as many of the debts as possible. You and your spouse are allowed to retain a specified equity in a home as well as other specified items such as a car, furniture, appliances, clothing, jewelry, and tools used for a livelihood. Once the process of straight bankruptcy has been completed, your debts are considered wiped out and you are judged free and clear. However, you cannot declare bankruptcy again for six years.

Under the *wage earner's plan*, you are permitted to keep your property, but you must set up a monthly budget plan, approved by the court, to pay off your creditors within a three-year period. The budget indicates how much you can afford to pay your creditors after paying your living expenses. Your payback may be ten cents or more on the dollar, depending on your income and essential living expenses. While you are in the process of repaying part or all of your debts, your creditors may not contact you about your financial obligations. After the plan is completed, whatever debts you had are considered eliminated. However, some debts—including taxes, fines, alimony, and child support—cannot be erased.

In some states, if you file for bankruptcy, your private pension accounts, including IRAs and Keoghs, may be subject to creditor's claims if you have access to the money, even with a penalty. Under the rules of bankruptcy, payments from stock-bonus, pension, profit-sharing, annuity, and similar plans are exempt only to the extent that they are necessary to support the account owner and his or her dependents.

If you are considering bankruptcy, contact a lawyer for advice and guidance even though you can file for bankruptcy on your own. The law is complex, and a lawyer can help you protect your property and advise you whether to file under Chapter 7 or Chapter 13.

Setting Up a New Business

Some retirees set up a small business to keep themselves occupied, to enjoy personal satisfaction, and/or to earn extra money. Free advice and guidance on small business is available from the federal government's Small Business Administration, 409 Third Street, S.W., Washington, D.C. 20416, or from any one of its field offices.

If you decide to set up a business, you can structure it as an individual proprietorship, a partnership, or a corporation. In both an *individual proprietorship*, a business structure in which one person owns and manages the enterprise, and a *partnership*, a business structure in which two or more individuals own and manage the enterprise, you have *unlimited liability*. This means that you are responsible to the full extent of your assets, both personal and business, for any debts incurred by the business. In a *corporation*, a business structure in which the enterprise is treated as a natural person and allowed to conduct business as such, you have *limited liability*, whereby you are liable only for the money you invest and not for any of your personal assets. Limited liability is, in fact, the principal feature of the corporate structure. To set up a corporation, you must have a lawyer draw up incorporation papers and other documents. For a partnership, the lawyer must draw up a detailed partnership agreement that covers all aspects of the business relationship and includes a suitable escape clause in case the partnership is dissolved.

Some points to check before starting a small business are the following:

■ *Taxes.* You will need a tax number for filing reports, a sales tax number for purchasing materials, and special records for state income and sales taxes as well as for local taxes. Also, you must pay Social Security taxes for yourself and your employees.

■ *Insurance.* You will have to purchase fire and liability insurance as well as workmen's compensation if you hire anyone.

■ *Licenses and permits.* You may need a special license or permit to operate your business.

No matter what type of business you choose to start or how many, if any, employees you plan to hire, it is essential that you retain a lawyer who is knowledgeable in the field of business law and regulations in your city and state.

Signing a Contract

You may wish to spend part of your retirement income to join a social club, to register in an exercise program, or to buy hobby equipment. These purchases may involve a contract requiring you to pay a large sum of money either in advance or on an installment plan. You must remember that a *contract* is a binding legal agreement. Before you sign it, be sure you understand what it says. You have the right to read the contract carefully first and check it with your lawyer.

A widely used type of contract is the *conditional sales agreement*. If you sign such an agreement, you are committing yourself to pay an agreed amount per month for a given number of months. The buyer takes possession of the purchased item—whether it is an automobile, home appliance, or furniture—but title, or ownership, remains with the seller until the final installment has been paid. Failure to meet the payments gives the legal owner, or seller, the right to repossess the item, resell it, and sue you for any deficiency plus whatever costs were incurred in the course of the court procedure.

In some cases, a *chattel mortgage* is used. The buyer acquires title to the purchased item but pledges it as security for the balance due. Again, failure to meet the payments gives the lender, usually a bank or finance company, the right to foreclose the loan, repossess the item, and sue for the remaining balance plus court costs.

Some Tips on Contracts

Because contracts closely touch your everyday life, it is important for you to be aware of their major pitfalls and how to avoid them. The following basic tips can save you time and money in the long run:

■ *Watch for blank spaces.* Do not sign a contract that has blank spaces in it. Be sure every space is filled in to your satisfaction.

■ *Retain the right to change a printed form.* You have the right to change a printed form to make the agreement meet the terms you are willing to accept.

■ *Reject oral promises.* Every provision agreed upon must be written into the contract in order to be enforceable. Do not accept oral promises.

■ *Check with your lawyer.* Most important, before you sign a contract, show it to your lawyer. Failure to do so can be costly and time-consuming.

CHOOSING AND USING A LAWYER

A lawyer is a highly trained professional who is qualified to assist you in handling your financial resources, property, housing arrangements, estate planning, and a variety of family affairs. Some lawyers specialize in one or more of these areas and are able to guide you when you begin to plan for retirement. Making a wrong decision can be very expensive, and when you pass age 50, the opportunities for correcting expensive errors are fewer. Therefore, it is wise to obtain as much expert legal advice as possible to assure yourself a problem-free retirement.

Laws today are much too complex to be correctly interpreted and applied by the layman. Many individuals practicing do-it-yourself law have found that they multiplied both their problems and the legal fees that had to be paid to resolve the problems. If you do not already have a lawyer, choose one to give you a legal checkup in the various areas of retirement planning—financial planning; estate planning; buying or selling a home; civil or criminal court actions; starting a business; and tax consequences of charitable contributions, bequests, medical expenses, and trusts.

More and more people are turning to lawyers for help during retirement and retirement planning. Many older citizens' problems center on the uncertainties and inequities in such government assistance programs as Medicare, Medicaid, and, on occasion, Social Security. Constantly changing rules and regulations make professional assistance mandatory.

Choosing a Lawyer

One way to select a lawyer is to find a satisfied client. You may be able to get a lead by talking to your family and friends. Be sure that the lawyer you choose handles your particular problem, since lawyers in larger cities generally specialize in certain branches of the law.

If you live in a rural area or small town, contact your local bank for the names of a few reliable attorneys. In larger towns or cities, call your local bar association. Most bar associations sponsor a lawyer referral service. For a small fee, you can arrange an interview to discuss your problem while, at the same time, getting to know the individual. If for any reason you are dissatisfied, you can look for someone else.

Most local libraries have a copy of the *Martindale-Hubbel Directory*, which lists lawyers, their specialties, and their ratings. Other directories include *Sullivan's Probate Directory, Markham's Negligence Counsel,* and *Best's Recommended Insurance Attorneys.* If you cannot afford a lawyer, contact your local legal aid society, which offers free legal services.

Legal Fees

Legal fees vary according to where you live and the complexity of your case. Ordinarily, a lawyer charges on the basis of the amount of time he spends serving you. This includes time spent talking to you in his office and on the telephone, looking up the law, preparing legal documents, writing letters, and negotiating with others in your behalf.

Sometimes a lawyer sets a flat fee for certain types of work, such as closing on real estate, drawing a will, and probating an estate. Many county and state bar associations have set up schedules of minimum fees for most common types of legal work. However, at your first contact with a lawyer, you should ask how much the charge will be in your particular case and what method of payment is requested. Payment possibilities include payment in advance, a deposit with the balance to come at the conclusion of the work, and periodic payments. Financial arrangements made in advance usually avoid disagreement and confusion later on. If you believe that a particular lawyer's fee is too high, you are free to solicit another lawyer whose charge may be more modest.

For certain kinds of legal work, a lawyer's fee is subject to approval by a court or by a state or federal agency. For example, lawyers' fees are controlled in cases involving guardianships and the estates of deceased persons and in proceedings concerning certain types of retirement benefits, such as Social Security.

KNOW YOUR RIGHTS

Many new rights and protections have been extended to older Americans by recent federal laws, as well as by state and local laws. If you believe that any of your rights have been violated, these laws spell out the ways in which you can obtain redress. Many laws permit you to file a suit against the party you believe injured you. However, filing a suit can be expensive and time-consuming and does not guarantee that you will win your case.

Several factors should be considered before filing a lawsuit. They include:

■ *Violation of a law.* You must consider with your lawyer whether a law has been violated. Even though you may not like something or think that it is unfair, it does not mean that a law has been violated. Your lawyer must carefully check the law's provisions.

■ *Payment of legal expenses.* In many cases, the court requires the losing side to pay all legal expenses. This means that if you lose, you must pay both your own and your opponent's legal fees. You must decide whether initiation of a lawsuit is worth this possible high cost.

■ *Proving your case.* In a lawsuit, you are required to prove to the satisfaction of the court that you have been harmed. While you may be certain that you have been injured, you and your lawyer must determine if you are able to prove it.

■ *Time and aggravation.* You must carefully weigh whether the time, costs, and aggravation of a lawsuit are worth the redress you *might* win. As you deliberate, you must also bear in mind that you may *lose*.

Initiation of a lawsuit should be made with great care and in consultation with your lawyer.

Self-Study
Evaluating a Lawyer

1. Which of the following qualifications do you consider essential in a lawyer?

Qualification	Essential	Not Essential
Communicative	❑	❑
Compassionate	❑	❑
Competent	❑	❑
Discreet	❑	❑
Forceful	❑	❑
Honest	❑	❑
Independent	❑	❑
Knowledgeable in field	❑	❑
Reasonably priced	❑	❑
Respected	❑	❑
Up-to-date	❑	❑

2. To what extent does your current lawyer meet these standards?

_____

_____

_____

_____

Glossary

Age discrimination. When an employer or other person makes a decision about an individual because of age alone, overlooking individual merit and competence. *See also* Age Discrimination in Employment Act.

Age Discrimination in Employment Act (ADEA). A federal law passed in 1968 and amended in 1978 that makes it illegal for employers to refuse to hire an individual because of age. *See also* Age discrimination.

Antenuptial agreement. A legal agreement usually prepared before a second or subsequent marriage that sets forth the details of property distribution in case of the death of one of the partners. Also known as a premarital agreement.

Bankruptcy. A court proceeding in which an individual declares that he or she is unable to pay his or her debts and seeks the court's guidance in removing or reducing those debts. *See also* Straight bankruptcy; Wage earner's plan bankruptcy.

Chattel mortgage. A type of sales agreement in which the buyer acquires title to the purchased property but pledges it as security for the balance due. The buyer's failure to meet the payments gives the lender, usually a bank or finance company, the right to foreclose the loan, repossess the item, and sue for the remaining balance plus court costs. *See also* Conditional sales agreement.

Common law. Law based on court decisions and customs rather than on written codes.

Community property. A form of concurrent ownership in which property acquired after marriage is considered to be owned equally—50 percent each—no matter who contributes the money to pay for its purchase or upkeep. *See also* Joint tenancy with right of survivorship; Separate property; Tenancy by the entirety; Tenancy in common.

Concurrent ownership. Ownership and control of property by more than one person. The various types of concurrent ownership are treated differently at death. Also known as plural ownership. *See also* Community property; Joint tenancy with right of survivorship; Sole ownership; Tenancy by the entirety; Tenancy in common.

Conditional sales agreement. A type of sales agreement in which the buyer agrees to pay a specified amount of money per month for a given number of months. Title remains with the seller until the final payment is made by the buyer. The buyer's failure to meet the payments gives the seller the right to repossess the item. *See also* Chattel mortgage.

Conservator. An individual who is court-appointed to look after the financial affairs of a person judged incompetent.

Contract. A legally binding agreement between two or more parties.

Corporation. A form of business organization in which the enterprise is a legal entity that is treated like a natural person. It can make contracts; own, buy, and sell property; incur debts; and engage in lawsuits in a court of law. The corporation enjoys perpetual life, and the stockholders enjoy limited liability. *See also* Individual proprietorship; Partnership.

Durable power of attorney. A power of attorney that remains in force even if the principal becomes incompetent. *See also* Power of attorney.

Incompetent. Unable to manage personal affairs such as handling mail, making bank transactions, and paying bills.

Individual proprietorship. A form of business organization in which one individual owns and manages the enterprise, assumes all the risks, and derives all the profits. *See also* Corporation; Partnership.

Intangible personal property. *See* Personal property.

Joint tenancy with right of survivorship (JTWROS). A form of concurrent ownership in which each spouse or partner owns an equal share of the property. When one owner dies, the property automatically passes to the survivors outside a will. *See also* Community property; Tenancy by the entirety; Tenancy in common.

Limited liability. The legal condition in which a stockholder cannot be held personally responsible for the debts of the corporation beyond the amount that he or she already invested in the enterprise. *See also* Unlimited liability.

Partnership. A form of business organization created through a contractual arrangement between two or more individuals, each of whom assumes unlimited personal liability for the debts of the joint enterprise. *See also* Corporation; Individual proprietorship.

Personal property. The things that people own other than land and the buildings on it. The two types are *tangible personal property*, which is something you can touch, such as clothing, a car, and a boat; and *intangible personal property*, which is a right or an interest protected by law, such as an invention, a stock certificate, or a savings account. *See also* Real property.

Plural ownership. *See* Concurrent ownership.

Power of attorney. A written instrument by which one person, known as the principal, appoints another person as an agent with the authority to perform certain specified acts on his or her behalf.

Premarital Agreement. *See* Antenuptial agreement.

Property. Things or rights that people acquire for the purpose of ownership. *See also* Personal property; Real property.

Real estate. *See* Real property.

Real property. Land and the buildings on it. Also known as real estate. *See also* Personal property.

Separate property. Property other than real estate that is acquired after marriage but owned by the individual spouse who purchased it. *See also* Community property.

Sole ownership. Ownership and control of property by one person who, upon death, leaves the property to chosen heirs. *See also* Concurrent ownership.

Straight bankruptcy. A form of personal bankruptcy in which the indebted individual is ordered by a bankruptcy court to liquidate a specified amount of assets to repay as much debt as possible. *See also* Bankruptcy; Wage earner's plan bankruptcy.

Tangible personal property. *See* Personal property.

Tenancy by the entirety. A form of concurrent ownership of real property in which each spouse owns the entire property in his or her own right. Upon death, the property passes to the surviving spouse the same way it does under joint tenancy with right of survivorship. Elimination of either party's right of survivorship can be accomplished only with the consent of both parties. *See also* Community property; Joint tenancy with right of survivorship; Tenancy in common.

Tenancy in common. A form of concurrent ownership in which each partner owns a specified percentage of the property but not a specific piece. There is no right of survivorship and no automatic transfer at death. The portion owned by each person can be sold, given away, used as collateral, or passed through the particular owner's will. *See also* Community property; Joint tenancy with right of survivorship; Tenancy by the entirety.

Title. Ownership; legal right to the possession of property, especially real property, or the instrument constituting evidence of such right.

Trust agreement. A legal document in which the maker of the trust (trustor) names a trustee to distribute income and/or principal to a beneficiary(ies) at specified times.

Unlimited liability. The legal condition in which owners of individual proprietorships or partnerships are held personally responsible for the debts of the business to the full extent of their assets and personal wealth. *See also* Limited liability.

Wage earner's plan bankruptcy. A form of personal bankruptcy in which the indebted individual is ordered by a bankruptcy court to set up a court-approved monthly budget plan to repay as much debt as possible within a three-year period while still retaining ownership of all real and personal property. *See also* Bankruptcy; Straight bankruptcy.

Ward. A person who is judged incapable of managing his or her personal affairs and for whom a conservator is court appointed.

PART TWO
Long-Term Funding for Retirement

6
Savings and Investments

More than most countries, the United States is a land of consumers. Of every dollar of income after taxes, the average American spends 95 cents and saves only about 5 cents. While the savings rate in the United States is only 5 percent, in Japan and Germany it is 15 to 20 percent. Many economists believe that the low savings rate in this country is responsible for restraining investment and for slowing down the growth of productivity.

In spite of our low savings rate, however, Americans recognize that income from savings is one of the important components of total retirement income. Individuals and couples who have accumulated a nest egg will enjoy a more financially secure retirement.

The average American accumulates a small personal nest egg for retirement by making monthly payments on a mortgage and by purchasing ordinary life insurance. Monthly mortgage payments build up equity in a family home; *equity* is the net investment in a home and represents ownership. *Insurance premiums*, which are installment payments toward the purchase of a life insurance policy, increase the cash value of the life insurance. In addition, the average family tries to save its

unspent cash income, banking between 5 and 7 percent of its disposable income per year. These savings are usually deposited in a savings bank, savings and loan association, or commercial bank. Other Americans build up their capital through investments in stocks, government securities, and real estate.

Some people make investments all during their working lives and acquire a general picture of the intricacies of the subject. Others are unable to save and invest and are, thus, novices in the field when they try to do so. However, many public pension systems permit lump-sum distribution of excess reserves or rollover of tax-deferred annuity funds at the point of retirement; many private pension plans also allow lump-sum distribution at this time. If your pension fund allows this, you will need to make some investment decisions. It is, therefore, essential that you understand savings and investment alternatives in terms of both safety and yield.

SAVINGS ACCOUNTS

Banks and savings and loan associations offer a variety of savings accounts. Some of the more popular are the passbook savings account, money market deposit account, Negotiable Order of Withdrawal account (NOW account), Super Negotiable Order of Withdrawal account (Super NOW account), and certificate of deposit.

Passbook Savings Account

Passbook savings accounts are offered by savings banks, savings and loan associations, and commercial banks. The money in these accounts is *liquid*, available for withdrawal whenever the need for cash arises. However, the accounts pay a relatively low interest rate, generally around 3 percent. These rates can rise or fall. *Interest* is the fee that banks pay to depositors for use of their money. The savings are safe, since up to $100,000 per account is insured by the United States Federal Deposit Insurance Corporation (FDIC).

Money Market Deposit Account

Money market deposit accounts (MMDA) pay a higher interest rate than passbook savings accounts do, but they also require that a minimum balance be maintained. If the balance in an MMDA falls below the bank's specified minimum, the lower passbook savings account interest rate is paid. MMDA accounts are offered by savings banks, savings and loan associations, and commercial banks, which use the account balances for investment in money market instruments. The savings are insured by the FDIC up to $100,000 per account, and the money in the account is liquid, available for withdrawal whenever the need for cash arises. Some MMDA accounts offer check-writing privileges. If your savings are in a passbook savings account, you might want to transfer your funds into a higher-yielding MMDA. Check the interest rates at several banks.

Negotiable Order of Withdrawal Account (NOW Account)

A new era in banking services began in 1981 when commercial banks, savings and loan associations, mutual savings banks, and credit unions were authorized to offer *Negotiable Order of Withdrawal accounts* (NOW accounts). NOW accounts can be viewed in two ways—as checking accounts that earn interest, or as savings accounts on which you can write checks. The balance requirements and interest rates of NOW accounts vary from bank to bank.

Super Negotiable Order of Withdrawal Account (Super NOW Account)

Since late 1982, banks have also been offering *Super Negotiable Order of Withdrawal accounts*, or Super NOW accounts, which are savings accounts with check-writing privileges. There is no limit on the amount for which a check can be written. Generally, Super NOW accounts pay an interest rate that is higher than that of an ordinary NOW account but less than that of a money market deposit account. They also require a higher minimum balance, with some banks applying a penalty fee if the balance falls below the minimum. Each bank sets its own rules and regulations governing Super NOW accounts, although all accounts are insured up to $100,000 each by the FDIC.

Certificate of Deposit

A *certificate of deposit* (CD) is a type of savings account in which a specified sum of money is deposited for a set period of time. CDs are also instruments of the money market (see page 96).

Since the deregulation of banking in 1983, each bank has been able to set its own interest rates, terms, and minimum deposit requirements. Most banks currently accept $500 minimum deposits, and many accept deposits as low as $100. The interest rates paid are competitive. In addition, your entire investment in CDs, as in any savings account, is insured up to $100,000 by the FDIC.

CDs of $100,000 or more feature *negotiable interest rates*, the rate of interest paid is negotiated between the investor and the institution. Individuals or institutions purchasing these CDs usually shop around for the highest interest rates available.

Since all bank interest is fully taxable, the interest earned on a CD is also fully taxable. In addition, if you withdraw any of the principal before maturity for any reason, you must pay a penalty. The minimum loss is thirty-one days' interest on accounts that are due in one year or less. If you have not earned sufficient interest to pay the penalty, you will have the penalty deducted from your principal.

CDs were instituted to induce savers to keep their money in banks, instead of shifting it to money market mutual funds. CDs are safe and yield competitive returns.

EMERGENCY SAVINGS FUND

All retirees should have an emergency savings fund as a cushion in case of an unforseeable crisis such as an accident or serious illness. An emergency savings fund will help you in situations in which something happens so suddenly that you are left totally unprepared. Emergency reserves are important because they give you protection against the unexpected. The amount set aside in an emergency savings fund should equal the retirement cost of living for a period of about three to six months. For example, a retired couple whose living expenses are $2,000 a month should have between $6,000 and $12,000 in an emergency savings fund. An emergency

fund is necessary even though Social Security and pension incomes are certain and will continue.

At least $5,000 of your emergency savings fund should be kept in a money market deposit account, which offers not only safety and a competitive yield but also allows you to tap the money quickly. The balance should be deposited in a mutual fund, which allows you to immediately redeem your investment by phone at any time. (See page 98 for information on mutual funds.)

STOCKS

The term "stock" actually refers to two types of investment instruments. One is known as common stock and the other is called preferred stock.

Common Stocks

Most investors should include at least some common stocks in their portfolios. Common stocks are the most popular form of investment in the United States. Over 25 million Americans own stocks directly, and many more are indirect holders through their interests in pension funds and other intermediaries, such as insurance companies.

When you buy shares of common stocks, you become a part owner of the enterprise that issued the stock and can expect to participate in the profits of the firm, if there are any. *Common stocks* can be defined as shares in a corporation that give their owners the right to control the enterprise and to share in the profits. The amount of the dividend paid to common stockholders out of the profits and the time of the payment are within the discretion of the board of directors of the corporation.

Traditionally, common stocks have been considered a means of protection against inflation, rising in value as prices increase. However, average stock prices are erratic. In some periods, stock prices decline while consumer prices rise. But in the *long term*, which is ten or more years, investments in stocks yield a higher return than do investments in bonds or in the money market. (See Table 6.1 and page 96 for a discussion of the money market and its instruments.)

Preferred Stocks

Preferred stocks are shares in a corporation that entitle their owners to receive fixed and stated dividends before any earnings are distributed to the common stockholders. However, the fixed return is not guaranteed. The company's board of directors has the authority to pay or not pay the preferred stockholders' dividends, depending on the amount of profits earned during the year. If the company does not pay dividends to the preferred stockholders, it cannot pay dividends to the common stockholders either.

Preferred stock is "preferred" not only because of its payment of dividends but also because of its payment to stockholders if and when the corporation is dissolved. When an enterprise is folded, the claims of the preferred shareholders are put before those of the common stockholders. However, the claims of bondowners come first.

Preferred stocks are not necessarily better than other types of investments.

BONDS

Bonds are written promises to repay a loan on a specified date, called the *date of maturity*, while paying the bondholder a specified amount of interest at regular intervals, which is usually twice a year. On the date of maturity, the borrower, either a company or a governmental unit, will return the investor's capital. Referred to as *fixed income assets*, bonds are usually issued in units of $1,000 or more and bear a fixed interest rate, known as the *coupon rate*. The *interest* is the fee that the company pays the bondholder for the use of his or her money. On the date of maturity, the borrower, either a company or a governmental unit, returns the bondholder's capital. The value of the bond fluctuates in the bond market in an inverse manner with interest rates, so that when interest rates are high, bond prices are low, and when interest rates are low, bond prices are high. Maturity dates extend from ten to thirty or more years.

When you buy a bond, you will know exactly how much you will receive when interest is paid. If you hold the bond until the date of maturity, you will get back your initial investment in full. If you sell your bond before maturity, you may earn a *capital gain,* making money on the sale, or take a *capital loss,* losing money, depending upon the bond's market price at the time of the sale.

A variety of bonds are available:

Government Bonds

A large variety of government bonds is available for sale to investors. Included are United States Savings Bonds, United States Treasury bonds; Unites States agency securities, such as those issued by the Government National Mortgage Association, the Federal National Mortgage Association, and the Federal Home Loan Mortgage Corporation; and municipal bonds, which are issued by states, counties, and municipalities, as well as their various agencies.

States may not tax the interest earned on United States government bonds, according to a Supreme Court decision of 1819. In *McCulloch v. Maryland*, Chief Justice John Marshall said that a state or local tax on a federal instrumentality is invalid. However, United States government bonds are not exempt from federal income tax. On the other hand, the federal government

Table 6.1
Advantage of Investing in Common Stocks

Growth of a $10,000 Investment
for Periods Ending December 31, 1991

Over the past	Total Value	Average Annual Total Return	Average Annual Rate
	Common Stocks		**Inflation**
10 years	$ 50,548	17.6%	3.9%
20 years	$ 94,469	11.9%	6.2%
30 years	$186,997	10.3%	5.2%
40 years	$857,332	11.8%	4.2%
	Corporate Bonds		
10 years	$ 45,133	16.3%	3.9%
20 years	$ 60,518	9.4%	6.2%
30 years	$ 82,086	7.3%	5.2%
40 years	$104,362	6.0%	4.2%
	U. S. Treasury Bills		
10 years	$ 20,894	7.7%	3.9%
20 years	$ 44,173	7.7%	6.2%
30 years	$ 68,484	6.6%	5.2%
40 years	$ 84,203	5.5%	4.2%

Source: *Stocks, Bonds, Bills, and Inflation 1995 Yearbook*, Ibbotson Associates, Inc., Chicago (annually updates work by Roger G. Ibbotson and Rex A. Sinquefield). Used with permission. All rights reserved.

The data above indicate that the stock market's performance over several decades is a fine illustration of the positive power of time. The table shows how dramatically a $10,000 investment in common stocks or stock mutual funds would have grown over the past 10, 20, 30, and 40 years, compared with investments in bonds or U.S. Treasury paper. It is obvious, therefore, that every portfolio should contain a common stock component.

may not tax the interest earned on a municipal bond, which is an instrumentality of a state, county, or local government, because of the general constitutional principle of mutual independence of the federal and state governments. These latter bonds are also tax-exempt in the states and municipalities in which they are issued. However, you are liable for taxes on the interest you earn on bonds issued by states other than the one in which you live. For example, if you live in New York and receive interest on a bond issued by the state of Colorado, you must report the income in your New York state tax return. But if you live in New York and own a bond issued by the state of New York, you will not have to pay federal, state, or city taxes on the interest.

United States Savings Bonds

Savings bonds are securities sold by the federal government that offer fixed income with minimum risk and investment. They are sold at a discount, and they earn interest over a designated time period. The United States government offers two types of savings bonds—the Series EE savings bond and the Series HH savings bond.

The **Series EE savings bond** is an appreciation-type security. The price you pay to purchase a bond is half the bond's face value. For example, you pay $50 for a $100 bond.

Series EE bonds purchased prior to May 1, 1995, reach maturity (full value) eighteen years from the date of purchase. This is because the guaranteed rate of interest was changed to 4 percent as of March 1, 1993, in response to a sharp drop in market interest rates. The last change in the guaranteed minimum rate before that had taken place on November 1, 1986, when the rate was reduced from 7 1/2 percent to 6 percent. Series E and EE bonds issued prior to

March 1, 1993, are retaining their previously guaranteed minimum rates until the end of their maturity periods.

Bonds purchased after May 1, 1995, will earn market-based interest rates with no guaranteed minimum yield through maturity—seventeen years. The Treasury will announce two interest rates for savings bonds each May 1 and November 1. The first will be the short-term or five-year rate, and the second will be the long-term rate that applies for years five through maturity. The short-term rate will be 85 percent of the average of six-month Treasury security yields. The long-term rate will be 85 percent of the average of five-year Treasury security yields. Bonds are guaranteed to reach twice their purchase price in seventeen years regardless of the average interest rate. If a savings bond were to fall short of its face value after seventeen years, the Goverment would make a one-time adjustment to achieve that price. Because the market-based rate changes, bonds may reach face value before seventeen years. They may be redeemed six months after the issue date and will receive interest for thirty years from that date. To obtain the latest interest rate, call 800–US–BONDS.

Series EE savings bonds are available in eight denominations—$50, $75, $100, $200, $500, $1,000, $5,000, and $10,000. They can be purchased through a payroll savings plan where you work or any bank. Reporting of interest for federal income tax purposes may be deferred until the bonds are cashed. The interest earned is exempt from state and local income taxes. Series EE bonds are excellent for building a savings nest egg.

Series HH savings bonds can only be purchased when you redeem your Series EE bonds. The redemption value of your EE bonds is simply converted into Series HH bonds, thus postponing your having to pay taxes on the accumulated interest from the EEs until you cash in the HHs. Series HH bonds are issued in four denominations—$500, $1,000, $5,000, and $10,000–and sell at full face value. The interest on Series HH bonds is paid semiannually by United States Treasury check at a rate of 4 percent a year, effective March 1, 1993. The semiannual interest is subject to federal income tax, but not to state or local income tax. HH bonds also reach maturity eighteen years after purchase.

United States Treasury Bonds

United States Treasury bonds are obligations of the United States government with maturities of ten or more years. The older United States Treasury bonds are *bearer bonds*, that is, the owner's name does not appear on the certificate and is not registered on the books of the issuer.

Since January 1983, all new Treasury bonds have been issued in *registered* form only, which means that the owner's name is inscribed on the certificate and is recorded on the Treasury's books. Ownership of these bonds may be registered to one person, to two or more persons, or to minors. These bonds are *coupon bonds*; attached to them are postdated interest coupons representing ownership. The owners clip these coupons as they come due and present them at a bank for deposit or in exchange for cash.

In the early 1980s, Treasury bonds paid 12 to 14 percent interest. Issues since then have been paying lower rates. Interest on registered securities is paid automatically by United States Treasury check every six months from the issue date. The return on United States Treasury bonds is about one percentage point less than the return on triple-A corporate bonds. This is to be expected because corporate bonds involve a somewhat greater risk than United States Treasury bonds do, and the interest on corporate bonds is fully taxable.

United States Treasury bonds are issued in denominations of $1,000, $5,000, $10,000, $100,000, and $1,000,000. Bonds that mature in fifteen years are issued in January, July, and October. Longer-term bonds are issued during quarterly financings—every three months, on February 15, May 15, August 15, and November 15.

For detailed information on purchasing a United States Treasury bond, contact the Federal Reserve Bank nearest you. The Federal Reserve Bank's twelve regional offices are located in Atlanta, Boston, Chicago, Cleveland, Dallas, Kansas City, Minneapolis, New York City, Philadelphia, Richmond, St. Louis, and San Francisco. The Federal Reserve Bank also sells United States Treasury bills and United States Treasury notes, which are described on pages 97 and 98.

United States Treasury bonds are a good choice for the investor seeking maximum safety of capital and a steady high rate of interest. When interest rates begin to fall, the astute investor seeks to lock in a high rate of interest by buying for the long term. You must carefully follow interest rate movement to determine the ideal time to buy United States Treasury bonds. You can find this information in the financial pages of your daily newspaper or by contacting the nearest branch of the Federal Reserve Bank.

United States Agency Securities

Some of the United States government agencies that raise funds through public offerings include the Government National Mortgage Association, the Federal National Mortgage Association, and the Federal Home Loan Mortgage Corporation. The bonds sold by these agencies are referred to in the investment world by the nicknames *Ginnie Mae, Fannie Mae,* and *Freddie Mac.* Ginnie Maes are backed by government-insured Federal Housing Administration (FHA) and Veterans' Administration (VA) mortgages, which add a safety feature for the individual investor. Fannie Maes and Freddie Macs are backed by conventional (uninsured) mortgages and are favored by institutional investors, not individual investors. All these bonds can only be purchased through a commercial bank or a stock brokerage firm, requiring payment of a commission; they cannot be purchased directly from the government agency that issues them.

The government agencies that issue the bonds buy the mortgages from financial institutions, which actually make the loans. The agencies then package a number of similar mortgages into pools amounting to millions of dollars. The agency securities backed by these mortgages are sold to investors, who receive a return that reflects the interest paid by the individual homeowners. Agency bonds are called *pass-through securities* because the homeowner's payments of interest and principal are *passed through* to the investors, who have bought shares in one or more of the mortgage pools. Holders of the bonds receive interest payments by check. The interest is subject to federal income tax but is exempt from state and local income taxes.

GINNIE MAES

The Government National Mortgage Association (GNMA) is a branch of the United States Department of Housing and Urban Development. It is the leading issuer of pass-through certificates, with over $447.6 billion worth outstanding, representing more than 333,000 separate pools of mortgages. The Ginnie Mae offers the highest interest rate of any government security and is generally sold in maturities of thirty years and minimum denominations of $25,000. Many mutual funds hold only Ginnie Maes. (See page 98 for a description of mutual funds.) A *unit*

investment trust is a mutual fund that sells units of ownership. The advantage of buying into a Ginnie Mae mutual fund or unit investment trust is that the monthly principal and/or interest can be reinvested when the fund or trust is instructed to do so.

Most government securities pay interest semiannually. Ginnie Maes, on the other hand, make payments monthly, which most retirees prefer. Investors, however, must realize that the monthly check includes principal as well as interest. If they spend the whole check, they will discover later that their principal has diminished. It is important that they spend only the interest each month, setting aside the principal for further investment. The principal is paid back because many homeowners try to repay their mortgages quickly or refinance existing mortgages at lower rates.

FANNIE MAES AND FREDDIE MACS

Fannie Mae and Freddie Mac, both government-sponsored, are siblings of Ginnie Mae. The Federal National Mortgage Association (Fannie Mae) and Federal Home Loan Mortgage Corporation also pool mortgages. These are conventional home mortgages, and are, therefore, a little less safe than the Ginnie Mae pools, which are composed of guaranteed home mortgages.

Through Fannie Mae and Freddie Mac bonds, investors receive principal and interest payments from homeowners' payments. Freddie Mac investors are guaranteed interest and principal payments every month even when homeowners skip payments. Fannie Mae investors are guaranteed only interest; the principal may come later. As a result, the interest paid on Fannie Mae bonds is a fraction higher than the interest paid by Freddie Mac bonds.

Fannie Mae and Freddie Mac certificates are bought through brokerage firms, not from the government. The bonds are available at $10,000 and $5,000 increments. You can purchase them by buying into a mutul fund, which generally has a lower entry fee.

Municipal Bonds

Municipal bonds are issued by a state, county, or city and are called *municipals* for short. They offer tax advantages that make them attractive to people in higher income-tax brackets. For example, a New York City resident who owns a New York City or New York state bond pays no taxes to the federal, New York State, or New York City governments on the interest earned. The decision to buy or not buy a municipal depends upon the stated interest rate, or coupon rate, and the investor's tax bracket.

Municipals, like taxable bonds, must be considered in terms of their safety. If a municipality is about to go bankrupt, a bond issued by it is not a sound investment. It is important to ascertain the bond rating of the municipal. Choose *high-grade bonds*, which are bonds that are rated triple-A. The risk-return relationship pertains to municipals just as it does to stocks—the higher the risk, the higher the interest return. If there is an element of risk involved, the state or city will give you a higher rate to make the offering more attractive.

There are two principal varieties of municipal bonds. *General obligation bonds* pledge the faith and credit of the government that issues them, meaning that the taxing authority of the issuer will insure the payment of interest and principal. The repayment of *revenue bonds* is tied to a particular source of revenue, such as a bridge, tunnel, or airport, or to a specific tax, such as a sales tax. Always check the bond rating before buying.

Since July 1, 1983, issuers of municipal bonds have been required to maintain records showing who owns the bonds and who receives interest payments. This is intended to discourage tax evasion. These recorded municipals are also called *registered bonds*. Before July 1983, issuers kept no records of ownership and paid interest on bearer bonds to whomever submitted an interest coupon.

Zero Coupon Bonds

A popular investment vehicle is the zero coupon bond. As the name implies, *zero coupon bonds*, called *zeros* for short, have no coupons. Zeros can be purchased at a fraction of their ultimate redemption value, perhaps at one-quarter or one-half of their *par value*, that is, their face value. The bond increases in value at a compound interest rate until maturity, at which time it can be worth several times what you paid for it.

Zeros are issued by the United States Treasury and other federal agencies, as well as by municipalities and corporations. If you own a federal zero coupon bond, you must pay federal income taxes but not state or city taxes each year on the interest that accrues, even though you do not receive any interest until the bond has matured. Buying a home-state municipal zero coupon bond eliminates the tax problem.

Many large brokerage firms package these securities and sell them to investors through investment trusts. Some examples of United States government zero coupon bonds are Treasury Investment Growth Receipts (TIGRs), Certificates of Accrual on Treasury Securities (CATS), and Separate Trading of Interest and Principal of Securities (STRIPS). Some of these issues are traded on the New York Stock Exchange and, therefore, can be bought or sold prior to maturity.

Most zero coupon bonds have a face value of $1,000. Some zeros can be purchased for as little as $100 to $200. Brokerage firms charge a commission that ranges from 2 to 5 percent of the purchase price. The main difference between zeros and other bonds is that zeros do not pay interest until maturity. Zero coupon bonds are attractive to small investors because the purchase cost is less than that of conventional bonds.

Zeros are recommended for long-term retirement planning if the maturity date coincides with the retirement date. They should not be purchased after retirement, however, since most retirees seek a regular monthly flow of income.

Corporate Bonds

Corporations issue a wide variety of bonds. For example, *mortgage bonds* are secured by a mortgage on a specific piece of property, which is usually of a durable nature such as land, buildings, or machinery. *General mortgage bonds* are secured by a blanket mortgage on a company's property. *Debenture bonds* are not backed by any specific piece of property but by the general credit of the corporation. *Convertibles* give their holders the right, at a particular time and under certain stated terms, to change the bonds into stock.

Bonds are bought and sold for the public by brokers and securities dealers. You do not need to keep a bond until it matures—you can sell a bond you hold or buy one previously held by someone else. In the process of trading, you may earn a capital gain or incur a loss.

An investor must be able to assess the financial soundness of a bond before buying it. A bond with a higher degree of risk may pay a higher interest yield to compensate the investor for assuming the higher risk. Individual investors do not have the expertise to rate bonds. They rely on independent bond-rating services. The two largest are *Moody's Investors Service* and *Standard & Poor's Corporation*. The best quality bond with the smallest degree of risk is rated

Aaa by Moody's and AAA by Standard & Poor's. These bonds are known as triple-A bonds. The scale used by Moody's continues Aa1, Aa2, Aa3, A1, A2, A3, Baa1, Baa2, and Baa3. The last three ratings designate medium grades, which are still investment grades. Below-investment-grade ratings are Ba1, Ba2, Ba3, B1, B2, B3, Caa, Ca, and C. If you are interested in buying a bond, tell your broker that you want an issue rated Aa1, Aa2, Aa3, or, preferably, Aaa.

MONEY MARKET INSTRUMENTS

Money market is the collective name for transactions involving the borrowing or lending of money for a short term by the government, banks, large corporations, securities dealers, or individual investors. In investment circles, *short term* is considered to be one year or less. When individuals or businesses have more cash on hand than they currently need, they often find the money market an attractive place to temporarily invest the funds to earn interest. At the same time, the government or a business may require funds for a short term and is willing to pay interest for the use of the money.

Some of the short-term instruments traded in the money market include United States Treasury bills, United States Treasury notes, certificates of deposit (see page 88), commercial paper, banker's acceptances, and repurchase agreements. Most of these money market instruments can be purchased by individuals through the banking system, but many require a minimum purchase amount ranging from $10,000 to $25,000. Much less is required to purchase a small portion of a portfolio of money market instruments through a money market mutual fund (see page 99).

The short-term credit instruments traded in the money market have two very important characteristics—a very high degree of safety and a high degree of liquidity. Short-term investments are responsive to current market conditions, such as interest rate changes.

United States Treasury Bills

The United States government sells securities that are of the highest quality. In today's uncertain market for investors, the ultimate safe haven for short-term funds is the United States Treasury bill, or T-bill. *T-bills* are short-term securities that mature in three, six, or twelve months and are backed by the full faith and credit of the United States government. They pay a yield that is not subject to state or local income taxes, only to federal income taxes, which are payable in the year the T-bill matures, not in the year in which you receive the income or discount. T-bills are almost as liquid as cash, since they may be sold at any time without interest penalty.

T-bills are unique in that you receive your interest as soon as the Federal Reserve Bank receives your money. Investments such as certificates of deposit, savings accounts, and most bonds pay interest after the institutions that issued them have had the use of your money. The reason that interest on T-bills is paid so promptly is that you buy the bills at a discount from their face value. For example, you send the Treasury $10,000, the minimum amount required to buy a T-bill. If the actual cost of a ninety-one-day (three-month) bill is $9,640, the Federal Reserve Bank within a few days sends you a check for $360. About a month before the T-bill matures, the Federal Reserve Bank sends you a form that gives you the options of getting back your full $10,000 investment or of rolling it over into a new bill and again getting a discount. You pay no commission or redemption fee.

Since you receive the discount well in advance of the maturity of the bill, the true yield on an annual basis works out to be higher than the discount. The difference can be a percentage point or more.

There are several ways in which to buy Treasury bills. You can buy a T-bill through your bank or broker, paying a fee of $25 or $50 per bill. Or you can buy it by mail or in person from any Federal Reserve Bank branch. To buy a T-bill, you must fill out an application known as a *tender*, or bid, which requires only your name, address, Social Security number, signature, date, whether you want to reinvest at maturity at whatever rate is then prevailing, and whether you are submitting a competitive or noncompetitive bid. A purchaser spending under $1,000,000 buys on a *noncompetitive* basis. This means that the buyer will receive a price or discount equal to the average bid of all the big-money bidders.

To buy a $10,000 bill, you need to send a cashier's check or certified personal check payable to the Federal Reserve Bank along with the completed tender. For purchases above $10,000, you can invest in $5,000 increments. You receive a receipt as evidence of ownership. Engraved certificates are no longer given, which is an advantage since they can be stolen or counterfeited.

Interest rates for three- and six-month T-bills are set by the Treasury at auctions held every Monday. Auctions for fifty-two-week T-bills are held by the Treasury every fourth Thursday. If you buy by mail, the envelope containing your application and check must be postmarked no later than midnight of the day preceding the auction. If it is late, your application and check automatically are held until the next week's auction. If you buy in person, you must hand in the application and check no later than 1 P.M. of the day of the auction to receive the week's rate. If you arrive late, your check and application will be held for the following week's auction.

The decision to buy short-term or relatively

long-term bills depends on your individual situation and your guess concerning the future course of interest rates. In a period of declining rates, you would be prudent to nail down current higher yields by buying longer-term bills. But in periods of uncertainty, many investors stick to short-term bills.

United States Treasury Notes

The United States government borrows billions of dollars each year by selling Treasury notes. *Treasury notes*, or T-notes, are IOUs backed by the full faith and credit of the United States government. They have maturities of two to ten years and are issued in denominations of $1,000, $5,000, $10,000, $100,000, and $1,000,000. The minimum investment for two- to four-year notes is $5,000, and for four- to ten-year notes, $1,000.

After you have sent in a completed application form and personal check payable to the Federal Reserve Bank, you will receive a receipt as evidence of ownership. The interest earned is automatically sent to you by the United States Treasury every six months from the issue date.

Treasury notes can be considered a money market instrument even though they run longer than one year. This is because they can be traded when they are close to maturity. They can be purchased through your bank or broker at a commission or through the Federal Reserve Bank without payment of a commission.

Commercial Paper

Corporations pay investors for the short-term use of cash. A corporate IOU is issued to raise funds for a limited period of time, usually thirty days or less. The certificates, called *commercial paper*, are generally issued in denominations of $100,000 or more. The investor receives no collateral for this loan, but the interest paid is above that of T-bills. Be sure to check the ratings of commercial paper. The highest ratings are F-1 (Fitch Investors Service), Prime-1 (Moody's), and A-1 (Standard & Poor's). Commercial paper is sold directly by issuers and by dealers, brokers, and investment bankers. It is not for amateur investors.

Banker's Acceptances

Import and export transactions involve a loan known as a *banker's acceptance*. In these transactions, a seller draws a *draft*, a document for transferring money, payable by the buyer within a stipulated period of time. The bank financing the transaction accepts the draft, guaranteeing payment at maturity and thereby making the draft salable in the open market. The money market fund can buy the acceptance at a discount and be paid the full amount at maturity.

Repurchase Agreements

Repo is the shortened name given to a repurchase agreement. In a *repurchase agreement*, a bank that is anxious to borrow money for a short period of time sells United States Treasury bills to a money market mutual fund with the promise that it will buy them back the next day or within an agreed-upon period of time. The bank must buy back the T-bills at a higher price or at a specified interest rate. Repos actually are loans with United States Treasury securities as the collateral.

MUTUAL FUNDS

A *mutual fund*, which currently is a popular investment, is a company that collects the funds of hundreds of thousands of small investors through the sale of stock and then uses the collected funds for investment purposes. The investment philosophy of a specific fund and the types of investments it makes are spelled out in its prospectus. Over 6,000 mutual funds currently operate in the United States.

Mutual funds can be classified according to their investment objectives. Some common types of mutual funds are the following:

■ *Growth funds.* These funds are the most popular form of mutual fund, investing primarily in common stocks and seeking capital appreciation.

■ *Aggressive growth funds.* These funds take more risk to earn higher returns.

■ *Income funds.* These mutual funds invest in quality bonds to maintain a high level of income for their shareholders. They are attractive to retired investors and specialize in particular types of bonds including corporate bonds, United States government bonds, Ginnie Maes, and municipal bonds.

■ *Growth and income funds.* These invest in both stocks and bonds to provide capital growth as well as regular, fixed income. Sometimes referred to as *balanced funds*, they combine the objectives of growth funds and income funds.

■ *Long-term growth funds.* These funds take less risk and seek long-term growth.

■ *Money market funds.* These mutual funds invest in instruments of the money market such as United States Treasury bills, commercial paper, and other instruments of the money market. These funds are popular today, but only for storage of money, not for income or capital growth.

■ *International and global funds.* These invest in corporations and businesses located anywhere in the world, such as in Europe in general or in specified countries, such as in France or Canada. Their objective is growth.

■ *Sector funds.* These funds invest in particular areas of the economy, such as energy, chemicals, or nonprecious metals.

■ *Specialized funds.* Some of these mutual funds invest solely in new businesses. Others invest in gold, gold bullion, or Eurodollars, which are American dollars deposited in foreign banks. Some seek maximum capital gains by investing in highly speculative items such as *call options*, which are the right to buy stock at certain prices within certain time limits; *put options*, which are the right to sell stock at certain prices within certain time limits; or *futures contracts*, which are contracts to buy or sell commodities at a certain price on a certain future date. Many of these funds are extremely risky and are not recommended for retiree investment.

In addition to their investment objectives, mutual funds can be classified according to whether they are closed- or open-ended funds and whether they are load or no-load funds. A *closed-end company* is a mutual fund that has issued a fixed number of shares of stock, which are traded at the prevailing market prices listed on one or more of the major stock exchanges. It issues new shares infrequently. In contrast, an *open-ended company* continuously sells new shares of stocks and purchases shares from people desiring redemption. It buys and sells its shares at a fixed price and uses whatever funds it has for its investments.

A *load fund* is a mutual fund that charges a commission, or *load*, on the shares you buy or sell. The load ranges from 7.5 percent to 8.5 percent, which is the maximum allowed by the United States Securities and Exchange Commission (SEC). A *no-load fund* charges no sales fee, has no sales force, and waits for investors to come to it to purchase shares. Both load and no-load funds charge a management fee, which amounts to 3 percent or less of the interest earned on the money you have invested in the fund.

There are many advantages to investing in a mutual fund. Among them are the following:

■ *Small investment.* Only a small investment is required by mutual funds. In fact, some accept initial investments of as little as $50, with subsequent investments as low as $25. Check the individual fund.

■ *Professional management.* Your money is managed by full-time, professional money managers whose education and experience qualify them to handle money prudently.

■ *Low management fee.* The usual management fee is small, ranging from 1 to 3 percent.

■ *No sales commission.* About half of all mutual funds do not charge a sales commission, or load. Your full investment works for you from the outset.

■ *Diversification.* Mutual funds offer a much larger measure of diversity than most investors can afford to achieve on their own. This reduces risk.

■ *Liquidity.* Redemption of your money often requires no more than a telephone call to the headquarters of your fund. You can receive your money quickly.

■ *Flexibility.* Some of the larger mutual fund companies that have a variety of mutual funds under the same overall administration allow you to transfer freely among the funds.

HOMES AND OTHER REAL ESTATE

Home ownership has always been a sound investment in terms of capital gains. The deductions you enjoy on your income taxes include the interest you pay on your mortgage loan as well as the payments you make on your property taxes. And after you reach the age of 55, you can enjoy a tax-free capital gain of up to $125,000 if you sell your home.

In addition to their homes, many older people and retirees have moderate investments in other real estate and in mortgages that earn extra retirement income.

Real Estate Investment Trust

Buying stock in a Real Estate Investment Trust (REIT) is considered an ideal way to participate in real estate investment if you do not want to buy property or make a mortgage loan on your own. Professionally managed, *REITs* make investments in big commercial properties and shopping centers. Individual investors are able to pull out anytime by selling their shares.

GOLD, SILVER, AND COLLECTIBLES

During the past several years, many investors have been putting their money into tangibles such as gold and silver and a variety of *collectibles* including diamonds and other precious stones, art, antique furniture, stamps, coins, rare books, antique cars, and Tiffany glass. Many investors turn to gold to counteract high rates of inflation, to diversify an investment portfolio, or to have an insurance policy against the day when all paper assets may be worthless. Some investors buy gold coins or gold bars. Others invest in gold commodity futures, gold-mining stocks, or shares in gold mutual funds, which probably invest in a combination of bullion, coins, and mining stocks. Silver prices have been following precisely the movement of gold prices. Investors in collectibles do so in the hope that their items will increase in value, yielding a profit.

INVESTMENT TIPS

The interest or dividend return that you can earn on an investment is directly related to the amount of risk you assume. An axiom of investing is that the greater the risk you take, the greater is the return you can expect. Very high risk investments will yield very high returns, *if* you select winners. But risk always involves the element of potential loss, and if you select a loser, you may lose all or most of what you have invested.

Each individual has a specific level of risk tolerance. To determine your own risk tolerance, take the "risk quotient" test on page 108. As an investor, it is your responsibility to stay in the risk zone that leaves you comfortable with your selection. High risk investments should not be undertaken by people who are concerned about the safety of their principal. Such investments should be undertaken only by wealthy individuals who have a high risk quotient and who will not suffer too much by significant losses.

As a prospective retiree, you begin to think about maximizing your retirement income and keeping your taxes as low as possible. In addition, you want to have the feeling of security that comes from knowing your monthly income is certain and uninterrupted. Therefore, you should take a conservative approach, seeking investments that offer safety, liquidity, and good yields with minimum risk (see Table 6.2).

The investment pyramid in Figure 6.1 shows the levels of risk. The foundation of the pyramid represents minimum risk investments, in which most of a retiree's portfolio should be stored. The items in this group are the financial instruments that are worry-free, can be easily converted into cash, and pay market interest rates—money market deposit accounts, money market mutual funds, certificates of deposit,

United States Treasury bills and notes, and any of the other forms of investment that are listed for Level 4. A much smaller portion should go into moderate risk investments, such as blue chip common and preferred stocks, real estate, and certain stock and bond mutual funds. *Blue chip stock* is stock in a company known nationally for the quality and wide acceptance of its product or services and for its ability to earn large profits and to pay dividends regularly. Again, the investor's risk tolerance must be considered. Average small investors should not risk capital in very high or high risk investments, which are the forms of investment included in Levels 1 and 2 of the Investment Pyramid. None of a retiree's money should be put into these investments.

Before deciding on an optimum portfolio mix, you should first analyze your current portfolio (see Self-Study, Analysis of Your Portfolio, on page 107). Next, calculate your risk quotient (RQ) to determine the level of risk you are economically and psychologically suited to undertake (see Self-Study, Calculate Your Risk Quotient, on page 108).

Table 6.3 presents a suggested investment strategy for the average small investor who is able to tolerate moderate risk. The percentage distributions can be modified to suit your individual needs or risk quotient. If you are planning for retirement, you should put a higher percentage of your assets into minimum risk investments than if you are still working. The mix of investments also depends on how close you are to your actual retirement.

Figure 6.1. The Investment Pyramid.

1. **Very high risk investments.** These are a sophisticated form of gambling. They include futures contracts, options, collectibles, oil and gas drilling ventures, raw land, foreign stocks, *penny stocks* (extremely low priced stocks), *margin accounts* (accounts with brokers to help pay for the purchase of stock), and gold, silver, and other precious metals.

2. **High risk investments.** These contain elements of speculation. They include common stocks of low quality, new issues of stocks and bonds, and speculative grade bonds with Standard and Poor's ratings of BB, B, CCC, CC, or D, or Moody's ratings of Ba, B, Caa, Ca, or C.

3. **Moderate risk investments.** These offer regular income and potential long-term growth. They include blue chip common stocks and preferred stocks, variable annuities (see Chapter 9), investment real estate other than your home, stock and bond mutual funds whose goals are income and long-term growth, and investment grade corporate and municipal bonds with Standard and Poor's ratings of AAA, AA, A, or BBB, or Moody's ratings of Aaa, Aa, A, or Baa.

4. **Minimum risk investments.** These offer safety, liquidity, and good yield. They include Series EE United States savings bonds, United States Treasury bills and notes, federal agency bonds such as Ginnie Maes and Fannie Maes, individual tax-exempt municipal bonds rated triple-A, money market mutual funds, tax-exempt bond mutual funds, and bank offerings such as certificates of deposit and money market accounts. They also include other safe items such as equity, or net investment, in your own home; fixed annuities (see Chapter 9); and cash value of life insurance.

Table 6.2
Investments Classified by Level of Risk

1. **Very high risk investments** (A form of gambling)
   Puts and calls
   Commodities futures
   Options
   Collectibles
   Raw land
   Oil and gas drilling ventures
   Gold, silver, and other precious metals
   Penny stocks
   Foreign stocks
   Margin accounts

2. **High risk investments** (Contain elements of speculation)
   Common stocks of low quality
   New issues of stocks and bonds
   Speculative grade bonds with the following ratings:
       Standard and Poor's ratings: BB, B, CCC, CC, D
       Moody's ratings: Ba, B, Caa, Ca, C

3. **Moderate risk investments** (Offer regular income and potential long-term growth)
   "Blue Chip" common stocks and preferred stocks
   Investment grade corporate and municipal bonds with the following ratings:
       Standard and Poor's ratings: AAA, AA, A, BBB
       Moody's ratings: Aaa, Aa, A, Baa
   Variable annuities
   Investment real estate other than your home
   Stock and bond mutual funds whose goals are income and long-term growth

4. **Minimum risk investments** (Offer safety, liquidity, and good yield)
   Bank money market deposit accounts
   Money market mutual funds
   Insured Certificates of Deposit
   U.S. Treasury paper: Bills and Notes
   Tax-exempt bond mutual funds
   Individual tax-exempt municipal bonds rated AAA
   U.S. Government savings bonds
   Federal agency bonds: Ginnie Maes (GNMA) and Fannie Maes (FNMA)

(Other investments in this category include the equity in your home, fixed annuities, and cash value life insurance)

Table 6.3
Asset Allocation for Moderate Risk Investors

Goals and Investments	Portfolio Composition		
	More Than 5 Years to Retirement	**Within 5 Years of Retirement**	**Retired**
Safety of Principal			
Money market mutual funds			
United States Treasury bills	20%	25%	30%
Certificates of deposit			
U.S. Savings Bonds			
Income			
United States Treasury bonds			
Corporate bonds	30%	35%	45%
Municipal bonds			
Bond mutual funds			
Ginnie Maes			
Growth			
Common stocks			
Stock Mutual funds	50%	40%	25%
Real estate			
Total	100%	100%	100%

CONSUMPTION OF SAVINGS

The savings and investments you accumulated while working are significant sources of retirement income. If, after retirement, you withdraw a portion of your capital every month for living expenses, how long will your nest egg last? The answer depends on the interest rate the money is earning and on the amount you withdraw monthly.

Table 6.4, prepared by the United States League of Savings Associations, answers the question. Regardless of the amount of capital you consume, if the interest rate paid by the savings institution equals the percent of principal you withdraw, the fund will last indefinitely. For example, if you have $10,000 invested, earning 8 percent interest, and you withdraw just 8 percent a year, your capital will last indefinitely because you are withdrawing only the interest that you are earning. On the other hand, if you have $10,000 invested, earning 8 percent interest, and you withdraw 12 percent a year, your $10,000 will last only about 14 years.

In short, your savings will last as long as you live if you withdraw only the interest earned.

Table 6.4
Number of Years Money Can Last at Various Interest Rates and Percentages of Principal Withdrawn Annually*

Interest Rate Paid	Percent of Principal Withdrawn Annually										
	5%	6%	7%	8%	9%	10%	11%	12%	13%	14%	15%
5%	∞	37	26	20	16	14	12	11	10	9	8
6%		∞	34	24	19	16	13	12	10	9	9
7%			∞	31	22	18	15	13	11	10	9
8%				∞	29	21	17	14	12	11	10
9%					∞	27	20	16	13	12	10
10%						∞	26	19	15	13	11
11%							∞	24	18	14	12
12%								∞	23	17	14
13%									∞	22	16
14%										∞	21
15%											∞

*Assumptions made in this table are the following:

1. Withdrawals are made at the end of each month.
2. There are no penalties for premature withdrawal.
3. Interest is compounded daily, which provides the highest return possible under current banking regulations. *Compounding* is the process of earning interest on the interest already earned on an investment.

∞ Indefinitely (the symbol means "infinity").

Source: Reprinted with permission of the United States League of Savings Associations.

Self-Study
Calculate the Status
of Your Emergency Savings Fund

Your financial retirement plan should include an emergency savings fund equal to three to six months of your annual cost of living. Calculate the status of your emergency savings fund and set a goal for achieving the required amount as follows:

For a single retiree or a couple:

Yearly cost of living in 19_____	$_____
Emergency savings fund should be	$_____
Actual savings are	$_____
Surplus or shortage is	$_____

If your savings are short, divide the shortage by the amount of money you can afford to save each week to determine the number of weeks you need to reach your goal. For example:

$$\frac{\$3{,}000 \text{ shortage}}{\text{Can save } \$30 \text{ a week}} = 100 \text{ weeks, or about 2 years.}$$

Self-Study
Analysis of Your Portfolio

Before deciding on an optimum portfolio mix, you should first analyze your current portfolio. Using the format on the following page, enter the current dollar value of each of your assets. Then, compute the percentage of your portfolio in each type of investment. This will enable you to determine whether the proportions conform with your needs or desires.

Current Value and Percentage Distribution of Your Assets as of _____
(Date)

Assets	Current dollar value	Percent of total
Safety of Principal		
Savings accounts	_____	
Certificates of Deposit	_____	
U.S. Savings Bonds: Series EE	_____	
U.S. Treasury paper: Bills and Notes	_____	
Money Market Mutual Funds	_____	
Total	_____	_____
Income		
U.S. Treasury Bonds	_____	
Corporate Bonds	_____	
Corporate Bond Mutual Funds	_____	
Municipal Bonds	_____	
Ginnie Maes (GNMA)	_____	
Ginnie Mae Mutual Funds	_____	
Total	_____	_____
Growth		
Common Stocks	_____	
Common Stock Mutual Funds	_____	
Preferred stocks/mutual funds	_____	
Equity in your home(s)*	_____	
Real Estate Investment Trusts	_____	
Other real estate	_____	
Total	_____	_____
Other Investments		
Gold, silver, collectibles	_____	
Itemize: _____	_____	
_____	_____	
Total	_____	_____
Grand Total	_____	_100%_

* Estimated market value of your home(s) minus mortgage balance.

Self-Study
Calculate Your Risk Quotient

Now that you know the types of investments that are available, the level of risk associated with each, and the distribution of investments in your personal portfolio (see page 107), you can calculate your *risk quotient* (RQ). This exercise will enable you to determine the level of risk that you are economically and psychologically suited to undertake.

To determine your RQ, circle the response for each item that most closely describes you and enter the score in the final column. Then, add all the individual scores for a total score, which will give you your RQ and an approximate indication of your most suitable portfolio mix.

If your RQ is between 31 and 80, you can be classified as a moderate risk investor. See page 104 for a suggested portfolio mix. If your score is 81 or higher, you can handle a larger percentage of high risk investments. And if your score is 30 or less, you would do best with minimum risk investments, remembering that some proportion of your portfolio should be in growth type investments, which in the long run outperform other types of investments.

Item						Score
Your age	21–30 4	31–40 5	41–50 7	51–60 5	Over 60 1	
Total family income	$10,000–20,000 1	$20,001–30,000 2	$30,001–50,000 4	$50,001–75,000 6	Over $75,000 8	
Savings	$2,000–5,000 1	$5,001–15,000 3	$15,001–40,000 5	$30,001–75,000 8	Over $75,000 10	
Your home (Equity)	$20,000–60,000 1	$60,001–100,000 2	$100,001–150,000 3	$150,001–200,000 4	Over $200,000 5	
Life insurance	$10,000–20,000 1	$20,001–50,000 2	$50,001–100,000 3	$100,001–200,000 4	Over $200,000 5	
Dependents	Only yourself 10	One additional 6	2–3 4	4–5 2	More than 5 1	
Investment income used for living costs	Never 10	Seldom 8	Occasionally 5	Often 3	Always 1	
Employment and income security	Very stable 10		Fairly stable 5		Unstable 1	

Item				Score
Major medical or disability income	Have both 10	Have one 4	Have neither 1	
Attitude toward risk	Enjoy risk-taking 10	Will take occasional risks 5	Avoid risk 1	
Investment principal earmarked for major goals	Yes: for education and retirement 1	No: but need for overall security 4	Could afford to lose my principal 15	
Total				

Source: Reprinted with permission of R. & R. Newkirk, P.O. Box 1727, Indianapolis, Indiana.

Glossary

Aggressive growth mutual fund. A growth mutual fund that takes more risks than normal to earn higher returns.

Balanced mutual fund. *See* Growth and income mutual fund.

Banker's acceptance. A type of loan used in international trade. A seller draws a draft that is payable by a buyer within a stipulated period of time. A bank accepts the draft, guaranteeing payment of it at maturity and thus enabling it to be sold in the open market.

Bearer bond. A bond that does not have the owner's name registered on the books of the issuing company or governmental agency or noted on the certificate. Interest and principal, when due, are payable to the holder. *See also* Coupon bond; Registered bond.

Blue chip stock. Stock in a company known nationally for the quality and wide acceptance of its products or services and for its ability to earn large profits and to pay regular dividends.

Bond. A written promise to repay a loan on a specified date while paying the bondholder a specified amount of interest at regular intervals, usually twice a year; basically an IOU or promissory note. *See also* Bearer bond; Convertible; Coupon bond; Debenture bond; General mortgage bond; Registered bond.

Call option. The right to buy a fixed number of shares of a particular stock at a specified price within a limited period of time. The purchaser hopes that the stock's price will go up by an amount sufficient to provide a profit when the option is sold. If the stock's price remains the same or goes down, the investment in the call option is lost. *See also* Put option.

Capital gain. The profit from stocks, bonds, real estate, and other investments.

Capital loss. The loss resulting from the sale or exchange of a capital asset.

Certificate of Accrual on Treasury Securities (CATS). Securities that represent ownership of interest or principal payments made on United States Treasury notes or bonds. CATS are taxable zero coupon securities that are extremely liquid. *See also* Zero coupon bond.

Certificate of deposit (CD). A type of savings account in which a specified sum of money is deposited for a set period of time. Each bank has its own rates, terms, and minimum deposit requirements, and most charge a penalty for the early withdrawal of funds.

Closed-end mutual fund. A mutual fund that issues a fixed number of shares, which are traded at the prevailing market price and listed on one or more of the major stock exchanges. New shares are issued infrequently. *See also* Open-end mutual fund.

Collectible. An item purchased by an investor for its value. The investor hopes that the value of the collectible will increase and thus yield a profit when the item is sold. Collectible items include jewelry, diamonds, rare books, paintings, other art works, stamps, antiques, and Oriental rugs.

Commercial paper. A corporate promissory note, usually issued in denominations of $100,000 or more. It is used to raise funds for a limited period of time, usually sixty days or less. Higher risk loans pay higher interest rates.

Common stock. A security that represents an ownership interest in a corporation and the right to share in profits. Owners of common stock have the potential of earning not only dividends but also capital appreciation. *See also* Preferred Stock.

Common stock mutual fund. *See* Growth mutual fund.

Compounding. The process of earning interest on interest already earned on an investment. When interest is left to accumulate, compound interest is earned.

Convertible. A corporate bond or preferred stock that may be exchanged by the owner for common stock or another security, usually of the same company, in accordance with the terms of the issue.

Coupon bond. A bond that has postdated interest coupons attached. The coupons are clipped as they become due and presented at a bank for deposit or cash. The bank is then reinbursed by the issuing corporation or government agency. *See also* Bearer bond; Registered bond.

Coupon rate. Interest rate of a coupon bond.

Date of maturity. Date on which a loan matures, or becomes due.

Debenture bond. A corporate bond that is backed by the general credit of the issuing corporation and not by any specified piece of property.

Diversification. The allocation of investment funds among stocks, bonds, and instruments of the money market in order to reduce the risks associated with the volatility of the market. Most studies show that to achieve adequate diversification in stock investments, you must buy eight to twelve stocks in unrelated industries. A growth mutual fund offers this type of diversification.

Dividend. The payment that a corporation makes to the holders of its common stock or preferred stock. On common stock, the dividend varies with the fortunes of the company and may be skipped if business is bad. On preferred stock, the dividend is usually a fixed amount. *See also* Common stock; Preferred stock; Interest.

Draft. Document for transferring money.

Emergency savings fund. A cash reserve that will serve as a cushion in case of an unexpected emergency, in an amount equal to the cost of living for about three to six months, depending on individual needs.

Equity. The net investment in a home or a business enterprise that represents ownership, or that portion of borrowed funds or a mortgage that the owner has amortized.

Eurodollars. American dollars invested in banks in foreign countries, especially in Europe.

Fannie Mae. The nickname for a bond issued by the Federal National Mortgage Association (FNMA), a private corporation created by Congress to serve as a secondary mortgage market. Fannie Mae bonds may be purchased through a bond broker or by buying into a mutual fund that specializes in them. *See also* Ginnie Mae; Unit trust.

Fixed income asset. An asset, such as a bond, that has a fixed rate of return or interest.

Freddie Mac. The nickname for a bond issued by the Federal Home Loan Mortgage Corporation.

Futures contract. A contract to buy or sell a given commodity on a future date for a specified price. The market that handles futures contracts is known as the futures market and trades in agricultural products such as wheat, soybeans, and pork bellies; metals; and financial instruments. Businesses utilize futures as a hedge against price changes. Speculators buy and sell futures to profit from price changes.

General mortgage bond. A corporate bond that is secured by a blanket mortgage on the borrowing company's property. *See also* Mortgage bond.

General obligation bond. A municipal bond whose payment of interest and repayment of principal are backed by the full faith and credit of the issuing government. *See also* Revenue bond.

Ginnie Mae. The nickname for a bond issued by the Government National Mortgage Association (GNMA), a subsidiary organization of the United States Department of Housing and Urban Development, which guarantees funds invested in the mortgage market by institutional investors such as pension funds. Ginnie Mae bonds may be purchased through a bond broker or by buying into a mutual fund that specializes in them. *See also* Fannie Mae; Unit investment trust.

Growth and income mutual fund. A mutual fund whose investment holdings are balanced among common stocks, preferred stocks, and bonds, giving the investor a balanced risk and return. Also known as a balanced mutual fund.

Growth mutual fund. A mutual fund whose investments are primarily in common stocks. It is the most popular type of mutual fund.

High-grade bond. A bond that is rated triple A.

Income mutual fund. A mutual fund that seeks to return a higher level of dividends than other types of mutual funds do by investing in high-yielding common stocks, preferred stocks, and bonds.

Insurance premium. Installment payment to-

ward the purchase of a life insurance policy. It increases the cash value of the insurance policy.

Interest. The fee a borrower pays a lender for the use of money. A corporation pays interest on its bonds to its bondholders. Banks pay interest to depositors. *See also* Bond; Dividend.

Liquid. Readily converted into cash. Used to describe an asset such as a savings account.

Load mutual fund. A mutual fund that maintains a sales force and charges a commission, or load, for the purchase of shares. In most cases, no commission is charged when shares are sold. About half of all mutual funds are load funds. *See also* No-load mutual fund.

Long term. Ten or more years.

Long-term growth mutual fund. A growth mutual fund that takes less risk and seeks long-term growth.

Margin account. A brokerage account in which an investor maintains a deposit of money. When an investor buys stock, he or she pays only part of the purchase price with cash; the investor borrows the rest of the purchase price from the broker. The investor buys on margin in the hope of a price advance, enabling him or her to repay the loan and make a profit. If the market declines, however, the investor may be asked by the broker to make an additional deposit in the margin account. If the investor cannot make the deposit, the broker can sell the stock to liquidate the loan, and the investor suffers a loss.

Money market. The collective name for transactions involving the borrowing or lending of money for a short term by the government, banks, large corporations, securities dealers, or individual investors. A short term is considered to be one year or less.

Money market deposit account (MMDA). A

type of savings account offered by savings banks, savings and loan associations, and commercial banks, which then invest the savings in money market instruments. The depositor in return earns a relatively high rate of interest.

Money market instruments. Short-term paper traded in the money market. Examples are United States Treasury bills, certificates of deposit, commercial paper, banker's acceptances, and repurchase agreements.

Money market mutual fund. A mutual fund whose investment holdings are in high-yield money market instruments. The purpose of the fund is to make high-yield money market instruments, which are normally purchased by institutions in denominations of $100,000 or more, available to individuals of moderate means, who can buy into the fund with as little as $250.

Moody's Investors Service. A well-known stock and bond rating service.

Mortgage bond. A corporate bond that is secured by a mortgage on a specific piece of the borrowing company's property, which is usually of a durable nature, such as land, buildings, or machinery.

Municipal bond. A debt security issued by a state, county, or city that pays interest which is usually exempt from federal income taxes and from the income tax of the state that issued the bond. Bonds issued by counties or other subdivisions within a state are exempt from the income tax of the home state as well as from federal income taxes. Also known as a municipal. *See also* General obligation bond; Revenue bond.

Mutual fund. A company that collects the funds of hundreds of thousands of small investors through the sale of stock and then uses the funds for a variety of investments. Mutual funds are classified according to their investment objectives. *See also* Growth and income mutual fund; Growth mutual fund; Income mutual fund; Specialized mutual fund.

Negotiable interest rate. An interest rate that is negotiated between investor and institution.

Negotiable Order of Withdrawal (NOW) account. A checking account that earns interest, or, viewed another way, a savings account on which checks can be written. The minimum balance and interest paid vary from bank to bank. *See also* Super Negotiable Order of Withdrawal account.

No-load mutual fund. A mutual fund that does not have a sales force, does not charge a commission or sales fee, and waits for investors to buy its shares. About half of all mutual funds are no-load. *See also* Load mutual fund.

Open-end mutual fund. A mutual fund that continuously sells new shares of stocks and purchases the shares of investors desiring redemption. It buys and sells shares at a fixed price and uses whatever funds it has for investment. *See also* Closed-end mutual fund.

Option. The right to buy or sell a certain number of shares of a particular stock at a specified price within a limited period of time. *See also* Call option; Put option.

Over-the-counter stock. Stock of companies that do not have sufficient shares, stockholders, or earnings to qualify for listing on a major exchange, that is, they are traded directly by the buyer and seller, not through a broker.

Par value. The face value printed on a stock certificate or bond instrument. It is assigned at the time of original issue. Many stocks are issued with no par value.

Pass-through security. A United States agency

bond such as a Fannie Mae or Ginnie Mae. The homeowner's payments of interest and principal are passed through to the investors, who have bought shares in one or more of the mortgage pools.

Passbook savings account. A basic savings account. It usually pays a relatively low interest rate.

Penny stock. An issue that sells for less than $1 a share. This low-priced stock is often highly speculative.

Preferred stock. A security that entitles its holder to receive fixed and stated dividends before earnings are distributed to the common stockholders. Preferred stock represents an ownership interest in a corporation and gives its holder the right to vote when preferred dividends are in default for a specified period. In case of bankruptcy or liquidation, preferred stockholders have priority over common stockholders in the division of the company's assets. However, the claims of bondholders come first. *See also* Common stock; Convertible; Cumulative preferred stock; Participating preferred stock.

Put option. The right to sell a fixed number of shares of a particular stock at a specified price within a limited period of time. The purchaser hopes that the stock's price will go down by an amount sufficient to provide a profit when the option is sold. If the stock price remains the same or goes up, the investment in the put option is lost. *See also* Call option.

Real Estate Investment Trust (REIT). An investment fund that is similar to a mutual fund. Small investors buy shares in a REIT, which then uses the funds collected to invest in real estate including shopping centers and large commercial properties. Return on investment is liberal. However, because of the nature of the real estate market, a REIT is highly speculative.

Registered bond. A bond that has the owner's name registered on the books of the issuing company or governmental agency and noted on the bond. A registered bond can be transferred only when endorsed by the registered owner. *See also* Bearer bond; Coupon bond.

Repurchase agreement. A type of loan, also known as a repo, in which a bank in need of money for a short period of time, usually one or more days, borrows money from a money market mutual fund using United States Treasury securities as collateral. In effect, the bank sells the Treasury paper to the money market fund with the provision that it will buy the paper back within the specified period of time.

Revenue bond. A municipal bond designed to raise money for a specific municipal facility, such as an airport, bridge, or tunnel. The payment of interest and repayment of principal are backed by the income earned by the facility. *See also* General obligation bond.

Rollover. When you receive a lump-sum payment from a pension or profit-sharing plan because you have quit your job or retired or because the employer has terminated the plan, you have the option of trasnferring or "rolling over" the money into an individual retirement account. By so doing, you can avoid paying taxes on the money.

Savings bond. A security sold by the United States government that offers a fixed income with minimum risk and minimum investment. The bonds are sold at a discount, and the interest accumulates over a designated time period.

Sector growth mutual fund. A growth mutual fund that invests in particular areas of the economy, such as energy, chemicals, or nonprecious metals.

Short term. One year or less.

Specialized mutual fund. A mutual fund whose investment holdings are concentrated in one or two fields such as gold, Eurodollars, commodities, options, or foreign stocks.

Standard & Poor's Corporation. A well-known stock and bond rating service.

Super Negotiable Order of Withdrawal (Super NOW) account. A savings account with check-writing privileges. It pays an interest rate somewhere in between those of a NOW account and a money market deposit account. A minimum balance must be maintained or the bank applies a penalty fee.

T-bill. *See* United States Treasury bill.

T-note. *See* United States Treasury note.

Tender. Bid.

Unit investment trust. A mutual fund whose investment holdings are a diversified but fixed portfolio of securities including corporate bonds, municipal bonds, and preferred stock, which provide a steady, guaranteed income. Ownership in the trust is purchased in units.

United States Treasury bill. A short-term security, maturing in three, six, or twelve months, that is backed by the full faith and credit of the United States government. Also known as a T-bill, it pays an attractive yield, which is exempt from state and local income taxes and subject only to federal income taxes. It is sold at a discount from its $10,000 face value.

United States Treasury bond. A bond issued by the United States government that is backed by the full faith and credit of the federal government. Treasury bonds mature in ten or more years, sell at face value, and pay a fixed rate of interest twice a year throughout ownership. The interest is exempt from state and local income taxes and is subject only to federal income taxes.

United States Treasury note. A security that matures in two to ten years. The minimum investment for a two- to four-year note is $5,000, and for a four- to ten-year note, $1,000. Also known as T-notes, they are backed by the full faith and credit of the United States government. The interest is exempt from state and local income taxes and is subject only to federal income taxes.

Zero. *See* Zero coupon bond.

Zero coupon bond. A bond that makes no coupon, or interest, payments. It is sold at a substantial discount and, through the buildup of accrued interest, pays its face value at maturity.

7

Social Security

The philosophy of the American government for its first 150 years of existence was that responsibility for the care of the poor and the aged was a private matter, one that belonged to the family. State and local communities did help on occasion in cases of dire need. When the Social Security Act was signed into law by President Franklin D. Roosevelt in August 1935, responsibility for the aged was transferred from the individual family to society. This was a giant step forward for the United States, taken long after the industrial nations of Europe had adopted some form of retirement benefits for their citizens.

Today, our Social Security program is an integral part of the American economic system. It is a federal program that provides comprehensive benefits for you and your family, a package of benefits that would otherwise be unaffordable. Benefits are paid for with funds derived by taxing the earnings of working people. This package includes retirement, disability, and survivors' benefits. Supplemental Security Income, a fourth program, is payable to the blind, disabled, and people age 65 or older whose principal sources of income are insufficient to provide a minimum standard of living. Medicare, a fifth program, provides hospitalization

and medical expense benefits to those 65 or older. (For a thorough discussion of Medicare, see Chapter 16.)

The Social Security system provides benefits under the Old Age (Retirement), Survivors, and Disability Insurance program (OASDI):

■ Monthly benefits to retirees and their spouses.

■ Monthly benefits for the survivors of deceased workers.

■ Monthly benefits for disabled workers and their dependents.

■ A lump-sum death benefit payment for certain insured workers.

The Health Insurance portion of the system, known as Medicare (see pages 229 through 241), includes both hospital insurance benefits (Part A) and medical insurance benefits that pay for doctor bills (Part B). The medical benefits program is a voluntary supplementary program that is partially financed by each person who enrolls. The monthly premium covers about a quarter of the cost with the rest paid for by general tax revenues of the federal government.

Until 1983, the Social Security program operated as a *pay-as-you-go system* with each year's income used to pay for that year's beneficiaries. Since 1983, as a result of amendments to the Social Security Act, the program has been operating under a *partial reserve* method of funding, accumulating reserves. The system's current income is greater than its current expenditures.

Social Security had a $60 billion *surplus* in 1994. The system is currently so well funded that annual surpluses will continue for many years, with a $70 billion surplus in 1995, rising to $100 billion by 1999. The Social Security Trust Funds will reach nearly $3 trillion by 2020. Currently, these trust funds have over $400 billion in reserves that earned $29 billion in interest in 1994.

A notable change affecting the Social Security Administration comes from the Social Security Independence and Program Improvement Act of 1994. According to this act, on March 31, 1995, the Social Security Administration was removed from the United States Department of Health and Human Services and became an independent agency. An immediate benefit was greater visibility and accountability. Independence will insulate the agency from politics and enable it to help the public understand that Social Security will be a healthy program for generations to come.

Social Security/Medicare Financing

Social Security and Medicare Part A are financed by matching contributions from employees and employers, currently (1995) 7.65 percent of a person's wages. Of this amount, 6.2 percent of earnings up to maximum wages of $61,200 goes into two separate trust funds—5.6 percent goes into the Old Age and Survivors Insurance (OASI) Trust Fund and 0.6 percent into the Disability Insurance (DI) Trust Fund.

Together, the funds are called the OASDI program.

There are also two Medicare trust funds: the Hospital Insurance (HI) Trust Fund pays for the services covered under the hospital insurance (Part A) provisions of Medicare. HI is financed by matching contributions from employees and employers; each pays 1.45 percent of a worker's earnings with no limit on salary. (If an individual earns $300,000 a year, 1.45 percent of $300,000 is taxed.)

Finally, the Supplemental Medical Insurance (SMI) Trust Fund is used to pay for services, primarily physician services, covered under the medical insurance (Part B) provisions of Medicare. SMI derives no revenues from Social Security payroll taxes. About three-quarters of SMI revenues come from the general fund of the United States Treasury; the remainder derives from premiums paid by enrollees, $46.10 a month in 1995.

At the present time, the federal government borrows Social Security surpluses to pay its operating expenses. The spending of these surplus funds by the government hides the true size of the federal deficit, which is attributable to other spending programs, not to the payment of Social Security benefits. In exchange for these monies, the government issues United States Treasury bonds that the Social Security Trust Funds hold as reserves.

In 1994, Social Security paid benefits of $325 billion to over 42 million men, women, and children. At the same time, it collected $60 billion more than it spent. Benefits are paid to approximately:

29 million retirees and their spouses
6 million widows or widowers
4 million disabled workers and their spouses,
and
3 million children of retired, deceased,
or disabled workers

More than 138 million workers in the United States who are contributing to the Social Security system through earnings deductions are building the *earned right* to future retirement benefits for themselves and their dependents; disability benefits to protect them and their dependents in the event of severe, long-term disability; and, when they die, survivor benefits for thier spouses and dependent children and/or dependent parents. In addition, Social Security offers Supplemental Security Income for the needy and Medicare hospital benefits for people aged 65 and older.

THE SOCIAL SECURITY SYSTEM

Many people see the Social Security system as complex and confusing. The following explanations may help to make it easier to understand.

Social Security Payroll Deductions

The benefits paid by Social Security are derived by taxing the earnings of working people. In addition, for every dollar you pay, your employer contributes an equal amount. If you are self-employed, you pay twice what individual employees pay because you do not have an employer to match your contribution. On your paycheck, the abbreviation "FICA," which stands for Federal Insurance Contributions Act, identifies your Social Security payroll deductions. Social Security taxes are collected by the Internal Revenue Service, which transmits them to the United States Treasury.

The amount of money collected by the Social Security system depends on two factors— the *tax rate*, which is a percentage figure, and the *earnings base*, which is the maximum amount of earnings that can be taxed. This limit on taxable earnings is called the *maximum taxable amount*, and you do not pay any taxes on amounts higher than this maximum. Table 7.1 presents the tax rates and maximum taxable amounts for the years 1990 through 1995.

When Congress decides to increase the Social Security tax rate or maximum taxable amount, it simply amends the Federal Insurance Contributions Act (FICA) for employees and employers, and the Self-Employment Contributions Act for the self-employed. Although increases in the tax rates and taxable amounts mean that workers in the higher income brackets pay more into Social Security, higher paid workers also are able to count on greater benefits later. This is because benefit amounts are based upon earnings credited for Social Security.

Table 7.1
Social Security Tax Rates and Maximum Taxable Amounts Since 1990

Year	Employee Tax Rate	Employer Tax Rate	Self-Employed Tax Rate	Maximum Taxable Amount
1990	7.65%	7.65%	15.30%	$51,300
1991	7.65	7.65	15.30	53,400
1992	7.65	7.65	15.30	55,500
1993	7.65	7.65	15.30	57,600
1994	7.65	7.65	15.30	60,600
1995	7.65	7.65	15.30	61,200

Soundness of the Social Security Program

The surpluses that are accumulating in the form of United States Treasury bonds ($60 billion in 1994, $70 billion in 1995, $100 billion by 1999) actually help finance the federal deficit. The more than $400 billion in the Social Security Trust Funds earned $29 billion in interest in 1994. Under current law and at current contribution rates, with no change in the way benefits are assigned, the trust funds will continue to grow until 2020. At that time, or earlier, an increase of 1.9 percentage points in the contribution rate for both employees and employers and an adjustment in retirement age (see page 124) will carry the system for least 75 additional years. Such a tax increase is not trivial, but is supportable, offsetting about a 14 percent growth in earnings projected between now and 2020. The *baby boomers*, those born between 1946 and 1964, can be reassured that Social Security, with a few minor adjustments, is financially sound to the end of the 21st century.

Tax and Legal Status of Benefits

Beginning with returns filed in 1995 for 1994 income, better-off Social Security recipients will see a larger share of their benefits (up to 85 percent as opposed to the former 50 percent) subject to the ordinary income tax. The boost was one of a number of tax changes approved by Congress in 1993 as part of the Omnibus Budget Reconciliation Act (OBRA). The increase became effective January 1, 1994.

Some things remain the same. As before, single beneficiaries with "provisional adjusted gross income" from $25,000 through $34,000 and couples with income from $32,000 through $44,000 will pay federal income taxes on 50 percent of their Social Security benefits. *Provisional adjusted gross income* is adjusted gross income plus tax-exempt interest plus one-half of

Social Security benefits, less alimony, IRA and KEOGH contributions.

The new 85 percent rate applies to those with provisional adjusted gross income above $34,000 for singles and $44,000 for couples. It has been estimated that the higher Social Security tax will affect roughly 5.4 million people, or 13 percent of beneficiaries.

As for the legal status of benefits, they are not subject to garnishment or attachment, except for delinquent federal taxes, child support, or alimony payments.

RETIREMENT BENEFITS

Several factors are involved when retirement benefits are calculated. You should understand these factors and be aware that the benefits to which you are entitled are also available to your spouse, children, and dependent parents.

Qualifications for Retirement Benefits

To qualify for retirement benefits, you must satisfy three requirements:

1. You must have reached *retirement age*. Retirement age is currently set at 65. However, at any point from age 62 on, you can retire and receive a monthly benefit for life.

2. You must be *fully insured*, having worked the required number of *quarters of coverage (QC)* for your age. A quarter is one-fourth of a year, or three months. The four quarters in the year are January 1–March 31, April 1–June 30, July 1–September 30, and October 1–December 31. For 1995, you must earn a minimum of $630 within a specified quarter to earn one QC. (To keep pace with inflation, the minimum earnings per quarter are adjusted annually.) If you have ten years of work credit, or forty QC, you are fully insured and will never

need additional QCs no matter what your age. For any type of benefit, you must have a minimum of six QC, but the benefit will be scaled down. "Fully insured" does not mean that you will get the highest monthly benefit. It merely means that you have enough QC to be eligible to receive benefits when you retire or for your survivors to receive benefits when you die.

3. You must file an application, since benefits are not paid automatically when you retire.

Steps in Figuring a Social Security Retirement Benefit

The *Primary Insurance Amount* (PIA) is the largest benefit a worker can receive at age 65 based upon his/her earnings over a lifetime. This amount is equivalent to *full benefits*. A Social Security retirement benefit is derived from a three-level formula that is applied to your average indexed monthly earnings (AIME).

To derive *AIME*, actual earnings over past years are adjusted, or indexed, to take account of changes in average wages that increase over the years due to inflation. For example, average earnings for 1995 were about five times greater than average earnings for 1964. To make 1964 earnings comparable with 1995 earnings, those earnings are multiplated by five. Earnings are adjusted for each year up to the year in which you reach age 60. The adjustment factor becomes smaller the closer you get to the present. After you reach age 60, *actual earnings* are used to compute the retirement benefit. By this method, called *indexing*, the value of earnings in past years is increased to reflect current dollar value. In practice, a computer does all the work, and the final set of annual earnings is used to compute your retirement Primary Insurance Amount.

Five steps are involved in the computation of your primary insurance amount:

1. First, your earnings covered by Social Security are listed starting with 1951.

2. Your earnings are indexed or adjusted to take account of changes in average wages since the year you received the earnings.

3. From the years listed, the thirty-five years with the highest earnings are used to figure your retirement benefits. If an individual's working years do not total thirty-five, the procedure will add years of "zero" earnings to total thirty-five years.

4. The earnings for these years are totaled and divided by 420, the number of months in thirty-five years, to get your average monthly earnings. This is the number used to figure your benefit rate.

5. A three-level formula is applied to your average monthly earnings to arrive at an actuarial benefit rate. The three percentages used are 90 percent, 32 percent and 15 percent. These percentages are applied to your AIME against specified amounts that are changed every year. (The current amounts are $422 and $2,123.) The formula for computation is based on the year you turned 62 even if you do not retire until later.

Let's look at an example:

Mr. Smith, born April 1, 1929, filed an application for retirement benefits on April 12, 1994, at age 65. His AIME is $2,600. Actually, he became eligible for retirement benefits in April 1991 when he reached 62, but he chose to continue working, thus becoming eligible for his full benefits. Mr. Smith's Primary Insurance Amount (PIA) is calculated as follows:

90 percent of $422	=	$ 379.80
32 percent of $2,123	=	$ 679.36

15 percent of any remaining		
amount ($55)	=	$ 8.25
Mr. Smith's AIME	=	$2,600.00
Mr. Smith's PIA	=	$1,067.41

Social Security benefits are paid in even dollar amounts, in this case $1,067. This is the basic full benefit rate at retirement age.

Each year, a new formula is established for people who reach 62 that year. The percentages (90, 32, and 15) remain the same, but the dollar amounts change. For Mr. Smith in this example, the dollar amounts are $422 and $2,123. Even if you do not retire at 62, Social Security will figure your benefits based on the year you turned 62.

You are eligible for cost-of-living increases in benefits starting with the year you become 62. This is true even if you do not get benefits until 65 or even 70. This means your benefit is increased by all the cost-of-living adjustments starting with the year you reach 62 until the year you start getting benefits. In effect, this means that your PIA of $1,067 will be increased by the total cost-of-living increases granted over the previous three years.

You can start receiving benefits as early as age 62, but at a reduced rate. At age 62, you get 80 percent of your PIA; in Mr. Smith's case 80 percent of $1,067 is $853.60. Your benefit is reduced five-ninths of 1 percent for each month you get benefits before age 65. The closer you are to 65 when benefits start, the smaller the reduction. For example, the reduction is 13 1/3 percent at age 63 and 6 2/3 percent at 64.

Disability and survivors benefits are figured a little bit differently.

Cost-of-Living Adjustments (COLAs)

When most people retire, one of their main concerns is protecting their retirement income against inflation. Fortunately, some protection is built into the Social Security payment system in that the payments are raised each year on a scale that is tied to the increase in the cost of living. The United States Congress approved these automatic increases in Social Security benefits, called *cost-of-living adjustments (COLAs)*, starting in 1975. Using the United States Consumer Price Index as the guideline, Social Security makes the adjustment once a year.

Table 7.2 shows what the cost-of-living adjustments have been since 1980. Originally, the adjustment was made effective July 1, and the dollar increase was included in the July benefit check. The Social Security Amendments of 1983, however, postponed the payment of the cost-of-living increase for six months, moving it from July 1983 to January 1984. Since then, January has been the permanent month for COLA increases.

It is comforting for benefit recipients and potential retirees to know that benefit payments will continue to rise as living costs increase.

Table 7.2
Cost-of-Living Adjustments Since 1980

Date of Payment	Percent of Increase in Benefits
June 1980	14.3
June 1981	11.2
June 1982	7.4
December 1983	3.5
December 1984	3.5
December 1985	3.1
December 1986	1.3
December 1987	4.2
December 1988	4.0
December 1989	4.7
December 1990	5.4
December 1991	3.7
December 1992	3.0
December 1993	2.6
December 1994	2.8

Retiring at 62 Versus 65

The earliest age at which you can receive Social Security benefits is 62. If you take an early retirement, you will lose five-ninths of 1 percent of your primary insurance amount for each month that you receive your benefit before age 65. If, for instance, you retire at age 62, you will have to settle for only 80 percent of your full benefits. This reduction is permanent; your benefit will not increase to your full PIA at normal retirement age. Furthermore, your benefits will be reduced because your Social Security contributions will have been less. (For information on calculating retirement benefits, see page 121.) If, however, you retire at age 65, you will get 100 percent of your full benefits.

The principal advantage of retiring at 62 on a reduced benefit is the collection of several thousand dollars during the three years before you reach 65. If you defer retirement until 65, it will take you several years to reach the break-even point, that point at which you will have made up the amount you would have received between 62 and 65. Table 7.3 illustrates this point. Whether it is better for you to retire at age 62 or wait until age 65 depends on how long you will live, which is something that most people cannot predict.

Table 7.3
How Long It Takes to Reach the Break-Even Point

Age	80% of Primary Insurance Amount Amount Received		100% of Primary Insurance Amount Amount Received	
	Annual	Cumulative	Annual	Cumulative
62	$ 8,000	$ 8,000	0	0
63	8,000	16,000	0	0
64	8,000	24,000	0	0
65	8,000	32,000	$ 10,000	$ 10,000
66	8,000	40,000	10,000	20,000
67	8,000	48,000	10,000	30,000
68	8,000	56,000	10,000	40,000
69	8,000	64,000	10,000	50,000
70	8,000	72,000	10,000	60,000
71	8,000	80,000	10,000	70,000
72	8,000	88,000	10,000	80,000
73	8,000	96,000	10,000	90,000
74	8,000	104,000	10,000	100,000
75	8,000	112,000	10,000	110,000
76	8,000	120,000	10,000	120,000
	120,000		120,000	

Effects on Benefits of Continuing to Work

If you are a retiree between the ages of 62 and 64 in 1995, you are permitted to earn up to $8,160 a year, or $680 a month, and still receive full Social Security benefits. Retirees age 65 through 69 can earn up to $11,280 a year, or $940 a month, without losing any Social Security benefits. There is no earnings limitation for retirees age 70 or above under current Social Security rules.

If you are age 62 through 64 and earn more than $8,160 in 1995, you will lose $1 of your Social Security benefits for each $2 of excess earnings. If you are 65 through 69 and earn more than $11,280 in 1995, you will lose $1 of your Social Security benefits for each $3 of excess earnings. For example, assume that you are 67 years old in 1995 and are earning $15,000 per year. You are permitted to earn $11,280. Your actual earnings of $15,000 minus your permitted earnings of $11,280 yields an excess of $3,720. One-third of $3,720 is $1,240, which must be paid back to Social Security. At income tax time (April 15), you are required to submit a report to the Social Security Administration indicating your previous year's earnings if your income exceeds the aforementioned limits. Filing an income tax return does not take the place of filing this report with the Social Security Administration. A substantial penalty is levied if you do not report these earnings.

Delayed Retirement Credit

If you take a *late retirement*, working between the ages of 65 and 70, and do not collect any Social Security benefits before retiring, your retirement benefits will be increased by a specified percentage. If you are age 65 in 1994 or 1995, the increase will be 4.5 percent of your PIA. If you work all five years (age 65 through age 70), you will receive 22.5 percent, or 4.5

percent for each of the five years. This benefit, known as the *delayed retirement credit*, increases every two years and will be 8 percent a year for people born in 1943 or later. In other words, for each year beyond your full retirement age you delay receiving Social Security benefits, you will receive an additional 2/3 percent per month as detailed in Table 7.4.

Table 7.4 Delayed Retirement Credit

Year of Birth	Year You Reach 65	Monthly %
Prior to 1916	Prior to 1982	1
1917–1924	1982–89	3
1925–26	1990–91	3.5
1927–28	1992–93	4
1929–30	1994–95	4.5
1931–32	1996–97	5
1933–34	1998–99	5.5
1935–36	2000–01	6
1937–38	2002–03	6.5
1939–40	2004–05	7
1941–42	2006–07	7.5
1943 or later	2008 or later	8

Raising the Retirement Age

Between the years 2000 and 2022, the retirement age for full benefits will be raised gradually from 65 to 67. This change, under the Social Security Amendments of 1983, will be made for two reasons—to assure the long-term financial solvency of the Social Security trust funds and to adjust the retirement age to the increased life expectancy over the years. It will still be possible to retire at age 62, but the benefits that can be collected will gradually be reduced from 80 percent of the PIA in 1999 to 75 percent in 2005 and ultimately to 70 percent in 2022. Table 7.5 presents the timetable for raising the retirement age from 65 to 67.

Retirement Benefits for Your Spouse

If a spouse has never worked at paid employ-

Table 7.5
Timetable for Raising the Retirement Age
From 65 to 67

Year of Birth	Age Necessary for Full Benefits
1937 or earlier	65 years
1938	65 years, 2 months
1939	65 years, 4 months
1940	65 years, 6 months
1941	65 years, 8 months
1942	65 years, 10 months
1943-1954	66 years
1955	66 years, 2 months
1956	66 years, 4 months
1957	66 years, 6 months
1958	66 years, 8 months
1959	66 years, 10 months
1960 and after	67 years

ment and, therefore, is not entitled to his or her own Social Security benefits, then the spouse at age 62 would get 37.5 percent of the worker's *primary insurance amount* (PIA). The spouse at age 65 would get 50 percent of the worker's PIA. If a spouse has worked a little and is entitled to retirement benefits equalling less than 50 percent of the worker's PIA, the spouse will, nevertheless, receive 50 percent. If a spouse has worked enough to be entitled to a benefit greater than 50 percent of the worker's PIA, then the spouse will collect benefits based on his or her own earnings. In other words, if a husband and wife both worked and paid Social Security taxes, each would be entitled to his or her own benefits, whichever is higher.

Benefits for a Divorced Woman

A divorced woman who has not remarried can receive benefits on her former husband's record if they were married at least ten years. Benefits will be the same as if they had remained married. This means she and her former husband must be of retirement age, 62 or older. A divorced woman who has reached retirement age may claim benefits on her own record until her former husband retires and then file later for the spousal benefit if it is higher.

Retirement Benefits for Your Children

Each dependent child or grandchild is entitled to receive 50 percent of the retired worker's PIA. A *dependent child* is a person under 18 years of age, a full-time elementary or secondary school student up to age 19, or an older child with a disability that began before age 22. A *dependent grandchild* is a child under the age of 18 both of whose parents are disabled or deceased.

Widow's or Widower's Benefits

A widow or widower can begin collecting benefits at age 60. If the person waits, the amount increases until it reaches 100.0 percent of the member's PIA at age 65. If a widow or widower is 60, he/she gets 71.5 percent of the deceased member's PIA; 61, 77.2 percent; 62, 82.9 percent; 63, 88.6 percent; 64, 94.3 percent; and at age 65, 100.0 percent.

At age 62, the widow or widower must decide whether to continue collecting as a survivor or take his/her own entitled benefits. The survivor will, of course, take the larger of the two.

Retirement Benefits for Your Parents

A dependent parent who is at least 62 years of age is entitled to receive 82.5 percent of the retired worker's PIA. If both parents are dependent, each can get 75 percent of the retired worker's PIA. A *dependent parent* is one who is receiving at least 50 percent of support from his or her offspring.

Filing for Retirement Benefits

If you are ready to retire, you should apply for retirement benefits approximately three months before your actual retirement date. You must file your application at your local Social Security office. To get the address of your nearest social security office, call 1-800-772-1213 or any social welfare agency in your community. Your benefits will become effective as of the month you reach retirement age. Benefits are retroactive only for the twelve months before the date of filing. Therefore, a delay for any reason, even a disabling illness, may cause loss of benefits.

The following is a list of records you must present when filing for retirement benefits. These records should be certified documents bearing the official seal of the agency from which you obtained them. Photocopies are not acceptable. Your representative will return the documents to you after making a copy for Social Security's records. Documents in foreign languages are acceptable.

■ *Social Security card* or record of Social Security number.

■ *Proof of age.* Most people submit their birth certificates or baptismal certificates made before the fifth birthday.

■ *Form W-2.* The Form W-2 should show your earnings for the year prior to the year in which you are applying for Social Security retirement benefits. For example, if you are applying for benefits in 1995, you should bring your Form W-2 for 1994. If you are self-employed, bring a copy of your last federal income tax return.

■ *Proof of marriage.* Your marriage certificate is required if you are applying for benefits as a spouse. A divorced woman needs proof of divorce in addition to proof of marriage.

The following records are needed when filing for benefits for children:

■ *Social Security card* or record of Social Security number.

■ *Proof of age.*

■ *Proof of adoption*, if applicable.

■ *Marriage certificate* of natural parent and stepparent if applying for stepchild benefits.

Refer to Table 7.6, Social Security Fact Sheet, for a concise guide to information regarding your benefits.

SURVIVORS' BENEFITS

When you die, certain members of your family may be eligible for benefits on your Social Security record if you earned enough credits while you were working. These family members include:

■ Your widow or widower, 60 or older.

■ Your widow or widower, aged 50 or older and disabled.

■ Your widow or widower of any age if he or she is caring for a dependent child who is receiving Social Security benefits.

■ Unmarried children under 18, or under 19 but a full-time student in elementary or secondary school, or a child who became disabled before age 22.

■ Your parents, if they were dependent on you for at least half of their support.

The amount payable to your survivors is a percentage of your basic Social Security benefit,

Table 7.6
Social Security Fact Sheet*

	1995	1994
Maximum taxable wages	$61,200	60,600
Withholding tax:		
Employee	7.65% [a]	7.65%
Employer	7.65% [a]	7.65%
Self-employed	15.30% [b]	15.30%
Maximum earnings while receiving benefits:		
Ages 65–69	$11,280/year [c] ($940/month)	$11,160/year ($930/month)
Ages 62–64	$8,160/year [d] ($680/month)	$8,040/year ($670/month)
Age 70 or more	No limit	No limit
Cost of living adjustment (COLA)	2.8%	2.6%
Quarters of coverage required if you reach age 62 in year shown	40	40
Quarter of coverage (earnings)	$630	$620
Maximum benefit starting at age 65	$1,199/month	$1,147/month
Average benefit retired workers	$698/month	$679/month
Lump sum death benefit	$255	$255

*For Social Security information, call 1-800-772-1213.

a The 1995 FICA (Federal Insurance Contributions Act) tax remains at 7.65 percent; 6.2 percent goes for OASDI on wages up to $61,200 and 1.45 percent on all wages earned in 1995 for HI, which is a tax that pays for Medicare, Part A.
b Of the 15.30 percent, 12.4 percent goes for OASDI on wages up to $61,200 and 2.9 percent goes for HI on all wages for 1995.
c Beneficiaries earning over this amount will lose $1 of their benefits for each $3 in earnings above the limit.
d Beneficiaries earning over this amount will lose $1 of their benefits for each $2 in earnings above the limit.

the Primary Insurance Amount, usually in a range from 75 to 100 percent for each beneficiary. However, there is a limit to the amount of money that will be paid each month to a family. The limit varies, but is generally equal to about 150 to 180 percent of your benefit rate. If the sum of the benefits payable to your surviving family members is greater than this limit, then the benefits to your family will be reduced proportionately.

Even if you are not fully insured when you die, your family may still be eligible for benefits. You may be *currently insured*, which means that you earned six quarters of coverage (QC), or six units of Social Security credit, in the three years before your death. If you had enough credits, a special one-time payment of $255 also will be made after your death. This benefit, called a *lump-sum death benefit*, is paid only to your widow(er) or minor children.

Benefits for Widow(er)s

If you are receiving widows' or widowers' benefits (including divorced widows or widowers benefits), you should remember that, as early as age 62, you can switch to your own retirement benefits, assuming you are eligible and your retirement rate is higher than your widow(er)'s rate. In many cases, a widow(er) can begin receiving one benefit at a reduced rate and then switch at age 65 to the other benefit at an unreduced rate. The rules are complicated and vary depending on the situation so you should talk to a Social Security representative about the options available to you.

Benefits to Divorced Widows and Widowers

If you are divorced, even if you have remarried, your ex-spouse may be eligible for benefits on your record when you die. In order to qualify, your ex-spouse must:

■ Be at least 60 years old, or 50 if disabled, and have been married to you for at least ten years.

■ Be any age if caring for a child who is eligible for benefits on your record.

■ Not be eligible for an equal or higher benefit on his or her own record.

■ Not be currently married, unless the remarriage occurred after age 60, or 50 for disabled widows. In cases of remarriage after the age of 60, your ex-spouse will be eligible for a widow(er)'s benefit on your record or for a dependent's benefit on the record of his or her new spouse, whichever is higher. It is important to note that if your ex-spouse receives benefits on your account, it does not affect the amount of any benefits payable to your other survivors.

DISABILITY BENEFITS

You can plan for retirement and even for death, but you cannot plan for sudden catastrophe—an illness or injury that immobilizes you for several months or many years. When total disability occurs, the economic impact on the worker and family members is generally severe. As protection against such a crisis, disability insurance is probably the most important form of Social Security coverage.

Disability benefits were added to the Social Security Act in 1956, and in the years since then, Congress has substantially liberalized the provisions of the law. Today, the United States government through the Social Security system provides a noncancellable disability policy to almost all its employed citizens. Such a policy purchased from a private insurance company would be prohibitive in cost, unless you were very wealthy.

With disability insurance, you and your family are assured of a monthly income for the length of time you are disabled. Social Security computes these benefits as if you had retired in the year the disability began. The program provides major protection against financial disaster.

Qualifications for a Disability Benefit

An individual is considered to be under a *disability* if the following conditions prevail:

■ He or she is unable to do any substantial gainful work anywhere in the national economy because of a physical or mental impairment.

■ The physical or mental condition is expected to last, or has lasted, for at least twelve months or is expected to result in death.

If you are disabled and cannot engage in either your usual work or any other work, you, your spouse, and your dependent children are eligible for disability benefits at any age. To qualify for a disability benefit, you must have earned twenty quarters of coverage sometime during the ten years before you become disabled. If you become disabled before age 31, you only need to have earned six to ten QC, depending on your age, between the time you were 21 and the time you become disabled.

To collect benefits, you must file an application and include proof of disability. You must also be willing to accept vocational rehabilitation, if required.

Disability Benefit Amounts

The amount of your monthly disability payment is the same amount you would receive if you were retiring. The disability insurance benefit is, therefore, equal to your average covered monthly earnings (see page 121) over a period of years determined by your birthdate. It is calculated the same way in which retirement benefits are calculated. If you start to receive disability benefits before age 65, your PIA is not reduced.

For disabled widows, disabled surviving divorced wives, and disabled widowers between 50 and 62, reduced benefits ranging from 50 percent to 82.9 percent of the deceased spouse's full benefit may be paid if the survivors' disability prevents any substantial gainful work. Widows and widowers are found disabled if they satisfy the requirements of an impairment listed in the "Listing of Impairments" in *Disability Evaluation Under Social Security*, available in any Social Security office.

The maximum family benefits for disabled workers who first became entitled to disability benefits after June 1980 are 85 percent of the worker's average indexed monthly earnings before becoming disabled or 150 percent of the worker's disability benefits, whichever is less. Maximum family benefits are the total benefits that all the members of one family may receive based upon one worker's earnings. Average indexed monthly earnings are past earnings adjusted to reflect today's dollar and economy; see page 121 for a complete explanation.

No benefits are paid for the first five months of disability, which is the required waiting period. The first payment, therefore, is for the sixth full month of disability.

SUPPLEMENTAL SECURITY INCOME

Supplemental Security Income (SSI) became effective January 1, 1974, to assure a basic level of cash income to the aged, blind, and disabled under conditions that promote self-respect and dignity. The program is designed for people in financial need and provides eligible individuals with monthly payments from the federal government. Even though the Social Security Administration runs the program, SSI is not the same as Social Security. There are two main differences.

First, although SSI is administered by the Social Security Administration, SSI is financed by general funds from the United States Treasury rather than from contributions of workers, employers, and self-employed people. Second, SSI limits the value of the assets and income you are permitted to have and still be eligible for payments; Social Security imposes no limits on the amount of money or property you can have and still receive Social Security payments. However, you can receive both Social Security and SSI if you satisfy the eligibility requirements of each.

SSI checks are payable the first of every month and cover the benefit for that month. For example, an SSI check dated February 1 is for the month of February. This is different from Social Security checks, which cover the benefit for the prior month. For example, a Social Security check dated February 3 is for the month of January.

Qualifications for SSI Payments

If you apply for SSI, you will be asked five questions. First, are you 65 or older, blind, or disabled? Second, have you resided for a minimum of thirty consecutive days in one of the fifty states, the District of Columbia, or an American possession? Third, are you a citizen of the United States or a legally admitted alien seeking permanent residence in the United States? These first three questions cover the basic requirements.

In addition, you will be asked a fourth question about your income, which must be under the allowable limit. You may have some income and still be eligible for SSI. Monthly income includes money received from Social Security, the Veterans Administration, workers' compensation, pensions, annuities, gifts, or anything similar.

The final question you will be asked concerns the dollar value of your assets. Your assets are the things that you own, such as property, savings accounts, stocks, bonds, jewelry, and other valuables. Assets that are basic necessities of life are not, however, counted. A home that is a primary residence, for example, does not count as an asset, and the government does not ask for a lien on it. A car is not counted at all if it is used to travel to work or to receive regular treatment for a specific medical problem.

For the year 1995, a single person can own assets worth up to $2,000 and still be eligible for SSI. A couple can own assets worth up to $3,000 and still be eligible. If you own a car that is not used for employment or medical treatments, the portion of the market value that exceeds $4,500 is counted as an asset. Up to $1,500 may be set aside for burial expenses and does not count as an asset.

SSI Payment Amounts

The maximum monthly SSI payment varies according to whether the recipient is an individual or a couple and whether the recipient is living alone or with others. In 1995, federal SSI payments for an individual living alone are $458 a month and for a couple, $687. States supplement this amount, and the SSI check varies from state to state because each state contributes a different amount to the basic benefit provided by the federal government. In addition, the monthly check is reduced if the recipient has other income. Furthermore, special payment rates have been established for individuals who are blind, physically disabled, or mentally disabled. Call your local Social Security office for information about specific SSI payment amounts.

IMPORTANT TIPS

You should do several things to assure that you receive all the Social Security benefits to which you are entitled. The steps to take include the following:

1. **Check Your Earnings Record Biennially.** To protect your investment in Social Security, you should check your Social Security earnings and quarters of coverage in your personal account every two years. You want to be sure that the government's records are correct. To obtain this information, phone your local Social Security Administration office and ask for a Request for Earnings and Benefit Estimate Statement. When you receive the form, fill it out and mail it to the Social Security Data Operations Center serving your state. The addresses of the Social Security Data Operations Centers are as follows:

■ For Alabama, Arkansas, Colorado, Illinois, Iowa, Kansas, Louisiana, Mississippi, Missouri, Nebraska, New Mexico, Oklahoma, Texas, or Wisconsin:

P.O. Box 4429, Albuquerque, NM 87196.

■ For Alaska, American Samoa, Arizona, California, Guam, Hawaii, Idaho, Minnesota, Montana, Nevada, North Dakota, Oregon, South Dakota, Utah, Washington, and Wyoming:

100 East Alvin Drive, Salinas, CA 93906.

■ For Connecticut, Delaware, District of Columbia, Florida, Georgia, Indiana, Kentucky, Maine, Maryland, Massachusetts, Michigan, New Hampshire, New Jersey, New York, North Carolina, Ohio, Pennsylvania, Puerto Rico, Rhode Island, South Carolina, Tennessee, Utah, Virginia, Virgin Islands, West Virginia, and all foreign countries:

P.O. Box 20, Wilkes-Barre, PA 18703.

In response to the request form, you will receive an official statement from Social Security listing your earnings covered by Social Security and your estimated future benefits. When you receive your earnings record from Social Security, check the annual figures shown against your Forms W-2 or other earnings records to make sure that they are accurate.

It is important to verify your Social Security records every two years because the law sets a time limit for making corrections easily. That time limit currently is three years, three months, fifteen days after the year in which the wages were paid or the self-employment income was earned. Mistakes can be corrected after this time limit, but it is more difficult to do. The importance of accurate Social Security records increases as you get closer to retirement.

2. **Estimate your benefits.** In retirement planning, it is important to estimate your expected Social Security retirement allowance in advance. Therefore, as you approach your retirement date, you should visit or write your local Social Security office to have an experienced representative make the final and exact calculations for you.

3. **Apply for benefits.** Under Social Security law, you will not receive benefits automatically. You must apply for them, and you should do this during the three months before the month in which you will reach retirement age. Your benefits will become effective as of the month you reach 65.

4. **Gather the required documents.** The documents you will need in order to apply for Social Security benefits are listed on page 126. You will need similar documents when applying for benefits for children.

5. **Inform your family members.** Inform your spouse and children of the Social Security

benefits for which they may be eligible under various conditions. Furthermore, make sure that your family members know where your proofs and documents are located.

6. **Decide on retirement date.** If you retire at age 65, you will receive 100 percent of your Primary Insurance Amount. If you retire at 62, you will receive only 80 percent of this amount. However, retiring at age 62 is financially beneficial as compared with retirement at age 65. (See Table 7.3) It takes 14 years for a person who waits until 65 to retire to catch up with a similarly covered person who begins to receive benefits at age 62. Some individuals, for a variety of reasons, prefer to work until age 70 or beyond. For those who delay retirement beyond age 65, present law provides a delayed retirement credit, which amounts to 4.5 percent per year in 1995 (see Table 7.4).

Your Social Security benefits can be an important source of income during your retirement years. Your efforts to make sure that your account is accurate and to apply properly for your benefits are well worth the time.

Glossary

Any substantial gainful work. Any significant physical or mental duties or a combination of both that is productive in nature.

Average covered monthly earnings. A basic measure of a worker's earnings derived from *average indexed monthly earnings* over most of a worker's lifetime. Average covered monthly earnings is used to compute an individual's Social Security retirement allowance.

Average indexed monthly earnings (AIME). Monthly income for past years adjusted and then averaged; used to calculate Social Security benefit rates. Monthly earnings from the 1950s and 1960s are adjusted to reflect the impact of inflation and the current higher earnings levels. The adjusted earnings are then averaged to obtain a benefit rate that is more in line with today's earnings.

Cost-of-living adjustment (COLA). Annual increases in Social Security benefits designed to protect retirement income against the inroads of inflation.

Currently insured. A person is currently insured if he/she has at least six quarters (one and one-half years) of coverage during the full thirteen-quarter (three years and three months) period ending with the calendar quarter in which he/she dies; or most recently became entitled to disability benefits; or became entitled to retirement benefits.

Delayed retirement credit (DRC). An additional cash benefit awarded for each year of work after the normal retirement age during which an eligible individual does not draw Social Security benefits. Under current law, the annual DRC is 4.5 percent of the primary insurance amount. *See also* Primary insurance amount.

Dependent child. A person under 18 years of age, a full-time elementary or secondary school student up to 19 years of age, or an older child with a disability that began before age 22.

Dependent parent. One who is receiving at least 50 perent of support from an offspring.

Disability. A condition in which you are so severely disabled physically or mentally that you are unable to do "any substantial gainful work." The condition must be expected either to last at least twelve months or to result in death. *See also* Disability insurance.

Disability insurance (DI). A Social Security benefit that protects you, your spouse, and your children during your working years by providing benefits if you become unable to work because of an extended illness or other disability. The amount of your disability benefit is your primary insurance amount at the time you become disabled. *See also* Disability; Primary insurance amount.

Early retirement. Retirement before age 65. You can retire as early as age 62 and receive retirement benefits, if you are fully insured. But if you retire at 62, you will receive only 80 percent of your primary insurance amount. This reduction is permanent; your primary insurance amount will not increase to the full amount when you reach normal retirement age. *See also* Fully insured; Primary insurance amount.

Earnings base. The maximum amount of wages that can be credited to a worker's Social Security record for a specific year. In 1995, the earnings base is $61,200.

Earnings limitation for employees (retirement test). The amount of money you are allowed to earn after retirement without losing any Social Security benefits. There is no earnings limitation for retirees age 70 or above.

Federal Insurance Contributions Act (FICA). The federal law that sets the tax rate and maximum taxable amount for Social Security taxes. *See also* Maximum taxable amount; Self-Employment Contributions Act; Tax rate.

Fully insured. Completely eligible for Social Security benefits. When you are fully insured, you have worked the required number of quarters of coverage (QC) for your age. Being fully insured does not mean that you will get the highest monthly benefit; it means that you will be eligible for benefits when you retire and that your survivors can get benefits when you die. *See also* Quarters of coverage.

Hospital insurance (HI). Part A of Medicare. Medicare is one of the two separate programs in the Social Security structure; the other is the Old Age, Survivors, and Disability Insurance program. HI pays for hospitalization. (Each program sets an individual tax. The two taxes are added together and collected as one amount. When you become eligible for this benefit, you no longer pay the tax, unless you are still working.)

Indexing. Adjusting of past earnings to account for changes in average wages since the year the earnings were received. Part of the current method for calculating Social Security retirement benefits. *See also* Average indexed monthly earnings.

Late retirement. Retirement after age 65. For each year you work beyond retirement age but do not collect benefits, you can earn a bonus benefit that currently is 4.5 percent of the primary insurance amount. *See also* Delayed retirement credit; Primary insurance amount.

Lump-sum death benefit. A one-time, lump sum of money paid by Social Security upon the death of an insured individual, either working or retired. Currently, the death benefit is $255, and it is paid to the the surviving spouse or minor children.

Maximum family benefit. The limit on the total amount of benefits that all members of one family may receive based on the earnings record of one worker. This limit varies with the primary insurance amount. *See also* Primary insurance amount.

Maximum taxable amount. The maximum amount of an individual's earnings that can be taxed each year. You do not have to pay any taxes on earnings over this amount.

Medicare. A federal health insurance program for people 65 or older and certain disabled people under 65. It is run by the Health Care Financing Administration of the United States Department of Health and Human Services and paid for through Social Security taxes. Social Security Administration offices across the country take applications for Medicare and provide general information about the program.

Old Age, Survivors, and Disability Insurance (OASDI). One of the two separate programs in the Social Security structure.

Pay-as-you-go system. The system by which almost all of the taxes paid by workers into Social Security in a particular year were paid out to that year's Social Security beneficiaries. The Social Security Amendments of 1983 replaced this system with a partially funded pension system.

Primary insurance amount (PIA). The largest benefit a worker can receive upon retiring at retirement age. All Social Security benefits are based on this amount.

Quarter of coverage (QC). A designated time period during which you must earn a certain amount of money to receive credit toward being eligible to receive Social Security benefits. The number of QC you must accrue depends upon your age, with forty being the maximum number required. One quarter is one-fourth of a year. In 1995, you must earn a minimum of $630 within a specified quarter to earn one QC.

Retirement age. Refers to the age at which an individual becomes eligible to receive Social Security benefits—age 62. "Full retirement age" is 65, at which time an individual can begin to collect full Social Security benefits.

Retirement insurance. A Social Security benefit that enables you to retire at age 62 or over and receive a monthly payment for life.

Self-Employment Contributions Act. The federal law that sets the tax rate and maximum taxable amount for the self-employed. *See also* Federal Insurance Contributions Act; Maximum taxable amount; Tax rate.

Social Security. A federal program established in 1935 to provide retirement, survivors', disability, and medical benefits through a payroll tax paid by both employers and employees. *See also* Federal Insurance Contributions Act.

Social Security Administration (SSA). The agency that administers the Old Age, Survivors, and Disability Insurance programs.

Social Security trust funds. Separate trust funds set up to hold the money allotted for old age and survivors insurance, disability insur-ance, and health insurance. Employers and self-employed individuals remit their contributions to the United States Treasury, which credits them to the separate trust funds. A fourth trust fund, for Supplementary Medical Insurance (SMI), receives Medicare Part B premiums and general revenue payments, which are used to fund that program.

Supplemental Security Income (SSI). A sepa-rate Social Security program that provides a basic cash income for people age 65 or older who are in financial need and for the needy of any age who are blind or disabled.

Survivors' insurance. A Social Security benefit that is a form of life insurance, providing income to your dependent spouse, children, and parents, if they are qualified, in the event of your death.

Tax rate. The percent of your earnings that is paid by both you and your employer into the Social Security program each year. A self-em-ployed individual pays a higher rate than does a non-self-employed person. The tax rates are set by Congress.

Widowers' benefits. A Social Security program that provides monthly benefits to a father whose wife died while insured under Social Security. To be eligible, the father must not have remar-ried and must be caring for an unmarried child under 18 or an older child who was disabled before 22.

8

Pensions

Analysts in income security for the elderly refer to a "three-legged stool." Social Security is the most important source of income for retirees and covers the greatest number of people. It is, therefore, the first leg. The second leg consists of pensions, including private employer pension plans, public plans for government workers, and individual plans for the self-employed or for employed persons wishing to supplement their employer plans. The third leg consists of a variety of income sources such as savings and investments. A good pension is one that, when added to Social Security and third-leg income, will help retirement income to roughly match working income. Individuals and couples who can count upon adequate income from these three legs are indeed fortunate and can look forward to a secure retirement.

Current statistics indicate that only 10 to 20 percent of women over 40 receive or expect to receive a pension. And if they receive a retirement allowance, the amount is between one-third and one-half of that received by their male colleagues. The reasons for this include the following: Women leave and rejoin the work force more frequently than men because of maternity leave or to provide care when family members

are in need; they change jobs more frequently than men; they usually work in jobs less likely to have employer-provided retirement plans.

Women can achieve economic security in retirement only if they start planning for it while still working in order to provide for the shortfall of a pension. This requires that they initiate and maintain an active savings program that will accumulate an adequate retirement nest egg. A portion of the funds saved should be prudently invested to achieve growth. Retirement planning is the key. Guidelines are suggested in Chapter 6, Savings and Investments. A secure and successful retirement depends on the steps you take early in your working years to provide for your future.

The Retirement Equity Act of 1984 and the recent Supreme Court decision on equal pensions for men and women are a step in the right direction.

TYPES OF PENSION PLANS

A pension plan, subsidized and regulated by the government, is a benefit of most jobs in the private sector. The federal government regulates *private pension plans* by granting favorable tax treatment to employers whose plans meet certain standards. Approved plans are government-subsidized, with the total subsidy for all plans currently around $10 billion a year. This total represents the amount of taxes the companies would pay if they were not granted this tax exemption.

The plans set up by self-employed people, known as *Keogh plans*, and the plans set up by employed and other individuals wishing to accumulate retirement savings, known as *Individual Retirement Accounts* (IRAs), are voluntary plans. Under Keogh and IRA plans, the individual decides if he or she wants to set up a plan, how much to put into it (within statutory limits), and how the funds should be invested (again within statutory limits). Because these plans are subsidized by the government through tax deferment, there are penalties for withdrawing funds before retirement age.

About 90 percent of all government employees—including federal, state, and local, both military and nonmilitary—are covered under some form of *public pension plan*. Government plans pay benefits to about 10 percent of people over 65. Some government employees are also covered by Social Security.

Around 40 percent of people over 65 will eventually receive some retirement income from private employer pensions. An additional small percentage of people, mostly in the higher income brackets, will get significant retirement income from Keogh plans and IRAs. One or more of the plans discussed in this chapter can provide important supplementation to Social Security.

GROUP PRIVATE PENSION PLANS

The history of private pension plans in industry reveals that they grew slowly and were often controversial. A major expansion of the private plans occurred after World War II, particularly for workers in organized industries. Currently, about 41 million people, about half of all nongovernmental employees in the United States, are covered by a private pension system. Because of abuses that became prevalent in the 1960s and 1970s, Congress in 1974 passed the Employee Retirement Income Security Act, known as ERISA, to provide some protection for private pension plan members. A Supreme Court decision in 1983 outlawed sex discrimination in pension plans, and in 1984, Congress passed the Retirement Equity Act to make it easier for women to participate in pension plans and receive retirement benefits. A detailed discussion of these developments follows, as does a description of the basic features of group private pension plans.

Background

Before the Social Security Act of 1935, few employers thought they were obligated to do more than pay wages for work performed. Their philosophy was simply that they were buying work and they could not be good businessmen and also be held responsible for what would happen to their workers in retirement. Organized labor tried to establish pension plans tied to unions but was unsuccessful. In fact, until the mid-1940s, some unions actually opposed the establishment of private pension plans by employers. They thought that such plans would bind the worker to the industry and employer rather than to the union.

After World War II, circa 1945, there was a major expansion of private pension plans, particularly for workers in organized industries. By 1955, over 14 million workers were covered. The unions in this period supported the establishment of pension plans in industry to supplement the meager retirement allowances (averaging $25 a month) paid by Social Security. Moreover, with wage and price controls in effect during World War II and for a time thereafter, pensions were one of the few things for which unions could fight to improve the living standards of their members. Industry discovered that a good pension plan could attract and hold employees. Currently, about 50 million people, or approximately half of all nongovernmental wage and salaried workers in the United States, are covered by a private pension system.

In the 1960s and early 1970s, many workers discovered to their dismay that the benefits they had been expecting to receive were not to materialize. The rules were stacked in favor of employers, and minor deviations, such as *breaks in service* (temporary leaves of absence from employment) or job changes, nullified a member's right to a pension. Abuses were so prevalent that Congress took action in 1974 to provide some protection for pension plan members by passing the Employee Retirement Income Security Act, better known as ERISA.

Employee Retirement Income Security Act of 1974

The pension reform act approved by the federal government in 1974 established rules regarding eligibility for a pension, funding of pension plans, and day-to-day operations. These rules affect thousands of employers and millions of employees. As the name of the law implies, the primary goal of ERISA is to increase the probability that employees who are covered by a retirement plan during much of their working careers will, in fact, receive benefits upon retirement. ERISA covers nearly all pension and retirement plans created by private employers engaged in interstate commerce. Its provisions do not apply to plans sponsored by governments, charitable organizations, or firms involved exclusively in intrastate commerce. The law regulates plans that are in existence; it does not require firms to initiate retirement plans. Moreover, ERISA does not force companies to pay any minimum amounts to employees other than those specified in the plan.

ERISA was intended to put private pension programs on a secure financial footing and to assure millions of workers that they can depend on receiving retirement payments. It prescribes minimum standards that covered plans must meet. Among the major items addressed by the law are vesting, benefits, financing, funding, survivors' benefits, and disclosure to participants. ERISA also established the *Pension Benefit Guarantee Corporation* (PBGC), which guarantees benefits to plan members even when a plan's assets are insufficient to fulfill its commitments. As of 1995, PBGC guarantees the basic pension benefits of 41 million American workers and retirees participating in about 66,000 plans. The framers of the law also have provided for employees of companies that do not have a pension plan. Such persons can set up their own retirement system in the form of an IRA that offers substantial tax benefits to encourage saving for retirement. A 1981 law expanded the concept of the IRA to permit individuals who are already covered by a private or public pension to set up an account. The Tax Reform Act of 1986 restricts contributions to IRAs.

Retirement Equity Act of 1984

Proponents of the Retirement Equity Act of 1984 argued that many women were hurt economically by provisions of the ERISA law of 1974, which they said benefited men but not women. The Retirement Equity Act has made it easier for women to participate in private pension plans and to receive retirement benefits, either their husband's or their own.

Under the 1984 legislation, an employee's spouse must give written permission before the employee can choose a retirement plan that will stop pension payments upon his or her death, as opposed to continuing the payments to the surviving spouse. Until passage of this law, employees did not need a spouse's permission to waive the payment of benefits. Usually, payments to an employee are slightly greater if he or she waives payments to a surviving spouse. Another provision of the law is the payment of benefits to the surviving spouse of a worker who dies before the early retirement age of 55 but who is fully or partially vested in the pension plan. In a divorce case, the newer law authorizes a court to award an individual a portion of the former spouse's pension as part of the divorce settlement if the individual has not remarried.

In an effort to adjust private pension plans for women who enter the work force relatively early but interrupt their careers to have children, the law lowered from 25 to 21 the age at which workers must be allowed to participate in such plans. The 1984 law also requires that when eligibility for a retirement pension is calculated, the *years of service* from the time the employee turned 18 must be counted. Under the 1974 law, the age used for that calculation was 22.

The 1984 law also allows employees who have worked fewer than five years to stop working for five years without losing their pension credit. It also bars pension plans from counting a one-year maternity or paternity leave as a break in service.

The 1984 law has provided a more secure old age for thousands of American women who had been deprived of pension benefits by loopholes that did not recognize their contribution either inside or outside the home. In pension matters of the private sector, this newer law has been a major step toward true economic equity for women.

Sex Discrimination in Employee Pension Plans

In July 1983, the Justices of the United States Supreme Court issued a 5-to-4 decision in the case of *Arizona Governing Committee v. Norris*, which outlawed sex discrimination in pension plans. Up to that time, retirement annuities paid men and women different amounts. The payment schedule was based on the fact that, on average, women live nearly eight years longer than men. Therefore, pension plan administrators reasoned, women should get smaller payments since these payments will naturally be spread out over a longer period. The Supreme Court ruling required that the future pension checks of women be increased and that the checks for men be reduced. Because the decision was based on employment-bias law, it affects only company pension plans and not those offered by insurance companies on the open market.

Age Discrimination in Employee Pension Plans

In October 1986, President Reagan signed the Omnibus Budget Reconciliation Act (OBRA), which addresses the issue of employers' continuing retirement plan contributions after normal retirement age. OBRA amended ERISA and the Internal Revenue Code (IRC) to prohibit discrimination on the basis of age in employee pension benefit plans. The OBRA amendments require employers to continue pension plan benefit accruals and contributions after normal retirement age. The OBRA amendments also prohibit pension plans from excluding from participation employees hired at or after the plan's normal retirement age if those employees meet the other requirements. OBRA is generally effective for plans that began on or after January 1, 1988.

Types of Group Private Pension Plans

Essentially, there are two types of group private pension plans—the *defined contribution plan* and the *defined benefit plan*. In government employment, the defined benefit plan is dominant. In the private sector, as of 1994, 39.5 million workers were in defined benefit plans and 39.2 million workers were in defined contribution plans. These plans have several variations.

Defined Contribution Plan

In a defined contribution plan, you and your employer, or the employer alone, contribute to a retirement fund. In many cases, the administrator of the plan is responsible for investing the money in a variety of ways. In other cases, the employees have the opportunity to select the types of investments. When you retire, the contributions and earnings that have been accumulated over the years are used to purchase an annuity, which provides regular monthly payments for a specified time period, usually the recipient's lifetime. The retirement income you receive is determined by the size of the annuity bought with the money credited to your account.

An outstanding example of a defined contribution plan is the Teachers Insurance and Annuity Association-College Retirement Equities Fund (TIAA-CREF). This plan was founded in 1918 to provide retirement benefits for the staff of colleges, universities, independent schools, and certain other nonprofit and tax-exempt educational and research institutions. Today, about 5,250 educational institutions have TIAA-CREF retirement plans. Some 1,700,000 participants are accumulating future retirement income in annuity contracts, and another 300,000 participants are receiving annuity income benefits. The TIAA-CREF defined contribution plans for higher education are fully portable, fully and immediately vested systems. They are designed to permit, perhaps even encourage, the transfer of academic talent from one institution to another without concern about forfeiting pension benefits.

Defined Benefit Plan

In a defined benefit plan, a formula is used to determine your pension, and your employer is required to contribute enough into the pension fund over the years to insure that your retirement allowance equals the amount prescribed by the formula. The pension usually is tied both to years of credited service and to salary. The best pension plans base your retirement allowance upon your earnings in your last year or in your final few years of service, when you are likely to earn the most. Least favorable is a plan that gears your pension to the average earnings for all years.

Variations

Both defined contribution and defined benefit plans may require or allow contributions by employees. If a pension plan is financed entirely by the employer, it is referred to as *noncontributory*. In a *contributory pension plan*, the employer and employee share the cost in some prescribed proportion. The majority of corporate pension plans are noncontributory. Some plans are administered solely by a union and are financed by union dues or assessments.

In contrast, most federal, state, and local government pension plans are contributory. In a contributory plan, if you leave your employer before your rights have vested, you are legally entitled to remove your own contributions with interest. The employee share of costs in a contributory plan is usually between 3 and 10 percent of wages and is generally paid through payroll deductions.

Some pension plans are tied in with Social Security benefits. These plans are called *integrated plans*. In integrated plans, a participant's monthly pension amount is computed according to the pension plan's benefit formula, then a percentage of the participant's monthly Social Security benefit is subtracted from the monthly pension amount.

Tax Considerations

In a contributory plan, you pay income taxes on the amount you contribute. When you collect your retirement allowance, the amount you contributed over your working life is, therefore, not taxed. However, you must pay income taxes on the contributions of your employer and on the interest earned by all contributions.

According to rules developed by the Internal Revenue Service under provisions of the Internal Revenue Code, employer contributions to qualified pension plans—up to certain limits—can be deducted as a current business expense. Another tax advantage is that the investment income of a qualified pension plan is allowed to accumulate untaxed. Qualification standards apply only to private pension plans and not to retirement plans of governmental or charitable organizations because these last organizations are tax-exempt.

Eligibility Requirements for Group Private Plans

Most pension plans require employees to meet certain eligibility requirements before they can participate. ERISA approved four age-service eligibility standards, depending on other characteristics of the plan—age 25 and one year of service; age 25 and three years of service; age 30 and one year of service; and no age requirement but three years of service. The last requirement applies to Keogh plans, which are the plans used by self-employed people for themselves and their employees (see page 148). These eligibility standards constitute the maximum restrictions that an employer can apply to a pension plan. An employer has the right to make an employee a participant sooner.

For defined benefit plans, ERISA recognized a special provision of which you should be aware, especially if you are in your 50s and contemplating a job change. The law permits a defined benefit plan to exclude from membership any person who begins work within five years of the plan's normal retirement age.

Credit for Years of Service

How you earn benefits is usually determined by the number of years you work for your employer. You must know exactly how your employer counts a year of service and how any breaks in that service can affect the benefits you have accumulated. You must check to be sure that you have earned the pension benefits you think you have and that any breaks in service you may have taken have not jeopardized your benefits. Under most plans, you will have a year of service if you work at least 1,000 hours in a twelve-consecutive-month period. Some plans, however, use other standards for measuring years of service. Your plan may provide that you will have a break in service if you do not work at least 500 hours in a twelve-consecutive-month period.

Some plans give you credit for work performed before you became a plan participant, while others do not. Under some plans, you stop earning pension credits when you reach the plan's normal retirement age, even if you continue to work. Other plans give credit for years of service after retirement age. To avoid losing some or all of your accumulated benefits because of a break in service, read—particularly for breaks in service—your Summary Plan Description (SPD), a booklet issued by the employer explaining the pension plan's provisions.

In a defined contribution plan, your accrued benefit at any point equals the amount credited to your account. If the plan puts the money into a cash value life insurance policy, the amount for which the policy can be surrendered represents your accrued benefit.

In a defined benefit plan, the accrual process is different because your retirement allowance is not a special sum set aside for you in the pension fund but a fixed monthly income that will be paid on retirement. For example, according to one arrangement, if the plan requires thirty years of service and you leave the company after twenty years of covered service, you are entitled to two-thirds of your estimated pension. Another arrangement computes benefits at a fixed percentage each year. The law permits a plan to use a flat rate of not less than 3 percent a year so that an employee accrues 100 percent of his or her projected pension after no more than thirty-three and one-third years of covered service. ERISA also allows plans to apply different percentages for early and later years.

Time Required for Vesting

When an employee is *vested* in a pension plan, it means that the employee has the right to receive money from the plan—even if he or she resigns or is fired—based upon the employee's and employer's contributions. Employees' contributions vest immediately and can be withdrawn when the employee leaves the job. However, the rights of employees to employer contributions are generally subject to limitations, including service-time requirements (usually seven years) and amount limits.

The Tax Reform Act of 1986 accelerated the minimum vesting requirements set by ERISA. The 1986 vesting rules became effective in 1989. Three of the more popular vesting plans are the following:

1. **Cliff vesting.** ERISA provides full retirement benefits after ten years of employment. The Tax Reform Act of 1986 provides full benefits after five years of employment, starting January 1, 1989. Short of ten years under ERISA or five years under the 1986 Tax Reform Act, employees receive nothing.

2. **Vesting upon entry.** Under prior law, a plan could require a three-year waiting period for plan entry, with 100 percent vesting immediately upon entry. Effective in 1989, the Tax Reform Act of 1986 replaced the three-year/100 percent alternative with a two-year/100 percent provision.

The Tax Reform Act of 1986 is notable for its impact on pension reform. Acceleration in vesting schedules has provided the following benefits:

■ More workers have become eligible for pensions at retirement.

■ Working women, who on average change jobs more often than men do, have increased probability of ultimately receiving a pension.

■ The younger work force has a more secure retirement ahead.

The 1986 law provided another benefit. Pension plans until 1986 covered only about half of the work force. The 1986 law requires private pension plans to cover 70 percent of employees, thus benefiting more low-income employees.

Under current law, you must be given a statement telling you the amount of vested benefits you have earned if you request such a statement. If you leave your job, you should receive such a statement automatically.

Types of Benefits

Most pension plans provide retirement benefits and survivors' benefits.

Retirement Benefits

The three types of retirement benefits are as follows:

1. **Normal.** Most pension plans have designed their benefit programs for retirement at age 65, which is considered the *normal retirement age*. But despite this, the federal age discrimination law prohibits an employer from requiring employees to retire before age 70. The law forbidding age discrimination does not require an employer to increase pensions for work after 65. Nevertheless, a member of a defined benefit pension plan usually receives a higher retirement allowance for additional time served on the job.

2. **Early.** Many pension plans allow employees to take *early retirement*, which is retirement sometime prior to the plan's normal retirement age. If you retire early, you will receive a monthly retirement allowance, called an *early retirement benefit*, that is smaller than what you would receive if you retired at the usual retirement age. Because the contribution period is shorter, the monthly income at early retirement is reduced by an actuarial formula that takes into account the likelihood that you will receive the pension for more years than you would if you retired at 65. Some firms encourage early retirement by paying more than the actuarial equivalent or by offering other incentives, such as a lump-sum payment.

3. **Disability.** Some plans provide benefits if an employee is unable to work because of illness or disability. These benefits are known as *disability benefits*. Pension plans vary in the definition of disability as well as in the age and service requirements that determine eligibility for these benefits. Each plan specifies eligibility requirements and the amount of disability benefit you will receive if you are disabled.

Survivors' Benefits

Most pension plans that pay monthly benefits are required by law to include a provision for survivors' benefits, called *a joint and survivor annuity*. This provision allows an employee to designate an individual, usually the spouse, to receive benefits if the employee dies. It gives the survivor a minimum of 50 percent of the benefit that would have been payable to the retired employee. In order to provide for a survivor, the retired employee must accept a lower pension while alive.

An employee does not have the right to waive the survivor's option without obtaining the prior approval of his or her spouse. As explained earlier in this chapter, under the Retirement Equity Act of 1984, a member of a private pension plan must get the written consent of a spouse before electing not to take a joint and survivor annuity. If this option is not taken, the retiree can receive a higher pension, but the survivor will receive nothing when the retiree dies. The 1984 law also provides that private pension plans must now pay benefits to a surviving spouse if the employee dies after becoming vested, that is, after having worked long enough to earn the right to receive benefits.

Pension plans have a variety of provisions relating to death benefits. Death benefit provisions usually are related to an employee's age and years of service, with a varying schedule of survivors' benefits also depending upon these factors. Some pension plans have no death benefit. Instead, they pay a survivor a lump sum provided by a group life insurance policy.

Insurance for Plan Terminations

ERISA provides an important element of protection in the form of pension plan termination insurance. A provision of the ERISA law has established the Pension Benefit Guarantee Corporation (PBGC), whose purpose is to guarantee that pension benefits will be paid to eligible workers even if their employer's plan has insufficient assets to fulfill its commitments. Funding for PBGC is derived from charges levied against company pension plans regulated by ERISA.

PBGC has the power to seize up to 30 percent of a company's net worth if the company terminates its defined benefit retirement plan. When a company pension plan is unable to meet its commitments to beneficiaries, the agency will pay the pensions. It will pay up to $750 in monthly retirement benefits per person.

PBGC is similar to savings bank deposit insurance. However, the number of weak pension plans is much larger than the number of weak savings banks. Potential claims against PBGC, even considering the agency's ability to seize company assets, far exceed the millions in reserves that have been built up since 1974.

Funding of Group Private Plans

The law now requires that every company with a qualified pension plan each year contribute to the plan an amount that will cover the obligations for future benefits that build up during the year. A plan so structured is known as a *fully funded pension plan*. Prior to ERISA, many pension plans were unfunded or underfunded. In these, a company's pension reserves were nonexistent or inadequate to meet future pension benefits. Such pension plans paid benefits directly from the company's operating budget as claims arose. ERISA requires unfunded and underfunded pension plans to build up their reserves for past obligations over a period of thirty

to forty years. It also requires that pension funds be invested in safe assets. Most trustees of private pension funds invest in blue-chip company stocks or in fixed-return bonds rather than in more speculative investments.

Unfortunately, some employers have grossly and willfully underfunded their defined benefit pension plans. The General Accounting Office, the Congressional Budget Office, and the House Ways and Means Oversight Subcommittee estimate that as of 1994, about 15,000 businesses in the United States have a collective shortfall of $71 billion. This is up from $53 billion in 1992 and $27 billion in 1987, and the funding deficit is continuing to grow.

The federal government insures defined benefit plans through the Pension Benefit Guarantee Corporation (PBGC), collecting premiums from all employers who offer such plans. About 85 percent of American businesses adequately fund their pension plans, and their premiums to PBGC pay the costs to cover the collapse of the few irresponsible corporations. Many corporations with inadequately funded plans are converting their defined benefit plans into defined contribution plans, further endangering the federal system's financial soundness.

The Administration in Washington recognizes the issue and has promised to address it. However, pension reform requires cooperative efforts by corporate management, corporate employees, and taxpayers to let their Congressional representatives know how they feel about this issue.

Summary Plan Description

The 1974 pension reform law requires employers to provide each employee covered by the pension plan with a summary description of the plan and of any changes in the plan in a form that can be readily understood by the average participant. This requirement is very important. It means that you have a legal right to obtain the operating details of your private pension plan from your company. You can contact the personnel department and ask for the company's pension booklet. A small company may not have such a document. If you belong to a union, you can probably find out about your pension plan by contacting the union representative responsible for this aspect of your company's benefits.

The pension plan summary is called the *Summary Plan Description* (SPD). It must explain the eligibility requirements for benefits, how you accumulate benefits, how you can lose benefits, whether the plan is covered by plan termination insurance, and how you file a claim for benefits. If there are significant changes in your plan, you are entitled to an updated SPD. Reading your SPD carefully will help you to answer the questions in the Self-Study section of this chapter (see page 151).

Your plan administrator is also required to provide you with a Summary Annual Report, which is based on a more comprehensive report filed annually with the United States Department of Labor. The Summary Annual Report contains information on the financial activities of your plan for that particular year. If you have difficulty obtaining information about your plan, contact the nearest area office of the Labor-Management Services Administration.

Instructions for Applying for Benefits

Your Summary Plan Description must explain the procedures for filing a claim for benefits and for appealing a denied claim. The explanation must include such necessary information as whom you should contact, what documents you must provide, and how long you may have to wait for a decision to be made on your claim.

INDIVIDUAL PRIVATE PENSION PLANS

Most individuals do not plan for a secure retirement by saving enough to generate supplemental post-retirement income. To help ensure financially sound retirement, the federal government is encouraging individuals to save. The Economic Recovery Tax Act of 1981 tried to stimulate increased personal savings by allowing every employed person to put away money in an *Individual Retirement Account* (IRA) and subtract that contribution from his or her taxable income as long as he or she had earned income and was under the age of 70 1/2.

Self-employed individuals have a special option, known as a *Keogh plan*, to make large tax-deductible payments for themselves to a pension plan fund.

Simplified Employee Pension (SEP) plans, authorized in 1978, allow nongovernment employers with twenty-five or fewer employees to contribute to the pension funds of their workers and benefit from appropriate tax deductions.

In addition, *Tax Sheltered Annuities* (TSAs) were designed to help employees save retirement nest eggs. The principles guiding the operation of these annuities are included in various sections of the Internal Revenue Code—Section 401(k), for employees of private companies; Section 403(b), for employees of public schools and nonprofit organizations including hospitals and religious organizations; and Section 457, for employees of municipalities and state governments. (For a discussion of tax-sheltered annuities, see page 162.)

Individual Retirement Account

An *Individual Retirement Account* (IRA) is a personal retirement fund that can be set up by an individual. The individual can then make annual contributions of up to $2,000 a year, which may be fully tax-deductible, partially tax-deductible, or non-tax-deductible depending on the pension plan membership and individual or family income.

Under current law, if *neither* you nor your spouse is covered by a pension plan, regardless of the amount of income you both earn, each of you can contribute up to $2,000 tax-deferred every year. If your spouse is not employed, a *spousal IRA* permits you to contribute $2,250 annually. If *either* you or your spouse is covered by a pension plan:

■ Each of you can contribute up to $2,000 tax-deferred each year if married with joint income below $40,000 or if single with individual income below $25,000.

■ Each of you can contribute up to the amounts shown in Table 8.1 if married with joint income between $40,000 and $50,000 or if single with individual income between $25,000 and $35,000. As the table shows, the permitted tax-deferred contribution is reduced as income rises.

■ Each of you can make a non-tax-deductible contribution of up to $2,000 a year if married with joint income over $50,000 (both working) or if single with individual income over $35,000.

Until 1991, withdrawals before age 59 1/2 resulted in a 10 percent penalty plus payment of the income tax due. A 1991 revision permits withdrawals before age 59 1/2 without penalty, but the account must be depleted during your lifetime or the joint life expectancies of you and your spouse. The purpose of the revision is to assist individuals seeking early retirement by helping supplement income until Social Security can be collected at age 62; to help parents pay a child's college bills; and to help workers who, because of layoffs, are forced into lower-paying jobs and need extra income.

Table 8.1
Extent of Deductible for $2,000 IRA Contribution If Covered by Pension Plan

Individual Income	Family Income	Maximum Tax-Free Deductible per Individual	Voluntary Non-Deductible Contribution per Individual
$25,000 or less	$40,000 or less	$2,000	$ 0
26,000	41,000	1,800	200
27,000	42,000	1,600	400
28,000	43,000	1,400	600
29,000	44,000	1,200	800
30,000	45,000	1,000	1,000
31,000	46,000	800	1,200
32,000	47,000	600	1,400
33,000	48,000	400	1,600
34,000	49,000	200	1,800
35,000 or more	50,000 or more	0	2,000

Keogh Plan

The Keogh plan, named for Congressman Eugene J. Keogh of New York who sponsored the law (H.R. 10. Self-Employed Individuals Tax Retirement Act of 1962), is designed for self-employed individuals—professionals such as doctors, dentists, lawyers, and accountants; small business owners; and members of partnerships. The two basic types of Keoghs are the defined benefit plan and the defined contribution plan.

The first type of plan, the *defined benefit plan*, provides a set payout after retirement. An actuary calculates the annual deposits you must make to achieve your predetermined retirement allowance. These annual deposits are tax-deductible.

In the second type of Keogh, the *defined contribution plan*, you decide by yourself how much of an annual contribution you will make. The plan's investment performance then determines the ultimate payout. Your annual tax-deductible contribution may equal 25 percent of your earned income from self-employment, up to a maximum of $30,000 a year.

Specifically, if you do part-time or free-lance work, you can open a Keogh account on your part-time or free-lance earnings, even if you also work full-time for a firm that has a qualified pension, profit-sharing, or other retirement plan. For example, accountants who work for a corporation but prepare tax returns as a sideline may establish a Keogh account and contribute income based on what they earn from their sideline work. A Keogh plan can be established in any financial institution, including a bank, brokerage firm, or insurance company.

An account holder's contributions plus accumulated interest become payable upon his or her retirement, but not earlier than age 59 1/2 or later than 70 1/2. Distribution will not be made before age 59 1/2 without penalty, except in cases of disability or death. If you withdraw money from a Keogh plan early, the withdrawal is subject to a 10 percent penalty tax as well as regular income tax. Under the plan, the account holdings may be distributed in a lump sum or in payments spread over a specified period of time. The period cannot exceed, but may be spread over, the individual's life expectancy or the joint life expectancy of the individual and spouse. These periods are determined using published actuarial tables.

Should the account holder die before reaching age 59 1/2, payment will be made to a designated beneficiary. If the Keogh holder suffers permanent disability before age 59 1/2, the money is immediately payable to the account holder without penalty.

Simplified Employee Pensions

Many small businesses have been reluctant to establish a retirement plan for their employees because of the legal and administrative costs of setting up and maintaining such a plan and of complying with federal regulations. Congress sought to remove these obstacles for small businesses, those with a maximum of twenty-five employees, through a tax-favored retirement plan aimed specifically at small employers—the *Simplified Employee Pension* (SEP).

In an SEP plan, an employer establishes and finances, in part or in whole, an Individual Retirement Account for each eligible employee. The employee generally controls the investment of the money, in which he or she is immediately vested. These arrangements are sometimes called SEP-IRAs. The major difference between an SEP and an employer-sponsored IRA is the larger annual contribution that employers and employees can make to a SEP.

Acceptance of SEPs was extremely slow. To increase their attractiveness, Congress added a salary reduction feature in the Tax Reform Act of 1986. The modified plan, known as the *Salary Reduction Simplified Employee Pension* (SARSEP), is an affordable pension plan for small businesses. SARSEPs resemble 401(k) plans in that both the employer and the employee can contribute money. The contribution limit for the employee is the same as in 401(k) plans—for 1995, $9,240 or 20 percent of gross salary, whichever is less. As with a 401(k), the money comes out of the employee's salary before taxes, "reducing" the salary for tax purposes. The employer is allowed to contribute up to 25 percent of the salary, provided the total does not exceed $30,000. The payment is tax-deductible to the company. SARSEPs are not available to tax-exempt organizations or to state or local governments.

PUBLIC PENSIONS

Public pension systems probably began with the British Superannuation Act of 1834. In the United States, New York City established a pension fund in 1857 for policemen. Part of the financing for this early plan came from the proceeds of sales of confiscated and unclaimed property. In 1911, Massachusetts became the first state to establish a retirement system. At about the same time, many cities began to introduce pension systems for their general municipal employees. Both Philadelphia and Pittsburgh set up pension plans in 1915. In 1920, the United States government approved the Retirement Act to set up a pension system for federal civil service employees.

Since then, both the number of public pension plans and their membership have grown rapidly. Currently, about 2,500 public pension plans cover almost all the employees of the federal, state, and local governments—about 10.2 million active members. Almost 2 million more members of public pension plans in the United States are currently receiving benefits.

In 1983, a development affecting public pension systems (as well as private pension systems) related to the elimination of sex discrimination in pension benefits. As mentioned on page 140, the United States Supreme Court handed down a decision in the case of *Arizona Governing Committee v. Norris* requiring that pension benefits be gender-neutral. It ruled that sex-based mortality tables violate Title VII of the 1964 Civil Rights Act. It held that the longer life span of women may not be used to justify the payment of lower monthly benefits when they retire.

Federal Civil Service Plans

One of the most favorable features of employment by the federal government is its retirement system. Since 1920, employees have been covered under the Civil Service Retirement System (CSRS). In 1986, President Reagan signed into law an act creating the Federal Employees Retirement System (FERS). The need for a new retirement system for federal employees began with Public Law 98-21, which provided that federal employees hired after December 31, 1983, would be covered by Social Security.

A second law, Public Law 98-168, provided for a transition period from January 1, 1984, to January 1, 1986, for employees hired after December 31, 1983. During this period, employees were fully covered under CSRS and Social Security benefits. This transition period was extended to December 31, 1986, with the passage of Public Law 99-335, which established FERS.

FERS became effective January 1, 1987. All employees hired after December 31, 1983, have been automatically covered by FERS. Federal employees hired before December 31, 1986, and not covered by FERS have the option to transfer into FERS.

Active members of CSRS and FERS number about 2.8 million, and about 1.7 million retired and disabled civilian federal employees draw pensions.

Federal Employees Retirement System

FERS is a three-tier retirement plan. The three tiers are:

1. Social Security.
2. Basic Benefit Plan.
3. Savings Plan.

You pay full Social Security taxes and a small contribution to the Basic Benefit Plan. In addition, you can make tax-deferred contributions to the Savings Plan, with a portion matched by the government.

The three components of FERS work together to give you a strong financial foundation for your retirement years. FERS has the following advantages over CSRS:

■ Members can join a tax-deferred savings plan.

■ The government matches a portion of the members' savings.

■ Members have a choice among three different types of investment funds.

■ Individuals who leave the system with at least five years of service qualify for benefits.

■ Survivor and disability benefits are available after eighteen months of service.

Civil Service Retirement System

Members of CSRS were brought under Social Security by the 1983 Social Security Amendments. Employees hired on or after January 1, 1984, have been automatically covered by FERS and Social Security.

Most workers qualify for retirement at age 55 with thirty years' service including time in the military. (Credit for military service applies to federal employees and varies for state and local employees.) The amount of required service drops to twenty years at age 60 and to five years at 62.

Pensions are based on average salary in the three consecutive highest-paid years and can amount to as much as 80 percent of that figure. A recent tabulation reveals that the average retiree draws about $1,000 a month. Pensions are increased once a year to reflect increases in living costs.

Special Groups of Employees

Firefighters, law enforcement officers, and air traffic controllers receive an unreduced FERS benefit at age 50 with twenty years of service, or at any age with twenty-five years of service. Other groups eligible to join FERS and to receive retirement benefits include military reserve technicians and part-time employees. Members of Congress and congressional employees are also eligible for coverage.

Public Pension Reform

A proposal is introduced periodically in the United States Congress to establish federal reporting and disclosure requirements and fiduciary standards for public employee pension plans. Known as the *Public Employee Retirement Income Security Act* (PERISA), the proposal would subject federal, state, and local government pension plans to many of the same standards required of private pension plans under the terms of ERISA.

PERISA addresses itself to such problems as unfunded liabilities; rules for operation and administration; disclosure of the status of plans to members, taxpayers, and government decisionmakers; and prevention of fraud and dishonesty by requiring bonding of the trustees who are responsible for investing a plan's assets.

Self-Study
Your Pension Plan

The following questions should help you to better understand your pension plan, whether it is a private or public plan. If you are a member of a private pension plan and do not know the answer to a particular question, contact the individual in your company who handles the pension plan. If the answer is still not clear, contact the nearest office of the United States Department of Labor, Labor-Management Services Administration. If you are a member of a public pension plan, contact your personnel office for answers.

1. **Type of Plan**
   a. What type of plan is your pension plan?
      ❏ Defined benefit plan
         ❏ Integrated with Social Security
         ❏ Nonintegrated
      ❏ Defined contribution plan
         ❏ Integrated with Social Security
         ❏ Nonintegrated

   b. How is your pension plan financed?
      ❏ By employer contributions only
      ❏ By employer and employee contributions
      ❏ By union dues and assessments

   c. What is your contribution to your pension plan?

      $_____ per ❏ month
                     ❏ week
                     ❏ hour

      _____ percent of your compensation

2. **Credit for Service**
   a. How is a year of service earned under your pension plan?

      ❏ By working _____ hours in a twelve-consecutive-month period
      ❏ By meeting other requirements. Specify:

   _____

   _____

   _____

b. When does your plan year (twelve-month period for which plan records are kept) end each year? On _____
    _{date}

c. Does your pension plan give credit for work performed before becoming a participant in the plan?
    ❑ Yes
    ❑ No

d. Does your pension plan give credit for work performed after the plan's normal retirement age?
    ❑ Yes
    ❑ No

e. As of now, _____, how many years of service have you earned? _____ years.
    _{date}

f. What are your plan's *break-in-service* rules?

_____

_____

_____

3. **Vesting**
    a. Which vesting plan applies to you?
        ❑ Full and immediate vesting
        ❑ Cliff vesting
        ❑ Other _____
    b. How many additional years of service do you need to be fully vested? _____ years.

4. **Benefits**
    a. Will working beyond the normal retirement age increase your pension?
        ❑ Yes
        ❑ No
    b.   How is the normal retirement benefit computed?

_____

_____

_____

    c. What are the requirements for early retirement?
        _____ years of age; _____ years of service.
    d. Assuming you have met the age requirement, how many more years of service do you need to be eligible for early retirement benefits? _____ years.

e. How is the early retirement benefit computed?

_____

_____

_____

   f. Will your Social Security benefit be deducted from your pension benefit?
- ❑ Yes
- ❑ No

If yes, what percent of your Social Security benefit? _____ percent.

   g. How will your retirement benefit be paid?
- ❑ Monthly for life
- ❑ In a lump sum
- ❑ Adjusted periodically for cost-of-living increases
- ❑ To your survivor in the event of your death

5. Disability

   a. Does your plan provide disability benefits?
- ❑ Yes
- ❑ No

   b. How does your plan define *disability*?

_____

_____

   c. What are your plan's eligibility requirements for disability benefits?

_____ years of age; _____ years of service.

   d. Disablement by which of the following conditions would make you ineligible for disability retirement benefits?
- ❑ Alcoholism
- ❑ Drug addiction
- ❑ Mental incompetence
- ❑ Self-inflicted injury
- ❑ Other _____

   e. Who decides whether your condition meets your plan's definition of disability?
- ❑ Doctor chosen by you
- ❑ Doctor chosen by the plan director

   f. How is the disability retirement benefit computed?

_____

_____

g. Where do you obtain an application for disability retirement?

_____

_____

To whom must you send it? _____

_____

By when? Within _____ months after termination of work.

h. If you are qualified for disability benefits, for how long will your benefit be paid?
   ❑ For life, if your disability continues
   ❑ Until retirement age
   ❑ Until you return to your former job
   ❑ Until you are able to work

6. Survivors' Benefits

a. Does your pension plan offer a joint and survivor option or a similar provision for death benefits?
   ❑ Yes
   ❑ No
b. Has the joint and survivor option been waived by your spouse?
   ❑ Yes
   ❑ No
c. If death occurs before retirement, what will your survivor receive?

_____

_____

d. Electing a joint and survivor option will cause your pension benefit to be reduced by what percent? _____ percent.
e. If death occurs after retirement, what will your survivor receive? $_____ per month
   ❑ For life
   ❑ For _____ years
   ❑ Until Social Security payments begin
   ❑ Other _____

_____

7. Funding of Your Pension Plan

a. What is the funding status of your pension plan?
   ❑ Fully funded
   ❑ Underfunded but building up its reserves

    b. Have the auditors of your pension fund certified that its reserves are invested in high quality assets?

      ❑ Yes

      ❑ No

8. Insurance for Plan Termination

    a. Are your benefits insured by the Public Benefit Guarantee Corporation?

      ❑ Yes

      ❑ No

9. Summary Plan Description

    a. Has your company or union given you a Summary Plan Description?

      ❑ Yes

      ❑ No

    b. Has your company given you a copy of the latest Summary Annual Report?

      ❑ Yes

      ❑ No

10. Applying for Benefits

    a. Will your employer automatically send you a pension application?

      ❑ Yes

      ❑ No

    b. Must your application for pension benefits be made on a special form?

      ❑ Yes

      ❑ No

    c. Where and when should the application form be obtained? From _____ within _____ months before retirement.

    d. Where should your application for pension benefits be sent?

_____

_____

_____

    e. What documents must you present when applying for benefits?

_____

_____

    f. If your application for benefits is denied, what is the appeal procedure?

      An appeal may be made in writing to _____

_____

      within _____ days.

Glossary

Annuity. A tax-favored investment that generates a series of regular payments guaranteed to continue for a specific time, such as ten years or twenty years, or any other time period, or usually for the recipient's lifetime, in exchange for a single payment or a series of payments.

Break in service. A temporary leave of absence from employment.

Cliff vesting. A type of vesting in which an employee with ten years of service (or five years, starting January 1, 1989) has a nonforfeitable right to 100 percent of the accrued benefit derived from employer contributions, with no vesting before then. *See also* Graded vesting; Vesting.

Contributory pension plan. A type of pension plan in which both the employer and employee share the cost of the contribution in some prescribed proportion. *See also* Noncontributory pension plan.

Defined benefit plan. A type of pension plan in which the monthly retirement allowance is tied to both years of credited service and salary. The employee usually contributes to the plan, but the employer is responsible for contributing enough into the pension fund to buy an annuity that will provide the defined benefit. *See also* Defined contribution plan.

Defined contribution plan. A type of pension plan in which the employer and/or employee contributes a fixed amount each year to a fund that is then invested in some way by the plan's administrator to earn income. At retirement, the money credited to your account is used to purchase an annuity, which provides the monthly pension. You receive only as much of an annuity as the accumulation in your account will buy. *See also* Defined benefit plan.

Disability benefits. The benefits provided by some plans if an employee is unable to work because of illness or disability. Plans vary in their definitions of "disability" as well as in the age and service requirements that determine eligibility for the benefits.

Early retirement benefits. The benefits provided by some plans if an employee retires before the normal retirement age. Retirement at an age before 65 will bring a smaller monthly retirement allowance. This is because you will have contributed less money to the pension plan and will probably collect benefits for more years than someone who retires at the usual age of 65.

Employee Retirement Income Security Act (ERISA). A federal pension reform act, approved in 1974, that established rules for private employers engaged in interstate commerce regarding eligibility for pensions, funding, vesting, financing, survivors' benefits, and disclosure to participants.

Fully funded pension plan. A pension plan that has enough funds contributed each year to cover the obligations to pay future benefits built up during the year. *See also* Underfunded pension plan; Unfunded pension plan.

Graded vesting. A type of vesting that provides 25 percent vesting after five years of service with an additional 5 percent for each additional year up to ten years, plus an additional 10 percent for each year thereafter, or 100 percent vesting after fifteen years of service. The Tax Reform Act of 1986 requires that companies vest workers 20 percent after three years, then 20 percent per year thereafter, until the workers are fully vested after seven years, starting January 1, 1989. See also Cliff vesting; Vesting.

Individual Retirement Account (IRA). A personal retirement fund that an individual can establish by making tax-deductible contributions of up to $2,000 per year, subject to the restrictions of the Tax Reform Act of 1986.

Integrated pension plan. A type of pension plan that is tied in with Social Security. A participant's monthly pension amount is reduced by a percentage of his or her monthly Social Security benefit.

Joint and survivor annuity. A benefit in which an individual designated by the covered employee, usually the spouse, receives the pension benefits if the worker dies. It gives the survivor a minimum of 50 percent of the benefit that would have been payable to the retiree. However, to pay for this coverage, the retiree must accept a lower pension while alive.

Keogh plan. A type of retirement plan for self-employed individuals. It was established under the Self-Employment Individual Retirement Act of 1962.

Noncontributory pension plan. A type of pension plan financed entirely by the employer. The majority of corporate pension plans are noncontributory. *See also* Contributory pension plan.

Normal retirement benefits. The benefits received when retiring at the normal age of 65. Most pension plans have designed their benefit programs for retirement at age 65. While some employees work beyond 65, the federal law forbidding age discrimination does not require an employer to increase pension benefits for work after 65.

Pension. A benefit, usually monthly, paid to an individual who has retired from active work.

Pension Benefit Guarantee Corporation (PBGC). An agency established by the Employee Retirement Income Security Act

(ERISA) of 1974 that guarantees benefits to private pension plan members even when a plan's assets are insufficient to fulfill the commitments.

Qualified pension plan. A type of pension plan that meets a set of criteria developed by the Internal Revenue Service. An employer with a qualified plan can deduct contributions to the plan from taxable income as a business expense.

Simplified Employee Pension (SEP). A type of retirement plan authorized by the Revenue Act of 1978 that allows employers to contribute to IRAs set up for their workers and to take appropriate tax deductions.

Summary Plan Description (SPD). A summary description of a pension plan that the Employee Retirement Income Security Act of 1974 requires be given to each employee covered by the plan. It must include information on eligibility requirements for benefits, accumulation of benefits, loss of benefits, termination insurance, and the method for filing a claim for benefits.

Survivors' benefits. Benefits paid to the surviving spouse or other designated individual of a deceased plan participant. *See also* Joint and survivor annuity.

Tax Sheltered Annuity (TSA). A type of pension plan in which employees are allowed to earmark a portion of their salary for deposit into the plan, thus lowering their salary and deferring income taxes until the money is withdrawn, usually at retirement. Also known as a salary reduction plan, 401(k) plan, or 403(b) plan.

Underfunded pension plan. A pension plan with inadequate reserves to meet future pension benefits. *See also* Fully funded pension plan; Unfunded pension plan.

Unfunded pension plan. A pension plan that does not have any reserves to meet future pension benefits. *See also* Fully funded pension plan; Underfunded pension plan.

Vesting. The absolute right of an employee to receive money from a retirement plan even if he or she resigns or is fired. Employees' contributions vest immediately and can be withdrawn when the employee leaves the job. However, the rights of employees to employer contributions are generally subject to limitations, including service time requirements and amount limits. *See also* Cliff vesting; Graded vesting.

Year of service. Achieved when an employee works a full year (a twelve-month period) at a job.

9

Annuities

Annuities are essentially the opposite of life insurance. While life insurance pays off when the policyholder dies, an annuity contract, sold by insurance companies, is designed to pay off while the policyholder is still living.

Annuities serve an important role in retirement planning. They can serve as an investment vehicle by enabling you to save money and taxes at the same time. And in retirement, annuities can provide you with a guaranteed income each month for the rest of your life. Retirement income from annuities is part of your income from investments and supplements your pension and Social Security benefits.

At retirement, you can cash in your annuity and withdraw the accumulated value in a lump sum or in monthly payments as lifetime income. The lump sum withdrawal will enable you to invest the money, spend it, or pass it on to your heirs. By arranging to collect the monthly payments for life, you *annuitize,* which is an irrevocable choice between you and the insurance company. The money is no longer yours, but you have guaranteed income for life, and you will never have to fear that you will outlive the payments.

HOW ANNUITIES WORK

When making your financial plans for retirement, you should not forget to consider an annuity. An annuity can guarantee you a lifetime income, eliminating the fear that you will outlive your savings. Assume that you are planning to retire at age 65 with a $100,000 nest egg. If you keep the money in a bank paying 3 to 5 percent interest, it will produce an income of between $250 to $417 a month. If you draw on the principal every month in order to raise your level of living, you will run the risk of using up your money before you die.

The annuity was invented to help solve this type of problem. When an individual buys an annuity, he or she exchanges a sum of money for a promise to be paid back an agreed amount at a set schedule. This payout can begin either immediately or at a designated age, and will continue until death. You can look at an annuity as being like a life insurance policy but in reverse. With life insurance, survivors are paid when the annuitant dies. With an annuity, you receive payments while you live.

Annuities are usually purchased from insurance companies. In calculating how much to charge for an annuity, an insurance company uses actuarial tables, just as it does to set the premium on a life insurance policy.

Actuarial tables give "average" life expectancies. Some annuitants will live longer than others. Those who die sooner receive fewer payments. The unexpended funds are then used to pay those who live longer. While this may not seem fair to the ones who die early, it insures that everyone will have an equal guarantee of complete income protection for life.

Since women live longer than men, the monthly payments to women are lower than for a man of the same age. For example, a company may offer a 65-year-old man $9.30 per $1,000 of accumulated value while offering a woman of the same age only $8.50. This is referred to as a sex-distinct rate.

On the other hand, if you are in a *qualified* plan, one in which your contributions were made with no income taxes paid, and you annuitize, the company must use unisex rates. This means that the company must pay the same amount per $1,000 of accumulated value to both men and women.

An annuity, therefore, is a guaranteed income plan usually purchased from a life insurance company and paid back to the purchaser, or annuitant, during retirement. When you buy an annuity, you are lending money to the insurance company that you will get back with interest at a later date. The company, meanwhile, lends out your money at a higher interest rate.

TYPES OF ANNUITY PLANS

Annuities incorporate a variety of distinctive features. The money you give the issuing company can be paid in one of three different ways. To purchase a *single premium annuity*, you give the issuing company one single large payment, often using the proceeds from a lump-sum settlement of a pension fund or insurance policy. You buy a *fixed premium annuity* by making a series of fixed, equal payments on a monthly or annual basis. A *variable premium annuity* is purchased by installment payments, the size of which may be changed at your discretion.

Annuities also vary in how the payments are made to the annuitants. With an *immediate pay annuity*, you make the total premium payment and begin receiving a monthly check the next month. This is related to the single premium annuity. If you prefer to have the payments begin at a later date, you can select a *deferred annuity*. In this annuity, you can arrange for the payments to start at an age specified in your annuity contract.

Other arrangements focus on the time span of the payments made to you. A *straight life annuity* guarantees a stipulated monthly income to one person for life. It pays no death benefits to survivors, nor does it have a cash surrender value. A life annuity with a *term certain* guarantees one person lifetime income, but if that person dies within the designated "term certain," or guaranteed period, such as ten years or twenty years, the designated beneficiary will receive the payments for the remainder of the term. A variation is the *installment-refund annuity*. Here, the payments are guaranteed for life, but if you die before the total of the payments equals the purchase price, the payments will be continued to your beneficiary until the payments equal the purchase price. With a *cash refund annuity*, your designated beneficiary will receive a lump-sum payment. Finally, a *joint and survivor annuity* guarantees lifetime income to two persons with the cost of the annuity depending on the age and sex of each person. Table 9.1 shows the actual life expectancies for men and women as well as the gender neutral figures

Table 9.1
Life Expectancies of Men and Women
Ages 40–85

Age	Average number of years remaining		
	Men	Women	Unisex[a]
40	40	45	43
45	36	40	38
50	31	36	33
55	27	31	29
60	23	26	24
65	19	22	20
70	15	18	16
75	12	14	13
80	9	11	10
85	7	8	7

[a] In *Arizona v. Norris*, 1983, the United States Supreme Court ruled that sex-based mortality tables discriminate against women and that retirement benefits must be calculated on a "unisex basis," that is, *gender neutral basis*.

that, by law, must be used in the computation of retirement benefits.

Three types of annuities differ in what is done with the money you pay to the issuing company. With a *wraparound annuity*, you control the investment of the funds in your account. You can invest your money in a mutual fund; you can invest in stocks or bonds; or you can switch back and forth to take advantage of changes in market conditions. In a *fixed dollar annuity*, your funds are invested in a portfolio of bonds paying a set amount of interest. Your annuity, therefore, will pay you an amount that will remain unchanged over the years. Differing slightly is the *variable annuity*, in which you buy a certain number of "units." The value of the units will fluctuate each month because the issuing company will invest your payments in the stock market, and stock prices fluctuate daily.

Your monthly annuity will depend on the value of the units you own that month.

In a *tax-deferred annuity*, your payments to your account will be made with pre-tax dollars, which will become tax sheltered. In addition, you will pay no taxes on the interest that accumulates. You will eventually pay the income taxes when you withdraw your money after you retire, but at that point, you presumably will be in a lower tax bracket. In this sense, a tax-deferred annuity is similar to an IRA or Keogh plan. (For a more detailed discussion of tax-deferred annuities, see page 162.)

ADVANTAGES AND DISADVANTAGES OF ANNUITIES

Annuities as a source of retirement income have both advantages and disadvantages. Among the advantages of an annuity are the following:

■ It is the safest way in which to guarantee a fixed monthly income for life.

■ It is structured in such a way that you will never outlive your capital.

■ It requires no medical examination, a practice that would benefit the issuing company since you would probably collect fewer payments if you were not in tiptop health.

■ It frees you from the responsibility of money management and the headache of having to make investment decisions.

■ It offers a tax benefit in that some part of each annuity payout qualifies as a return of capital, which is tax-free.

Some of the disadvantages of annuities as a source of retirement income are significant. They include the following:

■ Because the monthly payment is fixed for the

rest of your life, you have no protection against inflation, which takes its toll every year to a greater or lesser degree.

■ The money you invest is tied up forever, because an annuity contract is irrevocable by either side once payments to you have begun.

■ If you should need a large sum of money in an emergency situation, you cannot borrow against your annuity once payments to you have begun.

■ Sales charges and management fees can be very large and, thus, can make quite a dent in your potential return.

WHO SHOULD BUY AN ANNUITY?

Who, then, is likely to buy an annuity? One prospective customer is an individual with a large sum of money who wants to avoid the responsibility of money management and needs maximum income but who wants absolute safety in terms of guaranteed monthly payments. Or perhaps a couple has sold the family home at a good profit and is satisfied to have a fixed monthly income for life under a joint and survivor annuity. In any case, shop around and compare contracts. Watch out for disclaimers and qualifiers in the contract, and make sure your net monthly income is clearly stated.

TAX-SHELTERED ANNUITIES

Now that you understand the rules governing IRAs, Keogh plans, and Simplified Employee Pension plans (discussed in Chapter 8), it might be useful to look at tax-sheltered annuities (TSAs), which were designed to help a company or government employee save a retirement nest egg. TSAs are often referred to as salary reduction plans. Under the plan, you authorize your employer to deduct a set amount from your check each pay period and to save the money for you. This deduction is considered deferred sal-

ary and is, therefore, excluded from current income taxation. The government collects income taxes only when you withdraw the money from the plan, which is usually at retirement. The plans discussed here are the 401(k) plan, the 403(b) plan, and the 457 plan.

Section 401(k) Plan

In 1978, Congress authorized Section 401(k), which was added to the Internal Revenue Code. A salary reduction plan, the 401(k) is designed to encourage retirement savings, permitting employees in private companies to make contributions of pre-tax dollars. A salary reduction plan differs from other employer-sponsored thrift plans or profit-sharing plans in that employee contributions up to the last two are made with after-tax dollars.

Each year, the employee can contribute a maximum tax-deferred amount. In 1995, that amount was $9,240. The employee pays no income taxes on the amount contributed and does not report the contribution on his or her income tax return. However, Social Security taxes must be paid on the contribution. Employees can make additional but non-tax-deferred contributions, amounting to the lesser of $30,000 a year or 25 percent of their compensation. And 401(k) plans give the employer the opportunity to "match" the employee's contributions. The typical employer match is fifty cents for every dollar, and some employers match dollar for dollar. The Internal Revenue Service allows a tax deduction to the employer for matching contributions based upon a formula set by the Internal Revenue Code. In general, the sum of the employee's pre- and after-tax contributions, plus any matching contributions by the employer, cannot exceed 25 percent of the employee's annual earnings or $30,000, whichever is less.

The employee contributions and matching

employer contributions are invested by an institution selected by the employer, typically an insurance company, mutual fund, or bank. Employee members of 401(k) plans usually are allowed to change their investment choices periodically.

To be legally "tax qualified," 401(k) plans must meet specified requirements. They must be voluntary, they must be nondiscriminatory (lower paid workers must be given the same opportunity to join as higher paid employees), and all employee contributions and earnings on contributions must vest immediately. Employer contributions must vest in accordance with vesting rules specified in applicable current law.

Section 403(b) and Section 457 Plans

Section 403(b) of the Internal Revenue Code is similar in concept to Section 401(k) except that it covers tax-deferred contributions to retirement savings plans by employees of public schools and nonprofit organizations, including hospitals and churches. The 403(b) tax-deferred savings plan actually preceded the 401(k) plan by many years and served as a model for the development of the Individual Retirement Account.

Section 457 of the Internal Revenue Code covers tax-deferred savings plans for employees of municipalities and state governments, following the same general principles of Section 403(b). As of 1995, the 403(b) plan permits eligible employees to contribute up to $9,500 a year to a tax-deferred savings plan, which is higher than the $9,240 maximum for 401(k) plans. The higher maximum was set because public sector employees have fewer opportunities to participate in thrift and savings plans than private-sector employees do.

Unlike 401(k) plans, 403(b) and 457 plans do not need to be nondiscriminatory to be legally tax qualified. This allows employers to offer the plan to some employees and to exclude others, such as part-time workers.

Handling Tax-Sheltered Money at Retirement

One of the questions individuals must address when they are about to retire concerns the handling of the tax-sheltered money they have saved during their working years. For some, the amount accumulated may be just a few thousand dollars, but for others, it may be as much as $100,000, $200,000, or even more. What are the alternatives available for retiring individuals? The choices are to either withdraw, rollover, or annuitize the funds, or defer the decision.

Withdrawing Tax-Sheltered Money

All 401(k), 403(b), and 457 plans permit you to withdraw part or all of your money without penalty starting at age 59 1/2. Withdrawals prior to age 59 1/2 are subject to a 10 percent penalty tax as well as regular income taxes. These withdrawals are permitted without penalty only if you separate from service, encounter "hardship," or are disabled. If you die before age 59 1/2, your beneficiary can withdraw the money without penalty.

In 1988, the Internal Revenue Service issued final regulations that define "hardship" for the withdrawal of money from a tax-sheltered annuity account. The two factors that determine hardship are:

1. The participant must have an immediate and heavy financial need.

2. Other resources to meet that need are not reasonably available.

Expenses that meet the requirements of "immediate and heavy financial need" are limited to medical expenses for the employee, spouse, or dependent; purchase of an employee's primary residence; post-secondary education tuition for the next semester or quarter for the employee, spouse, or dependent; and payments needed to prevent eviction or foreclosure.

A 1991 revision permits withdrawals before age 59 1/2 without penalty if you arrange to deplete your account over your life expectancy or the joint life expectancies of you and your spouse.

Since January 1, 1993, any withdrawal or lump-sum settlement from an employee retirement plan directly to you is subject to a 20 percent withholding tax by the payor for federal income tax purposes (see below). You can avoid the 20 percent withholding by choosing the *direct rollover option* under which an eligible rollover distribution must be transferred by the employer directly to an IRA or to a new employer's plan.

Rollovers and Tax-Sheltered Money

A *rollover* is a tax-free transfer of money from one investment program to another. Since January 1, 1993, the employer giving you a lump-sum payment from an employee retirement plan is required to withhold 20 percent of the amount for income taxes. For example, if the lump sum were $100,000, you would receive $80,000 and have $20,000 withheld. The lump-sum distribution for income tax purposes will be included as regular income for the year in which it is received, and the $20,000 withheld will be included with all other money withheld for taxes that year.

The only way to avoid the withholding of $20,000 is to have your employer directly transfer the entire lump sum into an IRA or into a new employer's plan. This law attempts to discourage the withdrawal of lump sums from retirement plans.

Annuitizing Tax-Sheltered Money

To *annuitize* means to convert accumulated savings into an annuity, from which you can draw a regular, usually monthly, benefit. Most people seek annuity payments for life, thus insuring that they will not outlive their savings.

Several standard arrangements are offered for lifetime payout—a one-life, or maximum-life, annuity for one individual; a joint and survivor annuity, to take care of a surviving spouse or other beneficiary when the annuitant dies; or a guaranteed-minimum annuity, to insure payment for five, ten, fifteen, or twenty years for at least a minimum payback on the investment.

Under the *one-life annuity*, when the annuitant dies, all the remaining money in the account reverts to the fund, unless the annuitant chose a guaranteed period of payment to continue beyond the date of death. This money would go to a beneficiary.

The Internal Revenue Service requires that you begin receiving your tax-sheltered annuity income by April 1 of the calendar year following the year you reach 70 1/2. If you fail to annuitize when required, you are subject to a 50 percent penalty on the minimum amount *not taken* plus regular income tax on what is taken out.

Deferring Your Decision

You can retire at any age and leave your tax-sheltered annuity account intact. The account will continue to grow because of the compounding of interest over a relatively long period of time.

After retirement, you can make withdrawals from the account and pay income taxes on the withdrawals, or you can choose annuitization, but you must do so no later than April 1 of the year after you turn 70 1/2. Deferral to age 70 1/2 is permitted by Sections 401(k), 403(b), and 457 of the Internal Revenue Code.

Deferring a decision on the accumulation in your tax-sheltered annuity (TSA) allows you to devote more time to making decisions regarding your basic retirement plan, such as how to allocate your accumulations among fixed and variable funds, and what payout option to choose.

The choices available can be confusing. Seek guidance from counselors who are knowledgeable and specially trained to answer such questions.

Is a Tax-Deferred Account for Everyone?

A tax-deferred account is not necessarily for everyone. It depends on age, needs, and financial resources. For example, individuals who anticipate receiving a large inheritance from relatives may find that investment in a tax-deferred program will tend to increase their tax rate after retirement rather than decrease it.

In addition, while the money in a tax-deferred annuity can be withdrawn before age 59 1/2, the penalty charge is significant. Because of this, the money is not readily available when you may need it. In some instances, it is important for you to keep your assets liquid because they will be needed in the near future. For example, a young person may be trying to save money for a down payment on a house, for a potential business opportunity, or for getting married and furnishing an apartment.

A tax-deferred account, like every good investment, has much to offer, if you can afford it. However, each person's situation must be analyzed on an individual basis in order to develop the best possible retirement program. Bear in mind that some type of savings plan is beneficial as a supplement to Social Security and a private or public pension.

Self Study
Your Annuity(ies) Inventory

1. Organize your annuity(ies) information in the following format. If you are not certain of the details, contact your insurance agent or the personnel department of your employer in the case of tax-sheltered annuities, Sections 401(k), 403(b), and 457 plans.

	Annuity		
	1	**2**	**3**
Name of annuity owner	_____	_____	_____
Name of company	_____	_____	_____
Address of company	_____	_____	_____
Premium amount	_____	_____	_____
Premium due date(s)	_____	_____	_____
Payout plan	_____	_____	_____
Income per month	_____	_____	_____
Beneficiary(ies)	_____	_____	_____
Survivor's rights	_____	_____	_____
Name of agent	_____	_____	_____
Address of agent	_____	_____	_____
	_____	_____	_____
	_____	_____	_____
Telephone number of agent	_____	_____	_____
Location of policy(ies)	_____	_____	_____

2. Handling tax-sheltered money at retirement is a matter that should be addressed in your planning. Your choices for the accumulation are to withdraw, roll over, annuitize, or defer the decision. Consider these alternatives; select the choice that seems reasonable at this time and list the reasons for your choice. (You may wish to discuss your decision with a financial planner.)

_____

_____

_____

_____

_____

_____

_____

Glossary

Annuity. A type of investment that guarantees a fixed income for a specific period of time to the annuitant or, in some cases, to a beneficiary. *See also* the individual types of annuities.

Cash refund annuity. A type of annuity that pays income for life, but if the annuitant dies before the payments equal the amount he or she put into the annuity minus specified administrative charges, the balance is paid to the designated beneficiary in a lump sum. *See also* Installment refund annuity; Joint and survivor annuity.

Deferred annuity. A type of annuity that begins making payments to the annuitant at a later date. *See also* Immediate pay annuity.

Fixed dollar annuity. A type of annuity that pays a fixed amount every month because the funds in the annuity account are invested in a portfolio of bonds that pays a set amount of interest. *See also* Variable annuity.

Fixed premium annuity. A type of annuity purchased by making a fixed payment each month or each year. *See also* Single premium annuity; Variable premium annuity.

Immediate pay annuity. A type of annuity that begins making payments to the annuitant immediately. *See also* Deferred annuity.

Installment refund annuity. A type of annuity that pays income for life, but if the annuitant dies before the payments equal the amount he or she put into the annuity minus specified administrative charges, the balance is paid to the designated beneficiary in regular payments. *See also* Cash refund annuity; Joint and survivor annuity.

Joint and survivor annuity. A type of annuity that guarantees income for life to two or more people, generally a husband and wife, so that the survivor can receive the same monthly income or some percentage of the monthly income as long as he or she lives. *See also* Cash refund annuity, Installment refund annuity.

Life annuity with a term certain. A type of annuity that guarantees income for life, but if the annuitant dies within the designated "term certain," or guaranteed period, such as ten years or twenty years, the designated beneficiary will receive the payments for the remainder of the term. *See also* Straight life annuity.

Single premium annuity. A type of annuity purchased with a single lump-sum payment. *See also* Fixed premium annuity; Variable premium annuity.

Straight life annuity. A type of annuity that guarantees a stipulated monthly income for life, with no death benefits paid to beneficiaries and no cash surrender value. May be appropriate for individuals who have no dependents and want maximum income. *See also* Life annuity with a term certain.

Tax-deferred annuity. A type of annuity purchased with pre-tax dollars, which become tax-sheltered. The annuitant pays no income taxes on the amount deposited in the annuity account or on the interest earned by the principal. When the annuitant eventually begins to withdraw the money after retirement, he or she pays income taxes on the amounts withdrawn.

Variable annuity. A type of annuity that pays a different amount every month because the funds in the annuity account are invested in a portfolio of stocks, and stock prices fluctuate daily. If average stock prices rise, the annuitant receives a higher annuity, and vice versa. *See also* Fixed dollar annuity.

Variable premium annuity. A type of annuity purchased by monthly or annual installment payments, the size of which may be changed at the annuitant's discretion. *See also* Fixed premium annuity; Single premium annuity.

Wraparound annuity. A type of annuity in which the annuitant controls the investment of the funds in the account. The funds can be invested in stocks or bonds or a mutual fund, and can be switched from one form of investment to another to take advantage of changing market conditions. *See also* Fixed dollar annuity; Tax-deferred annuity; Variable annuity.

PART THREE
Day-to-Day Financial Considerations

10
Budgeting

In retirement planning, it is essential to know your financial goals. The first step is to calculate your *net worth*, which requires that you list your *assets* and *liabilities*. Knowing your financial situation at a given point will enable you to plan ahead and to decide where you would like to be financially one year from now, five years from now, and on into retirement. The tool for accomplishing this is a *budget*.

DEVELOPING A RETIREMENT BUDGET

A *budget* is essentially a spending plan to help you manage your money effectively. Most people can benefit from spending their income more wisely, especially in a period of inflation. Whether you have had experience with a budget or not, it is essential that you plan a budget before you retire. This will enable you to estimate how much money you will need and to compare your estimate with the income you expect to have.

Most retirees find that they must adjust their spending to fit a reduced income. Fortunately, many expenses diminish or disappear entirely. For example, savings accrue in job-related expenses, such as income taxes, trans-

portation, clothing, and meals away from home. Additional free time will allow you to do those tasks that you previously paid others to do, such as yard work. However, other expenses may increase or arise for the first time, such as hobby and recreational expenses and certain medical costs.

HOW MUCH RETIREMENT INCOME IS ENOUGH?

Many experts claim that retired people require less income than employed people do. While it is true that certain expenses—such as transportation, food away from home, and clothing—decline, it is also true that retirees have expenses that they did not have when employed. For example, medical, dental, and pharmaceutical costs are greater. People planning for retirement should, therefore, strive to match their working incomes.

HOW MUCH OF A "NEST EGG" DO YOU NEED?

A problem that many retirees face is that they cannot meet their retirement-income target. Social Security benefits alone are inadequate for a comfortable retirement. Other sources of income—including pensions, savings, investments, cash value of life insurance, and annuities—are necessary to supplement Social Security benefits.

By planning financially and budgeting long enough in advance of retirement, you can ensure that your retirement income will be enough to allow you to live at the level you desire. If necessary, you will have time to develop additional sources of income or adjust to the idea of living on less by reducing expenditures.

A TYPICAL RETIREMENT EXPENSE BUDGET

Table 10.1 presents a typical retirement budget for a couple. It shows the allocation of the money left after the payment of personal income taxes. The indicated percentages may vary by plus or minus 5 percent, since a budget for expenses is a very personal matter. No two people think precisely the same way about this matter. However, the percentage distribution among the groups can be useful as a benchmark for evaluating your own expenditure pattern, whether your annual retirement income is $20,000, $40,000, or more. The percentages are derived from actual annual budgets of retired couples and are an approximation.

THE BUDGETING PROCESS

The budgeting process can be summarized in the following six steps:

1. **Calculate your net worth.** Before you attempt to develop and implement a budget, you must learn where you currently stand financially. To get a clear picture of their assets, liabilities, and net worth at a given moment in time, businesses prepare a finan-

**Table 10.1
Annual Budget of an Average Retired Couple**

Budget Item	Percent*
Housing	30
Food	22
Recreation and hobbies	20
Medical and dental care	10
Transportation	8
Clothing and personal care	5
Gifts and contributions	5
Total	100

*Percentages are approximate.

cial statement known as a balance sheet at least once a year. Understanding your present financial position by determining your *assets* (the financial and material possessions you own), your *liabilities* (your debts, or the amounts you owe), and your *net worth* (your assets minus your liabilities) allows you to plan for your future more intelligently. Your net-worth position, if it is adequate, can provide a cushion on which you can draw if any special need or emergency arises. An adequate net-worth position can also give you an inflation cushion, which may help you someday to restore your budget to balance, if necessary. Worksheet 10.1 on page 178 will help you to compute your net worth.

You should draw up a net-worth statement at least once a year. This way, you can study your current financial position, determine whether it has improved or worsened since the previous year, and set goals and take steps to help you to improve your position. Your net worth changes every year in the same way that your income and spending patterns change.

2. **Record your current expenditures.** Before you can draw up a budget, you must

learn what your current spending pattern is by keeping a record of all your expenditures. You will be surprised at how much a record of your expenses will tell you, particularly if you have never previously kept such data. You may already be using a formal written budget, or you may be functioning just from experience and logic. In any case, before you devise a retirement budget, you must analyze precisely how you are currently spending your money.

To determine your spending pattern, you must keep an exact record of every expenditure you make every day of the month. No amount expended, no matter how small, should be omitted. You need to keep these records for at least a year before you can use the figures for any projection. A year is a reasonable yardstick, since month-to-month expenses vary for such items as clothing, insurance, and even entertainment. This data will reveal much about your personal habits, likes, and dislikes. And certainly, such a record will answer the popular question, "Where does all my money go?"

Worksheets 10.2 and 10.3 on pages 179 and 180, respectively, provide a format for keeping track of your expenditures. Worksheet 10.2 shows you how to record daily expenses. Purchase large worksheet paper from a stationery store and, using Worksheet 10.2 as a model, note all the days of each month across the top of the worksheet paper and list the expense items in the first column.

Worksheet 10.3 is a model for a monthly expense record. Again, using a large worksheet purchased in a stationery store, copy the format of Worksheet 10.3, noting the months along the top of the paper and listing all the expense items in the first column. At the end of each month, total the daily figures for each expense item and transfer the totals to your monthly worksheet. At the end of the year, total the monthly figures for each expense item and note the amounts in the "Total" column. Finally, to calculate the monthly average expenditure for each expense item, divide the totals by twelve and enter the results in the final column.

3. **Estimate your retirement spending pattern.** Once you have completed Worksheet 10.3, you can transfer the year's totals and monthly averages to columns 2 and 3 of Worksheet 10.4 on page 181. This will enable you to estimate your first year's retirement-spending pattern, noting your estimates in columns 4 and 5 of Worksheet 10.4. Some of your expenses, particularly those that are job-related, will cease or almost cease when you retire. For example, you will no longer be paying for lunches and coffee breaks at work. However, remember that at-home food costs will counterbalance this reduction. Other expenses will continue but may be lower after retirement. For example, your clothing costs will probably be lower since retirees generally dress more casually. Your federal income taxes may be lower because you will probably be in a lower tax bracket. However, concerning income taxes, bear in mind that fortunate individuals enjoy a retirement income that is equal to or higher than their preretirement income.

Starting at age 65, all individuals enjoy some income tax benefits, such as an extra income tax exemption. Your housing cost will be less if you have paid off your mortgage by the time you retire. But other expenses may be higher after retirement, such as health insurance to fill in the Medicare gaps. Also, you will probably increase your expenditures for hobbies, recreation, and travel.

4. **Estimate your first year's retirement income.** Worksheet 10.5 on page 182 helps you to estimate your income for your first year of retirement and to compare it with your current annual income. For most retirees, the three major sources of income are Social Security, pensions, and interest and dividends from savings and investments. Additional sources of income include the following:

■ *Annuities.* Regular monthly income paid to an insured over a specified period of time or for life.

■ *Rent.* Income derived from the ownership of residential or commercial property.

■ *Royalty.* A share of the proceeds or profits paid to the owner of a patent, oil or mineral rights, or copyright.

■ *Veterans' benefit.* Income from a disability or pension benefit paid to a veteran by the United States Department of Veterans Affairs.

■ *Reverse mortgage.* Income derived by borrowing against the equity in a home, yielding regular monthly payments.

■ *Workers' compensation.* A disability benefit paid to a worker for a job-related injury or illness.

■ *Hobby income.* Income derived from the sale of handcrafted articles or in payment for hobby services rendered.

5. **Reconcile your income and expenses.** Worksheet 10.6 on page 182 is a summary table that you can use to balance your estimated retirement income and expenses. If your income is greater than your expenses, you have a *surplus*. What an ideal situation! However, if your income is smaller than your expenses, you have a *deficit*. If you have a deficit, you will need to make some

adjustments. You can increase your income, reduce your expenses, and/or consume some of your available *capital*. Capital is money or its equivalent in property or securities. To consume some of your capital, you can sell securities or real estate or withdraw money from your emergency savings fund or money market mutual fund. However, your future income will be reduced, and you will need to make further adjustments in your calculations. Use Worksheet 10.7 on page 183 to record possible solutions for a deficit in your anticipated retirement budget.

6. **Review and adjust budget items.** Use Worksheet 10.8 on page 184 to keep track on a monthly basis of your actual expenditures for each budget item and to compare your monthly outlays with your monthly projections. Take the projections from column 5 of Worksheet 10.4 on page 181. Use Worksheet 10.9 on page 185 to keep track of your monthly income and to compare it with your estimated income, taken from column 4 of Worksheet 10.5 on page 182.

Every two or three months, you can look at your spending pattern to check whether you are in line with your averages or are overspending and building up a deficit. A two- or three-month period is adequate for spotting where problems lie. You may find, for example, that your telephone bills and meals outside the home are larger than you had anticipated. To keep your budget in balance, you must reduce your expenditures in the problem categories or, if you cannot do this, you must cut back on other expenses.

In some instances, you may find it necessary to reexamine your priorities. If you were saving for a vacation and a new refrigerator, you may decide that you cannot save for both at the same time. If your savings schedule is not on target, you can use devices such as automatic payroll deductions, if still employed, or monthly transfers from your checking account to your savings account.

TIPS ON BUDGETING

Try not to become bogged down in nickel-and-dime details. Round your budget entries to the nearest dollar. Remember, a budget is a tool that, if used correctly, can give you a realistic picture of your income and expenditures and of how you handle your money. Your budget plan should reflect your retirement goals as well as your goals for the current year, and it should be flexible enough to allow you to adapt to changing circumstances.

Every household, especially a retiree's, needs a financial plan that incorporates specific savings programs for achieving stated goals. Your budget is a very personal tool. It should reflect your own needs and goals and should be based on your own experiences. Do not permit the needs and goals of others to influence your budget. Your current income as well as your projected retirement income should be reflected in your budget. The expectations of others, either family or friends, should play no role in the budget decisions that you make. A budget will help you to think about and plan for the future. At the same time, it will help you to live within your means. A budget can make your retirement years secure and satisfying.

Good money-management habits can be developed with time and effort. Once you have mastered the techniques, you will find that you can live free of money problems.

Self-Study
Plan Your Budget

Use the following worksheets to plan and adjust your retirement budget. For detailed directions, see pages 174 to 177.

Worksheet 10.1: Net Worth Statement

As of _____ 19_____

Assets	Amount
Cash on hand	$ _____
Savings accounts	_____
Checking accounts	_____
Life insurance (cash value)	_____
Investments	_____
Stocks	_____
Bonds	_____
Mutual funds	_____
Real estate (market value)	_____
Automobiles (Blue Book values)	_____
Furniture	_____
Home appliances	_____
Other assets	_____
_____	_____
_____	_____
Total assets	$ _____

Liabilities	
Mortgage balance	$ _____
Auto loan balance	_____
Credit card balance	_____
Other debts	_____
Total liabilities	$ _____

Net worth (total assets minus total liabilities) $ _____

Worksheet 10.2: Daily Expense Record
Month of _____ 19_____

Expense	Date						Total
	1	2	3	...	30	31	
Groceries	_____	_____	_____	...	_____	_____	_____
Food away from home	_____	_____	_____	...	_____	_____	_____
Total food				...			
Rent/mortgage payment	_____	_____	_____	...	_____	_____	_____
Property/local taxes	_____	_____	_____	...	_____	_____	_____
Heat, electricity, gas	_____	_____	_____	...	_____	_____	_____
Telephone	_____	_____	_____	...	_____	_____	_____
Water	_____	_____	_____	...	_____	_____	_____
Home insurance	_____	_____	_____	...	_____	_____	_____
Home maintenance	_____	_____	_____	...	_____	_____	_____
Total housing				...			
Auto payments	_____	_____	_____	...	_____	_____	_____
Gasoline, oil	_____	_____	_____	...	_____	_____	_____
Auto insurance	_____	_____	_____	...	_____	_____	_____
Auto maintenance	_____	_____	_____	...	_____	_____	_____
Public transportation, taxis	_____	_____	_____	...	_____	_____	_____
Total transportation				...			
Clothing	_____	_____	_____	...	_____	_____	_____
Dry cleaning	_____	_____	_____	...	_____	_____	_____
Laundry	_____	_____	_____	...	_____	_____	_____
Clothing repair	_____	_____	_____	...	_____	_____	_____
Total clothing				...			
Barber, beauty shop	_____	_____	_____	...	_____	_____	_____
Toiletries, cosmetics	_____	_____	_____	...	_____	_____	_____
Other personal items	_____	_____	_____	...	_____	_____	_____
Total personal care				...			
Medical	_____	_____	_____	...	_____	_____	_____
Dental	_____	_____	_____	...	_____	_____	_____
Pharmaceutical	_____	_____	_____	...	_____	_____	_____
Hospital/health insurance	_____	_____	_____	...	_____	_____	_____
Other health-care items	_____	_____	_____	...	_____	_____	_____
Total medical care				...			
Loan/installment payments	_____	_____	_____	...	_____	_____	_____
Life insurance	_____	_____	_____	...	_____	_____	_____
Recreation, vacation	_____	_____	_____	...	_____	_____	_____
Education	_____	_____	_____	...	_____	_____	_____
Gifts, dues, contributions	_____	_____	_____	...	_____	_____	_____
Other expenses	_____	_____	_____	...	_____	_____	_____
Total miscellaneous expenses				...			
Social Security taxes	_____	_____	_____	...	_____	_____	_____
Personal income taxes	_____	_____	_____	...	_____	_____	_____
Savings, pensions	_____	_____	_____	...	_____	_____	_____
Total expenditures	_____	_____	_____	...	_____	_____	_____

Worksheet 10.3: Monthly Expense Record
Year of 19_____

Expense	Month						
	Jan	Feb	Mar	...	Dec	Total	Monthly Average
Groceries	____	____	____	...	____	____	____
Food away from home	____	____	____	...	____	____	____
Total food							
Rent/mortgage payment	____	____	____	...	____	____	____
Property/local taxes	____	____	____	...	____	____	____
Heat, electricity, gas	____	____	____	...	____	____	____
Telephone	____	____	____	...	____	____	____
Water	____	____	____	...	____	____	____
Home insurance	____	____	____	...	____	____	____
Home maintenance	____	____	____	...	____	____	____
Total housing							
Auto payments	____	____	____	...	____	____	____
Gasoline, oil	____	____	____	...	____	____	____
Auto insurance	____	____	____	...	____	____	____
Auto maintenance	____	____	____	...	____	____	____
Public transportation, taxis	____	____	____	...	____	____	____
Total transportation							
Clothing	____	____	____	...	____	____	____
Dry cleaning	____	____	____	...	____	____	____
Laundry	____	____	____	...	____	____	____
Clothing repair	____	____	____	...	____	____	____
Total clothing							
Barber, beauty shop	____	____	____	...	____	____	____
Toiletries, cosmetics	____	____	____	...	____	____	____
Other personal items	____	____	____	...	____	____	____
Total personal care							
Medical	____	____	____	...	____	____	____
Dental	____	____	____	...	____	____	____
Pharmaceutical	____	____	____	...	____	____	____
Hospital/health insurance	____	____	____	...	____	____	____
Other health-care items	____	____	____	...	____	____	____
Total medical care							
Loan/installment payments	____	____	____	...	____	____	____
Life insurance	____	____	____	...	____	____	____
Recreation, vacation	____	____	____	...	____	____	____
Education	____	____	____	...	____	____	____
Gifts, dues, contributions	____	____	____	...	____	____	____
Other expenses	____	____	____	...	____	____	____
Total miscellaneous expenses							
Social Security taxes	____	____	____	...	____	____	____
Personal income taxes	____	____	____	...	____	____	____
Savings, pensions	____	____	____	...	____	____	____
Total expenditures	____	____	____	...			

Worksheet 10.4: Estimate of First Year's Retirement Expenses

Expense (1)	Current spending pattern		Estimated retirement spending pattern	
	Monthly average (2)	Year 19__ (3)	First Year (4)	Monthly average (5)
Groceries	_____	_____	_____	_____
Food away from home	_____	_____	_____	_____
Total food	_____	_____	_____	_____
Rent/mortgage payment	_____	_____	_____	_____
Property/local taxes	_____	_____	_____	_____
Heat, electricity, gas	_____	_____	_____	_____
Telephone	_____	_____	_____	_____
Water	_____	_____	_____	_____
Home insurance	_____	_____	_____	_____
Home maintenance	_____	_____	_____	_____
Total housing	_____	_____	_____	_____
Auto payments	_____	_____	_____	_____
Gasoline, oil	_____	_____	_____	_____
Auto insurance	_____	_____	_____	_____
Auto maintenance	_____	_____	_____	_____
Public transportation, taxis	_____	_____	_____	_____
Total transportation	_____	_____	_____	_____
Clothing	_____	_____	_____	_____
Dry cleaning	_____	_____	_____	_____
Laundry	_____	_____	_____	_____
Clothing repair	_____	_____	_____	_____
Total clothing	_____	_____	_____	_____
Barber, beauty shop	_____	_____	_____	_____
Toiletries, cosmetics	_____	_____	_____	_____
Other personal items	_____	_____	_____	_____
Total personal care	_____	_____	_____	_____
Medical	_____	_____	_____	_____
Dental	_____	_____	_____	_____
Pharmaceutical	_____	_____	_____	_____
Hospital/health insurance	_____	_____	_____	_____
Other health-care items	_____	_____	_____	_____
Total medical care	_____	_____	_____	_____
Loan/installment payments	_____	_____	_____	_____
Life insurance	_____	_____	_____	_____
Recreation, vacation	_____	_____	_____	_____
Education	_____	_____	_____	_____
Gifts, dues, contributions	_____	_____	_____	_____
Other expenses	_____	_____	_____	_____
Total miscellaneous expenses	_____	_____	_____	_____
Social Security taxes	_____	_____	_____	_____
Personal income taxes	_____	_____	_____	_____
Savings, pensions	_____	_____	_____	_____
Total expenditures	_____	_____	_____	_____

Worksheet 10.5: Estimate of First Year's Retirement Income

Income	Current working income		Income for first year of retirement	
	Monthly	Year 19_____	Monthly	Year 19_____
(1)	(2)	(3)	(4)	(5)
Husband's wages or salary	_____	_____	_____	_____
Wife's wages or salary	_____	_____	_____	_____
Social Security	_____	_____	_____	_____
Pensions	_____	_____	_____	_____
Interest	_____	_____	_____	_____
Annuities	_____	_____	_____	_____
Rents	_____	_____	_____	_____
Royalties	_____	_____	_____	_____
Other income	_____	_____	_____	_____
Total income	_____	_____	_____	_____

Worksheet 10.6: Surplus or Deficit in First Year's Retirement Budget

Income	Amount	
	Monthly	First Year
Total income	$_____	$_____
Total expenses	$_____	$_____
Surplus or deficit	$_____	$_____

Worksheet 10.7: Alternative Solutions for a Deficit

1. Increase income

	Gross income	Costs arising from work
Full- or part-time employment	$ _____	$ _____
Other	$ _____	$ _____

2. Reduce expenses

Item to be reduced	Means of reducing	Amount of reduction
_____	_____	$ _____
_____	_____	$ _____
_____	_____	$ _____
_____	_____	$ _____

3. Consume capital

Item to be consumed	Amount available	Resulting future reduction in income
_____	$ _____	$ _____
_____	$ _____	$ _____
_____	$ _____	$ _____
_____	$ _____	$ _____

Worksheet 10.8: Retirement Expense Budget
Month of _____ 19____

Expense	Projected	Actual
Groceries		
Food away from home		
Total food		
Rent/mortgage payment		
Property/local taxes		
Heat, electricity, gas		
Telephone		
Water		
Home insurance		
Home maintenance		
Total housing		
Auto payments		
Gasoline, oil		
Auto insurance		
Auto maintenance		
Public transportation, taxis		
Total transportation		
Clothing		
Dry cleaning		
Laundry		
Clothing repair		
Total clothing		
Barber, beauty shop		
Toiletries, cosmetics		
Other personal items		
Total personal care		
Medical		
Dental		
Pharmaceutical		
Hospital/health insurance		
Other health-care items		
Total medical care		
Loan/installment payments		
Life insurance		
Recreation, vacation		
Education		
Gifts, dues, contributions		
Other expenses		
Total miscellaneous expenses		
Social Security taxes		
Personal income taxes		
Savings, pensions		
Total expenditures		

Worksheet 10.9: Retirement Income and Surplus/Deficit
Month of _____ 19____

Income	Projected	Actual
Take-home pay (if employed)		
Husband	$ _____	$_____
Wife	_____	_____
Pension		
Husband	_____	_____
Wife	_____	_____
Social Security benefits		
Husband	_____	_____
Wife	_____	_____
Annuities	_____	_____
Royalties	_____	_____
Interest	_____	_____
Dividends	_____	_____
Veterans' benefits	_____	_____
Rents	_____	_____
Profit-sharing plans	_____	_____
Other income		
_____	_____	_____
_____	_____	_____
Total income	$ _____	$_____

	Projected	Actual
Total income	$ _____	$_____
Total expenses (from Worksheet 10.8)	$ _____	$_____
Surplus or deficit (Total income minus total expenses)	$ _____	$_____

Glossary

Assets. All money, investments, and other property owned by an individual, a family, or a business.

Blue Book. A publication of the National Automobile Dealers Association (N.A.D.A.) that lists the average prices paid for used cars at a specified time.

Budget. A spending plan designed to help you efficiently manage your income.

Capital. Money or its equivalent in property and/or securities.

Deficit. The amount by which expenditures exceed income.

Liabilities. All forms of indebtedness for which an individual, a family, or a business are legally liable.

Net worth. Monetary value of an individual, a family, or a business. It is equal to total assets minus total liabilities.

Surplus. The amount by which income exceeds expenditures.

11

Credit

The advice that Polonius gave to his son, "Neither a borrower nor a lender be," was eminently sound. That advice remains paramount today. However, there are times when the exigencies of life make it necessary to seek *credit*, which is a type of loan to an individual, business, or organization from the savings of individuals, businesses, or organizations. If you must borrow, you must also remember that credit costs something—you will have to pay back what you borrowed and you must also pay interest and other charges. If you are planning to borrow, you must first find out how much it will cost and then decide whether you can afford it.

COST OF CREDIT

Credit costs vary significantly. Under the terms of the Federal Truth in Lending Law, *creditors*, the sellers or lenders who provide credit, must tell you the finance charge and the annual percentage rate (APR) in writing and before you sign an agreement. The *finance charge* is the total dollar amount you must pay when you borrow a specified amount of money. It includes interest costs, service charges, insurance premiums, and possibly appraisal fees. *Interest* is the annual cost of borrowed money. The *annual percentage rate* is the percentage cost of credit on an annual basis.

All creditors—including banks, stores, car dealers, credit card companies, and finance companies—must give you these two pieces of information before you sign a credit contract. These two facts about a loan will enable you to compare credit costs to be sure that you are getting the best deal. Shop around; do not accept the first offer.

Creditors look for the three Cs of credit to evaluate a borrower. The three Cs are:

1. Capacity—Can you repay the debt?
2. Character—Will you repay the debt?
3. Collateral—Is the creditor fully protected if you fail to repay the debt?

Some creditors use *credit-scoring*, a statistical system that helps to predict whether a potential borrower is a good credit risk. They rate applicants on a scale and then decide either to make or to deny the loan.

AGE DISCRIMINATION

The Federal Equal Credit Opportunity Act says that age, sex, marital status, race, color, religion, national origin, or the fact that someone is poor, on welfare, or collecting Social Security may not be a basis for discrimination in any part of a credit transaction. While this law does not guarantee that you will be given credit, it clearly states that a creditor may not use any of the aforementioned grounds as an excuse to refuse you a loan if you qualify. Furthermore, creditors may not lend you money on terms different from those granted another person with similar income, expenses, credit history, and collateral.

Prior to the implementation of this law, many older persons complained that they were denied credit because of age. Many retirees also found that their credit was suddenly cut off or reduced. The Federal Equal Credit Opportunity Act changed this because under the law, a creditor may ask your age but may not deny you credit because of your age. Creditors may use a credit-scoring system and score your age, but, if you are 62 or older, you must be given at least as many points for age as a person under 62.

An older individual applying for a mortgage loan, such as a 65- or 70-year-old person seeking a twenty-five- or thirty-year mortgage, may have some difficulty, however. In this situation, the law permits creditors to require specific information related to age, including when the applicant plans to retire or how long he or she will continue to earn the current salary. On the other hand, an older individual who is prepared to make a large down payment on a house might qualify for a relatively small mortgage loan, assuming that the home is a sound investment. Remember that a lending institution owns a mortgaged home until the very last monthly payment of principal (the amount of money borrowed) and interest is made.

WOMEN AND CREDIT

Usually, women get credit under their spouse's names. If a woman divorces or her spouse dies, a credit problem may arise. If you don't have credit in your own name, you must begin the application process immediately. Credit is a necessity for everyone.

The first step is to apply for credit. If you have a problem, find out what is in your credit file. You can obtain this information from a credit reporting agency. The three major consumer credit reporting agencies are Equifax Credit Information Services, the Trans Union Corporation, and TRW Information Services Division. Their addresses and phone numbers are in your telephone directory under "Credit Reporting Agencies," or you can ask your creditors to which credit bureaus they report.

If you have never had credit in your own name before, you may have a problem initially because of lack of a credit history. The Equal Credit Opportunity Act and the Consumer Protection Act make it illegal to deny you credit due to marital status or sex. These laws allow you to rely on the credit history of a spouse or former spouse if you can show that you helped build that history.

If you are still having a problem getting credit, a good start is to open a department store credit account, the easiest type of credit to get. After using the store's credit card for a few months, you will have established some credit history. You can strengthen your financial position by opening a checking and savings account in your name. Your attorney may be helpful in getting you a major credit card.

You can also build a credit history by paying off a consumer loan. Buy a car or other large purchase and make a large down payment. This will make it easier to apply for credit to pay off the balance. Make regular, prompt payments to enhance your credit history.

BORROWING AGAINST ASSETS

A widely used method of borrowing is the *home equity loan*. With this type of loan, you borrow against the value of your home. However, you run the risk of losing your home if you fail to make payments because your home is your collateral. (For a further discussion of home equity loans, see page 41.)

Borrowing against the value of a home is traditionally done by *refinancing* the original mortgage. Lending institutions are often pleased at the opportunity to take back an old low rate mortgage and issue a new first mortgage at a higher rate. Your lender may even offer you a few percentage points less than the going rate of mortgage interest or possibly even forgive part of your indebtedness. Another possible source of retirement income is the *second mortgage*. However, the interest rate charged may be two or three percentage points higher than the current mortgage rates, and the repayment period is usually limited to between five and fifteen years. Monthly mortgage payments, therefore, can be quite high.

A *reverse mortgage* is another potential source of retirement income in which you borrow against the value of your home. This mortgage reverses the normal flow of money in a home loan, with the lending company making periodic payments to the homeowner based on the value of the home (see page 42). Essentially, a reverse mortgage takes advantage of the increase in the value of your home over the years.

Other possible sources of collateral when borrowing against your assets are negotiable securities such as stocks or bonds, savings in a passbook account, certificates of deposit, and credit union shares. When you use your passbook savings as collateral, the interest rate charged on the loan is generally low, usually just a point or two above the interest you collect on your account.

Most banks, credit unions, and consumer finance companies accept a car, boat, or plane as collateral for a loan. However, interest rates are at about the level charged on *installment loans*, which are loans repaid with a series of payments, and the repayment periods are short.

Individuals approaching retirement or already retired usually find that their best bet for a modest-sized loan is a *credit union*, a type of bank formed as a cooperative by a group of individuals. For a larger loan, the lowest rates are generally charged by commercial banks.

CREDIT CARDS

If financial planning for retirement is to be effective, individuals in their working years must learn the meaning of discipline in credit and money management. American society is geared to the philosophy of "buy now, pay later." This inflationary psychology has led people to believe that if they buy now and pay later, they will pay their bills with cheaper dollars. Unfortunately, the dollars are not always available when the bills come due. In addition, personal bankruptcy law, which was liberalized in 1979, encourages people to go deeper into debt. According to this law, if you are unable to extricate yourself from your debts, you can go to a bankruptcy attorney and possibly have your debts declared null and void.

The wisest way to use a credit card is to pay off the full amount of the balance due every month. There is no denying that credit card shopping is convenient. In addition, it can be a "free loan" because there is often a thirty-day grace period during which no interest accrues. However, only about one-third of credit card users pay their outstanding balances every month.

The maximum percentage of a family's take-home pay that should be used for credit payments is 10 to 15 percent. Mortgage payments should not be greater than 25 to 30 percent of take-home pay. When credit card debt begins to exceed 15 percent, it has passed the danger point; you must begin immediately to take remedial steps. The best prescription is to cut up and discard your credit cards. The next step should be to set up a strict budget that incorporates a schedule for paying off your creditors. These are the only ways to develop an effective financial plan for retirement. Effective personal money management is an essential ingredient for avoiding the many problems associated with excessive debt.

Self-Study
Determine the State of Your Credit

Take the following test to determine whether your outstanding credit card debt and/or installment loans are within reasonable limits.

1. Determine your grand total monthly debt repayment by filling in the following table:

Credit cards	Outstanding balance	Monthly payment
_____	$ _____	$ _____
_____	_____	_____
_____	_____	_____
_____	_____	_____
_____	_____	_____
_____	_____	_____
_____	_____	_____
Total monthly credit-card-debt repayment		$ _____

Loans	Outstanding	Monthly
_____	$ _____	$ _____
_____	_____	_____
_____	_____	_____
Total monthly loan-debt repayment		$ _____
Grand total monthly debt repayment		$ _____

2. Determine the percent of your monthly income that you owe to creditors by using the following formula:

$$\frac{\text{Grand total monthly debt repayment}}{\text{Take–home pay for one month}} = \text{Percent of your monthly income owed to creditors}$$

If the percent of monthly income that you owe to creditors is greater than 15 percent, you must begin immediately to take remedial steps (see page 190).

Glossary

Annual percentage rate (APR). The finance charge over a full year expressed as a percentage, reflecting all the costs of a loan. *See also* Finance charge.

Balance due. The amount still owed on a credit account or for a cash loan.

Collateral. Something that a creditor has the legal right to take from you if you fail to repay the loan. When you finance a car, the automobile is collateral. Other types of collateral may be stocks, bonds, or jewelry.

Consumer Credit Protection Act. A federal act that includes the Fair Credit Billing Act, Equal Credit Opportunity Act, Fair Credit Reporting Act, Consumer Leasing Acts, and Truth in Lending Act.

Credit. Loans to individuals, businesses, or governments from the savings of individuals and businesses.

Credit card. A plastic card displaying the account number of a line of credit extended by a bank or store that allows the holder to purchase items on credit from businesses that accept the card.

Credit charge. *See* Finance charge.

Credit contract. A signed agreement between a borrower and a lender that tells the amount owed and how it is to be paid.

Credit history. A record of the way an individual has handled credit, kept by credit bureaus and creditors.

Credit life insurance. A type of insurance that pays the balance due on an account if the debtor dies.

Credit-scoring. An objective method of evaluating whether an individual is a good credit risk. *See also* Three Cs of credit.

Credit union. A depository institution formed as a cooperative by a group of individuals that meets specific credit union requirements.

Creditor. A seller or lender who provides credit.

Debtor. A person, business, or organization that owes money for an item bought or for money borrowed.

Finance charge. The total amount paid for items or services purchased on credit or for money borrowed, always stated in dollar amount and annual percentage rate. Also known as a credit charge.

Home equity loan. A loan on the value you actually hold in your home. If your home is worth $200,000 (what you can sell it for) and you still owe $100,000 on your mortgage, your home equity is $100,000.

Installment loan. A loan repaid with a series of payments.

Interest. Annual cost of borrowed money. *See also* Annual percentage rate; Finance charge.

Maturity date. The day the last payment is due.

Points. An additional fee charged by some lenders at the time a mortgage is issued, with each point charged representing one percent of the total mortgage amount.

Principal. The amount of credit given.

Reverse mortgage. A mortgage that reverses the normal flow of money in a home loan, with the lending company making payments to the homeowner based on the value of the home and the duration of the payments.

Second mortgage. A loan on a home that already has an outstanding mortgage. The second mortgage is junior to a first mortgage in the event of default.

Three Cs of credit. Three points on which creditors evaluate potential borrowers to help in determining whether to make a loan. They are *capacity* (sufficient income to enable a borrower to repay a loan), *character* (personality traits that generally make a borrower want to repay a loan), and *collateral* (sufficient assets to ensure that a borrower can repay a loan).

12

Inflation

Inflation in economic terms means that the general level of prices for goods and services is on the rise. People understand this very well. They know that a shopping trip to the supermarket may cost more than the previous visit. In 1942, bread cost 9¢ a pound and coffee was 28¢ a pound. Today, a pound of bread costs over $1 and a pound of coffee is approximately $3. In 1942, you could buy a Cadillac for $3,000; today, the price is about $35,000. Not only have the costs of these items risen, but it is more expensive to go to a movie or a play; to take a vacation; to buy heating oil; to purchase clothing, furniture, and household appliances; and to obtain medical and other services.

Increases in living costs have been especially serious since 1973, although they have shown a downward trend in the last several years as shown in Table 12.1. Four categories of necessities—food, shelter, energy, and medical care—make up about 60 percent of the total market basket of expenditures of the typical urban family. In 1973, the costs of goods and services in these categories began increasing sharply and at an accelerated rate, hitting retirees forcefully because they are so dependent on these necessities.

Another way of looking at inflation is as a loss in real income at a percentage equivalent to the inflation rate. For example, if the inflation rate were 4.3 percent, a retiree with a $10,000 income would lose 4.3 percent of real income, which is $430. Or, the $10,000 would buy just $9,570 of goods and services. Continuing inflation eats away at fixed incomes, making it more and more difficult to make ends meet.

Also affected are nest egg savings accounts. Such accounts shrink in value when the rate of inflation exceeds the interest rate. This hurts retirees and those approaching retirement.

IMPACT ON RETIREES

As prices rise, retirees find that they must spend more for necessities and other items and services. If you are living on a budget, the problem becomes obvious immediately because your spending pattern is based on costs that apply to an earlier period. You must revise your budget to accurately reflect the new economic picture. In a noninflationary situation, you can revise your budget annually, but in an inflationary period, you should adjust it on a monthly basis.

Table 12.1
Annual Rate of Inflation, 1960-1994

Year	% Increase	Year	% Increase	Year	% Increase	Year	% Increase
1960	1.4%	1970	5.6%	1980	12.5%	1990	6.1%
1961	0.7	1971	3.3	1981	8.9	1991	3.1
1962	1.3	1972	3.4	1982	3.8	1992	2.9
1963	1.6	1973	8.7	1983	3.8	1993	2.7
1964	1.0	1974	12.3	1984	3.9	1994	2.7
1965	1.9	1975	6.9	1985	3.8		
1966	3.5	1976	4.9	1986	1.1		
1967	3.0	1977	6.7	1987	4.4		
1968	4.7	1978	9.0	1988	4.4		
1969	6.2	1979	13.3	1989	4.6		
Average 1960s	2.1%	*Average 1970s*	6.2%	*Average 1980s*	4.3%		

Source: U.S. Department of Labor, Bureau of Labor Statistics, as measured by the Consumer Price Index for All Urban Consumers, U.S. City Average, All Items, December to December. 1982-1984=100.

Retirees living on fixed incomes should react to price increases immediately.

If you have been operating without a budget, you are probably also aware of inflation, whether you are retired or still in the work force. Your money seems to simply evaporate more rapidly. This, of course, may be caused by carefree spending and overuse of credit cards. If this is the case, you must curb your spending. An inflationary situation will alert you to this need more quickly.

In an inflationary period, many older workers' dreams of retirement become unaffordable. They find it difficult to make ends meet while fully employed and become seriously concerned about trying to live on a lower retirement income. Most stay at work longer and postpone retirement in the hope that conditions will return to a more normal situation.

It is obvious, therefore, that high rates of inflation have a detrimental financial impact on fixed-income retirees. The argument that retirees are well off is not always valid.

MEASURES AGAINST INFLATION

The options available to people living on limited or fixed incomes are few. The three alternatives are to consume capital, to increase income, and to reduce expenses. Consuming capital is hardly a long-term solution to the problem of coping with inflation unless you are sure that your capital supply will not be consumed in your lifetime. The average person does not have a very large nest egg to begin with. But even for those who have managed to accumulate some savings and investments, consuming capital is not a recommended solution.

One of the soundest ways to keep your nest egg from withering after you retire is to increase your income by adding a fresh flow of new, inflated earnings. To earn an income after you retire, you do not have to keep on doing what you did before retirement. You can work part-time, possibly through one of the new job-sharing or flextime systems that some companies are adopting to make part-time employment more attractive. You can also set up your own business or expand a favorite hobby or pastime into a money-making proposition (See Chapter 1, Working in Retirement, for more detailed information.)

The third alternative is to reduce expenses, which simply means studying all of your major budgetary items—including food, clothing, shelter, and health care—and cutting the amount you spend on them. This means you must sharpen your shopping skills. You must learn to time your purchases to sales, to use discount stores, to avoid impulse buying, to carefully examine your purchases for quality, and to make your clothing and other items last longer by following the care instructions. Energy costs and medical costs, important in everyone's budget but especially in those of retirees, will probably continue to exceed the inflation rate in the 1990s. You will have to adopt cost-saving energy tactics, including installing insulation, updating your heating system to make it more efficient, and possibly lowering the thermostat setting. Solutions for controlling rising medical costs are not readily available. Perhaps the expansion of health maintenance organizations, known as HMOs, can be of some assistance.

If you are unable to cope with inflation, you can seek professional assistance. Financial counseling is available through credit unions and some banks, among other institutions. Check with your local senior citizens center.

13

Taxes and Tax Shelters

Taxes and tax shelters can be confusing subjects for all taxpayers, not just older ones. In this chapter, we will try to briefly explain both.

INCOME TAXES

The first tax bill of the Clinton Administration represented the most significant tax legislation since the 1986 Tax Reform Act. The Omnibus Budget Reconciliation Act of 1993 (OBRA 1993) focused primarily on individuals, with upper-income taxpayers shouldering most of the tax burden.

Tax Rates and Brackets

A 36 percent tax bracket was added to the existing tax rate structure of 15, 28, and 31 percent. The new tax rate applies to taxable income in excess of $140,000 for married individuals filing jointly and in excess of $115,000 for single taxpayers. The 36 percent rate was retroactive to January 1, 1993.

Beyond the new tax rate, a surtax was added, thereby creating a maximum tax rate of 39.6 percent for taxable income in excess of $250,000, applicable to married individuals fil-

ing jointly ($125,000 for married persons filing separately) as well as to single taxpayers.

The 1994 limits for the lower brackets have been increased for inflation by approximately 3 percent. Therefore, on joint returns, the 28 percent rate will not apply until the taxable income exceeds $38,000. (The 1993 amount was $36,900.) The 31 percent rate will not apply until taxable income exceeds $91,850. (In 1993, it was $89,150.) Table 13.1 provides the 1995 income tax rates.

Personal and Dependency Exemptions

The personal exemption is the amount you subtract from your taxable income for yourself and your dependents. Since 1990, a taxpayer's personal exemption has been adjusted annually for inflation. For 1994, the personal exemption was $2,450, and for 1995, $2,500. The personal exemption may be reduced or eliminated if your Adjusted Gross Income (AGI) exceeds specified limits.

Standard Deduction

The standard deduction is the maximum amount of income that an individual can earn

Table 13.1
1995 Income Tax Rates

Single
Taxable Income

Over	But Not Over	Amount of Tax	Rate on Excess	Of the Amount Over
$ 0	$ 23,350	15% of income		
23,350	56,550	$ 3,503	28.0%	$ 23,350
56,550	117,950	12,799	31.0%	56,550
117,950	256,500	31,833	36.0%	117,950
256,500		81,711	39.6%	256,500

Married Filing Jointly
Taxable Income

Over	But Not Over	Amount of Tax	Rate on Excess	Of the Amount Over
$ 0	$ 39,000	15% of income		
39,000	94,250	$ 5,850	28.0%	$ 39,000
94,250	143,600	21,320	31.0%	94,250
143,600	256,500	36,619	36.0%	143,600
256,500		77,263	39.6%	256,500

Married Filing Separately
Taxable Income

Over	But Not Over	Amount of Tax	Rate on Excess	Of the Amount Over
$ 0	$ 19,150	15% of income		
19,150	47,125	$ 2,925	28.0%	$ 19,150
47,125	71,800	10,660	31.0%	47,125
71,800	128,250	18,309	36.0%	71,800
128,250		38,631	39.6%	128,250

Head of Household
Taxable Income

Over	But Not Over	Amount of Tax	Rate on Excess	Of the Amount Over
$ 0	$ 31,250	15% of income		
31,250		$ 4,688	28.0%	$ 31,250
80,750		18,548	31.0%	80,750
130,800	250,000	34,063	36.0%	130,800
256,500		79,315	39.6%	256,500

that is not subject to income tax. If your taxable income after you deduct your personal exemptions does not exceed the standard deduction, you need not file a return. For 1994, the standard deductions were $3,800 for single returns; $6,350 for joint returns; and $5,600 for head-of-household returns. For 1995, the standard deductions are $3,900 for single returns; $6,550 for joint returns; and $5,750 for head-of-household returns.

Personal Deductions

The rules for personal deductions in 1995 were as follows:

■ Mortgage interest was deductible only for your first and second homes. If you owned additional homes, the mortgage interest was not deductible.

■ Property taxes and state income taxes were deductible.

■ Interest on credit card loans and auto loans was *not* deductible.

■ Medical expenses are an allowable deduction if they exceed 7 1/2 percent of the Adjusted Gross Income.

■ Unreimbursed business expenses, union dues, and tax preparer fees are an allowable deduction if the total exceeds 2 percent of the Adjusted Gross Income.

Adjusted Gross Income

Adjusted Gross Income is calculated by adding all your sources of income—salary or wages, dividends, interest, rents, and royalties—then subtracting your Individual Retirement Account contributions and alimony payments, if any, for the year. Under current federal law, retirees are required to include half of their Social Security income and all of their income from tax-exempt bonds when calculating AGI. Recipents of Social Security pay a tax on up to 85 percent of their Social Security benefits, depending on income (see page 120.)

Taxable Income

Taxable income is derived by subtracting personal exemptions, mortgage interest, property taxes, state income taxes, and charitable gifts from AGI. By law, your tax rate is applied to your taxable income, not to your AGI. Taxable income is typically much lower than AGI.

Profit on the Sale of a Home

Under present law, up to $125,000 of profit from the sale of a home is exempt from taxes for older Americans. This tax benefit can make the retirement years more financially secure and can add new flexibility to retirement planning.

To be eligible for this tax exclusion, you must be 55 or older when you sell your home. The home must have been your principal residence, and you must have owned and lived in it for at least three of the five years preceding the sale. For married couples, only one spouse must meet the age, ownership, and residency tests. To elect the exclusion, file Form 2119, Sale or Exchange of Personal Residence.

You can take advantage of the home-sale exclusion only once in your lifetime. For purposes of this limitation, married couples are treated as one. If one spouse used the exclusion before marriage, the other spouse forfeits the right to the tax break.

In addition, the $125,000 limit is not cumulative. For example, if you exclude from taxation $65,000 of the profit on the sale of one home, the remaining $60,000 is forfeited. You cannot carry an unused portion forward for application against the gain on the sale of another home.

If you realize a $150,000 gain, you can

escape the tax on the first $125,000 and postpone the tax on the remaining $25,000 if you buy a new home that costs at least $25,000. The gain you roll over into the new home will not be taxed until such time as you give up ownership of any home, that is, sell a house for the last time and do not reinvest your equity in another, more costly home.

Special Tax Concerns for Women

While the federal income tax applies to everyone regardless of gender, women should take note of a few pertinent items. Divorce, for example, quite common nowadays, carries with it several financial implications, such as division of marital property, alimony, and child support. Although the property divided in a divorce is not taxable, a hidden tax consequence may arise if an asset is subsequently sold showing a capital gain. And, if you receive alimony, it is included in your taxable income but tax deductible in your husband's tax return. Finally, child support money is not taxable to you nor deductible by your former husband.

A host of other tax issues arise through divorce including treatment of legal fees relating to the divorce, home mortgage interest, job-hunting expenses, and educational expenses required to maintain or improve your existing job skills. These various expenses are deductible if your miscellaneous total exceeds two percent of your Adjusted Gross Income.

Widowhood also has tax implications in terms of filing status. Both widowhood and divorce have a variety of rules and tax rates. Single filing status applies if you are unmarried or legally separated with no children at home. Head-of-household status applies if you maintain a home for a child, children, or another dependent. If you are widowed, you can file as married filing jointly for the year of your husband's death, and qualifying widow for the next two years, if you have a dependent child(ren) and you do not remarry. If you are currently married, you can file as married filing jointly, but you may file a return of your own as married filing separately. Each filing status has its own rules and tax rates.

Income Tax Filing Assistance

Many of the almost 33 million Americans who are 65 or older run into problems accomplishing the annual chore of filing an income tax return with the federal government. Some of the basic difficulties faced by these people include confusion over which forms to use, how to fill them out, whether or not to itemize deductions, and whether to file jointly with a spouse or separately. If you have a problem, the Internal Revenue Service is available to help you, even to the extent of computing your taxes so that you pay the smallest amount possible. Call or visit your nearest IRS office.

You may wish to obtain a free copy of Internal Revenue Publication Number 17, *Your Federal Income Tax*, from the IRS. You can also get free tax advice nationwide from volunteer tax counselors trained by the Internal Revenue Service to counsel retirees. For the location of the counselor nearest you, write to AARP-NRTA, Tax-Aide Program, Department RG, 1909 K Street, N.W., Washington, DC 20049. If you would like to obtain the details of a particular state's laws on income taxes or any other taxes, contact the Public Information Division of the Department of Revenue or Taxation in that particular state's capital.

You will need to get professional help if you do not wish to prepare your own tax return. A reputable preparer will be able to handle your return if you are salaried and have relatively few itemized deductions. If your return is more complex, you may wish to hire a Certified Public Accountant (CPA), licensed to practice accounting in your state, or an Enrolled Agent, an individual who has passed an examination administered by the Internal Revenue Service (IRS). Both CPAs and Enrolled Agents are qualified to represent you at an IRS audit. If you decide to use a professional accountant or tax attorney, you must be prepared to pay the required fee.

TAX SHELTERS
FOR RETIREMENT PLANNING

A *tax shelter* is an investment that legally enables you to defer taxes or, ultimately, to diminish taxes. These goals can be accomplished by investing soundly in assets that you leave untouched for a long period of time. This seasoning process in conjunction with compounding of interest steadily increases the size of an investment.

If you are an average small investor, you can benefit from a tax-shelter investment by putting your money into one or more of the following:

■ *Individual Retirement Accounts and Keogh plans.* The Tax Reform Act of 1986 made changes in IRAs and Keogh plans for self-employed people. However, these retirement plans still allow money to grow, and taxes on deductible deposits and earnings are deferred until the money is withdrawn. The tax-deferred feature enables your investment to grow faster than it would as an ordinary investment.

■ *Home ownership.* When you own your home, your mortgage interest and property taxes are deductible. Moreover, you have the one-time exclusion of a $125,000 capital gain when you sell your home if you are 55 or older.

■ *Pensions.* The money contributed to your pension account by your employer is tax-de-

ferred. You will not be required to pay taxes on it until you retire.

■ *Tax-deferred annuities.* The money you invest in a tax-deferred annuity is not taxed when you put it in and is tax-free while it is accumulating. Only when you begin to receive payments are you required to pay the taxes due. (For an in-depth discussion of this subject, see page 162.)

■ *Municipal bonds.* These are among the best tax shelters, particularly for people in the 28, 31, or 36 percent tax bracket. The interest earned is not taxable by the federal government and is exempt from the state income tax of the state in which the bond was issued. (For an in-depth discussion of this subject, see page 95.)

■ *United States government savings bonds.* Series EE and HH United States savings bonds offer the advantage of tax deferral. You pay taxes on the interest you have earned only when you cash in the savings bonds. (For an in-depth discussion of this subject, see page 92.)

Tax Shelters Not for Small Investors

Tax shelters that are not designed for the average small investor because of their high risk and the possible loss of all the invested money include oil and gas drilling, cattle raising, mineral excavation, and real estate development. The Tax Reform Act of 1986 severely restricts the tax write-offs that have long been a major appeal for investors in these types of activities. These tax shelters are now less attractive even to investors willing to assume such a risk.

The Rollover as a Tax Shelter

Anyone who takes a lump-sum settlement or withdrawal from an employee retirement plan or profit-sharing plan is subject to a 20 percent withholding tax on the withdrawal. This federal law, a part of the Unemployment Compensation Act of 1992, requires that 20 percent of the withdrawal amount be withheld by the payor for federal income tax purposes. Therefore, when you request a withdrawal or distribution from a qualified retirement plan, you will receive only 80 percent of the amount you requested. If you live in a state with mandatory state tax withholding, the payor must also deduct the state income tax, and you will receive an amount less than 80 percent of the withdrawal amount requested.

To retain the account as a tax shelter and to avoid the mandatory 20 percent withholding tax, you can rollover or transfer the entire account to another employee retirement plan or to an Individual Retirement Account.

Some distributions are not subject to the mandatory 20 percent withholding. They include:

■ Periodic payments made over the participant's single or joint life expectancy or over a period of not less than ten years.

■ Minimum distributions required when you attain age 70 1/2.

■ Loans.

■ Rollovers to another qualified employee retirement plan or to an IRA, as noted above.

The average small investor can benefit significantly by putting money into one or more of the tax shelters discussed above. Any of these tax shelters enables you to defer taxes or, ultimately, to diminish taxes.

Glossary

Adjusted gross income (AGI). The total of your annual wages, interest, dividends, and capital gains or losses minus allowable deductions such as alimony, business expenses, moving expenses, and IRA or Keogh contributions.

Standard deduction. The maximum amount of income that an individual can earn that is not subject to income tax. It is the threshold, or floor, for determining whether or not you can itemize on your tax return.

Tax. A contribution exacted from individuals, businesses, or organizations by the government, according to law, for the general support of the government and for the maintenance of public services.

Tax shelter. An investment that legally enables you to defer taxes or ultimately to diminish taxes.

PART FOUR

Insurance

14

Life Insurance

Many people in the early and middle years of their lives purchase life insurance policies without clearly understanding how much they need and how the policies meet the long-term needs of their families. As time elapses, needs and goals change, and the life insurance policies purchased earlier may no longer fulfill current requirements. As you begin to plan for retirement, it is appropriate to review and analyze the life insurance policies you own. Decide whether you need what you have and whether you can invest your accumulated cash values more profitably.

THE CHANGING ROLE OF LIFE INSURANCE

As your retirement time approaches, you must make certain decisions about your insurance: How much financial protection do you still need for your dependents? Do you still need insurance as a means of saving money? Is this an opportune time to cash in some of your policies and use the proceeds for other investments or purposes?

In general, life insurance serves two functions during the course of an individual's work-ing years. First, it provides financial protection for survivors in case of a breadwinner's death. Second, some types assist the insured in building a nest egg, hopefully for retirement.

The principal test of whether you need life insurance is the number of dependents you have. If your death would cause economic hardship for your spouse, children, parents, or someone else you want to protect, then insurance provides you with the ability to fulfill your obligations.

The need for life insurance is great in the case of a husband and nonworking wife who have two young children. Three people are dependent on the husband for their total support so insurance coverage is essential. If the wife were to die, the husband would have to pay for day care for the children, which is quite expensive. Perhaps, the wife should also have a life insurance policy.

A young, unmarried student whose parents are financing the student's education has little or no need for insurance. From an economic point of view, the student's death would create no burdens. An argument may be made for the young student to buy a policy because younger people pay lower rates.

During our working years, advertisements and insurance agents tell us that every breadwinner with a young family should carry life insurance. This concept has assumed the strength of a golden rule in financial planning. As the years pass, however, children grow to adulthood, retirement becomes imminent, and finances usually improve. As a result, near-retirees are almost certainly faced with premium payments for insurance that is no longer needed or wanted. Funds available from old policies can be converted into investments offering lifetime income.

If your children are self-supporting, your mortgage paid off, other income-producing investments made, and retirement rights under Social Security and your pension plan achieved, you may discover that you need only a relatively small insurance policy to cover your final medical and burial expenses.

On the other hand, you may have a situation in which you would be well served by a life insurance policy. If you have a physically handicapped or mentally retarded child or a spouse without adequate retirement income, a life insurance policy will provide a lump-sum payment to him or her as the beneficiary when you die. This sum, if properly invested by your beneficiary, can yield a safe, regular monthly income. If you are in a high-income bracket, life insurance can pay any federal and state inheritance taxes for your heirs, preventing the forced and uneconomical, unwanted sale of estate assets to pay these taxes. Thus, life insurance can help to preserve your estate.

TYPES OF LIFE INSURANCE

All the different policies offered by insurance companies fit into one of two major categories: those that build savings and those that do not. *Term insurance*, also known as *pure insurance*, is life insurance that does not include saving for the future. The insurance company pays only in the event you die during the time the insurance is in force. The beneficiaries of the insured will receive nothing if premium payments are discontinued.

Life insurance that includes a savings feature is called *cash value* or *permanent*. This type of insurance is popular among those who believe they can collect the savings if they live a long life and cancel the policy prior to their death. Permanent life insurance requires policyholders to pay higher premium charges. The factors that determine the premium rate include age, sex, health, family history, status as a smoker or nonsmoker, and the amount of the death benefit.

Term Insurance

Term life insurance contains no savings component and expires at the end of a specified term. The policy can be renewed at the end of the term, but a higher premium is assessed because the policyholder is older. The premium for a term life insurance policy is significantly less than that for a cash value life insurance policy, but term life insurance is a good buy. In case of death of the insured, the beneficiary will receive the face value of the policy, the amount specified in the contract as the death benefit.

Guaranteed renewable term insurance is purchased for a period ranging from one to five years. It offers the right to renew without proof of insurability. If an individual suffers a heart attack six months before renewal, the policy can be renewed. The premium cost, related to age, is increased at each renewal. A five-year term policy has a constant premium for the five-year period.

Decreasing term insurance allows you to pay a fixed premium and receive coverage that decreases each year. If it is purchased to guarantee paying off a mortgage for the benefit of the surviving spouse and children, the policy is a good selection, reducing insurance as the mortgage balance is reduced.

Convertible term insurance allows you to convert to some form of insurance that builds cash values. A medical examination is not required for conversion. The change, of course, will result in a much higher premium compared with the premium for term coverage. Convertible term allows you to convert to cash value insurance but does not require you to do so.

Cash Value Life Insurance

Cash value life insurance requires premium payments for a set number of years, until a specified age, or for life, depending on the specific type of policy. Cash value, or permanent, life insurance policies remain in effect even after you have finished paying the premium. Life insurance policies build cash values because the fixed premiums exceed the insurance company's cost of providing you with coverage. Several types of this popular form of insurance are offered by insurance companies. *Whole life insurance*, also known as *straight life insurance*, provides lifetime coverage in exchange for premiums that continue throughout your life, usually to age 100. The premium is lower for younger people, who have a longer life expectancy and will be paying premiums for a longer time. Straight life insurance offers the lowest premium for a specified amount of coverage as compared with other cash value policies. Because of lower premiums, cash values grow more slowly. The policy pays the face value if the insured dies or lives to 100.

Single premium life insurance requires payment of a single, relatively large premium at the time the policy is purchased. No other payment is required to keep the policy in force.

Limited payment life insurance policies in-

clude twenty-pay life for which you contract to pay twenty annual premiums, and thirty-pay life for which you must make thirty annual payments. When all required premiums have been paid, the policies are said to be *paid up*. Paid-up policies continue to provide insurance coverage and to accumulate cash values.

Endowment life insurance guarantees payment of the face value of the policy to your beneficiary(ies) if you die during the period the policy is in force. If you outlive the contract period, you will be paid the face value. These are very expensive policies, requiring very high annual premiums that generate rapid buildup of cash values. They are useful, for instance, in providing college tuition if purchased when your child is young.

Universal life insurance is a newer insurance product that became available in 1981. It divides premium payments into life insurance and savings, promising a fixed, competitive rate of return to be paid for one year on the investment portion. At the end of the year, a new rate is set for the next twelve months and a minimum rate is guaranteed. Premium payments are flexible, permitting increases, decreases, or even skips in payments. The amount of death benefits is also flexible. The insurance company's administrative expenses are deducted from the earnings.

Variable whole life insurance charges fixed premiums, offering a fixed minimum death benefit no matter what the performance of the investments. These policies offer a new freedom to policyholders, who can now choose the investments they want the insurance company to make with their premiums (e.g., money market, stocks, bonds, and real estate). Policyholders can choose more than one mutual fund and also have the option of switching from one fund to another. Shifts between funds are not taxed because they are made inside a tax-sheltered life insurance product.

Universal variable life insurance is a new and hybrid form of both universal and variable life unsurance. The policyholder can set most of the terms and conditions of the policy. Instead of paying fixed, level premiums at a specific time as with variable life, you can tell the insurance company exactly how much you would like to pay and when. You can direct how the money will be invested, and you have the right to change the face amount of the policy.

Vanishing premium life insurance has as its goal the production of enough income to pay for premiums after a set period of time such as ten years. Dividends, generally higher than traditional returns, are automatically reinvested. After a specified number of premium payments, the policyholder no longer has to pay premiums and is fully covered by the policy's death benefit.

Survivorship whole life insurance, also known as *second-to-die life insurance*, insures two lives—usually husband and wife—under one policy. Death benefits are paid on the death of the last of the two named insured. This policy is generally less expensive than two separate policies and is useful for planning the payment of estate taxes.

Options Offered by Cash Value Life Insurance

Life insurance that builds a cash value provides you with several options that are unavailable with a term policy.

■ *Loans.* You can borrow all or a portion of the cash value at favorable rates in the event you have a need for cash. You pay interest as long as the loan remains outstanding. If you die while a policy loan remains outstanding, the death benefit to beneficiaries is reduced by the amount of the loan.

■ *Withdrawal of cash value.* If you are willing to cancel your life insurance coverage, you can withdraw the cash value.

■ *Conversion to a term policy.* You can convert your cash value insurance to a term insurance policy that provides the same coverage. You instruct the insurance company to use the cash value to pay premiums on a term insurance policy. The greater the cash value accumulated, the longer the term policy will last.

WHAT BENEFICIARIES SHOULD KNOW

To collect the proceeds of life insurance if you are a beneficiary, you should contact your insurance agent and advise him/her to prepare the claim form. If you no longer have an insurance agent, you can contact the company directly.

Insurance companies offer a number of options for paying the face amount of the policy. The most popular option is the *lump-sum payment.* This settlement gives you the opportunity to invest the money and to earn a good return. For prudent money managers, this is the recommended option. The other choices include *life-income,* a specified amount of income paid periodically for life; *fixed-period option,* a specified amount paid periodically over a fixed number of years; or a *fixed-amount option,* a specified amount paid periodically until the insurance fund is exhausted. Among these three options, each payment will include payment of principal and interest. The principal you receive will be tax-free but the interest earned on the money being held for you by the insurance company is subject to income taxes.

LIFE INSURANCE AND TAXATION

Life insurance offers some tax advantages to policyholders and beneficiaries.

■ *Income tax.* Policyholders are not required to

pay income tax on the annual buildup in cash value, unless and until the money is withdrawn and the policy is surrendered. However, you will then have to pay tax only on the amount of cash value that exceeds the total amount of premiums you paid for the insurance policy.

Life insurance death benefits are not taxable to the beneficiary(ies). However, if the proceeds are received in yearly installments, the amount of interest included in the payment is subject to tax. The interest paid on loans from your policy is not tax deductible.

■ *Estate taxes.* Proceeds payable to a beneficiary or to your estate on a policy you own are part of your estate and subject to estate taxes. Proceeds payable to your spouse, qualifying for the marital deduction, are not subject to the estate tax.

Estate taxes can be avoided if the policy you own is transferred to someone else, wife or children, or to an irrevocable insurance trust more than three years prior to your death. Transferring ownership, however, results in the loss of your right to change beneficiaries, to make a loan, or to surrender the policy for its cash value. A transfer may be subject to gift tax.

REVIEWING YOUR INSURANCE NEEDS

Cash value life insurance policies usually include a table in the document that indicates the amount of cash the insurance company would pay if the policy were surrendered. This amount is the *cash value*. The amount becomes larger the longer the policy is owned, but it is less than the face value of the policy or the amount to be paid in case of death. The amount of money you receive upon surrender is equal to the total premiums you have paid plus the interest earned by those payments over the years.

If you have been paying premiums on a cash value life insurance policy for twenty to twenty-five years, the cash value of the policy is usually about half the face value. This cash-value sum can be withdrawn and invested in a way that will yield a higher interest rate than that paid by the insurance company.

An alternative is to convert the cash value of your life insurance policy into an annuity contract. Although you can buy the annuity from the company that issued the life insurance policy, you are not obligated to do so and may be able to get a better return from another company. The company from which you intend to buy the annuity should arrange the withdrawal of the cash value and the surrender of the policy in such a way that you avoid the income tax that would be imposed for a straight withdrawal of the cash value.

Investigating the many alternatives open to you is a major facet of retirement planning. The best time for a searching review of your insurance program is when your retirement is within sight. You may wish to seek the help of a trusted financial advisor or insurance agent to review and evaluate the available alternatives.

Self-Study
Your Life Insurance Policy(ies) Inventory

Filling out the following form will enable you to inventory your life insurance policies. Organizing your policy information in this way will be helpful in determining whether you are overinsured and whether the cash values are large enough to be invested in a way that will yield significantly greater returns. If you do not know the type of policy you own, call your insurance agent.

	Policy		
	1	2	3
Name of insured	_____	_____	_____
Name of company	_____	_____	_____
Policy number	_____	_____	_____
Type: term, cash value, endowment, specialized	_____	_____	_____
Face amount	_____	_____	_____
Beneficiary(ies)	_____	_____	_____
Current loan, if any	_____	_____	_____
Current cash value, if any	_____	_____	_____
Premium amount	_____	_____	_____
Premium due date(s)	_____	_____	_____
Name of insurance agent	_____	_____	_____
Address of agent	_____	_____	_____
Telephone number of agent	_____	_____	_____
Location of policy(ies)	_____	_____	_____

1. What is the total amount of life insurance you currently own?
2. What is the ideal amount of life insurance coverage you should have at this stage of your life? (Discuss this with a financial planner.)
3. Are you over or under the ideal amount?
4. What steps will you take, if any, to achieve the ideal amount of life insurance coverage?
5. What is your total accumulation of cash value at this time?
6. List alternative forms of investment for some portion of your total cash value. (Discuss this with a financial planner.)

Glossary

Annuity. A policy that guarantees its owner a specified lifetime income in return for a payment to the insurance company that may be in a single lump sum or spread out over a period of years.

Beneficiary. The person designated to receive the proceeds of a life insurance policy.

Cash value. The dollar value of a life insurance policy that has a savings component as part of the premium. The cash value is equal to the amount accumulated plus the interest earned.

Cash value life insurance. Also known as permanent life insurance, it requires premium payments for a specified number of years or for life and, over the years, builds up savings, referred to as "cash value." The policy's face value is paid at the insured's death, regardless of the policy's cash value.

Convertible term insurance. A term policy that allows you to convert the policy to some type of cash value life insurance policy without a medical examination.

Decreasing term insurance. A term policy whose face value is reduced in stages over a prescribed period. The reduction is often tied to the unpaid balance of a mortgage or other type of loan so as to pay off the debt at the insured's death.

Endowment life insurance. A cash value life insurance policy for which premiums are paid for a specified number of years. At the end of this time, the cash value of the policy equals the face value, which is paid to the insured by the insurance company. The death benefit is equal to whatever has been paid in plus accrued interest. This type of policy is usually used to help fund a child's college education or to build a retirement nest egg.

Face value. The amount of a life insurance policy that is scheduled to be paid at the death of the insured or at the maturity of the policy.

Guaranteed renewable term insurance. A policy that is purchased for a term of one to five years, offering the right to renew without proof of insurability, namely a medical examination.

Life insurance. Protection for an insured's dependents against the hardships they might suffer due to the loss of the insured's income because of death.

Limited payment life insurance. A cash value life insurance policy that is similar to a whole life insurance policy except that the premium payments are paid for a specified number of years or until a specified age. The policy remains in effect after the premiums have all been paid.

Paid-up life insurance. Cash value life insurance that remains in force even though no additional premiums are required.

Permanent life insurance. Any type of life insurance other than term.

Policyholder. The person who owns an insurance policy.

Premium. The monetary payment required to be paid to an insurance company for a specific amount of insurance.

Second-to-die life insurance. *See* Survivorship whole life insurance.

Single premium whole life insurance. A cash value life insurance policy for which the insured makes a single premium payment. No further payments are required.

Straight life insurance. *See* Whole life insurance.

Survivorship whole life insurance. Also known as second-to-die life insurance, the policy insures two lives, usually husband and wife. Death benefits are paid upon the death of the last of the two named insured.

Term life insurance. A type of life insurance policy that covers the insured for a specified number of years, paying the beneficiary(ies) the face value of the policy if the insured dies within that specified period. The premium is less than that for any cash value life insurance policy because the policy has no cash value and represents only the cost of pure insurance plus a charge for administration. The policy may be renewable at the end of each term, but not beyond age 65 or 70.

Universal life insurance. A new type of life insurance policy that allows the policyholder to vary both the amount of the premium payment and the amount of the death benefit to fit the changing needs of his/her growing family. The cash value grows at a competititve market interest rate.

Universal variable life insurance. A hybrid form of both the universal life policy and the variable life insurance policy.

Vanishing premium life insurance. After paying the specified number of premiums, the policyholder no longer has to pay premiums and is fully insured by the policy's death benefit.

Variable life insurance. A new type of life insurance policy for which the insured is assessed a fixed premium but which allows the insured to direct the investment of the cash accumulation among a variety of mutual funds or other types of investment while providing a guaranteed minimum death benefit.

Whole life insurance. Also known as a straight life insurance policy, whole life is a cash value life insurance policy that covers the insured for life, as long as the premiums are paid. It includes a savings feature against which the insured can borrow, paying interest on the loan. In addition, the insured can withdraw the cash value completely if he/she terminates the insurance. When the insured dies, the beneficiary collects the face value of the policy.

15

Health Insurance

You buy health insurance for the same reason you buy any other type of insurance, namely, to protect yourself and your family from financial loss if a dreaded event occurs. Illness and disability can wreak havoc at any age.

As you begin to plan for your golden years, you should investigate whether your health insurance protection can be carried over into your retirement. You should also determine whether you have correct and adequate protection. This chapter analyzes the principal and specialized types of coverage available as well as the kinds of organizations that offer them. The chapter also discusses special situations that need to be considered when selecting coverage and ends by offering basic advice on health insurance.

TYPES OF GENERAL HEALTH INSURANCE

The principal types of health insurance available today for an individual, a family, or a group include the following:

Hospitalization Insurance

Hospitalization insurance covers you for the expenses you incur while you are a patient in a hospital. Most plans cover daily room and board as well as regular nursing services in the hospital for varying periods of time, usually from 21 to 365 days. Some plans also pay for X-rays, laboratory tests, and medications.

Hospitalization is a basic form of health insurance that everyone should have. It is usually provided by employers and unions for their members.

Basic Medical/Surgical Insurance

Basic medical/surgical insurance covers you for doctors' visits in and out of the hospital, diagnostic and laboratory tests, and certain surgical procedures. The plans itemize the maximum benefit they will pay for each. Many plans have an annual deductible and coinsurance clause.

Basic medical/surgical insurance is usually provided by employers and unions. It is very often offered in conjunction with hospitalization insurance.

Comprehensive Major Medical Insurance

Comprehensive major medical insurance picks

up where basic health insurance ends, covering the high costs of serious long-term illness. Some plans have very high deductibles and provide benefits of up to $500,000 or $1,000,000. Other plans provide first-dollar coverage of some health care services. Some employers and unions provide this insurance on a contributory basis, while other groups offer noncontributory plans. In a *contributory plan*, the employer makes a contribution and the employee also contributes some portion of the premium cost that varies from plan to plan. In a *noncontributory plan*, the employer pays all.

Comprehensive major medical insurance is an appropriate form of insurance for people of any age. It can be purchased instead of Medigap insurance (see Chapter 17) by those over 65 who are on Medicare. If comprehensive major medical is provided by your employer, find out whether it can be carried over into retirement and, if yes, whether it would be contributory or noncontributory. For an individual 65 or older, the combination of Medicare Parts A and B and Medicare supplementary insurance may still require the additional coverage of comprehensive major medical.

Catastrophic Major Medical Insurance

Catastrophic major medical insurance provides compensation for extraordinary medical costs not covered by hospitalization insurance or by basic medical/surgical insurance or comprehensive major medical insurance. One such policy, after a $10,000 deductible, pays as much as $2,000,000 for three to ten years from the date an initial medical expense is incurred. Some plans offer a $25,000 deductible. The insured must select the deductible he/she feels will best supplement basic major medical or hospital coverage. All current reasonable and customary expenses count in full towards your chosen deductible. Even those eligible expenses paid for by your basic health insurance policy as well as those paid out of your own pocket count towards meeting your deductible.

After your deductible is met, the plan pays 100 percent of all eligible expenses, including all hospital charges for a semi-private room and board or intensive care; miscellaneous hospital services and operating room charges; treatment by a currently licensed physician, surgeon, or physiotherapist whether in a hospital, at home, or in the office; private duty nursing services; dental treatment if a jaw is fractured or natural teeth are injured by accident; x-ray, physiotherapy, or laboratory services for diagnosis and treatment; anesthetic and its administration; ambulance service; prescription drugs; oxygen and rental equipment such as wheelchairs or hospital beds; mental or nervous disorders, and alcoholism or drug addiction treated in a hospital. For all these expenses, the plan pays up to $2,000,000 up to ten full years from the date your first eligible expense is incurred.

Disability Income Insurance

Disability income insurance pays a percentage of your regular monthly income when you become disabled because of illness or injury and are unable to work for an extended period of time. This type of insurance is provided by the Social Security system at no extra cost to you, by commercial insurance companies usually at a high cost to you, and by some retirement systems. (In New York City, for instance, covered employees can retire under disability provisions when they are no longer capable of fulfilling their normal job functions.) The best disability coverage begins to pay a monthly allowance after 60 or 90 days of disability and continues until age 65 or retirement, whichever comes first. Provisions vary.

Most people tend to pay too much attention during their working years to life insurance and too little to disability income insurance. The need for disability insurance disappears after retirement when you begin to collect a pension and Social Security.

INSURANCE FOR SPECIAL NEEDS

Most people, whether actively employed or retired, can use specialized insurance coverage that is generally excluded from basic and major medical plans. Some popular types of special needs insurance include the following:

Dental Insurance

At a time when the family budget is under severe strain, the cost of dental care is becoming less of a burden for many American households. The reason for this is the rapid growth of dental insurance financed either wholly or partially by employers as a fringe benefit. Dental expense insurance covers necessary dental health care including oral examinations, X-rays, cleanings, fillings, extractions, inlays, crowns, bridgework, dentures (prosthodontics), oral surgery, treatment of gums (periodontics), root canal (endodontics), and teeth alignment (orthodontics).

The American Dental Association estimates that 100,000,000 people are covered by dental insurance. One of the reasons for this level of coverage is labor unions' support of dental protection.

The estimated 25,000 plans now in operation pay varying amounts for dental work. While some pay 100 percent, most pay less—about 33 to 50 percent. To reduce expenses, some dental insurance plans require members to pay part of the monthly premium. The coinsurance is usually 20 percent.

Optical Expense Benefits

An optical expense program provides eyeglasses to eligible members and their dependents. In one such plan, each eligible individual may obtain a pair of eyeglasses every two years from a participating optical outlet free of charge. The glasses can be either single-vision or bifocal lenses of standard prescription within a standard frame. The group administering the program reimburses the participating optician with set fees. If the member uses a nonparticipating optician, the member can be reimbursed directly for a specified amount that is usually less than the actual cost.

Hearing Aids

The process of aging is the most common cause of hearing loss, and about half of all purchases of hearing aids are made by people 65 or older. It is estimated that about 3,000,000 Americans currently use hearing aids.

Many older people find the cost of a hearing aid prohibitive. Some employer health insurance packages include a subsidy for the purchase of a hearing aid, and some of the programs carry this benefit over into retirement. In general, however, most do not offer this benefit at all. To help offset costs, a Federal Task Force on Hearing Aid Health Care recommended in 1990 that the United States Department of Health and Human Services consider the possibility of subsidizing the purchase of hearing aids for elderly persons.

Prescription Medication Plan

Some employers and unions provide a prescription medication plan that may be carried over into retirement. The full cost of prescription medications is covered provided the prescription is filled by a participating pharmacist. If a nonparticipating pharmacist is used, reimbursement of charges is made in accordance with a schedule of allowances.

In one plan, prescriptions may not exceed a thirty-day supply, and if the physician so specifies, one or more refills are allowed. Medications, vitamins, and diet supplements that can be purchased without a prescription usually are not covered. To reduce costs without sacrificing quality, members are advised to ask doctors to prescribe generic medications when possible as a substitute for brand-name products. Covered members are issued identification cards and may be required to use special prescription blanks that request identifying data from the member, the doctor, and the pharmacist.

Blood Program

Many large employers, both public and private, offer membership in a blood program. An enrolled employee or a substitute is required to donate one pint of blood annually. Some of the plans provide unlimited blood credit for the member, spouse, unmarried children of any age, unmarried brothers and sisters of any age who live with the member, and member's and spouse's parents and grandparents regardless of residence. If you donate more than a pint of blood a year, you can build up credit for future years. Some of these programs carry over into retirement and help in providing the first three pints of blood not covered by Medicare (see page 236).

Long-Term Care Insurance

The major gaps in health insurance coverage for the elderly are long-term nursing home care and custodial home health care (see Chapter 17). About 80 percent of catastrophic health care expenses are for long-term care provided outside of a hospital. Long-term care insurance covers these expenses, which are the primary cause of

financial ruin among the elderly, the young, and the middle-aged. Medicare does not provide this coverage.

Nursing home costs can quickly erode lifetime savings, often causing bankruptcy. Long-term nursing home care costs about $30,000 a year per resident in lower-cost areas. In some parts of the country, these costs run as high as $70,000 to $90,000 a year. For the 1,600,000 Americans living in nursing homes and the estimated 2,500,000 Americans afflicted with Alzheimer's disease, such costs are prohibitive. The only option for many of these Americans is to exhaust all of their resources in order to become eligible for Medicaid.

A large proportion of chronically ill people prefer long-term care at home. Home care services include nursing care, homemaker/home health aide services, medical social services, rehabilitation therapies, medical supplies (other than medications and biologicals), and education, training, and counseling for the patient and caretakers.

Diseases and conditions that often result in a necessity for long-term care in a nursing home or at home include advanced Alzheimer's disease and Parkinson's disease, chronic lung impairment, stroke, long-term cancer, and paralysis due to accident, injury, or disease.

SOURCES OF HEALTH INSURANCE COVERAGE

Health insurance is available from three types of organizations—Blue Cross and Blue Shield, health maintenance organizations (HMOs), and commercial insurance companies.

Blue Cross and Blue Shield

Today, Blue Cross and Blue Shield serve every state and are coordinated through the Blue Cross and Blue Shield Associations. The Blues, as they are sometimes called, protect approximately 67,500,000 people in private and public programs.

Blue Cross plans, initiated in 1929, offer insurance for hospital expenses and have contracts with more than 90 percent of the nation's general, nonfederal, acute-care hospitals. The Blue Shield plans, initiated in 1946, offer insurance covering surgical and general physician expenses and have a working relationship with about 80 percent of the nation's practicing medical doctors.

While commercial insurance carriers provide all forms of health-care protection, Blue Cross and Blue Shield organizations are the pioneers in this type of insurance coverage. The basic goal of these plans has always been to offer high quality, effective, and economical health-care services. Blue Cross and Blue Shield usually return between 85 and 90 percent of premiums paid, making these plans excellent.

Health Maintenance Organizations

Your best coverage can most likely be obtained by joining a health maintenance organization (HMO), if one is operating in your area. *HMOs give you medical care and hospitalization coverage without deductibles or coinsurance.* Everything is prepaid, and there are no out-of-pocket expenses.

An HMO consists of one or more hospitals and a group of doctors and other health-care personnel joined together to provide necessary health maintenance and remedial services to the organization's members. The group practice plans of HMOs offer complete office and hospital care to an optimum number of members for a fixed monthly fee. Because of reduced costs and federal subsidies, the fees are reasonable when compared to those of other forms of health-care delivery systems. HMO members receive all necessary health care, including periodic checkups, X-rays, laboratory tests, mental health treatment, and twenty-four-hour emergency services. No additional fees are paid after the monthly fee has been paid.

The federal government's financial support of health maintenance organizations began in 1973 in an effort to curb the quickly rising costs of health care. The 1973 law as amended in 1976 requires that a company with twenty-five or more workers offer HMO membership as an alternative to any existing health-care program the company might have. The nation's 546 HMOs now have about 47,000,000 members.

The nation's first prepaid health care plan for physician visits and hospitalization was established in 1929 at the Roos-Loos Clinic in Los Angeles. The second was started in the 1930s in the West by Henry Kaiser to care for the workers at his isolated industrial sites. The first HMO-type organization in New York was established in the 1940s. Known as the Health Insurance Plan of Greater New York, or simply HIP, it was designed to provide complete medical services for employees of New York City, which paid the premiums. Currently, it is known officially as HIP/HMO.

The biggest and best known HMO is the Kaiser Foundation Health Plan, which functions in California and five other Western states. This HMO has more than 3,000,000 members, operates its own hospitals, and employs more than 3,000 physicians. The smallest HMOs have only a few staff members, most often internists, obstetricians, and pediatricians. If a member needs the services of another kind of specialist, the HMO will send him or her to one and pay the charges.

The main criticisms of HMOs are that patients have limited choice of doctors, that the relationship between patient and doctor is impersonal, and that the organizations operate on an assembly-line basis. The principal advantage is that the cost of paying for each visit to the doctor is eliminated, thus encouraging people to seek early detection and treatment of disease. It has been estimated that HMO members are admitted to hospitals 30 to 60 percent less often than are nonmembers, helping to reduce overall costs and, presumably, reflecting better health maintenance.

Since 1973, Medicare beneficiaries have been allowed to join health maintenance organizations. Certain HMOs are eligible for Medicare reimbursement. Such eligible organizaitons provide physicians' services; inpatient services; laboratory, X-ray, emergency, and preventive services; and out-of-area coverage.

Commercial Insurance Companies

A large number of commercial insurance companies offer a variety of health insurance plans to fill most buyers' needs. However, as with any purchase you make, you must be a wise and careful shopper. You should study not only the insurance company but also the plan.

Some questions you should ask about the insurance company are:

■ What are the financial resources of this company?

■ How does the company compare in size to other health insurance companies?

■ Does the company enjoy a good reputation?

■ Is it licensed to do business in your state?

■ Does the company pay claims promptly?

■ What is the percentage of premiums that this company returns as benefits to its policyholders? (This is known as the company's *loss ratio*, or *rate of return*.)

You can get some of these answers from your state insurance department, local Better Business Bureau, or *Best's Insurance Reports*, which is available in most public libraries.

Questions you should ask about the insurance plan include the following:

■ What does the plan cover?

■ What expenses and conditions does the plan not cover? (These are known as the plan's *exclusions*.)

■ Is the plan a *service benefit contract* paying a percentage of charges and therefore keeping up with inflation, or an *indemnity benefit contract*, paying fixed dollar amounts?

■ What is the maximum amount that the plan will pay for each service?

■ How does the plan handle conditions that existed before the contract goes into force? (These are known as *pre-existing conditions*.)

You can get some of these answers by studying the policy. The *policy* is the legal contract that sets forth the rights and obligations of both the policyholder and the insurance company.

SPECIAL CONSIDERATIONS FOR RETIREMENT PLANNING

In your retirement planning, you should be aware of special situations related to health insurance coverage. For example, if you are under 65, still working, and not yet covered by Medicare, you must make a special effort to obtain adequate health insurance at a reasonable price. Similarly, if you are 65 through 69 years of age, covered by Medicare, but still working, federal law requires that your employer's health insurance plan be the *primary payer*, with Medicare serving as the *secondary payer*. Finally, if you are retiring and your spouse is under 65, you must make sure that your spouse has adequate health insurance coverage. A discussion of each of these situations follows.

If You Are Under 65 and Still Working

For people under 65 who are still working and not yet covered by Medicare, essential health care coverage includes basic Blue Cross hospitalization insurance, basic medical/surgical insurance, a comprehensive major medical plan to supplement the basic coverage, and disability income insurance if it is offered by your employer or union or if you can afford it on your own.

Most people are offered some degree of health insurance as an employment benefit. Those not so fortunate have a major problem in getting adequate health insurance at a reasonable price. Private coverage purchased by an individual from a commercial insurance company is very expensive. Moreover, most private plans have a deductible and a 20 percent coinsurance provision.

An individual or couple without basic health insurance coverage (hospitalization and medical/surgical protection) should join either an HMO, which will provide full coverage without deductibles or coinsurance, or Blue Cross and Blue Shield, which are nonprofit groups whose premiums reflect actual costs.

If You Are 65 Through 69 and Still Working

If you are age 65 through 69 and still actively employed, the Tax Equity and Fiscal Responsibility Act (TEFRA) changed health insurance coverage for you in 1982. TEFRA amended the Age Discrimination in Employment Act and the Social Security Act in two ways. First, employers of 20 or more people must give 65-and-over workers the same health insurance coverage offered to younger employees and under the same conditions. This is true even for older employees covered by Medicare. To reduce an older employee's benefits in any way is considered age discrimination and is, therefore, illegal.

Second, TEFRA stipulates that Medicare is no longer the insurer of first resort for older employees. Instead, the employer's plan must be the primary payer, with Medicare serving as the secondary payer. An active employee between the ages of 65 and 69 has the right to reject the employer's plan, making Medicare the primary payer with no benefits paid by the employer's plan. However, even though Medicare may be chosen as the secondary payer between ages 65 and 69, it becomes the primary payer at age 70.

These changes, which became effective in 1983, have been saving the federal government hundreds of millions of dollars a year by transferring the primary insurance bill to the private sector.

If You Are Retired and Your Spouse Is Under 65

If you are retiring and your spouse is under age 65, check your employer's health insurance coverage, if it carries over into retirement, to determine whether your spouse will still be covered as a dependent. Most employer group health insurance plans that carry over into retirement continue coverage for the spouse and other eligible dependents. If yours does not, however, you may be able to convert from group coverage to an individual self-pay plan. If not, you may need to purchase individual hospitalization and medical/surgical insurance for your spouse from a commercial carrier. In any case, make sure that your spouse has adequate health insurance.

If You Are a Surviving Spouse

A spouse whose status changes from dependent

to survivor should check the deceased's health insurance coverage to determine whether protection is still in effect. If the coverage terminates, the survivor will need to purchase an individual hospitalization/health insurance plan on a self-pay basis.

COBRA COVERAGE

The *Consolidated Omnibus Budget Reconciliation Act*, known as COBRA (Public Law 99-272), has been in effect since 1986. Under *COBRA*, businesses that have more than twenty employees and offer health insurance must continue coverage at group rates for up to eighteen months for employees who retire, quit, switch from full-time to part-time status, or are laid off. These former employees must pay the full cost of the group insurance plus a 2 percent surcharge to cover administrative expenses.

In addition, companies are required to continue coverage for three years, at a premium rate of 102 percent of the employer's group rate, for an employee's spouse and dependents if the employee dies or becomes entitled to Medicare. COBRA also applies in the event of a legal separation or divorce. Moreover, an employer must offer to provide the same three years' continued coverage to a dependent who reaches the maximum age for dependent coverage. Those eligible have at least sixty days to decide if they want to continue their health insurance protection.

Before COBRA, employees and dependents usually lost their health insurance benefits upon job termination. Similarly, widows, divorcees, and spouses of retired employees who qualified for Medicare also lost their health insurance coverage.

About 38,000,000 men, women, and children in the United States are currently without health insurance; this is 7,000,000 more than in 1980, and the number is growing. These people are predominantly young, poor, and in worse health than the general population. COBRA's purpose is to provide some protection for people who are eligible according to the law. Severe penalties are imposed on employers who fail to meet COBRA requirements.

BASIC ADVICE ON HEALTH INSURANCE

The following six guidelines concerning health insurance should be helpful for people of all ages and employment status:

1. If you are under 65, are still working, and have an individual or group health insurance plan, you should:

   ■ Determine what benefits your coverage will provide when you reach 65 and whether you can carry the coverage over into retirement.

   ■ Consider buying disability income insurance. Most people insure their home, car, and jewelry, but it is their regular income that makes these kinds of amenities possible.

2. Consider purchasing a comprehensive major medical plan to cover both you and your spouse.

3. You should be insured for as many other health-care needs as you can afford, including dental care, prescription medications, optical expenses, and hearing aids.

4. In general, you should avoid mail-order health insurance plans and cancer or other dread disease insurance.

5. Protect your health insurance policies by keeping them in a safe place and letting a close relative or friend know where they are. In a separate place, keep a list of your policy numbers, the companies that issued them,

and the name of your agent, in case the originals are lost.

6. Keep a record of your medical expenditures and reimbursements. This is the only way you can follow up on open items to be sure you receive what you are owed.

In summary, you can never have too much medical insurance. If you don't believe it, ask someone who has recently returned home following an extended hospital stay. People will always tell you about the exorbitant charges for their care.

Self-Study
Checklist for Your Health Insurance

1. To ascertain the gaps in your overall health care coverage, check what you have and what you lack and note whether the coverage you have carries over into retirement.

Type of health-care insurance	Do you have the coverage indicated?		If you are covered, will it carry over into retirement?	
	Yes	No	Yes	No
Hospitalization	❑	❑	❑	❑
Basic medical/surgical	❑	❑	❑	❑
Comprehensive major medical	❑	❑	❑	❑
Disability income	❑	❑	❑	❑
Blood	❑	❑	❑	❑
Dental	❑	❑	❑	❑
Hearing aids	❑	❑	❑	❑
Long-term care	❑	❑	❑	❑
Optical expenses	❑	❑	❑	❑
Prescription medications	❑	❑	❑	❑

2. List the gaps in your present health insurance coverage.

_____

_____

_____

_____

3. List the health insurance coverage you have that will not carry over into retirement.

_____

_____

_____

_____

4. How do you plan to fill the gaps in your retirement health insurance package that you noted in questions 2 and 3 above?

_____

_____

_____

_____

_____

_____

_____

5. You should maintain a record of medical expenditures and reimbursements for yourself and for your spouse and other dependents. The following worksheet shows you what kind of details you should keep track of and provides a convenient form for doing so. If you are not reimbursed within a reasonable period of time, it will show up clearly on this type of record and you can follow up on the claim. The worksheet provides room for keeping track of claims submitted to Medicare, if you are a member, and to one supplementary plan. If you are not covered by Medicare, change that column heading to the name of the coverage you have. If you have additional coverage, such as dental insurance, the form can be expanded by adding columns similar to the two included. You can purchase multi-column worksheet paper in a stationery store to make your own forms.

Record of Medical Expenditures and Reimbursements

Patient_____Year_____

Date of visit or service	Name of doctor, hospital, lab, or other	Illness or treatment	Paid			Medicare				Supplementary policy or other coverage			
			Amt.	Date	Check No.	Claim submitted		Check received		Claim submitted		Check received	
						Date	Amt	Date	Amt	Date	Amt	Date	Amt

Glossary

Basic medical/surgical insurance. A type of health insurance that provides coverage for doctors' visits in and out of the hospital, diagnostic and laboratory tests, and certain surgical procedures.

Blood program. A type of health insurance program that provides unlimited blood credit for members and their eligible relatives in return for a donation of one pint of blood annually. Some of these programs carry over into retirement and help in providing the first three pints of blood not covered by Medicare.

Blue Cross and Blue Shield. Not-for-profit insurance associations that pioneered health insurance coverage. Blue Cross provides hospitalization insurance. Blue Shield provides surgical and general physician expense insurance.

Catastrophic major medical insurance. A type of health insurance that provides compensation for extraordinary medical costs not covered by hospitalization insurance or by basic medical/surgical insurance or comprehensive major medical insurance.

Comprehensive major medical insurance. A type of health insurance that covers the high costs of serious long-term illness, picking up where basic health insurance ends. Some plans have very high deductibles and provide benefits of up to $500,000 or $2,000,000. Other plans provide first-dollar coverage of some health-care services. *See also* Basic medical/surgical insurance; Catastrophic major medical insurance.

Consolidated Omnibus Budget Reconciliation Act (COBRA). A law passed in 1986 that requires businesses that have more than twenty employees and offer health insurance to continue coverage at group rates for up to eighteen months for employees who retire, quit, switch from full-time to part-time status, or are laid off.

Contributory insurance plan. The employer makes a contribution and the employee also contributes some portion of the premium cost that varies from plan to plan.

Dental expense insurance. A type of health insurance that provides coverage for necessary dental care including oral examinations, X-rays, cleanings, fillings, extractions, inlays, crowns, bridgework, dentures (prosthodontics), oral surgery, treatment of gums (periodontics), root canal (endodontics), and teeth alignment (orthodontics).

Disability income insurance. Provides a percentage of your regular income when you are unable to work for an extended period of time because of illness or injury.

Exclusion. An expense or condition that the plan does not cover and toward which it will not pay.

Health maintenance organization (HMO). Any organized system of health care that provides a full range of health maintenance and treatment services to an enrolled population in return for a fixed sum of money agreed upon and paid in advance.

Hospitalization insurance. A type of health insurance that provides coverage for the expenses incurred while you are a patient in a hospital.

Indemnity benefit contract. A health insurance plan that pays fixed dollar amounts and, therefore, may not keep up with inflation. *See also* Service benefit contract.

Long-term care insurance. A type of health insurance that provides coverage for long-term nursing home care and long-term custodial home care.

Loss ratio. The amount an insurance company pays out in benefits compared to how much it collects in premiums.

Noncontributory insurance plan. The employer pays the full premium cost.

Optical expense program. A benefit plan that provides eyeglasses to eligible members and their dependents.

Policy. A legal contract that sets forth the rights and obligations of both the policyholder and the insurance company.

Pre-existing condition. A health condition that existed before the policyholder became insured.

Prescription medication plan. A type of health insurance that provides coverage for all or part of the cost of prescription medications.

Primary payer. The insurance company to which a medical bill is sent for payment first. *See also* Secondary payer.

Rate of return. *See* Loss ratio.

Secondary payer. After the first insurance company (primary payer) pays a benefit, the original bill and an explanation of the payment by the primary payer are sent to another company (the secondary payer) to pay the balance or some portion of the balance. *See also* Primary payer.

Service benefit contract. A health insurance plan that pays a percentage of charges and, therefore, keeps up with inflation. *See also* Indemnity benefit contract.

16

Medicare and Medicaid

Successful retirement depends not only on a sound financial base but also on good health. While the maintenance of good health is a life-long project, older Americans are generally more vulnerable to health problems than younger people. In the 1960s, the government enacted two programs, Medicare and Medicaid, that provide health benefits for the elderly and the poor. This chapter offers a detailed analysis of both of these programs.

MEDICARE

Americans enjoy the comforting thought that starting at age 65, the government pays their medical bills. While it is true that Medicare provides significant amounts of financial assistance and some peace of mind, the program was not designed to cover *all* medical expenses for the elderly. Rather, it was intended to provide *basic* hospital and medical services at the *lowest possible cost*.

In 1965, Congress approved amendments to the Social Security law that, among other things, established the insurance program that became popularly known as Medicare. Along with Medicaid, Medicare was one of the Great Soci-

ety programs enacted that year to provide health benefits to the elderly and the poor. President Lyndon Johnson signed the Medicare-Medicaid bill into law on July 30, 1965, in Independence, Missouri, with former President Harry S. Truman at his side.

Medicare is a federal health insurance program for people 65 or older and for certain disabled people under 65. It is run by the Health Care Financing Administration of the United States Department of Health and Human Services. Social Security Administration offices across the country take applications for Medicare and provide general information about the program.

Medicare is a two-part program. *Part A* provides hospital insurance and *Part B* provides supplementary medical insurance. People who have reached age 65 and are eligible for Social Security benefits, whether or not they are still working, are entitled to Part A coverage without having to pay any *premiums*, or fees. However, they must meet certain deductibles and make coinsurance payments. A *deductible* is an annual maximum amount you must pay on claims before the insurance carrier begins to calculate benefit allowances due to you. *Coinsurance* is the percentage of a covered expense that you are required to pay. Part A of Medicare pays for services received as an inpatient in a hospital, skilled nursing facility, or hospice, and for home health services.

Part B supplementary medical insurance is voluntary, requiring recipients to pay a monthly premium either directly to the Health Care Financing Administration or as a deduction from their monthly Social Security check, if they receive one. After a deductible and *copayments*, which are the specific coinsurance payments, Medicare Part B pays a "reasonable and customary" amount for doctors' services, outpatient hospital services, and specified medical items and services not covered under hospital insurance.

Part A is financed through Social Security taxes paid by people who are still working and by their employers. Part B is financed through premiums paid by Medicare beneficiaries and, in addition, is subsidized by the federal government.

The Catastrophic Coverage Act

Significant changes in Medicare were mandated by the Medicare Catastrophic Coverage Act of 1988. The goal of the act was to protect some 33 million elderly and disabled individuals from "catastrophic" hospital, doctor, and prescription-medication bills. It limited the amount a Medicare beneficiary had to pay for hospital care, physicians' services, medical supplies, and prescription medications. At the same time, the new law expanded coverage for hospital, skilled nursing facility, home health, and hospice care. A *skilled nursing facility* is a nursing home that specializes in the care of patients recovering from an illness or injury. A *hospice* specializes in the care of terminally ill patients. New benefits included breast-cancer screening and out-of-hospital prescription medications.

Some of the new benefits were introduced

on January 1, 1989, while others were scheduled to begin on January 1, 1990. However, in November 1989, Congress repealed the Medicare Catastrophic Coverage Act of 1988 effective January 1, 1990. The repeal represented congressional response to the protests of hundreds of thousands of older Americans who resented having to pay a "seniors only" income tax to help finance a program that duplicated benefits many of them were receiving from their former employers. These older citizens were also angry that the program did not include long-term custodial care either at home or in a nursing facility. *Custodial care*, which is help in meeting personal needs such as bathing and eating, is the primary cause of financial ruin for the elderly. As of January 1, 1990, Medicare benefits reverted to their 1988 status.

However, when Medicare started in 1965, coverage for women was not as complete as it should have been. It excluded mammography and Pap tests. These were recently added to the list of covered procedures. Starting in July 1990, Medicare pays for a Pap test every three years and, effective January 1991, Medicare pays 80 percent of the $55 allowable amount for a screening mammography every two years.

According to the National Cancer Institute and the American Cancer Society, breast cancer incidence rates have increased about one percent each year since the 1970s. Nine percent of the adult female population, or one in every ten American women, will develop breast cancer, which is why medical examinations should not be overlooked. Mammography plays a critical role in detection of breast cancer, and preventive medicine saves lives.

The Costs of Sustaining Medicare

Medicare cost approximately $3.5 billion in 1967. In fiscal year 1993, it cost $142.9 billion—

$90.5 billion for hospital care and $52.4 billion for physicians' services. Despite the cost increase, the Medicare program enjoys strong bipartisan support in Congress. The number of people enrolled in Medicare increased from 19.5 million in 1967 to about 36 million today. The program helps not only the elderly but also many severely disabled people. A 1972 law expanded Medicare to cover disabled people under 65 years of age and people with chronic kidney disease requiring a kidney transplant or dialysis. It is estimated that today, Medicare pays about 48.8 percent of the medical costs of the elderly.

What Medicare does *not* cover, however, can mean financial disaster for the elderly, since they spend three times more for health care than younger people do. Present and future beneficiaries should, therefore, clearly understand who is eligible for Medicare, what Medicare does and does not provide, how to collect benefits, and what additional insurance is needed for maximum protection.

Eligibility for Medicare

More than 98 percent of the nation's 33 million elderly and disabled are covered by Medicare. Ineligible individuals may receive Part A and Part B Medicare benefits by paying monthly premiums—$261 for Part A and $46.10 for Part B for the 1995 calendar year. People are not eligible if they have reached age 65 without becoming eligible for Social Security retirement benefits. This includes individuals who have not been credited with a sufficient number of quarters of coverage, as well as noncitizens and people convicted of particular crimes. (For a full discussion of Social Security and its terminology, see Chapter 7.) Federal employees, originally ineligible for the Medicare program, have been eligible since January 1983.

Enrollment in Medicare

Enrollment in Medicare Parts A and B is automatic upon application for monthly Social Security benefits. You should apply for Medicare separately if you plan to continue working past age 65. You can do this at your nearest Social Security office about three months prior to turning 65. If you retire before age 65 and file an application for Social Security benefits, you do not have to file a separate application for Medicare.

Medicare coverage becomes effective the month you reach 65, even if you elect to begin receiving Social Security retirement benefits at age 62. When you apply for Social Security benefits or enroll in Medicare, you have the option of turning down Part B coverage. If you retire at age 65 and decline Part B coverage at that time, you will have to pay higher Part B premiums if you decide later to enroll. The penalty for late enrollment in Part B is a 10 percent increase in premiums for each twelve-month period in which you could have been enrolled but were not. If you have Medicare hospital insurance but not the medical insurance, you can sign up for the medical insurance during the general enrollment period. The general enrollment period is the same every year—January 1 through March 31. Your protection will begin the following July 1. For more information about obtaining the part of Medicare you do not have, contact your Social Security office.

If you continue working past age 65 and remain covered by an employer's group health-insurance plan, you may wait to enroll in Part B without penalty until either age 70 or retirement, whichever comes first.

If your spouse is under age 65 but already receiving Social Security benefits, his or her Medicare coverage will begin automatically at 65. A spouse not yet receiving Social Security benefits should file an application for Medicare at the nearest Social Security office three months before reaching age 65.

Medicare Benefits

The services and supplies covered under Medicare as well as the *benefit periods*, or periods of time during which the services and supplies are covered, vary for Part A and Part B. They also vary for the different types of care facilities covered in Part A. A detailed description of the benefits, benefit periods, and deductibles follows. For a quick review, see Table 16.1.

The following alphabetical list shows most of the major services and supplies usually *not* covered by Medicare. The items with an asterisk may be covered by Medicare under certain conditions.

- Acupuncture.
- Chiropractic services.*
- Christian Science practitioners' services.
- Cosmetic surgery.*
- Custodial care.
- Dental care.*
- Eyeglasses and eye examinations.
- Foot care that is routine.*
- Hearing aids and hearing examinations.
- Homemaker services.*
- Immunizations.*
- Injections that you can self-administer, such as insulin.
- Long-term care (nursing homes).
- Meals delivered to your home.
- Medications you buy yourself.*
- Naturopaths' services.
- Nursing care on full-time basis in your home.
- Orthopedic shoes.
- Personal items in hospital room such as telephone or television.
- Physical examinations such as annual checkup.
- Private duty nurses.
- Private room.
- Services payable by another government program.
- Services performed by relatives or members of your household.
- Services provided outside the United States.*
- Services that are not reasonable or necessary.

For information on the conditions under which the items with an asterisk are covered by Medicare, call your regional office of the Health Care Financing Administration.

MEDICARE HOSPITAL INSURANCE

Medicare hospital insurance (Part A) provides four types of benefits—inpatient hospital coverage, skilled nursing facility coverage after a hospital stay, home health care coverage, and hospice care coverage. It will pay for most but not all of the services you receive in a hospital, skilled nursing facility, or hospice, and for most home health services. *Covered services* are services and supplies for which Part A will pay. *Noncovered services* are services and supplies for which you must pay yourself.

The unit of measure used to keep track of consumption of services under Medicare hospital insurance is the benefit period. A *benefit period* starts the day you enter a hospital and is a maximum of 90 days long. In addition to the 90-day benefit periods, you are given a lifetime allotment of 60 *reserve days* to be used for hospital confinements of more than 90 days.

Table 16.1
Medicare Facts

	1995	1994
Part A premium[a]	$261/month	$225/month
Part B premium	$46.10/month	$41.10/month
Part B deductible	$100/year	$100/year
Part B coinsurance	20%	20%
A. *Hospital*		
Day 1 in hospital	$716	$696
Days 2–60	No charge	No charge
Days 61–90	$179/day	$174/day
Days 91–150 if you use 60 lifetime reserve days	$358/day	$348/day
Beyond day 150, or after day 90 if all 60 *reserve days* have been used	All charges	All charges
B. *Skilled nursing facility*	100 days after a minimum of 3 days in a hospital	
Days 1–20	No charge	No charge
Days 21–100	$89.50/day	$87.00/day
C. *Home health care if homebound*	Unlimited number of medically necessary home health visits or physical therapy, provided a doctor sets up the home health plan.	
D. *Hospice care*	210 days lifetime limit if the patient is certified as terminally ill and chooses to receive care in a Medicare certified hospice.	

[a] Persons age 65 who are not eligible for Medicare may enroll for Part A benefits by paying the monthly cost of coverage. Such individuals include noncitizens of the United States, people convicted of particular crimes, and those with insufficient quarters of coverage.

Once you have used up your 60 reserve days, your benefit periods are limited to the basic 90 days. There is no limit to the number of 90-day benefit periods you can have, but in order to be eligible for a new benefit period, you must have been out of the hospital for *60 consecutive days*.

If, after a hospital confinement of more than 3 days, you need additional care, Part A provides 100 days of skilled nursing facility benefits for each benefit period. These 100 days are in addition to the 90 days of hospital benefits. When you have been out of a skilled nursing facility for *60 consecutive days*, you are eligible to begin a new benefit period.

The covered services and benefit periods as well as the deductibles vary for each type of benefit.

Inpatient Hospital Care

Medicare hospital insurance will pay for inpatient hospital care if *all four* of the following conditions are met:

1. A doctor prescribes inpatient hospital care for treatment of your illness or injury.
2. You require the kind of care that can be provided only in a hospital.
3. The hospital is a Medicare participant.
4. The utilization review committee of the hospital or a peer review organization does not disapprove your stay. (For a full discussion of peer review organizations, see page 237.)

Covered Services

When you are an inpatient in a Medicare-approved hospital, the following services are covered:

■ A semiprivate room (a room with two to four beds).

■ All your meals, including special diets.

■ Regular nursing services.

■ Special care units, such as intensive care and coronary care.

■ Medications furnished by the hospital for use during your stay.

■ Blood transfusions after the first three pints.

■ Laboratory tests.

■ X-rays and other radiology services, including radiation therapy.

■ Medical supplies such as casts, surgical dressings, and splints.

■ Appliances such as wheelchairs.

■ Operating room and recovery room, including anesthesia services.

■ Rehabilitation services such as physical, occupational, and speech therapy.

Noncovered Services

The following hospital services are not covered by Medicare Part A:

■ Doctors' fees. (These fees are covered by Medicare Part B.)

■ Private duty nurses.

■ Personal convenience items in your room such as a television, radio, or telephone.

■ A private room, unless it is determined to be medically necessary.

Deductibles

You are entitled to receive up to 90 days of inpatient care in a Medicare-participating hospital during each benefit period. A *participating hospital* is a facility that accepts Medicare. For the first 60 days of a benefit period, Medicare pays for all covered services after the first $716

(1995 amount). This deductible is increased annually. For days 61 through 90, Medicare pays for all covered expenses except for $179 a day (1995 amount).

Up to all 60 reserve days can be used in one benefit period. Each reserve day you use permanently reduces your total number of lifetime reserve days. For every reserve day, Medicare pays for all covered services except for $358 a day (1995 amount).

After day 90 of the benefit period and if all reserve days have been used, you must pay all charges while Medicare pays nothing.

Psychiatric Hospitals

Medicare hospital insurance will not pay for more than 190 days of care in participating psychiatric hospitals in your lifetime. Once you have used your 190-day allotment, Part A will not pay for any further care in any psychiatric hospital.

Foreign Hospitals

Medicare generally cannot pay for hospital or medical services outside the United States. Along with the fifty states and the District of Columbia, the following are considered part of the United States—Puerto Rico, the United States Virgin Islands, Guam, American Samoa, and the Northern Mariana Islands. However, Medicare can help pay for care in a qualified Canadian or Mexican hospital if you are in one of the following three situations:

1. You are in the United States when an emergency occurs and a Canadian or Mexican hospital that can provide the care you need is closer than the nearest United States hospital.

2. You live in the United States but a Canadian or Mexican hospital is closer to your home than the nearest United States hospital and can provide the care you need, regardless of whether or not an emergency exists.

3. You are in Canada traveling by the most direct route to or from Alaska and an emergency occurs that requires you to be admitted to a Canadian hospital.

Skilled Nursing Facility Care

Medicare hospital insurance will pay for inpatient care in a skilled nursing facility if your condition requires daily skilled nursing or rehabilitation services that, as a practical matter, can be provided only in a skilled nursing facility. A *skilled nursing facility* is a specially qualified facility with the staff and equipment to provide skilled nursing care or rehabilitation services and other related health services.

To be eligible for care in a skilled nursing facility, *both* of the following conditions must be met:

1. A doctor certifies that you need skilled nursing or skilled rehabilitation services on a daily basis and then you actually receive them.

2. The Medicare intermediary or the facility's utilization review committee does not disapprove your stay.

Covered Services

When you are in a Medicare-approved skilled nursing facility, the following services are covered:

■ A semiprivate room (a room with two to four beds).

■ All your meals, including special diets.

■ Regular nursing services.

■ Medications furnished by the facility for use during your stay.

- Blood transfusions after the first three pints.
- Medical supplies such as casts and splints.
- Appliances such as wheelchairs.
- Rehabilitation services such as physical, occupational, and speech therapy.

Noncovered Services

The following skilled nursing facility services are not covered by Medicare Part A:

- Doctors' fees. (These fees are covered by Medicare Part B.)
- Private duty nurses.
- Personal convenience items in your room such as a television, radio, or telephone.
- A private room, unless it is determined to be medically necessary.
- Custodial nursing home care services for persons with chronic, long-term illnesses or disabilities.

Deductibles

You are entitled to receive up to 100 days of care in a Medicare-participating skilled nursing facility during each benefit period. Medicare pays all covered services for the first 20 days. For days 21 through 100 of continuous confinement, you pay $89.50 a day (1995 amount) and Medicare pays the balance. After day 100, you must pay all costs and Medicare pays nothing.

Home Health Care

If you need part-time skilled health care in your home for the treatment of an illness or injury, Medicare will pay for covered home health visits furnished by a participating home health agency. A *home health agency* is a public or private agency that specializes in giving skilled nursing services and other therapeutic services such as physical therapy in your home.

To be eligible for home health care, *all four* of the following conditions must be met:

1. The care you need includes intermittent skilled nursing care, physical therapy, or speech therapy.
2. You are confined to your home.
3. A doctor determines that you need home health care and sets up a home health plan for you.
4. The home health agency is a Medicare participant.

Covered Services

The following services provided by an approved home health agency are covered:

- Part-time or intermittent skilled nursing care.
- Physical therapy.
- Speech therapy.

In addition, if any of the above services are required, Medicare also pays for:

- Occupational therapy.
- Part-time or intermittent service by home health aides.
- Medical social services.
- Medical supplies and equipment provided by the agency.

Noncovered Services

The following services are not covered by Medicare Part A:

- Full-time nursing care at home.

■ Medications and biologicals.

■ Meals delivered to your home.

■ Homemaker services.

■ Blood transfusions.

Deductibles

Medicare pays the full approved cost of all covered home health care visits. You pay nothing. However, you may be charged for noncovered services and supplies. The home health agency will submit the claim for covered items to Medicare. You are not required to send in any bills yourself.

Hospice Care

Under the Tax Equity and Fiscal Responsibility Act of 1982, Medicare coverage was extended to hospice care services. A *hospice* is a facility, usually a home, that provides pain relief and supportive services for terminally ill patients. Hospice care in a patient's home provides nurses, medication, home helpers, counseling, and other assistance for terminally ill patients. Hospice care emphasizes relief of pain and suffering as opposed to hospital technology and cures.

Respite care is a short-term inpatient hospital stay that may be necessary for the patient in order to give temporary relief to the *caretaker*, who is the person who takes care of the at-home patient. Each inpatient respite-care stay is limited to five consecutive days.

To be eligible for hospice or respite care, *all three* of the following conditions must be met:

1. A doctor certifies that you are terminally ill.

2. You choose to receive care from a hospice instead of taking the standard Medicare benefits for terminal illness.

3. The hospice program is a Medicare participant.

Covered Services

When you are in a Medicare-approved hospice program, the following services are covered:

■ Doctors' services.

■ Nursing services.

■ Medications for pain relief and symptom management.

■ Physical therapy, occupational therapy, and speech-language pathology.

■ Home health aide and homemaker services.

■ Medical social services.

■ Medical supplies and appliances.

■ Short-term inpatient care including respite care.

■ Counseling.

Deductibles

Special benefit periods apply to hospice care. Medicare hospital insurance pays for a maximum of two 90-day periods and one 30-day period, which combine for a lifetime maximum of 210 days. During a hospice benefit period, Medicare pays the full cost of all covered services for the terminal illness. The only deductibles and copayments are for part of the cost of outpatient medications and for part of the cost of inpatient respite care. While receiving hospice care, if a patient requires treatment for a condition not related to the terminal illness, Medicare continues to help pay for all necessary covered services under the standard benefit program.

The Role of Peer Review Organizations

Peer review organizations (PROs) are groups of

practicing doctors and other health care professionals paid by the federal government to review the hospital care of Medicare patients. Each state has a PRO to help Medicare decide whether care is reasonable and necessary, is provided in an appropriate setting, and meets the accepted standards of the medical profession. PROs have the authority to deny payments if those conditions are not met. PROs also respond to requests for review of hospital notices of noncoverage issued to beneficiaries. In addition, they respond to hospital requests for reconsideration of PRO decisions and investigate individual patient complaints. If you are admitted to a Medicare-participating hospital, you will receive "An Important Message From Medicare," which explains your rights as a hospital patient and provides the name, address, and phone number of the PRO for your state.

If you feel that you have been improperly refused admission to a hospital or that you are being forced to leave the hospital too soon, ask for a written explanation of the decision. Medicare regulations require that a notice fully explain how you can appeal the decision and give the name, address, and phone number of the PRO to which you can submit your appeal or request for review.

Your Hospital Rights Under Medicare

Whether you go to a hospital emergency room on your own or are taken there by ambulance, the hospital must do certain things for you. The hospital is required by law to:

1. **Provide a medical screening examination** to determine if an emergency medical condition exists.

2. **Provide stabilizing treatment** to any individual with an emergency medical condition or any woman in active labor prior to transfer of the patient to another facility.

If a patient cannot be stabilized, he or she can be transferred to another hospital *only*:

■ If the responsible physician certifies in writing that the benefits of the transfer outweigh the risks.

■ If the receiving hospital has space and personnel to treat the patient and has agreed to accept the patient.

■ If the transferring hospital sends medical records along with the patient.

■ If the transfer is made in appropriate transportation with life support equipment if necessary.

Medicare Patient Bill of Rights

Medicare beneficiaries have complained that they were discharged from hospitals "too quick and too sick" because of pressures on hospitals to cut costs. Elderly patients are sometimes told by hospitals that their Medicare benefits have run out, and they are forced to leave before they are well. As a result, the Health Care Financing Administration of the United States Department of Health and Human Services has set up a "Medicare Patient Bill of Rights," which provides Medicare patients with a clear understanding of their rights when they are hospitalized.

Under the "Medicare Patient Bill of Rights," you have the following rights as a Medicare hospital patient:

■ *The right to proper care.* You have a right to receive all of the hospital care that is necessary for the proper diagnosis and treatment of your illness or injury. Your discharge date should be determined solely by your medical needs, not by Medicare payments.

■ *The right to information.* You have the right to be fully informed by the hospital about decisions affecting your Medicare coverage and the length of your stay.

■ *The right to appeal.* If the hospital wants to discharge you too soon, you have the right to appeal the decision to your local peer review organization. You cannot be dismissed before your appeal decision is made.

This "Medicare Patient Bill of Rights" is in force in hospitals throughout the country.

MEDICARE MEDICAL INSURANCE

Medicare medical insurance (Part B) helps pay for doctors' services—those of your regular doctor, as well as those you might need in a hospital such as anesthesiology, radiology, and pathology. Medicare medical insurance can also help pay for outpatient hospital care and certain medical services and supplies not covered under hospital insurance.

Medicare medical insurance payments for covered services or supplies are based upon approved, or reasonable, charges, not on your doctor's or supplier's actual, or current, charges. An *approved charge* is an amount set by the Medicare carrier in your area and based primarily on the customary charge in your locale for the service or supply in question. *Customary charges* are the fees that were most frequently charged by doctors and suppliers for specific services and supplies during the previous calendar year. *Actual charges* are the actual fees charged and are most often considerably higher. You must pay the full amount of all charges in excess of Medicare's approved allowance. In addition, every calendar year, you must pay as a deductible the first $100 (1995 amount) of approved charges. After you have met the deductible, Medicare pays 80 percent of the approved charge and you pay the remaining 20 percent, which is known as the *Part B coinsurance.*

Medical Insurance Payments

There are two ways in which Medicare medical insurance payments are made.

1. **Assignment Method.** When the *assignment method* is used, the doctor or supplier agrees that his or her total charge for the covered service will not be more than the charge approved by the Medicare carrier. Medicare pays your doctor or supplier 80 percent of the approved charge, first subtracting any part of the $100 deductible you have not yet met. The doctor or supplier can charge you *only* for the part of the $100 deductible (1995 amount) you have not met and for the coinsurance, which is the remaining 20 percent of the approved charge. Your doctor or supplier also can charge you for any services that Medicare does not cover.

2. **Payment-to-You Method.** The *payment-to-you method* is used if your doctor does not accept Medicare assignment. Under this method, the doctor bills you for his or her actual charge, which you pay. You or the doctor then submits a claim to your Medicare carrier, which decides on the approved charge for the service or supply. The carrier pays you 80 percent of the approved charge, first subtracting whatever part of the deductible remains.

An American Medical Association survey of payment methods in 1985 indicates that only 37.2 percent of patient-care physicians accept Medicare assignment 100 percent of the time. Whether your physician does or does not and no matter what payment method is used, Medicare will send you an "Explanation of Medicare Benefits." This notice shows which services are covered, what charges are approved, how much is credited toward your

$100 deductible, and how much Medicare has paid. You have the right to ask the carrier for a review of the decision.

Coverage

Medicare medical insurance covers some doctors' services but not all. Following is a list of services that are covered and a list of services that are not.

Covered Services

Medicare medical insurance covers the following services:

■ Medical and surgical services, including anesthesia.

■ Diagnostic tests and procedures that are part of your treatment.

■ Radiology and pathology services while you are a hospital inpatient or outpatient.

■ Services that are ordinarily furnished in a doctor's office and included in his or her bill, such as:

- X-rays that you receive as part of your treatment.
- The services of your doctor's office nurse.
- Medications and biologicals that cannot be self-administered.
- Transfusions of blood and blood components.
- Medical supplies.
- Physical therapy, occupational therapy, and speech pathology services.

Noncovered Services

Medicare medical insurance does not cover the following services:

■ Routine physical examinations and tests directly related to them.

■ Routine foot care.

■ Eye or hearing examinations for prescribing or fitting eyeglasses or hearing aids.

■ Immunizations except pneumococcal vaccinations or immunizations required because of an injury, immediate risk of infection, or increased risk of contracting hepatitis B.

■ Cosmetic surgery unless it is needed because of accidental injury or to improve the functioning of a malformed part of the body.

■ Dental care.

■ Services received outside of the United States.

■ Acupuncture.

■ Chiropractic services.

■ Christian Science practitioners' services.

■ Custodial care.

■ Medications that you buy with or without a doctor's prescription.

■ Homemaker services.

■ Injections that can be self-administered, such as insulin.

MEDIGAP

Medicare was never designed to cover the first-dollar costs of basic health-care services. From the outset, it usually paid about half the charges incurred, requiring the recipient of the services to pay the balance. These out-of-pocket expenses are referred to as *gaps*. Medigap coverage is discussed in detail in Chapter 17.

BASIC ADVICE ON MEDICARE

The following eight suggestions should guide you in your acquisition and use of Medicare:

1. Apply for Medicare coverage at your local Social Security office at least three months before your sixty-fifth birthday to make sure your benefits start on time.

2. Be sure to purchase Medicare medical insurance (Part B). It requires that you pay a monthly premium, but it is one of the best buys available.

3. Buy Medigap insurance, which pays for the gaps in Medicare coverage. A Medigap policy will reduce your out-of-pocket costs (see Chapter 17). If you can afford it, comprehensive major medical insurance is even better (see Chapter 15). *Comprehensive major medical insurance* provides coverage for the same types of services covered under basic health insurance plans—hospital, medical, and surgical—picking up where the basic protection ends.

4. In addition to subscribing to Medicare and Medigap insurance, set up a health emergency fund to cover out-of-pocket expenses connected with illness.

5. When shopping for Medigap insurance, compare the benefits of at least three companies to be sure that you get the specific coverage you want. Avoid policies with confusing language.

6. Avoid exploitive salespeople seeking to sell you coverage that you do not need or cannot afford. If you are in doubt about a policy or salesperson, contact your State Insurance Commissioner.

7. When visiting a physician or surgeon, do not hesitate to ask about the fees and how they are to be paid. If you think the fees are too high, check with other physicians or surgeons.

8. If your spouse is under 65 and dependent, be sure that he or she has adequate coverage for hospitalization and medical care (see Chapter 15). The coverage should be at least equal to the protection of Medicare Part A and Part B.

MEDICAID

Medicaid is a public-assistance program designed to provide benefits to people who are unable to pay for health care. The official name of Medicaid is *Medical Assistance*. While it has special provisions for persons 65 or older, Medicaid helps anyone in need of medical services they cannot afford.

Medicaid is part of the Social Security law, Title 19. This portion of the law provides for aid by local welfare departments to cover medical expenses of people who are unable to pay for such needed care. The program is financed primarily by the federal government. For its first full year of operation in 1967, Medicaid cost about $1.5 billion. The cost for 1993 was $102 billion for services to 33.4 million recipients.

Medicaid is administered as part of state or local welfare departments. Each state designs its own program in accordance with federal guidelines. With the exception of Arizona, all the states as well as the District of Columbia, Puerto Rico, and the Virgin Islands have Medicaid programs. A retired person who cannot afford the premium for Part B of Medicare and the additional expense of Medigap insurance should apply for Medicaid. Welfare no longer has the stigma it once had. However, finding where to apply might give you some problems. Your best first step is to contact your local welfare office, Red Cross office, or Social Security office, all of which are listed in the phone book. Or contact your representative in the local or state legislature.

Eligibility

Your local welfare office can tell you the qualifications for Medicaid. Basically, people earning low incomes meet the test. While for Medicare you must be age 65 to qualify, Medicaid covers people of all ages, including the 65-or-older group, some of whom are already receiving welfare benefits. Also eligible are the blind, the disabled, and members of low-income families, both adults and children.

Even though your income may fall within the limits prescribed by your state, the agency will check your savings account and assets. Most states permit you to keep some savings as a reserve and still consider you eligible for Medicaid.

If you are eligible, the welfare department will give you an identification card that you can use to get the medical services you need. The state's administrative agency will pay the doctors, pharmacists, and others who serve you. Simply present your card in advance of receiving the service to be sure that the fees set by the state are acceptable to the supplier.

A unique aspect of the Medicaid law is that adult children have been relieved of the legal responsibility for their parents' medical expenses. Even though your grown children may have provided financial assistance or are currently able to help you, this does not affect your eligibility for Medicaid. However, husbands and wives are still legally responsible for each other and must contribute to each other's support.

Covered Services

If a person is eligible for both Medicare and Medicaid, then Medicaid will cover all the gaps and deductible charges of Medicare. In many states, Medicaid pays for such additional services as dental care, prescription medication, eyeglasses, clinic services, intermediate care facility services, and other diagnostic, screening, and rehabilitative services.

Advice on Medicaid

If you need the financial support offered by Medicaid, apply for it. There is no shame in having inadequate resources. All levels of government are striving to fill people's needs and are available to process your application. With the costs of health care as high as they are and still rising, it is virtually impossible for an individual or family to cope with the expense of a catastrophic illness. If your income is low and you need financial support to cover the costs of an illness, you should apply as soon as the need arises.

Self Study
Your Medicare Coverage and Its Major Gaps

1. To obtain Medicare coverage, you must apply for it about three months before your sixty-fifth birthday unless you are already receiving Social Security checks. Medicare is not assigned to you automatically. To help you remember when to apply, write your sixty-fifth birthday below:

Month_____ Day_____ Year_____

Write the date that is three months before your sixty-fifth birthday:

Month_____ Day_____ Year_____

Visit your local Social Security office on or before the date that is three months before your sixty-fifth birthday to make your application for Medicare coverage. Failure to apply will cause coverage problems, including a 10 percent increase in your Part B premium.

2. If you already are a member of Medicare, write your claim number below:

_____

Write the effective dates of your Part A and Part B coverage:

Part A—Hospital insurance _____

Part B—Medical insurance _____

Glossary

Actual charge. The fee billed by the doctor or supplier. Also known as the current charge. *See also* Approved charge; Customary charge; Prevailing charge.

Approved charge. When a medical insurance claim is submitted, the carrier compares the actual charge shown on the claim with the customary charge and prevailing charge for that service or supply. The charge approved by the carrier will be whichever of the three is the lowest. Also known as the reasonable charge. *See also* Actual charge; Customary charge; Prevailing charge.

Assignment method. Method of payment in which the doctor or supplier agrees that his or her total charge for the covered service will not be more than the approved charge. The doctor or supplier can charge you only for the part of the deductible you have not yet met and for the coinsurance. *See also* Payment to you method.

Benefit period. The unit of measure used to keep track of consumption of services under Medicare hospital insurance. The benefit periods vary in length for the different facilities involved.

Coinsurance. The percentage of a covered expense that you are required to pay. With Medicare Part B, you pay 20 percent of the approved charge; the insurer pays 80 percent. *See also* Copayment.

Copayment. The specific dollar amount of an approved charge that you must pay. *See also* Coinsurance.

Covered services. Services and supplies for which Medicare will pay. *See also* Noncovered services.

Current charge. *See* Actual charge.

Custodial care. Help in meeting personal needs such as walking, getting in and out of bed, bathing, dressing, eating, and taking medication. Custodial care can be provided by persons without professional skills or training and is not covered by Medicare.

Customary charge. The fee that was most frequently charged by doctors and suppliers during the previous calendar year for specific services and supplies furnished to patients. *See also* Actual charge; Approved charge; Prevailing charge.

Deductible. The annual amount you must pay toward claims before the insurance carrier begins to calculate benefit allowances due to you.

Gaps. Out-of-pocket expenses, including deductibles and copayments.

Home health agency. A public or private agency that specializes in giving skilled nursing services and other therapeutic services such as physical therapy in patients' homes.

Hospice. A program through which a terminally ill patient is provided with pain relief and supportive services, either as an inpatient or at home.

Medigap insurance. A form of supplemental major medical insurance that covers some or all of the gaps in Medicare coverage.

Noncovered services. Services and supplies for which Medicare will not pay and you must pay yourself. *See also* Covered services.

Participating supplier. A physician, facility, or other supplier that accepts Medicare insurance.

Payment-to-you method. The method of payment in which the doctor or supplier bills you for his or her actual charge. You pay the bill, then you or your doctor submits a claim to your Medicare carrier, which decides on the approved charge for the service or supply and reimburses you 80 percent. *See also* Assignment method.

Peer review organization (PRO). Groups of practicing doctors and other health-care professionals paid by the federal government to review the hospital care of Medicare patients.

Reasonable charge. *See* Approved charge.

Reserve days. A lifetime allotment of 60 extra days for use to lengthen benefit periods for hospital confinements of more than 90 days.

Respite care. A short-term stay in a hospital of a hospice patient in order to give temporary relief to the person who regularly assists with the home care.

Skilled nursing facility. A specially qualified facility with the staff and equipment to provide skilled nursing care or rehabilitation services and other related health services.

17

Medigap and Long-Term Care Coverage

Medicare was not designed to cover the entire health care bill for the elderly. At the beginning, the gaps left by Medicare were small, and the premiums for supplemental policies were low. But as health care costs escalated, the gaps widened. Currently, Medicare supplement insurance has become a major expenditure of older Americans. About 80 percent of all Medicare beneficiaries own a supplemental policy.

One major gap in Medicare and Medicare supplement policies is long-term care, or custodial care. Senior citizens without long-term care insurance coverage are leaving themselves open to the loss of all their assets accumulated over a lifetime of work and saving if they have to enter a nursing home. Private insurance companies offer long-term care insurance to protect the elderly from such a catastrophe. The cost for such insurance is relatively high.

MEDICARE GAPS

Medicare provides basic coverage for hospital and medical expenses, but the huge gaps in coverage must be paid by the insured. Medicare recipients are responsible for paying the annual hospital and medical deductibles, which keep rising every year. The Part A hospital deductible has risen from $160 in 1979 to $716 in 1995. The Part B medical care deductible is $100 in 1995, and the insured is also responsible for the 20 percent coinsurance payment on Part B medical bills.

Medicare has other serious gaps. Hospital coverage can run out after a fixed number of days, leaving the patient exposed to significant financial liability in case of a serious illness. Medicare covers 90 days of hospitalization plus 60 *lifetime reserve days*. Therefore, for a first hospitalization, Medicare covers up to 150 days. You will then have used up your 60 lifetime reserve days. Medicare will cover 90 days of hospitalization (see page 234 for more information) for subsequent hospital stays. And if a physician charges more than the approved Medicare allowance for a particular procedure, the patient must pay the difference as well as the coinsurance. Medicare does not pay for any prescription drugs for outpatients and does not cover preventive medical care.

MEDIGAP INSURANCE: COVERING MEDICARE GAPS

Because of gaps in Medicare coverage, seniors are encouraged to supplement their Medicare coverage with an additional policy that pays all or part of the additional costs. This coverage is referred to as a *Medigap policy*, which is private commercial insurance.

In 1990, Congress passed a law requiring states to standardize Medicare supplement policies. It delegated the National Association of Insurance Commissioners (NAIC) to develop ten standardized Medicare supplement benefit policies. The ten plans developed by NAIC became effective July 1992 and are identified by letters A through J. Each state insurance department then decided which of the ten policies would be available for sale in that state.

Insurance companies in each state now offer only the prescribed plans. They must use the standardized designations (See Table 17.1) for the ten different plans, and the states are not allowed to change the combinations of benefits in any of the standard policies. This eliminates the confusion that previously existed in this insurance policy market.

Individual states may limit the number of plans for sale within their borders to fewer than ten, but every state that adopts the new regulations must approve the sale of Plan A, which offers certain basic minimum benefits. Those few states whose own standardized policy regulations predated the new federal law may retain their regulations if granted a waiver by the Secretary of Health and Human Services. These states must, however, offer the same basic minimum benefits in their benefit packages.

To determine the standardized policies available in your state, you should contact your state insurance department. The new regulations do not apply to Medigap policies in force before the requirements took effect in a particular state. Anyone owning such a policy does not have to switch to a new standard policy, but it's probably a good idea to do so. If you have such a policy, you should contact your insurance company to find out your options.

Core Benefits

Table 17.1 specifies the different benefits of each of the ten standard Medigap plans. All Medigap policies supplement Medicare benefits and all ten plans offer the same core benefits. These benefits pay the patient's 20 percent share of Medicare's approved amount for physician's services after the $100 annual deductible. Also covered is the patient's cost of a long hospital stay. (For 1995, a patient covered by Medicare will spend $179 a day for days 61 through 90, $358 a day for days 91 through 150, and all approved costs not paid by Medicare after day 150 to a total of 365 days lifetime.) Charges for the first three pints of blood, which are not covered by Medicare, are also part of the core benefits.

Additional Benefits

Additional benefits, as they appear in Table 17.1, include coverage for:

■ *Skilled nursing care.* This coverage in a skilled nursing facility pays the coinsurance amount (in 1995, $89.50 per day for days 21 through 100 per benefit period.) A *benefit period* starts when you enter a hospital and has a 90-day maximum. There is no limit on the number of 90-day benefit periods, but to be eligible for each benefit period, you must have been out of the

Table 17.1
The Medigap Guide: The Ten Standard Medicare Supplement Benefit Plans

Core Benefits	Plan A	Plan B	Plan C	Plan D	Plan E	Plan F	Plan G	Plan H	Plan I	Plan J
Part A Hospital (Days 61–90)	X	X	X	X	X	X	X	X	X	X
Lifetime Reserve (Days 91–150)	X	X	X	X	X	X	X	X	X	X
365 Life Hospital Days—100%	X	X	X	X	X	X	X	X	X	X
Parts A and B Blood	X	X	X	X	X	X	X	X	X	X

Additional Benefits	A	B	C	D	E	F	G	H	I	J
Skilled Nursing Facility Coinsurance (Days 21–100)			X	X	X	X	X	X	X	X
Part A Deductible		X	X	X	X	X	X	X	X	X
Part B Deductible			X			X				X
Part B Excess Charges						100%	80%		100%	100%
Foreign Travel Emergency			X	X	X	X	X	X	X	X
At-Home Recovery				X					X	X
Prescription Drugs								1	1	2
Preventive Medical Care					X					X

1 Coverage for 50 percent of the cost of prescription drugs up to a maximum annual benefit of $1,250. There is an annual $250 deductible.
2 Coverage for 50 percent of the cost of prescription drugs up to a maximum annual benefit of $3,000. There is an annual $250 deductible.

Source: US Department of Health and Human Services. *Guide to Health Insurance for People with Medicare.*

hospital for 60 consecutive days (see page 235 for additional information).

■ *Medicare Part A deductible.* The Medicare Part A inpatient deductible (in 1995, $716 per benefit period).

■ *Medicare Part B deductible.* The Medicare Part B deductible (in 1995, $100 per calendar year).

■ *Percentage of Part B excess charges.* This coverage pays either 100 percent or 80 percent of Medicare Part B excess charges. Excess charges are doctor's actual charges that are greater than Medicare's approved or reasonable charge. The amount that is above the approved charge is the excess charge, which is an out-of-pocket cost to the patient.

■ *Emergency care in a foreign country.* This coverage pays medically necessary emergency care when you are traveling in a foreign country.

■ *At-home recovery.* This benefit pays up to

$1,600 per year for short-term, at-home assistance with such activities of daily living (ADLs) as bathing and dressing for those recovering from surgery, illness, or an injury.

■ *Prescription drug option 1.* This benefit pays 50 percent of the cost of prescription drugs up to a maximum annual benefit of $1,250 after a $250 annual deductible.

■ *Prescription drug option 2.* This benefit pays 50 percent of the cost of prescription drugs up to a maximum annual benefit of $3,000 after a $250 annual deductible.

■ *Preventive medical care.* This benefit pays up to $120 per year for such things as flu shots, diabetes screenings, and physical checkups.

Cost of a Medigap policy

The cost of a Medigap policy depends on the carrier and where you live. The basic core benefits for Plan A cost about $400 a year while Plan J, the most comprehensive coverage, may cost $2,000 a year. Plan J includes coverage for preventive medical care and for 50 percent of the cost of prescription drugs up to a maximum annual benefit of $3,000 after a $250 annual deductible. Like all health care costs, these premiums are likely to increase annually.

When deciding what coverage to buy, you should evaluate the cost of the insurance versus the risk you are willing to take. If you can afford any of the additional benefits beyond the basic core coverage, you may not need to pay the premium cost for the extra coverage. Generally speaking, however, you should buy the additional coverage to minimize your risk exposure if you can afford that coverage. The helpful booklet *Guide to Health Insurance for People with Medicare* can be obtained by writing to the United States Department of Health and Human Services, Health Care Financing Administration, Baltimore, MD 21207.

Self-Study
Comparative Costs of Medigap Policies

This self-study will enable you to compare costs for the ten standardized Medigap policies.

Company name	Policy 1	Policy 2	Policy 3
Pre-existing condition waiting period (days)	_____	_____	_____
Guaranteed renewability	_____	_____	_____

Plan	Annual Premium		
A	_____	_____	_____
B	_____	_____	_____
C	_____	_____	_____
D	_____	_____	_____
E	_____	_____	_____
F	_____	_____	_____
G	_____	_____	_____
H	_____	_____	_____
I	_____	_____	_____
J	_____	_____	_____

Self-Study
Comparative Analysis of Different Companies' Medigap Policies

If you are considering the purchase of Medigap insurance to supplement your Medicare coverage, use the following worksheet to compare the costs of each company's policy.

Comparison of Medigap Insurance Policies

		Benefits and Premiums		
		______ Company	______ Company	______ Company
Medicare's Major Gaps (1995 figures)	You pay	______ Policy Type	______ Policy Type	______ Policy Type
Part A—Hospital insurance				
1. Hospital Deductible	$716	______	______	______
Days 61–90	$179/day	______	______	______
Days 91–150	$358/day	______	______	______
Beyond day 150	All costs	______	______	______
After day 90 if 60 reserve days have been used	All costs	______	______	______
2. Post-hospital skilled nursing care First 20 days	No charge	______	______	______
21st–100th day	$89.50/day	______	______	______
Part B—Medical insurance				
1. Excess charge	All	______	______	______
2. $100 annual deductible	All	______	______	______
3. Medicare's approved charge	20%	______	______	______
Other Gaps				
1. Long-term custodial care: a. At home	All costs	______	______	______
b. In a nursing facility	All costs	______	______	______
2. Homemaker services for individuals ill at home	All costs	______	______	______
3. Care outside the United States	All costs	______	______	______
Total annual premium		______	______	______

LONG-TERM CARE

Older Americans, age 65 and over, make up the fastest growing part of the population, and this trend will continue as the baby boomers, those born between 1946 and 1964, become seniors. In 1984, 12 percent of the American population was 65 or over. By the year 2030, it is estimated that over 21 percent of the population will be in this age group. This "graying of America" has brought new concerns to the forefront; one of the most vexing of these is the issue of long-term care.

A Common Story

A couple plans carefully for the future, saving money to put their children through college and to retire in comfort. As the couple grows older, one of them becomes seriously ill and must enter a nursing home. To the couple's surprise and dismay, they discover that neither their health coverage nor Medicare will cover the cost. Within months, their lifetime savings and assets are completely wiped out.

Unfortunately, this story is quite common. In fact, two out of five Americans age 65 or older will enter a nursing home at some time in their lives. While we automatically equate this story with growing older, even younger people are not immune. An unexpected accident or illness can make long-term care necessary at any age.

LONG-TERM COVERAGE

Long-term care generally refers to care that does not require a hospital stay and is less intensive, such as convalescent nursing and personal care services provided over an extended period of time. This type of care becomes necessary when a person needs assistance with life's daily tasks. Such assistance, commonly called *custodial care*, is the cornerstone of long-term care, ranging from all levels of nursing home care to at-home help with personal hygiene and getting around.

Medicare does not cover these services; it serves as insurance against the costs of acute care only. And Medicaid, the government program of social welfare that funds long-term care, does not merit the title of "insurance" in the accepted sense. Instead of sheltering you from the inroads that long-term care might make on your finances, Medicaid requires you to deplete your assets before you can be eligible for its funding. And Medicare supplement insurance or Medigap policies do not cover custodial or long-term care, the most significant gap in America's health insurance system. Nursing homes are the most expensive form of long-term care facility. One year's stay in a nursing home can cost $20,000 to $90,000 depending upon the geographical area in which the home is located.

Medicaid is means-tested health coverage provided by the government. In other words, you can be covered only if you are poor enough to qualify for public welfare. Because spouses have a legal responsibility to support each other, for an ill spouse to qualify for Medicaid, the healthy spouse must first spend the assets of both. Some middle income families resort to financial shuffling and become eligible for Medicaid by "spending down" their assets to state-required levels.

It is possible to qualify for Medicaid and still protect your assets by giving those assets to your children or other family members three years (thirty-six months) prior to entering a nursing home. You may keep your home without disqualifying yourself from Medicaid, but your home may be subject to a lien by Medicaid after the home is sold by the surviving spouse or the estate.

Some middle-class families use Medicaid for long-term care benefits without going into poverty by transferring assets into an irrevocable trust, specifying that the money and interest earned from it cannot be applied to nursing home costs. Some elder law attorneys specialize in this procedure.

Under current law and regulations, the best solution for a middle-income household is to buy long-term care insurance.

Private Insurance: One Solution to Long-Term Care Coverage

To obtain long-term care coverage, you can purchase long-term care insurance, a policy that pays a specified amount every day, whether you're in your own home, a nursing home, an adult day care center, or an assisted living facility. The policy covers benefits for all levels of care—skilled, intermediate, and custodial—and covers 100 percent of costs up to the daily benefit you select, regardless of where you receive care. A long-term care policy pays benefits even if there is no prior hospitalization.

More than 300 insurance companies sell long-term care insurance. Most policies are sold to people over age 65 by individual agents. Long-term care policies offer asset protection for middle income people, those with over $25,000 in assets, and above minimal income. On average, a person holds a policy for ten years before filing a claim. If you are convinced that you, or someone in your family, should purchase insurance to cover the cost of long-term health care, you should begin to consider the types of policies available and decide whether you can afford the annual premium.

Table 17.2 gives an example of one company's premiums for individuals at various ages. This policy provides for $100 daily nursing home benefit or $50 daily home care benefit payable for a period of five years. There is a forty-five-day waiting period and an inflation adjustment is offered every three years.

Table 17.2
One Company's Premiums
for a Long-Term Health Care Policy

Age	Premiums	
	Monthly	Annually
40	$ 17	$ 202
50	37	444
55	54	653
60	84	1,010
65	134	1,603
70	210	2,520
75	336	4,028
80	543	6,518
85	826	9,912
90 and over	1,093	13,118

Selecting a Long-Term Care Policy

Before purchasing a long-term care policy, it is important to compare features and prices. The Self-Study on comparative features (see page 257) should help you in recording information so that you can make the best choice. Space is provided for data from three insurance companies.

When purchasing a long-term care policy, consider the following key elements:

■ *The Company.* It is important to deal with a financially secure company that will provide good service. To be sure about your choice, you should select companies rated A++ or A+ by A.M. Best, a widely respected independent company that rates the financial stability of insurance companies. Look for an AA rating by at least one of the other major rating services: Standard & Poors, Moody's, or Duff and Phelps. You can obtain the ratings at your local library.

■ *Daily Benefits.* Most insurance companies offer a wide range of benefits, usually from $40 to

$250 a day. With some nursing homes charging over $200 a day, you should buy a benefit of at least $100 to $120 a day. It is suggested that you check actual costs in your area before making this decision. Be aware that a nursing home usually bills its patients monthly. Generally, to obtain the daily benefits, the insured must file a claim and the insurance company will pay the agreed amount to the insured. Some insurance companies send the payment directly to the nursing home.

■ *Maximum benefits in years.* Companies generally allow you to choose benefit periods of from one to six years, with some offering lifetime coverage. Statistics on nursing home patients indicate that the typical stay is two to three years. Based upon these figures, the coverage you purchase should be a minimum of three years.

■ *The elimination period in days.* Most policies have an elimination period, the number of days during which the nursing home charges will remain your responsibility. The insurance company will not pay costs until after the elimination period, which usually ranges from 20 to 100 days. If a nursing home charges $120 per day and you buy a policy with a 20-day elimination period, you will have to pay $2,400 out of pocket before the insurance company begins to pay. With a 50-day elimination period, you will have to pay $6,000, an amount that will not cause an upper middle income family financial catastrophe. The longer the elimination period, the lower will be the insurance premium.

■ *Gatekeeper mechanisms.* The goal of an insurance company is to minimize claims payments in order to earn a profit. To limit payments, the insurance company writes restrictions—*gatekeeper mechanisms*—into the policy contract, making it more difficult for the insured to qualify for a benefit. While these mechanisms protect the insurance company, they may be totally unacceptable to the buyer of the policy.

An example of a gatekeeper mechanism is the number of activities of daily living (ADLs) you must be unable to perform in order to be eligible for admission to a nursing home. ADLs include bathing, dressing, eating, transferring from a bed to a chair, continence, and toileting. Some policies require the inability to perform three of six ADLs, others two of six. Obtain a list of ADLs covered in the policy and also request definitions. Make sure the definitions are not too restrictive.

Other gatekeeper mechanisms include a requirement for prior hospitalization, a doctor's certification, and the exclusion of patients with Alzheimer's disease.

■ *Pre-existing conditions.* Pre-existing conditions refer to illnesses that were diagnosed and/or treated for some specified period before you purchased your policy. Most companies do not cover these conditions for a certain period of time after you purchase your policy. In any case, the time period should not exceed six months. Most companies cover ailments disclosed on the application so make certain the health portion of the application is completely filled out.

■ *Inflation protection.* Long-term care policies offer inflation protection to meet rising costs of nursing home care. Some policies include an automatic inflation adjustment for which the insured pays. The company usually offers a choice: a simple increase or a compounded increase.

In a *simple increase*, the policy may provide a 5 percent yearly increase of the original benefit. If the original benefit is $100 per day, a 5 percent increase will be a $5 increase each year. The second-year coverage will be $105; the third year, $110, and so forth. In fifteen years, a simple increase will raise the coverage to $175 per day.

With a policy that provides a 5 percent *compounded increase*, the benefit of $100 per day will rise to $208 in fifteen years. Of course, the annual premium cost is higher for the compounded increase.

Some companies offer an inflation adjustment annually for four years, indicating the amount of the increased benefit and the higher premium. If the insured accepts the higher benefit and the higher premium, the company will offer the inflation adjustment option for four more years. If the insured rejects the inflation adjustment for four consecutive years, it is no longer offered.

The inflation adjustment provision you buy depends on the cost you are willing to pay. Obtain figures on the coverage without inflation protection and with such protection. With this information, you are able to make an informed decision.

■ *Home care benefits.* Seek a policy that provides coverage for different kinds of care facilities. Some policies will pay for custodial care only if the insured is in a nursing home. Most people prefer home care. The policy should provide for skilled, intermediate, and custodial care. It should also provide for homemaker services. Some good policies also offer coverage for adult day care and respite care.

■ *Other features.* The policy should have a *waiver of premium* feature. Good policies waive the premium after an individual has been in a nursing home for a specified period of time, typically ninety days. Some policies also provide a *death benefit*. Usually payable only if the insured dies before a certain age, typically 65 or 70, this benefit refunds to the insured's estate any premiums paid less any benefits the company paid on the policyholder's behalf.

Final Tip

An excellent long-term care policy is one that will provide a minimum of $120 per day coverage after a fifty-day elimination period, coverage for three to six years, and an inflation adjustment feature. You should consider broader coverage if you can afford it. A rule of thumb is that premiums for a long-term care policy should not exceed 10 percent of your gross income. Buyers should look for a policy that is renewable for life and that cannot be cancelled for any reason other than failure to pay premiums, which should remain level over the policy's life.

The prime candidate for a long-term care policy is someone 50 to 60 years old. For those older, premiums rise sharply. Furthermore, if you wait until after retirement to buy a policy, you may be considered unacceptable. With age, the chances increase of being rejected because of a medical condition such as a stroke, Parkinson's disease, or failing vision. It's best to sign up while you are still young and healthy.

Self-Study
Comparative Features
of Three Long-Term Care Policies

	Policy 1	Policy 2	Policy 3
Company Name	_____	_____	_____
Daily Benefits for:			
Skilled nursing care	_____	_____	_____
Intermediate care	_____	_____	_____
Custodial care	_____	_____	_____
Home care	_____	_____	_____
Other noninstitutional care	_____	_____	_____
Maximum years for:			
Nursing home benefits	_____	_____	_____
Home care benefits	_____	_____	_____
Total lifetime benefits in dollars	_____	_____	_____
Elimination period in days	_____	_____	_____
Gatekeeper mechanisms	_____	_____	_____
Activities of Daily Livng (ADLs), number needed	_____	_____	_____
Are ADLs specifically defined?	_____	_____	_____
Is doctor certification required?	_____	_____	_____
Is Alzheimer's disease covered?	_____	_____	_____
Pre-existing conditions:			
Months before coverage starts	_____	_____	_____
Inflation protection:			
Type of inflation adjustment	_____	_____	_____
Is adjustment annual or periodic?	_____	_____	_____

	Policy 1	Policy 2	Policy 3
Home care benefits:			
Skilled care	_____	_____	_____
Intermediate care	_____	_____	_____
Custodial care	_____	_____	_____
Are homemaker services included?	_____	_____	_____
Other features:			
Waiver of premium	_____	_____	_____
Death benefit	_____	_____	_____
Annual premium with an inflation adjustment:			
Simple increase	_____	_____	_____
Compounded increase	_____	_____	_____
Annual choice option	_____	_____	_____

Glossary

Activities of Daily Living (ADLs). Activities that people do independently every day, such as bathing, dressing, eating, transferring from a bed to a chair, using the toilet, and maintaining bowel and bladder control.

Acute care. Medical care that is required for a short period of time to cure a certain illness and/or condition.

Adult day care. Health support and rehabilitation services provided in the community to people who are unable to care for themselves independently during the day but are able to live at home at night.

Custodial care. Help with bathing, dressing, eating, taking medication, and other personal needs. *See also* long-term care.

Death benefit. A refund to the policyholder's estate of any premiums paid, minus any benefits the company paid on the policyholder's behalf. This benefit is usually payable only if the policyholder dies before a certain age, typically 65 or 70.

Elimination period. The period between the time a policyholder becomes disabled and the date when payments by the insurance company begin.

Gatekeeper mechanisms. Restrictive clauses in a policy developed by insurance companies to reduce their exposure to policyholder's claims.

Home health care. A wide range of services, from skilled care and physical therapy to personal care delivered at home or in a residential setting.

Inflation protection. A type of protection offered by some insurance companies so that benefits paid will be adjusted to keep up with inflation.

Intermediate care facility. A type of care facility designed for residents who do not require the type of intensive care provided by a skilled nursing facility but need room and board along with medical, nursing, social, and rehabilitative services.

Long-term care. Long-term care is assistance, provided over a long period of time, to people with chronic health conditions and/or physical disabilities who are unable to care for themselves without the help of another person.

Long-term care insurance. Insurance available through private insurance companies as a means for individuals to protect themselves against the high costs of long-term care.

Medicaid. State-run health care programs for the poor or disabled jointly financed by federal and state funds.

Medicare. The federal health insurance program for individuals 65 and over and for those who qualify under Disability Rules.

Medicare supplement or medigap policies. Private commercial insurance that covers some of the gaps in Medicare coverage.

Nursing home. A facility that provides room and board and a planned, continuous medical treatment program, including twenty-four-hour-per-day skilled nursing care, personal care, and custodial care.

Personal care. Assistance provided to help a person with walking, bathing, eating, and other routine daily tasks. It is provided by aides who are not medical professionals but are trained to help with these tasks.

Policy. A legal contract that sets forth the rights and obligations of both policyholder and insurance company.

Pre-existing condition. A health condition that an individual had before becoming insured. Such conditions may not be covered by insurance policies.

Premium. The amount of money paid to the insurance carrier in return for insurance protection.

Renewability. An insurance policy that guarantees that the company cannot cancel your coverage as long as you pay the premium.

Residential care facility. Provides secure and healthful accommodations to individuals who are capable of meeting their own basic needs. These facilities pay special atention to the social, recreational, and spiritual requirements of the residents.

Respite care. A program that relieves a caregiver of continuous responsibility for taking care of the needs of a patient by providing time off to recoup energy and ability to perform.

Skilled nursing care. Nursing and rehabilitative care provided by and under the direction of skilled medical personnel.

Skilled nursing facility. A specially qualified facility that has the staff and equipment to provide skilled nursing care or rehabilitation services and other related health services. Most nursing homes in the United States are not skilled nursing facilities, and many skilled nursing facilities are not certified by Medicare.

Spending down. Refers to depleting almost all assets to meet eligibility requirements for Medicaid.

Waiting period. The amount of time that must pass after a person becomes insured before his/her policy begins to pay benefits.

Waiver of premium. A long-term care policy provision which provides that the insured may stop paying the policy premium after confinement in a nursing home for a specified period of time, typically ninety days.

PART FIVE
Final Facts

18

Estate Planning and Wills

Many people think that estate planning is a concern reserved for wealthy individuals. This is not true. The typical middle-class family owns a home, furniture and furnishings, an automobile—possibly two—and hobby items, and has savings, some investments, and life insurance worth a great deal. When you add it all up, the total is usually surprising. This is the package to be analyzed in estate planning.

Most people cringe at the thought of planning for death, and, therefore, procrastinate and postpone this effort. However, the head of a household and that person's spouse should have an estate plan. Anyone who fails to undertake estate planning will impose upon his or her heirs a host of unnecessary costs and problems.

In general, people usually think of family members as beneficiaries. However, beneficiaries may include friends, charities, educational institutions, and other objects of your bounty.

ESTATE PLANNING BASICS

Your *estate* consists of the assets you leave for your heirs. *Estate planning* is the process of managing your assets effectively during your lifetime, and arranging for the disposal of assets at your death so as to best serve the needs of your beneficiaries. The goal of estate planning is the establishment of an *estate plan,* the overall arrangement for disposing of your wealth both before and after death. It takes a lifetime to create an estate, yet at death, many estates are reduced by as much as 20 to 50 percent because of taxes and settlement costs resulting from poor planning. It takes careful planning to minimize estate shrinkage and to transfer as great a portion of your assets as possible to your heirs.

Objectives of Estate Planning

Estate planning has three principal objectives:

1. To make certain that your property is distributed according to your wishes and the needs of your beneficiaries. An effective estate plan will provide for the individuals about whom you care, leaving them what you want them to have. This is your primary objective.

2. To minimize federal and state estate and inheritance taxes, which are levied on an individual's estate at death.

3. To keep settlement costs to a minimum. The goal is to lower the nontax costs associated with dying, such as legal and accounting fees.

STEPS IN ESTATE PLANNING

The five basic steps you must take to prepare an effective estate plan are explained below.

1. **Inventory Your Assets and Their Value.** The first step in estate planning is to identify each of your assets and to estimate the value of each. You can take these directly from the net worth statement which you have already prepared (see page 178). This inventory of your assets should be compiled in cooperation with your spouse, and with your children, if they are old enough. A full and accurate inventory is helpful to your attorney in implementing your wishes correctly.

2. **Identify Your Heirs and Their Needs.** The major concern of most married men is their wives. Children grow up, get married, and pursue their own careers. At that point, a wife who has had a short-term career may have only a modest pension, and a wife who has not pursued her own career may be out of touch with the job market. Because of her age and lack of marketable skills, she may have a problem in obtaining paid employment. Therefore, your first responsibility is to take care of the needs of your spouse. Usually the home is owned jointly and full control of the home passes to the surviving spouse. This is known as *joint tenancy*. Individuals, usually two, hold property jointly with equal rights to share in its use. When one dies, the survivor receives the entire property. Property held this way avoids probate.

   If there is any question about prudent management of the balance of your assets, both of you should discuss this important matter together. The best interests of the children, grandchildren, and other heirs must also be considered in this discussion. Together, you must decide whether or not to place these assets in a *trust* to be managed by a *trustee*. (Trusts are discussed in Chapter 20.)

3. **Estimate Your Final Cash Requirements.** The *testator,* or maker of a will, must estimate cash requirements to cover the costs of the last illness and funeral expenses. In addition, several other obligations must be paid in cash shortly after the death of the estate owner. These are estate and inheritance taxes, if any; debts of the decedent, such as outstanding loans and unpaid bills; property taxes, if any; and legal fees for administering the estate. These obligations must be paid in full before any property can be distributed to the beneficiaries.

   If sufficient cash or near-cash assets are not available to satisfy these obligations as they fall due, the nonliquid assets of the estate must be sold to pay them. Funds should be available in the form of cash, highly marketable stocks or bonds, savings accounts, or life insurance.

4. **Select Appropriate Estate Planning Tools.** The fourth step in estate planning is to decide which tools you will need to achieve your objectives:

   - A will.
   - A durable power of attorney.
   - Advance directives.
   - A trust or trusts.

   Choosing the appropriate tool(s) requires the services of a lawyer, who must make the required decisions as to the most appropriate tools for your particular situation. You and your spouse will certainly need wills. Need for the other tools varies from one situation to another. These tools in combination will help you to meet your goals concerning distribution, property management, tax planning, and any other objective you may have. The following pages contain information on each of these elements.

5. **Consult With a Specialist in Estate Planning.** Theoretically, estate planning can be done by the individual on his or her own. You can probably save money. However, if you do it by yourself, you run the risk of making a costly error. Outside experts may save you more money than they cost you. Professionals will help you plan your estate while you are living, and, after your death, they will administer the estate to insure that your wishes are achieved. It is recommended, therefore, that you seek professional advice.

A lawyer who is a specialist in estate planning should be called upon to handle the details of an estate plan whether they seem simple or complex. A competent lawyer can be obtained by recommendation of a friend or by contacting your local bar association. Good rapport between you and your lawyer is essential. It is important to discuss fees before any work is initiated. You should be given a firm estimate of total costs in advance. If you do not feel comfortable with the lawyer you have chosen, find someone else. You have the right to look elsewhere.

While a lawyer specializing in estate planning is essential, advice can also be obtained from trust departments in banks as well as from life insurance salespeople, whose possible bias must always be kept in mind.

Self-Study
Data for Your Estate Plan

1. Refer to your net worth statement, which you prepared in Chapter 10, Worksheet 10.1. Review this inventory to be sure that the list of assets is complete and that the values are up-to-date.

2. List your heirs, including spouse, children, grandchildren, relatives, charities, and other beneficiaries you wish to consider. Based upon individual needs, estimate the proportion of your assets each beneficiary should receive. (Set up a worksheet.)

3. Estimate the cash required to cover costs of last illness, funeral expenses, and settlement costs. Remember that costs of illness may be covered in part or in full by medical insurance.

    $_____

4. List the names, addresses, and telephone numbers of two or three lawyers in your area who specialize in estate planning. You will need a lawyer's assistance in selecting appropriate estate planning tools.

    a._____

    _____

    _____

    b. _____

    _____

    _____

    c._____

    _____

    _____

WILLS

Most people recognize the importance of having a will, yet due to the human tendency to procrastinate, particularly when doing something with which they are uncomfortable, three out of four adults die without ever having finalized this most essential document. Failure to have a will is a serious oversight. If you die without a will, the probate court will appoint an administrator who will then act in accordance with the statutes of the state in which you are a legal resident. The actions that will be taken may not coincide with what you wanted or planned. Additionally, the estate will be charged for the services of the individuals who will be making decisions that should have been made by the deceased. If you want your heirs to benefit to the fullest from whatever wealth you may have accumulated during your lifetime, begin now to think about your will and to prepare one that will accomplish your personal goals.

A *will* is a legal document, almost always in writing and properly executed, which describes how a person (known as the *testator*) wants his or her property to be distributed after death, and which designates the person or institution that will carry out the terms of the will. In effect, your will is the center of your estate plan.

In the will, you designate an *executor*, known as a *personal representative* in some states, who is responsible for carrying out the provisions of the will. You should also designate an alternate executor to serve in case your original choice is unable or unwilling to serve.

In the will, you can designate a *guardian* and an alternate guardian who will have the responsibility to care for children under 18 (minors) or for an incompetent adult.

Why Make a Will?

A duly executed will reflects your wishes as it applies to your property and your family situation. Having a will offers the following advantages:

- It will guarantee that your property is distributed according to your wishes, which were based upon thoughtful planning.

- It will minimize taxes and other expenses in the distribution of your assets.

- It will accomplish the transfer of your estate to your heirs with a minimum of delay.

- It will take care of special problems, such as provision for children or an incompetent dependent.

- It will minimize the possibility of costly and family-disrupting lawsuits.

- It can provide for continued income to the family during the period in which the estate is being settled.

- It can direct that particular beneficiaries receive specified assets, known as *bequests*.

- It is the appropriate means for setting up a trust after death.

Some assets cannot be bequeathed or disposed of through your will because the beneficiaries for these assets have already been named. These assets include life insurance, pension benefits, and jointly owned property.

A wife should have her own will. Otherwise, if a couple dies in a common disaster, or if the wife dies shortly after the husband and does not have a will, her property will be distributed according to state law.

A will allows you to make bequests as percentages of your total estate. Because of the continuing problem of inflation, experts suggest that bequests be made as percentages of your estate, rather than in dollar amounts.

Risks of Dying Without a Will

When someone dies without a will, that individual is said to have died *intestate*. If you die leaving a valid will, you are said to have died *testate*. If you die intestate, the laws of the state in which you lived at the time of your death will provide for the distribution of your assets. These state laws determine who will inherit your property, which property, in what proportions, when, under what conditions, under whose auspices, and subject to what federal, state, and local taxes. This may not be the way you want your assets distributed, and may result in many inequities.

Dying without a will may create serious problems for your survivors. For example:

■ If you have a wife and three grown children, you may want your assets to go to your wife to support her for the rest of her life. Without a will, she may get only one-half or one-third, with the rest divided among the children. If your wife cannot live on her share, it will be necessary for the children to support her, working a real hardship on everyone.

■ If you are married and have no children, money meant for your wife may go instead to your parents or even your brothers and sisters, who may feel no obligation to support your wife.

■ Without a will, adopted children or stepchildren may inherit nothing.

■ Where no will exists, the court appoints an administrator to manage and distribute your estate. The fees he collects may be greater than the cost of making a will and then having the survivors pay probate costs.

The distribution of assets *by intestacy,* applicable to many states but not all, gives you a general idea of what can happen to your property. The wishes or financial needs of the survivors are not taken into account by your state's law, and this may be contrary to your wishes. Even if you have not made a will, your state has one tucked away for you. Table 18.1 illustrates one state's distribution of assets by intestacy.

Types of Wills

A will can take many forms. Among them are the following:

Do-It-Yourself Will

How often people ask, "Why do I need an attorney to help me write a will? I know what I want." In truth, you do not need an attorney to help you write your will. You can do it yourself by using a printed form that can be bought in a stationery store.

The state of California became the first state to approve a legal, standard will. It costs $1, and became effective January 1, 1983. It is called a *fill-in-the-blanks will,* and is intended for low- and middle-income people with fairly simple legal needs. The document was drawn up by the state bar of California and approved by the legislature. The bar still recommends that people see a lawyer before filling in the blanks. The terms of the document apply only to California residents.

Writing your own will certainly saves time and money, but it can also create serious problems for your heirs. These can be costly and time-consuming and may evoke family squabbles.

A Handwritten Will

A handwritten will is known as a *holographic will.* It is fully handwritten and, in the states where it is recognized, does not require witnesses. The risks and hazards of a holographic will are numerous. Only about half of the fifty states recognize this type of will. Lacking legal knowledge, you may fail to use language that

Table 18.1
Example of Distribution of Assets
by Intestacy

Survivors	Division of Assets
Surviving spouse, no children	Spouse, 100 percent

Surviving spouse, one or more children	First $50,000 to surviving spouse
	Rest of estate:
	    50 percent to surviving spouse
	    50 percent to child/children

One or more children, no surviving spouse	Child/children get 100 percent
Surviving parents, no surviving spouse or children	Parents, 100 percent
Surviving brothers and sisters, no surviving spouse, children, or parents	Divide among brothers and sisters, or to their issue, *per stirpes* (according to the line of descendants).
No surviving relatives	100 percent to state

can guarantee your estate is handled in the manner you intended. You may include an instruction such as providing for an action that is not permitted by your state's law, thereby invalidating the will. A seemingly inconsequential error, such as failure to include the date or part of the date, or use of a stamped date, may make a handwritten will worthless under the law.

Other technicalities by which a handwritten will may be invalidated are listed below:

■ Part of the will is handwritten and part is typed. How can anyone know whether the typed part was put in by you?

■ A sentence is deleted by crossing it out, but no initials appear next to it to show that you approved of the deletion. Anyone could have deleted the sentence, not necessarily the maker of the will.

■ After you had signed the will, an additional paragraph was added, leaving some of your property to another person. Could this individual have added the paragraph without your knowledge?

An Oral Will

An oral will is one made in military combat and within hearing of two witnesses. It is used primarily by soldiers or sailors in active service or by mariners at sea. Oral wills may be recognized only for a short time after the soldier, sailor, or mariner is discharged and usually provide for minimum estates. They always bear the risk that the witnesses may not recall accurately what was said.

A Will Drawn Up by Your Lawyer

Everyone needs a legally valid will; it is not a do-it-yourself activity. Executing a legally valid will is the job of a professional, and having a will can save your heirs numerous problems after your death and ensure that your property goes to the people you want to have it. A lawyer's fee for making a will may range from $75 to $250 and up, depending upon its complexity.

A will drawn up by a lawyer will meet the legal requirements for being valid, especially if the lawyer specializes in this area. He or she should have a knowledge of the laws of the state in which you reside, and be trained to give you advice and guidance to meet your goals.

Whatever type of will you have, review it periodically and keep it up-to-date. A will should be checked every two or three years to make sure that the provisions conform with changing federal and state laws, and your own resources and wishes.

Where Should Your Original Will be Stored?

You have several choices for the safekeeping of your will.

■ *In the lawyer's vault.* It is most common for the attorney who drew up the will to retain the original document in his/her vault where the wills of all the attorney's other clients are stored.

■ *In a locked file or safe.* Alternatively, if you feel more comfortable keeping the original will in your possession, you can store it at home in a locked file or safe to which your heirs have access.

■ *In a safe deposit box.* This is not the best choice. When a bank becomes aware that the renter of a safe deposit box has passed away, the box is sealed until its contents can be officially inventoried. This enables the state to collect estate or inheritance taxes on any valuable assets that may have been stored in the safe deposit box, but it will delay access to the will. To avoid

such delay, your will can be stored in a safe deposit box rented in your spouse's name and your spouse's will can be kept in a box rented in your name.

■ *In the probate court.* In localities where permitted, a will can be filed with the clerk of the probate court. Your heirs should be advised of this. After your death, your heirs can report to the court and initiate probate proceedings.

No matter where your will is stored, you may wish to keep a copy at home for easy reference. Remember, it is important for your heirs to know where the original will is kept.

FIDUCIARIES

A *fiduciary* is the individual or institution to whom you grant specific rights, duties, and powers to act in your behalf for the benefit of a survivor(s). The principal fiduciaries are as follows:

■ An *executor* (or *executors*), called *personal representative* in some states, is a person named in the will who is responsible for carrying out the provisions of the will.

■ A *guardian* (or *guardians*) is a person who has the responsibility to care for a minor or an incompetent adult, or to control his or her property, or both.

■ A *trustee* (or *trustees*) is responsible for managing the assets of a trust carefully and prudently. Often, a trustee is given discretionary authority in deciding whom to pay income from the trust. (See Chapter 20.)

■ An *administrator* is a court-appointed executor who is designated to serve when someone dies without a will, referred to in the law as dying *intestate.* An administrator is also appointed when a will does not name an executor; when a will cannot be located; or when a will is declared invalid. The responsibilities of an administrator and an executor are the same.

■ A *conservator* is a court-appointed representative of an incompetent person.

Before naming fiduciaries in your will, get the approval of those you plan to name. For every fiduciary you select, choose also an alternate (or successor) to serve in case your original choice is unable or unwilling to serve. This alternate should also be named in the will.

Executor

An *executor* or *executrix* is the person responsible for the management of property specified in the will until disposition of the estate is completed. The executor serves in a *fiduciary relationship* to the beneficiaries of the estate, meaning that the executor must comply with high standards of integrity and responsibility in managing the estate's property and carrying out the provisions of the will. The executor must make periodic reports to the probate court and actually make a final accounting to the court before being released from the fiduciary relationship.

Fees or commissions for executors vary from state to state; are computed on the gross value of the estate; are fixed by state law; and are paid only once.

The responsibilities of the executor are the following:

■ To prepare an inventory of all estate assets.

■ To pay all federal, state, and local taxes owed by the estate.

■ To pay all of the estate's debts and expenses incurred during the administration of the estate.

■ To decide on the validity of claims against the estate.

■ To represent the estate in case of lawsuits.

■ To fund and establish any trusts created under the will.

■ To manage any other financial matters pertaining to the estate.

■ To keep complete records of all transactions made on behalf of the estate or in accordance with the will.

■ To distribute according to the terms of the will the estate assets that remain after all settlement obligations are met and all specific bequests are satisfied.

■ To make a final accounting to the court and the decedent's beneficiaries.

Who should be the executor of a will? *Choose a competent executor.* It is important to choose an executor who is competent and has your confidence. You should also choose an alternate, in case the executor is unable to serve in this capacity.

The first consideration is the size of the estate. If the estate is relatively small, a spouse, a son, or a daughter can be the executor. If the estate is large, involving difficult tax and investment decisions, it would be best to select an estate lawyer or the trust department of a bank. A spouse may be called upon to serve as a coexecutor.

Special qualities of an executor that should be examined include the ability to get along with your heirs, the ability to command respect, availability or having the time to get the job done, and, finally, executive and administrative ability.

Before you select a professional fiduciary, discuss the fees, philosophy, and method of operation to be sure the individual meets your needs and those of your beneficiaries. You can change an executor during your lifetime, but once you die, your will is irrevocable and it is then very difficult to make a replacement. Only the probate court will be able to make a replacement.

Fees or commissions for executors vary from state to state. One of your relatives would probably not accept a commission. If your lawyer serves as your executor, he will charge a fee. The commission is computed on the gross value of the estate including income that passes through the executor's hands. The commission is fixed by state law and is payable only once during the administration of an estate. An example of an executor's commission charge is as follows:

5 percent on the first $100,000 ($5,000)
4 percent on the next $200,000 ($8,000)
3 percent on the next $700,000 ($21,000)
2.5 percent on the next $4,000,000
2 percent on the excess over $5,000,000

The commission on a $300,000 estate would, therefore, be $13,000—5 percent of $100,000 ($5,000) plus 4 percent of $200,000 ($8,000).

Guardian

A *guardian* is a person who has the responsibility to care for a minor or an incompetent adult, or to control his or her property, or both. A will usually names the person who will serve as guardian of minor children in the event of the death of you and your spouse. If the guardian(s) you select are deemed incompetent, the court has the power and authority to disregard the nomination set forth in the will and to appoint another guardian who will serve the best interests of the individual requiring this care.

In naming a guardian, many gravitate toward relatives, particularly their own parents. But estate attorneys caution against this. Your parents may make wonderful grandparents, but they may not wish or be able to assume the responsibility of child rearing. Moreover, do not assume that a married sibling who is childless will want to act as guardian. Often, friends with children of about the same age are a fine choice. Frequently, friends make reciprocal agreements, in which each couple agrees to act as the guardian of the other's children. In any case, be sure that you check with the persons you have selected before you name them in your will. Some lawyers think it wise to name guardians who reside in the same state because legal complications may arise if you select nonresidents. It is a good idea to name *successor guardians* in case your initial choices die or become divorced.

Choosing a guardian is a complex and personal matter. Choose the individual(s) who feel love for your children and who share your values and philosophy of life in raising children.

Guardianship lasts only until a child reaches the age of majority, typically eighteen. At that age, the child becomes fully entitled to whatever property is in the estate. In many cases, it is wise to establish a trust, stipulating that the eighteen-year-old receive a weekly or monthly allowance; at twenty-five he or she will receive one-third of the assets; half the balance at thirty, and the remainder at thirty-five.

Conservator

A *conservator* is appointed by the court to be responsible for the person and property of an incompetent person. The conservator looks after the financial affairs of an individual who is incapable of dealing with such matters as picking up mail, handling checks and bank transactions, and paying bills. In addition, a conservator can make decisions regarding health care. The court appointee might not be the individual of your choice. To ensure that decisions concerning your person and property are made by those you trust if you are declared incompetent, you should designate individuals who will have durable power of attorney and durable power of attorney for health care (see page 284).

Trustee

The job of a trustee is generally long-term; every trust requires maintenance of records, keeping custody of securities, and filing whatever tax returns are necessary. When very long service is required, the testator, or maker of the will, may designate an individual as the *first trustee* and another individual or a bank as a *contingent* or *successor trustee.*

An individual can act as trustee of his own trust in the case of a living trust that is created during his or her lifetime. In this case, the individual does not want to give up management of his or her own affairs, but wants to be sure that if he or she becomes ill, incapacitated, or dies suddenly, the terms of the trust will be carried out. Thus, a *successor trustee* or *alternate trustee* is available to step in and carry on.

The most important job of a trustee is to manage the assets of the trust carefully and prudently for the benefit of the beneficiary or beneficiaries. Often, a trustee is given discretionary authority in deciding whom to pay income from a trust or even, in some cases, whether to dip into the principal if income is insufficient to meet a beneficiary's needs. If, for example, an elderly person is in a nursing home and for a time has extremely large medical bills, then the trustee may use not only the income from the trust, in the case of a sprinkling trust, but also some of the principal to pay the medical bills.

Many individuals choose a relative or close friend as a trustee. If you are considering doing this, weigh the decision carefully. An individual may not have the time or inclination to properly manage a trust fund and, even more important, may not have the background and knowledge to do so.

If you do name an individual, remember to name a successor or alternate in case the first individual cannot fulfill the obligation. It is wise also to include a provision that, after your death, your spouse or another heir can name a successor or alternate to the original trustee.

While an individual family member or trusted friend probably will charge little or nothing to manage a trust, institutional managers do charge for this service. Any fees paid are tax deductible, however, and you have several important advantages:

■ The institution will undoubtedly continue doing business in the same city and state for many years to come, while an individual may move.

■ Trust officers devote their time to managing money and are among the most knowledgeable people in handling trust funds.

■ Your money is protected because banks and other financial institutions are subject to periodic state and federal audits, whereas individual trustees are not under any such scrutiny.

■ An institution provides continuity in the management of your funds. Even if your trust officer is unable to continue handling your account, another trained and knowledgeable individual will be available.

Self-Study
Data for Your Will

1. If you have no will and wish to have a lawyer draw up a will for you, you should contact a qualified lawyer and arrange to have an estate planning conference. In preparation for this conference, you should assemble all the facts concerning your estate and your family. Following is a list of the types of data you should assemble:

    ❑ Family information
    ❑ Beneficiary information
    ❑ Executor, guardian, trustee information
    ❑ Asset information

2. If you have a will, check your answers to the questions that appear below. You may have to amend your will by adding a *codicil*. A codicil must be signed with the same formality as a will. If the changes are major, it may be wiser to draw up a new will.
    a. Are the beneficiaries you named still alive and still worthy of your bequest?
    b. Have you moved to another state since making this will?
    c. Are you now living in a community property state?
    d. Do you still want to keep the same executor and alternate executor?
    e. Do you still own the same assets mentioned in your will?
    f. Do you wish to take advantage of and are you taking advantage of the maximum marital deduction allowable under the Economic Recovery Tax Act of 1981? (See Chapter 19.)
    g. Should this will be reviewed with your lawyer?

Estate Planning Conference

After setting up an appointment with the estate lawyer you have selected, you should compile the basic information that you will need for the conference.

Basic Information for Estate Planning Conference

Family Information

Date_____

Full legal name_____

Address and phone number_____

Birth date_____Social Security number_____

Employers (last two years)

_____

_____

Veteran?_____Service number_____

Disability: Service connected or nonservice connected _____

Marital status: Single, Married, Widowed, Separated, or Divorced _____

Do you have a will? _____

Legal name of spouse _____

Address and phone number _____

Birth date_____ Social Security number _____

Does spouse have a will? _____

Children, including those legally adopted:

Full name	Full address	Birth date	Extent of dependence
1. _____	1. _____ _____	1. _____	1. _____
2. _____	2. _____ _____	2. _____	2. _____
3. _____	3. _____ _____	3. _____	3. _____
4. _____	4. _____ _____	4. _____	4. _____
5. _____	5. _____	5. _____	5. _____

Parents

1. _____	1. _____ _____	1. _____	1. _____
2. _____	2. _____ _____	2. _____	2. _____
3. _____	3. _____ _____	3. _____	3. _____
4. _____	4. _____ _____	4. _____	4. _____

Brothers and sisters

	Full address	Birth date	Age (approximate)
1. _____	1. _____	1. _____	1. _____
2. _____	2. _____	2. _____	2. _____
3. _____	3. _____	3. _____	3. _____
4. _____	4. _____	4. _____	4. _____
5. _____	5. _____	5. _____	5. _____
6. _____	6. _____	6. _____	6. _____

Other next of kin: Nieces, nephews, etc.

	Full address	Birth date	Age (approximate)
1. _____	1. _____	1. _____	1. _____
2. _____	2. _____	2. _____	2. _____
3. _____	3. _____	3. _____	3. _____
4. _____	4. _____	4. _____	4. _____

Asset Information

Annual income: Salary_____Investment income _____

Cash

Checking accounts

Name of institution	Account number	Amount	Joint	Husband	Wife
1. _____	_____	_____	____	____	____
2. _____	_____	_____	____	____	____
3. _____	_____	_____	____	____	____

Check (√) ownership

Savings accounts
Name of bank

			Joint	Husband	Wife
1. _____	_____	_____	____	____	____
2. _____	_____	_____	____	____	____
3. _____	_____	_____	____	____	____

Stocks and Bonds

Name of company	Number of shares/ principal amount	Purchase cost	Current value	Check (√) ownership		
				Joint	Husband	Wife
1. _____	_____	_____	_____	_____	_____	_____
2. _____	_____	_____	_____	_____	_____	_____
3. _____	_____	_____	_____	_____	_____	_____

Real Property

Address	Purchase cost	Current value	Check (√) ownership		
			Joint	Husband	Wife
1. _____ _____ (primary residence)	_____	_____	_____	_____	_____
2. _____ _____ (Vacation home)	_____	_____	_____	_____	_____
1. _____ _____ (investment realty)	_____	_____	_____	_____	_____
2. _____ _____ (investment realty)	_____	_____	_____	_____	_____

Life Insurance

Name of company and policy number	Name of insured/ name of owner	Face value and cash value	Names of beneficiaries	Loans, if any
1. _____	_____ (Insured)	_____ (Face value)	_____	_____
# _____	_____ (Owner)	_____ (Cash value)	_____	_____

Life Insurance

Name of company and policy number	Name of insured/ name of owner	Face value and cash value	Names of beneficiaries	Loans, if any
2. _____	_____ (Insured)	_____ (Face value)	_____	_____
# _____	_____ (Owner)	_____ (Cash value)	_____	_____
3. _____	_____ (Insured)	_____ (Face value)	_____	_____
# _____	_____ (Owner)	_____ (Cash value)	_____	_____

Personal Property

(Autos, furniture jewelry, furs, hobby items, etc.)	Purchase cost	Current value	Check (√) ownership		
			Joint	Husband	Wife
_____	_____	_____	____	____	____
_____	_____	_____	____	____	____
_____	_____	_____	____	____	____
_____	_____	_____	____	____	____
_____	_____	_____	____	____	____
_____	_____	_____	____	____	____

Privately Held Business Interests

(Partnership, limited partnership, corporate)	Original investment	Current value	Check (√) ownership		
			Joint	Husband	Wife
_____	_____	_____	____	____	____
_____	_____	_____	____	____	____
_____	_____	_____	____	____	____
_____	_____	_____	____	____	____
_____	_____	_____	____	____	____
_____	_____	_____	____	____	____

Liabilities

Creditor and type of debt (loans, mortgages, consumer credit)	Current amount due	Interest rate	Due date	Check (√) debtor		
				Joint	Husband	Wife

1. _____ $ _____ _____ _____ _____ _____ _____
   (Creditor)

_____
(Type of debt)

2. _____ $ _____ _____ _____ _____ _____ _____
   (Creditor)

_____
(Type of debt)

Beneficiary Information

Names of individuals or charities	Bequest: Dollars or percent of estate
_____	_____
_____	_____
_____	_____
_____	_____

Executor, Guardian, Trustee Information

1. The following person and/or bank trust department should be the executor of my estate:

   Name and address of person and/or bank _____

   Name and address of alternate executor _____

2. The following person(s) should be the guardian(s) of my children:

   Name and address _____

   Name and address of alternate _____

3. The following person and/or bank trust department should be the trustee for any trust that may be established:

Name and address _____

Name and address of alternate _____

SUPPLEMENTAL LETTER OF INSTRUCTIONS

You should leave a *supplemental letter of instructions* to assist the individual who must begin to administer the will. It should contain the following types of information.

■ *Persons to be notified.* Names, addresses, and telephone numbers of those persons to be notified at the time of your death: relatives, friends, associates, others.

■ *Location of the will.* Include the names, addresses, and telephone numbers of your lawyer and the executor of your will, as well as the location of the will.

■ *Location of vital documents.* These include certificates of birth and of marriage; veteran's discharge; Social Security number and location of card; past tax returns, paid bills, cancelled checks, and bank statements for the last several years.

■ *Location of assets.* Safe deposit boxes, stock and bond certificates, insurance policies, pension documents, bank accounts, real property documents (e.g., mortgages, deeds, and title documents).

■ *Professional advisors.* Names, addresses, and telephone numbers of your lawyer, accountant, stockbroker, insurance agent, banker or trust officer, and minister or rabbi.

■ *Employment or business information.* Name, address, and telephone number of present or last employer; instructions relative to any business enterprises you may own or in which you have an interest.

■ *Personal Valuables.* List your personal valuables (e.g., jewelry, collections, cameras, antiques, and home furnishings) and name the recipient for each item.

■ *Funeral and burial instructions.* The testator should spell out instructions for disposition of the body; type of service desired; memorial donations to a selected charity.

After the letter is completed, make two copies and file the original with your will. Give one of the copies to your executor and retain one accessible to you and your spouse so that it may be kept up-to-date. If you are single, give one copy to your executor and/or to a close friend or relative.

Self-Study
Supplemental Letter of Instructions

Prepare a Supplemental Letter of Instructions by filling in the required information. Data for the Supplemental Letter of Instructions can be taken from Appendix A, Inventory of Personal and Financial Data.

The Supplemental Letter of Instructions

	Husband	Wife
Legal name	_____	_____
Permanent address	_____	_____
	_____	_____

1. **Persons to be notified of death**

   (Name, address, and telephone number of each.)

	Husband	Wife
	_____	_____
	_____	_____
	_____	_____
	_____	_____

2. **Location of the original will**

   (Name, address, and telephone)

	Husband	Wife
	_____	_____
	_____	_____
	_____	_____
❑ Safe deposit box	_____	_____
❑ Lawyer	_____	_____
❑ Bank trust department	_____	_____
❑ Executor	_____	_____

	Husband	Wife
3. **Vital document information**		
Birth certificate location	_____	_____
Birthdate	_____	_____
Birthplace	_____	_____
Father's name	_____	_____
Mother's name	_____	_____
Marriage certificate location	_____	_____
Date married	_____	_____
Place married	_____	_____
Prior marriages		
Names; dates	_____	_____
How terminated	_____	_____
Veteran's discharge certificate location	_____	_____
Service serial number	_____	_____
Date discharged	_____	_____
Place discharged	_____	_____
Social Security card location	_____	_____
Social Security number	_____	_____
Financial documents		
Location of paid bills	_____	_____
Location of past tax returns	_____	_____
Cancelled checks	_____	_____

	Husband	Wife

4. **Location of assets**

   Safe deposit boxes _____ _____

   Stock and bond certificates _____ _____

   Insurance policies _____ _____

   Pension documents _____ _____

   Bank accounts and books _____ _____

   Real property documents _____ _____

5. **My professional advisors**
   (Name, address, phone number)

   Lawyer _____ _____

   Accountant _____ _____

   Insurance agent _____ _____

   Broker _____ _____

   Banker or trust officer _____ _____

   Minister or rabbi _____ _____

6. **Employment or business data**

   Present or last employer
   (Indicate which) _____ _____

   Name, address, phone number _____ _____

7. **Personal Valuables**

   List your personal valuables _____ _____
   (e.g., jewelry, collections,
   cameras, antiques, home furnishings) _____ _____
   and name the recipient for each item.

   _____ _____

   _____ _____

   _____ _____

	Husband	Wife
8. **Funeral and burial instructions** Include disposition of the body (burial, cremation, donation of body or parts); types of burial service desired (religious or nonreligious); recipient of memorial donations; flag for casket from Department of Veterans Affairs.	_____ _____ _____ _____	_____ _____ _____ _____
	_____ (Signature)	_____ (Signature)
	_____ (Date)	_____ (Date)

DURABLE POWER OF ATTORNEY

In addition to a will and a supplemental letter of instructions, you should provide for a durable power of attorney. A durable power of attorney ranks higher than an ordinary power of attorney in that it enables the holder of the power to act when the maker or granter of the power becomes incompetent.

State law allows you to give someone a power of attorney. This enables the person who holds the power to act for you, on your behalf, as your legal representative. A power of attorney will terminate immediately upon incompetency or other disability of the maker. State law provides, however, that a power of attorney can contain appropriate language so that in the event of the maker's disability, the holder of the power may continue to act on bahalf of the person who granted the power. A power of attorney that contains this language is known as a *durable power of attorney*. Some financial powers that may be included in a durable power of attorney are:

- Handle banking transactions such as deposits and withdrawals.
- Buy, sell, or lease assets.
- Sue on the principal's behalf.
- Collect from creditors.
- Operate principal's business.

The durable power of attorney refers to financial affairs. A *durable power of attorney for health care* refers to medical decisions (see page 285). A power of attorney can be revoked as long as its maker is competent to act.

Tips on Durable Power of Attorney

After you have completed your will, ask your lawyer about drawing up a document designating someone to assume durable power of attorney for you. After it is drawn up, give copies to family members, your lawyer, and the executor of your will.

ADVANCE DIRECTIVES

Through advance directives, your wishes about life support systems will already be known in the event that you become terminally ill or incompetent. These advance directives include a health care proxy, a living will, and the durable power of attorney for health care.

■ *A Health Care Proxy.* A *health care proxy* gives an individual other than yourself the power to decide about medical treatment on your behalf in the event that you lose the capacity to decide for yourself. Your agent will then be able to apply your wishes and instructions in the light of changing medical circumstances. A health care proxy can be changed or revoked as long as you are competent to act.

A health care proxy is legally recognized in some states, but not all. Both spouses should have a health care proxy.

■ *The Living Will.* A *living will* serves the same function as a health care proxy, but expresses *your own personal wishes* about medical treatment in the event of a hopeless condition. It is suggested that each individual or spouse have both a health care proxy and a living will. Figure 18.1 is a sample living will.

■ *A Durable Power of Attorney for Health Care.* A *durable power of attorney for health care* is another form of advance directive. It is a signed, dated, and witnessed document naming another person to make medical decisions for you if you are unable to make them for yourself. This document is sometimes combined with the durable power of attorney discussed previously. This directive offers a potentially useful legal instrument by which you can protect your right to refuse life-sustaining procedures in the event of a hopeless condition and incapacity to make decisions. Without a durable power of attorney for health care, your physician or hospital will have to search for a family member or other individual and ask the court to approve that person's right to act in your behalf. That person is known as a *conservator*.

■ *Anatomical Gifts.* Donation of human organs can save lives and ease suffering. Through organ transplants, the life of a dying patient can be sustained. Transplant gifts include the heart, lungs, kidneys, pancreas, liver, corneas, skin, and bone. Nationwide, it has been estimated that more than 50,000 patients could benefit from transplants if gift organs were available.

If you wish to have your organs donated, you can sign and carry a Uniform Organ Donor Card, or you can indicate your wish to donate organs by marking the appropriate spot on your driver's license. Discuss your wishes with members of your family. Just as your family may have to make the decision after your death, someday you may be asked to donate the organs of a deceased member of your family who has died. Although this can be a difficult decision, many families find that when faced with such a tragedy, donating organs for transplantation provides consolation and comfort.

Everyone should be considered a potential donor, regardless of age or medical history. The suitability of donated organs and tissues will be determined by the medical team at the time of donation.

The following information may help you decide whether you should become a donor:

- Organ donation does not affect or delay customary funeral arrangements.

- The donation involves no cost or payment.

- Funeral expenses and hospital expenses incurred prior to the donation of organs remain the responsibility of the donor's family.

- Donation of the body to a medical school can save funeral expenses. Contact a medical school in your community.

- Individuals under the age of eighteen may sign a Donor Card with the consent of a parent or legal guardian.

- It is not necessary to mention organ donation in your will.

For further information, contact The United Network for Organ Sharing (UNOS), P.O. Box 28010, Richmond, Virginia 23228. The phone number is 1-800-446-2726.

You can request your estate attorney to prepare advance directives for you and your spouse at the same time that he draws up your will and durable power of attorney.

Figure 18.1   A Living Will

TO MY FAMILY, MY PHYSICIAN, MY LAWYER, MY CLERGYMAN
TO ANY MEDICAL FACILITY IN WHOSE CARE I HAPPEN TO BE
TO ANY INDIVIDUAL WHO MAY BECOME RESPONSIBLE FOR MY HEALTH, WELFARE, OR AFFAIRS

Death is as much a reality as birth, growth, maturity, and old age—it is the one certainty of life. If the time comes when I, _____ can no longer take part in decisions
(please print)

for my own future, let this statement stand as an expression of my wishes, while I am still of sound mind.

   If the situation should arise in which there is no reasonable expectation of my recovery from physical or mental disability, I request that I be allowed to die and not be kept alive by artificial means or "heroic measures." I do not fear death itself as much as the indignities of deterioration, dependence, and hopeless pain. I, therefore, ask that medication be mercifully administered to me to alleviate suffering even though this may hasten the moment of death.

   This request is made after careful consideration. I hope you who care for me will feel morally bound to follow its mandate. I recognize that this appears to place a heavy responsibility upon you, but it is with the intention of relieving you of such responsibility and of placing it upon myself in accordance with my strong convictions, that this statement is made.

Date_____   Signed _____

Witness_____   Witness_____
(please print)   (signature)

Witness_____   Witness_____
(please print)   (signature)

Copies of this request have been given to _____

_____

Directions for the Living Will

1. Sign and date before two witnesses. (This is to insure that you signed of your own free will and not under any pressure.)
2. If you have a doctor, give him a copy for your medical file and discuss it with him to make sure he is in agreement. Also give copies to those most likely to be concerned "if the time comes when you can no longer take part in decisions for your own future." Enter their names on the bottom lines of the living will. Keep the original nearby, easily and readily available.
3. Above all, discuss your intentions with those closest to you, *now.*
4. It is a good idea to look over your living will once a year, redate it, and initial the new date to make it clear that your wishes are unchanged.
5. Make a copy of the living will above for your spouse, if he or she desires. Attach the copy to this page for future reference.

The *Living Will* and directions appeared in *Your Vital Papers Logbook,* 1981 edition, and are reprinted with the permission of Action for Independent Maturity, a division of the American Association of Retired Persons.

Glossary

Administrator. The person appointed by a court to administer and settle the estate of a person dying without a will or the estate of a person whose will appoints an *executor* who cannot serve. (*See* Executor.)

Assets. All money, investments, and other property owned by an individual, a family, or a business. (*See* Liabilities, Net Worth.)

Beneficiary. A person or organization you designate to receive the income from a policy or a *trust*.

Bequest. A gift of property by *will*. Same as Legacy.

Codicil. An amendment to a will that must be signed and witnessed with the same formality as a will.

Coexecutor. An additional executor, perhaps your spouse, to work with the *executor*.

Conservator. A court-appointed administrator who is designated to look after the financial affairs of an individual who is incapable of dealing with such matters as picking up mail, handling checks and bank transactions, and paying bills.

Donee. A person to whom a gift is made.

Donor. A person who makes a gift.

Estate. The assets you leave to your heirs.

Estate planning. The process of analyzing your assets and liabilities, managing them effectively during your lifetime, and disposing of them at your death through a will so as to best serve the needs of your beneficiaries. (*See* Will.)

Executor (Executrix, if a woman). A person nominated by the individual who writes a *will* to

carry out the directions and requests in that will. (*See* Administrator.)

Fiduciary. The individual or institution to whom you grant specific rights, duties, and powers to act for you or in your behalf to carry out the provisions stipulated in your *will*. (*See* Administrator, Executor, Guardian, Trustee.)

Guardian. A person who has the responsibility to care for a minor or an incompetent adult or to control the property of such an individual, or to do both. (*See* Successor Guardian.)

Heirs. Those who inherit your property.

Holographic will. A handwritten will that is signed and dated by the person writing the will. Recognized in about half the states, *holographic wills* require no witnesses.

Intestate. One who dies without leaving a valid *will*. (*See* Testate.)

Legacy. A gift of property by *will*. Same as Bequest.

Liabilities. All forms of indebtedness for which an individual, a family, or a business is legally liable. (*See* Assets, Net Worth.)

Life insurance. Insurance to pay a named beneficiary or beneficiaries a specified dollar amount at the death of the insured. A life insurance policy can be used to provide income for the family at your death, or can be used to fund a trust or a business agreement.

Living will. A written request that the life of the individual not be prolonged by artificial means when death is inevitable.

Marital deduction. The amount of property that can be left to a spouse tax-free. The Economic

Recovery Tax of 1981 permits an *unlimited marital deduction.*

Net worth. Monetary value of an individual, a family, or a business. It is equal to total assets minus total liabilities. (*See* Assets, Liabilities.)

Oral will. Made in military combat and within hearing of two witnesses, it is used primarily by soldiers, sailors in active service, or mariners at sea.

Property. Includes cash, securities, real estate, and any other possessions.

Residuary. Property left in your estate after payment of your debts and distribution of specific bequests.

Successor guardian. An additional guardian listed in a will, who can assume the responsibilities of guardian in case your initial guardian dies or is otherwise unable to perform the functions.

Supplemental letter of instructions. A memorandum of personal details that should be attached to your will. The supplemental letter of instructions should include such information as location of vital documents, location of assets, employment or business information, disposition of personal valuables, and funeral and burial instructions.

Testate. One who dies leaving a valid will. (*See* Intestate.)

Testator (Testatrix, if a woman). The person who makes a will.

Unlimited marital deduction. Under present law, no limit exists on the size of the estate that one spouse can leave for the other, and the transfer is free of estate taxes. This change became effective January 1, 1982.

Will. A legal document, almost always in writing and properly executed, which describes how a person wants his or her property distributed after death and designates an *executor.*

19

Minimizing Estate Taxes

The *federal estate tax* is paid to the federal government by the executor of the decedent's estate. Some states also tax estates, but most states levy an inheritance tax, which is paid by the inheritor rather than the estate. Some wills specify that the inheritance taxes be paid out of the estate's funds in order to minimize the shrinkage of an individual's inheritance. The federal estate tax and state inheritance and estate taxes are referred to as *death taxes.*

In addition to taxing estates, the federal government levies a gift tax that applies to transfers—gifts between living individuals. Gift taxes are imposed in order to make the taxation of estates and gifts equitable. If there were no gift tax, wealthy individuals could make large gifts immediately prior to death, thus reducing their estates and the tax on those estates. The average citizen, on the other hand, has to maintain maximum assets until death; the estate tax is, therefore, levied on all accumulated property. In 1976, the federal government combined the gift and estate tax schedule and created a single, unified tax credit that minimizes the tax liability either on taxable gifts or on an estate. This deduction is applied against both estate and gift

taxes due the government, thus shielding both transfers from taxation. This tax credit is a direct reduction of the total taxes due, saving the taxpayer thousands of dollars. Approved by Congress in 1981, the *unified tax credit* increased from $62,800 in 1982 to $192,800 in 1987 and later years.

THE FEDERAL ESTATE TAX

The Economic Recovery Tax Act of 1981, known as ERTA, made several sweeping changes that not only affected estates and estate taxes but also gift taxes.

Unlimited Marital Deduction

The single most significant change in the tax structure is the unlimited marital deduction. All transfers between husband and wife became free of estate taxes. This allows estates of *any* size to be passed tax-free. This change simplifies estate planning for the initial transfer from one spouse to another, but requires very careful planning for the transfer when the surviving spouse dies.

Tax-Free Estate Transfers to Any Beneficiary Aside From Spouse

The amount of an estate that can pass tax-free to any beneficiary is currently $600,000. An estate tax return must be filed only if the decedent's estate exceeds $600,000.

Increase in Annual Gift Tax Exclusion

Currently, the gift tax annual exclusion is $10,000 per donee. This means that if a married couple agrees to make a split gift, they can give up to $20,000 per donee, each and every year without incurring any gift tax. The recipient pays no income tax on the gift.

Maximum Estate and Gift Tax Rates Are Reduced

The maximum tax rate on estates and gifts ranges from 37 percent to 55 percent on estates over $600,000. In effect, each spouse enjoys a $600,000 exemption from the federal estate tax.

Taxable Gifts

Under current law, a taxable gift is any gift of more than $10,000 (or $20,000 if each spouse makes a gift) made in any year. If you make one or more such gifts above the exempt amount, you must file a federal gift tax return so that the IRS can charge them against your exemption, the amount of your estate that can pass tax-free, shown previously. Gifts to a spouse are exempt from these limits.

If you exceed your annual exemption of $10,000/$20,000 per recipient, and file a federal gift tax return, no tax is payable until you exceed your lifetime exemption, either during your lifetime or after your death, when the value of your estate must be determined. Therefore, grandparents giving a joint gift can transfer to each of their children and grandchildren up to $20,000 a year.

INHERITANCE TAX

The inheritance tax differs from the estate tax in that the individual who inherits property pays the tax. Inheritance taxes vary greatly among the states. The state inheritance tax applies when the decedent lived in the state at the time of death, or if the property of the decedent is located in the state that levies the tax. The only state that does not levy a tax on inheritances is Nevada. The federal estate tax computation allows a credit for any inheritance taxes paid to a state or to the District of Columbia.

CASE STUDIES IN ESTATE PLANNING

■ *Small Estates ($600,000 or less).* If an estate is valued at $600,000 or less, assets can be held jointly with the right of survivorship. Each individual's will can leave all property to the surviving spouse or to children and/or grandchildren. Since up to $600,000 can pass tax-free, a small estate avoids estate and inheritance taxes.

■ *Medium-Sized Estates ($600,000 to $1,200,000).* Let's assume that an individual with a wife and two children has an estate that totals $1,200,000. Most of the assets of that estate—home, insurance, investments—are owned jointly with the right of survivorship. If the husband were to die, leaving everything to his wife under the unlimited marital deduction, the wife would then possess assets worth $1,200,000.

Under federal law, up to $600,000 can pass tax-free from a decedent to beneficiaries. In this case, the wife possesses $1,200,000 and, when she dies, can pass $600,000 of this total to her children tax-free, but the remaining $600,000 is taxable. The federal estate tax on $600,000 is $192,800, and a state estate tax and/or inheritance tax would be an additional cost, quite a tax bite.

With planning, all the taxes can be saved and the money transferred to the children. Each spouse should have a maximum of $600,000 of the assets held in sole ownership or tenancy in common. An attorney can set up a trust in *each* spouse's will to absorb $600,000 if the individual should die. The trust will guarantee income to the surviving spouse for life from the $600,000 invested by the trust, specifying that when the surviving spouse dies, the $600,000 should pass to the children. Since each spouse can legally pass up to $600,000 to the children tax-free, no taxes will be paid on this estate and either spouse can enjoy lifetime income from the trust if one spouse dies.

This solution is illustrated in Table 19.1. With planning, the assets will be divided equally between the husband and wife, with the couple owning their primary residence as tenants in common. All other assets will be divided between the husband and wife, with each owning 50 percent of the total assets in sole ownership. Planning will result in a net tax savings of over $200,000.

■ *Large Estates (Over $1,200,000).* If a couple's estate is valued at more than $1,200,000, it will be necessary for them to choose among several alternatives to avoid or reduce the size of the estate tax. For example, if a gross taxable estate is $2,000,000, only $1,200,000 can be sheltered, as previously indicated. The net taxable estate, therefore, is $800,000, subject to a federal estate tax of $267,800. Assuming a state tax of $39,000, the total taxes due amount to $306,800. What are the options available to this couple?

Options

It may be appropriate for them to consider shar-

Table 19.1
Case Study in Estate Planning

| | | With planning | |
| | | Sole ownership or tenancy in common | |
Asset	Survivor's estate	Husband	Wife
Cash	$ 30,000	$ 15,000	$ 15,000
Certificates of deposit	50,000	50,000	—
Stocks	200,000	125,000	75,000
Municipal bonds	100,000	—	100,000
Mutual funds	140,000	70,000	70,000
Primary residence	400,000	200,000	200,000
Vacation home	200,000	100,000	100,000
Individual retirement account	40,000	40,000	—
Autos, furniture, jewelry	40,000	—	40,000
Total	$1,200,000	$600,000	$600,000

ing their wealth with children, grandchildren, a charity, or an institution. This involves giving $10,000 a year as an individual gift, or $20,000 as a couple, to each child, grandchild, and/or charity, as permitted by law. Regular gift giving of this magnitude will reduce each individual's estate to the $600,000 level that is exempt from federal estate taxes. At the same time, the couple will see the family enjoy their largesse while they are alive. However, the couple should retain enough to ensure their own secure retirement.

Some well-to-do individuals prefer to retain all their assets and purchase a life insurance policy that will provide enough money to pay all estate taxes when they die. If you decide to purchase such a policy, you can also create an irrevocable life insurance trust to receive the proceeds of the policy. The trust will then be used to pay the estate taxes. The money will not be part of your estate when you die. You can arrange for your intended heirs to pay the policy premiums by making annual gifts to them, part or all of which can be used for the premiums.

Another route is to leave a portion of your estate to a favorite charity in the form of a charitable remainder trust. You can arrange to receive annual income from the trust as long as you live as well as a current income tax deduction for a charitable gift. The amount you leave to the charity in the trust will reduce your taxable estate when you die. The income from the trust can be given as annual gifts to your heirs if you do not need the money.

Self-Study
Understanding Your Estate Taxes

1. Assume that your estate is worth $350,000. Will the federal government levy an estate tax?
   ❏ Yes   ❏ No

   Explain._____

   _____

   _____

   _____

2. Would your answer change if the estate were worth $1,500,000? Explain.

   _____

   _____

   _____

   _____

Glossary

Death taxes. Those taxes imposed on the property that is transferred to another upon the death of an individual. Death taxes include the federal estate tax and state inheritance and estate taxes.

Estate tax. A tax levied upon the gross estate of a deceased person prior to its division. (*See* Inheritance Tax.)

Gift tax. A tax levied upon the value of a gift after certain specified exemptions.

Inheritance tax. A tax levied upon the property that individual beneficiaries receive from the estate of a deceased person. *See* Estate Tax.

Unified tax credit. The amount that can be deducted from the gross estate tax.

20

Trusts

A trust is an important tool of estate planning. It is a legal entity that holds assets for certain persons or other entities. A trust is similar to a life insurance policy in that the trust property is ultimately distributed to beneficiaries under the terms of the trust agreement. Trust property passes to beneficiaries outside an individual's will and avoids probate. Holding property in a trust is a form of ownership that may result in tax savings.

WHAT IS A TRUST?

A *trust* is a legal entity consisting of assets, such as money or property, that are administered by an individual or an institution (the *trustee*) for a beneficiary or beneficiaries who may be the owner of the trust. Any asset you own—including cash, securities, real estate, and proceeds of life insurance, annuities, or pension funds—can be put into a trust.

USES OF TRUSTS

Among possible uses of trusts are the following:

■ *To Provide Management of Funds Left to a Spouse.* A spouse may lack the ability or the knowledge to manage a large sum of money effectively. In such a case, assets can be set up in a trust to be managed by a trustee who does have this specialized knowledge and experience. The spouse is thus guaranteed income for life. At the spouse's death, the assets in the trust can be distributed to your children and/or grandchildren, or any other beneficiary you name.

■ *To Hold Money Until a Child Reaches Maturity.* Funds can be set aside in a trust until a child reaches maturity, usually 18 years of age. If you believe that this is too tender an age to assume the responsibility of money management, you can provide that the funds be paid out in installments, such as one-third at age 25, one-third at age 30, and the last third at age 35. Or, you can provide that the funds be paid out in a lump sum, at a specified age, or paid out at the discretion of the trustee.

■ *To Provide for a Retarded or Physically Handicapped Child.* In the case of a retarded child, you may wish to set up a trust that would provide income for the life of the retarded person. In this way, you can insure that the individual will have spending money, clothes, and incidentals. Federal and state programs pay for basic residential and medical costs for retarded children and adults.

■ *To Save on Estate Taxes.* The Economic Recovery Tax Act of 1981 provides for an unlimited marital deduction, which means that assets left to a spouse go completely untaxed. However, when the spouse dies, if the amount in the estate exceeds the limits set up by law, then taxes are imposed. This is discussed in Chapter 19. However, the spouse's will can set up a trust for the children and/or grandchildren for the amount that exceeds the tax-free portion. For 1987 and thereafter, the amount of an estate that can pass to heirs tax-free is $600,000.

■ *To Protect the Children of a First Marriage When a Second Marriage Takes Place.* Before marrying a second time, it is essential that you protect the children of your first marriage. This can be done by setting up a trust that will provide children with income, particularly during their college years, and ultimately with the principal at some specified time.

■ *To Pay for a Child's College Education or Other Needs.* Property may be placed in a trust for a minor child for the purpose of financing education or for other needs, such as medical emergencies. The trust can be set up so that income from trust property may be distributed to the child while he or she is a minor, and at age 21, the beneficiary may receive all the trust assets and accumulated trust earnings.

■ *To Avoid Probate.* Probate, the court procedure for validating a will and disposing of an estate at death, is often a very costly and time-consuming process. Many people, seeking to bypass probate, place assets in a living trust in order to transfer ownership to others and at the same time avoid probate.

Any of these goals can be achieved through setting up a trust. It is not a do-it-yourself project.

You should call upon an experienced lawyer who specializes in estate planning and trusts to guide you.

TYPES OF TRUSTS

The two major types of trusts are a *living trust* and a *testamentary trust*. A living trust, also known as an *inter vivos trust,* is created while you are still living. The Latin words *inter vivos* mean "among the living." A testamentary trust is arranged for in your will and comes into being after your death.

Living Trusts

Living trusts are of two types. A *revocable living trust* is one that can be changed or cancelled during your lifetime. This is a distinct advantage. Another advantage is that if you, the *truster* (or maker of the trust), die, the properties held in a living trust are not subject to the formalities of probate. An *irrevocable living trust* is one that cannot be amended or revoked during your lifetime.

When to Use a Living Trust

Living trusts are useful if your wealth is substantial enough to warrant professional management; if you are the key person in a family business; or if you do not have a spouse or child capable of managing your affairs in the event that you become incapacitated. It is advisable to combine a durable power of attorney (see page 284) with a living trust.

How to Implement a Living Trust

You may immediately endow a living trust with your assets. Alternatively, you may leave it empty but assign someone durable power of attorney with instructions to pour all your money into the trust if you become incompetent or die. With a revocable living trust, you control the assets while you are alive and competent. You can receive the income from the trust, which will be taxable to you. When you die, the assets will pass to your heirs without going through probate.

The *advantages* of a revocable living trust are as follows:

■ Offers flexibility because it can be changed or cancelled during your lifetime.

■ Avoids probate when assets are transferred after your death.

■ Takes over in case of your incapacity.

■ Enables you to see how well your trustee functions and to make changes, if necessary.

The *disadvantages* of a revocable living trust are as follows:

■ Income earned by the trust is subject to income tax.

■ When you die, trust assets are subject to estate tax.

■ You cannot make a loan against the assets of the trust.

The *advantages* of an irrevocable living trust are as follows:

■ Can shift income from the trust to a beneficiary in a lower tax bracket, resulting in income tax savings.

■ Capital appreciation of trust assets is free of estate taxes when you die.

■ Avoids probate when assets are transferred after death.

■ By avoiding probate, you gain privacy.

The *disadvantages* of an irrevocable living trust are as follows:

■ You lose control of the trust assets forever.

■ If the property is sold after your death, the profit is subject to income taxes.

■ Setting up the trust agreement involves a legal fee as well as the annual cost of commissions charged by the trustee.

Testamentary Trusts

A *testamentary trust* is created by the terms of a will. It, therefore, takes effect some time after your death and, consequently, is irrevocable. Estate planning is usually directed toward the creation of testamentary trusts rather than living trusts.

Examples of some testamentary trusts include the following:

■ *Qualified Terminable Interest Property Trust (or Q-Tip).* The *Q-Tip* enables you to provide income for your spouse for his or her lifetime, and allows you (the maker of the trust) to designate how the property should be distributed upon his or her death. The Q-Tip protects your assets from going to someone your spouse later marries. If you are in a second marriage, you can also insure that your assets will go to the children of your first marriage.

■ *Standard marital trust.* A *standard marital trust* provides trust benefits to your spouse for life. After the death of your spouse, your children and/or grandchildren become the beneficiaries.

■ *Sprinkling trust.* A *sprinkling trust* allows the trustee to distribute trust income to the children or other beneficiaries according to their needs rather than according to a specific formula. If one beneficiary has a greater need than another, the trustee has the power to *sprinkle* more of the money to the needier beneficiary.

■ *Life insurance trust.* The *life insurance trust* is designed to accept the proceeds of a life insurance policy of the decedent.

OTHER TYPES OF TRUSTS

Some trusts have characteristics of both the irrevocable and revocable trusts, and others are simply custodial accounts for minors. Examples of some of these are the following:

■ *Charitable remainder trust.* A *charitable remainder trust* can be set up as a living trust or as a testamentary trust. As a living trust, it gives you an immediate tax deduction for your charitable contribution and also provides income for you and/or your family while the property is in trust. In the trust agreement, you can arrange for the charity or institution to get the trust's assets at some future date, say at your death, or ten, twenty, or twenty-five years hence. If you set it up as a testamentary trust, you can specify that the trust provide income to your beneficiary for life, and that the remainder of the trust's assets go to a specified charity or institution at the beneficiary's death.

■ *Totten trust.* A *Totten trust* is a bank account that is "in trust for" a named beneficiary, such as "Jack Smith in trust for Jane Smith." As long as Jack Smith lives, he maintains control over the account with the right to withdraw funds. Jane Smith has no right to the funds in the account until Jack Smith dies, at which time the funds in the account go directly to Jane Smith, avoiding probate. Certificates of deposit and other investments can be registered in this manner. The Totten trust is an alternative to putting savings in joint tenancy, discussed in Chapter 5.

■ *Uniform Transfers to Minors Act.* The *Uniform Gifts to Minors Act* (UGMA) was in effect in the United States until 1983. Then the *Uniform Transfers to Minors Act* (UTMA) was introduced as a substitute and, so far, more than 30 states have adopted it. The rest still use UGMA.

There are two key differences between the old and the new acts. UGMA generally limited gifts to securities, cash, bank and money-market accounts, and, in some states, life insurance policies. Under UTMA, you can give any kind of property, including real estate, partnership interests, and even artwork. And UTMA does not limit donors to adults: trusts, estates, or other entities can give, too. With this added flexibility, you can now use UTMA to make gifts to a minor by will or provide income through a trust to the custodian.

Accounts for your children under UGMA are not affected if your state switches to UTMA. You can still add cash or securities to them. But you should use the UTMA designation for the title to securities: (Name of donor), as custodian for (name of minor), under the (name of state) Uniform Transfers to Minors Act.

Both UGMA and UTMA are subject to limitations. Gifts qualify for the annual exclusion from the gift tax. Under both acts, gifts are irrevocable—you part with the assets forever. In addition, UTMA or UGMA custodianships end as soon as your child becomes an adult (commonly at age 18 or 21) unless your state provides otherwise.

Under UTMA, each parent can contribute a gift maximum of $10,000 a year to each minor and the recipient pays no income, gift, or estate taxes. This state law permits a couple to give up to $20,000 a year to each minor without being taxed. The Tax Reform Act of 1986 added the Kiddie Tax. If the child is under 14, only the first $1,000 of income from an account is taxed at the child's rate. Income amounts above $1,000 are taxed at the rates of the parent/custodian until the child reaches 14. When the child is 14 or older, income from the account is taxed at the child's personal income tax rate.

Self-Study
Should You Set Up a Trust?

1. Based upon your reading of this introduction to the subject of trusts, do you believe that you have need for a trust in your estate plan?   ❑ Yes   ❑ No

   If yes, what type of trust are you considering?_____

   _____

2. Do you have a relative or close friend qualified to serve as a trustee?   ❑ Yes   ❑ No

   If yes, who? _____

   _____

   If no, you have the choice of any bank trust department.

   List your first choice _____

   List your second choice _____

   Present the above choices to your lawyer when you discuss your estate plan and will.

3. Are you interested in charitable bequests in order to:

   a. Help the causes you have always supported, the ones that will miss your help when you are gone.

   b. Make a charitable gift as a living memorial for a loved one.

   What charitable causes have you always supported?

   _____

   _____

Glossary

Charitable remainder trust. An arrangement with a charity under which it pays income to one or more persons for the lifetime of the persons named and at some future date, say at your death, or ten, twenty, or twenty-five years hence, the charity receives the trust's assets.

Gift. A voluntary transfer of property from one person to another. Gifts can be given to your children, grandchildren, relatives, other people, or charities while you are still living, or they can be given after your death through a charitable foundation or trust. A charitable foundation can be created during your lifetime or through your *will.*

Inter vivos trust. Created while you are still living. The Latin words *inter vivos* mean *among the living.* (*See* Living Trust.)

Irrevocable living trust. A trust that cannot be changed or cancelled during your lifetime. (*See* Living Trust, Revocable Living Trust.)

Living trust. A trust that becomes effective during the holder's lifetime. The property is placed in the hands of a *trustee* to be managed by the trustee for the benefit of one or more individuals. It does not pass through probate when the holder dies. (*See* Revocable Living Trust, Irrevocable Living Trust.)

Qualified terminable interest property trust (Q-Tip). An arrangement by which your spouse has a right to the income from the principal for life, but has no access to the principal. On the death of the surviving spouse, the property goes to such person(s) or organization(s) as determined by the spouse whose property it was and who was the first to die. The concept was developed by the Economic Recovery Tax Act of 1981 (ERTA).

Revocable living trust. One that can be changed or cancelled during your lifetime.(*See also* Living Trust, Irrevocable Living Trust.)

Sprinkling trust. The trustee has the power to make distributions according to a standard such as need rather than according to a preset percentage. This gives a trustee the power to distribute income, and possibly principal, according to the needs of each beneficiary.

Successor trustee. An additional trustee listed in a will who can assume the responsibilities of trustee in case your initial trustee dies or is otherwise unable to perform the functions.

Testamentary trust. One that is created by the terms of a will and that comes into being after an individual's death.

Totten trust. A *payable-on-death* bank account. The bank account will usually read *John Smith in trust for Jane Smith,* or vice versa.

Trust. A legal entity (the *trust*) created by the owner of property for the purpose of administering and distributing such property for the benefit of the owner and/or other persons.

Trustee. The person who holds legal title to property for the use and benefit of another person who is the beneficiary.

21

Probate

Probate is a state's court procedure for establishing the validity of a will and supervising the distribution of an estate's assets. The laws of probate have evolved over centuries and operate in all fifty states. Basically, the probate process serves an important function, namely, to make certain that your assets are distributed as specified in your will, thus protecting the interests of your beneficiaries. The probate process also serves to insure that the property of an individual who dies without a will is distributed in accordance with the laws of the state.

Criticisms of the probate process over the years include high costs, a slow and cumbersome system that is too time-consuming, and corruption among probate lawyers and probate judges. As a result, much has been written on how to avoid probate. The thrust of much of the writing is that the average layman can probably handle whatever probate proceedings are required without the assistance of a lawyer, and that assets can be legally transferred without going through probate.

With a little time and effort and a willingness to study a state's probate laws and procedures, a survivor can probably deal with the details of settling an estate as a do-it-yourself project. Relevant material on handling the simple, routine tasks can be found at your local library. Moreover, personnel at local probate courts are usually cooperative and will assist you in filling out and filing required forms. Even if you ultimately seek the assistance of a lawyer, you can probably complete most of the routine, preliminary paper work, thus reducing your lawyer's workload. This would significantly reduce the lawyer's fee, yielding large savings to you.

SMALL ESTATES (UNDER $10,000)

Even in the case of estates under $10,000, a will must be reviewed by a probate court. More than twenty states have instituted simplified probate proceedings by adopting, in whole or in part, the Uniform Probate Code (UPC). The procedure for the settlement of small estates is designed to eliminate a large part of a probate court's administrative requirements. In such states, if the gross estate is $10,000 or less of personal property, the simplified proceedings are fast and inexpensive. A filing fee may be charged, but it is minimal.

If an individual dies without a will (intestate), the probate court must still become involved in order to check the amount of assets left by the decedent and the number of beneficiaries related to the deceased. The court then applies the state's intestacy law in distributing the assets to the legitimate claimants.

In some jurisdictions, a layperson may be able to handle many aspects of the proceeding without an attorney. After a person dies, the executor of the will, or anyone who is handling matters for the deceased, must file a notification of the death with the probate court in the county where the person lived. Notification usually must be filed within nine months of the death.

METHODS OF TRANSFERRING PROPERTY OUTSIDE PROBATE

To bypass the probate process, you can arrange to transfer property to a beneficiary outside your will. Among the methods available are the following:

■ *Joint Ownership.* When you die, all property held in joint tenancy with the right of survivorship automatically goes to the survivor, usually your spouse, outside the probate process. Usually, joint ownership is used for your home, but the technique of joint ownership can be applied also to other types of property such as stocks and bonds, bank accounts, and mutual funds.

■ *Living Trusts.* The two types of living trusts, revocable and irrevocable, can also be used for transferring property outside the will and the probate process. The trust instrument specifies who shall receive the property when death occurs.

■ *Life Insurance.* Life insurance is not part of a probate estate because when you die, the proceeds of the policy are paid directly to a named beneficiary. The money is transferred by contract and is, therefore, nonprobated property.

■ *Gifts.* By giving gifts to your heirs before your death, you will reduce the size of your estate. The gifts may be subject to the federal gift tax, but the gifts themselves are not part of the probate estate.

ASSETS SUBJECT TO PROBATE

Assets subject to probate are those held in sole ownership that are usually included in your will, such as cash on hand, individual savings and checking accounts, certificates of deposit, government securities, mutual funds, stocks and bonds, money owed to you, life insurance to the estate, a share in a business, automobile(s), household furnishings, art and antiques, jewelry and furs, and other valuables, including a stamp or coin collection.

ROLE OF A PROBATE COURT

A *probate court* not only validates the will but also serves as a referee, resolving questions of interpretation of the wishes expressed in the will. A will may be poorly worded, and the heirs may question the interpretation. The court also considers whether undue influence was used to obtain particular benefits, whether the maker of the will was of sound mind, or whether the executor is handling the estate properly.

It has been estimated that almost three-quarters of the people who die each year leave no will. These are mainly wives and single people. In these cases, the probate court has the responsibility of appointing an administrator who must inventory the decedent's assets and then have them appraised to get an accurate value. The property is then distributed according to prescribed state law. No one knows what the wishes of the decedent were, nor is it possible to make allocations according to need. The law spells out what the spouse receives and what each child receives. The 8-year-old gets the same amount as an adult child; the affluent adult child gets the same amount as the retarded child.

The role of a probate court is to study the will of a decedent. It must be proven to the satisfaction of the court that the instrument before it is the decedent's valid will. If the court accepts the will as valid, then the property owned solely by the decedent in his or her own name at the moment of death is distributed. If the court rejects the will as invalid, the property of the decedent is distributed in accordance with the state's law of intestacy.

WHAT MAKES A WILL INVALID?

A will is invalid if it is handwritten in a state that does not accept handwritten wills. Or, the will may not have been properly witnessed: there may have been too few witnesses, or one of the witnesses may also be a beneficiary. Possibly all the heirs named in the will are deceased, or the property that was bequeathed in the will has been sold.

The probate court will generally try to weed out any parts of a will that are invalid and then will try to honor your instructions in the rest of the will as closely as possible. If this is not possible, the court may declare the entire will invalid and proceed as if you had died without a will, distributing your assets according to the law of intestacy.

If you wish to avoid this possibility, make certain that your will is valid and that it stays valid by having it drawn up by a qualified law-yer. Then, keep it up-to-date by reviewing it every two or three years.

ADVANTAGES AND DISADVANTAGES OF PROBATE

The *advantages* of using the probate process are as follows:

■ Determines the validity of a will.

■ Serves as a forum for settling disputes on the interpretation of a decedent's wishes.

■ Protects your beneficiaries by honoring their directives in your will.

■ Distributes property of an individual who dies without a will according to state law.

The *disadvantages* of using the probate process are as follows:

■ The probate process is expensive, involving legal fees, executor fees, court costs, and other fees and expenses.

■ The probate process takes a long time, possibly years, if the estate is diverse, if tax problems exist, or if disputes occur.

■ Records of the probate court are open to the press and public, leading to unwelcome publicity.

■ Charges are frequently heard that a particular probate system is corrupt.

Self-Study
List of Your Probate and Nonprobate Assets

On this worksheet, enter your probate and nonprobate assets.

Probate Assets	Nonprobate Assets
_____	_____
_____	_____
_____	_____
_____	_____
_____	_____
_____	_____

Glossary

Probate. The judicial process of establishing the validity of a will and supervising the distribution of an estate's assets.

Probate court. Acts as a referee and decision maker by answering pertinent questions and resolving conflicts of interpretation of a will.

22

Planning for the Inevitable

While many people prefer to ignore or overlook the subject, the fact remains that death is inevitable. Just as you make preparations for other facets of life so, too, you must make careful preparations for the final event. It is not easy to do. A death in the family is a deep wound. Survivors invariably react with shock and disbelief, even on those occasions when the death was anticipated. The grief and sense of loss are overwhelming, and people are not prepared to cope.

Thinking people who are concerned about the inevitable should prepare for it in every way possible. Planning will insure that you have a voice in your own disposition and will save your loved ones the headaches and problems of making decisions on matters they may be too bereaved to handle effectively.

This chapter provides a check list of things to consider before and after a death, details of arranging a funeral, funeral ceremonies and costs, things to do after the funeral and interment, and survivors' benefits.

WHEN DEATH OCCURS

It is precisely during this period of suffering that survivors are required to handle complex and often expensive business arrangements. Under normal conditions, this would require calm detachment and presence of mind. Yet when a death occurs and you become highly emotional, it is difficult to exercise sound judgment. Perhaps it might be sensible at such a time to call upon a close relative, friend, clergy member, or family lawyer to make the decisions that have to be made and to do the things that have to be done.

The following checklists of things to do after a death and after the funeral and interment should be helpful. This section also provides background material on the role of the death certificate.

A CHECKLIST OF THINGS TO DO AFTER A DEATH

After a death, some things must be done immediately and some things must be done after the funeral and interment.

Things to Do Immediately

Immediately following a death, you must do the following:

❑ **Obtain death certificate.** Get a death certificate from the physician attending at the time of death or from the physician who examines the body after death. (See page 309 for more details.)

❑ **Obtain copy of the will.** The will and/or supplemental letter may have directions concerning disposal of the body.

❑ **Notify religious leader.** A member of the clergy can help you to make decisions at this time and can offer spiritual comfort.

❑ **Dispose of the body.** Check whether the decedent had any specific wishes for disposal of the body, including possible donation of the body or organs for medical purposes. A Uniform Donor Card may have been prepared in accordance with the Uniform Anatomical Gifts Act. Check the decedent's will, driver's license, or the supplemental letter of instructions, if available. (See page 309 for more details.)

❑ **Notify burial or memorial society.** If the deceased was a member of a burial society or a memorial society, notify an official of that group. Find out what services the society provides.

❑ **Choose funeral home.** After comparing the costs of two or three funeral homes, hire one. The first service of the funeral home will be to transfer the body to the home's facilities.

❑ **Locate cemetery plot.** Determine whether the deceased owns a burial plot. If a *family plot* is to be the site of the burial, obtain the consent of the individual responsible for the interment. If no gravesite is available, it will be necessary to purchase one.

❑ **Make funeral arrangements.** Make final arrangements for the funeral and interment.

❑ **Notify relatives and friends.** Advise relatives and friends of the date, time, and place of the funeral and burial.

❑ **Prepare obituary notices.** Prepare an obituary notice and then place it in appropriate newspapers and other publications.

❑ **Notify decedent's employer.** Notify the decedent's employer. Also, notify fraternal orders or lodges in which the decedent was a member.

Things to Do After the Funeral and Interment

After the interment has occurred, the survivor should do the following:

❑ **Contact decedent's lawyer.** Inform the decedent's lawyer about the death. The original will may be in the lawyer's vault or in a safe deposit box. Probate proceedings should be initiated.

❑ **Collect official documents.** Collect the official documents left by the deceased (e.g., birth and marriage certificates, veteran's discharge, social security card, copies of tax returns) and turn them over to the lawyer and/or the executor or executrix so that settlement of the estate can be started. The locations of these documents may have been listed in the supplemental letter of instructions, attached to the will.

❑ **Funeral and burial allowances.** Prepare a list of funeral and burial allowances to which the survivors may be entitled. Sources of such allowances are: Department of Veterans Affairs, Social Security Administration, a labor union, a fraternal organization, an employer, burial insurance purchased from an insurance company, or other sources. Obtain and prepare the necessary applications.

❑ **Tombstone.** Begin to make arrangements for a tombstone or grave marker.

The Death Certificate

A *death certificate* stating the date, time, place, and cause of death is required in all states. The document is prepared by a physician, medical examiner, or coroner who examines the body. It must be filed in the appropriate county office. Depending upon state laws, the certificate must be filed within a few days of death. It is important that you obtain several certified copies of the death certificate. These are required as proof of death in order to arrange for probate of the will and to secure Social Security benefits, life insurance payments, and pension benefits. A death certificate is also required to gain access to the decedent's safe deposit box and to obtain possession of the decedent's assets. Additional certified copies of the death certificate can be obtained later if they are required. It is important that the cause of death be correctly entered on the death certificate since accidental death, if this were the case, might elicit higher life insurance benefits for the survivors.

In most cases, death is due to natural causes. However, if death were due to an accident or other unnatural causes, such as murder or suicide, a medical examiner or coroner would determine the date and probable cause of death. An autopsy may be performed if the cause of death is doubtful, or to provide the medical profession with additional information about any illness from which the decedent may have suffered. An autopsy requires the consent of surviving relatives, except in the case of murder or suicide.

DISPOSAL OF THE BODY

State laws generally require that a dead body be buried or otherwise legally disposed of within a specified number of days. Generally, these laws further specify that only a licensed funeral director is authorized to move the decedent.

The family or the executor of a decedent's estate is not legally bound to follow the decedent's wishes regarding the funeral and burial, such as cost of the funeral, or how the body should be prepared, or where it should be buried. The law, however, usually does honor a decedent's right to donate the body or specific body organs. Every effort, of course, should be made to satisfy the decedent's wishes as specified in the will or supplemental letter of instructions.

The choices of disposal of the body for the typical family are:

■ *Earth Burial.* In the United States and Canada, earth burial is the most widely used form of disposition, involving interment in a grave or crypt of uncremated remains, generally in a casket.

■ *Entombment.* In entombment, the casket with the remains is placed in a mausoleum or in an above-ground tomb.

■ *Cremation.* In cremation, the body is reduced to ashes that are then buried or scattered, depending on your wishes or local ordinances. While most religious groups approve cremation, some, such as certain Protestant denominations, Islam, Eastern Orthodoxy, and Orthodox Judaism, do not.

■ *Whole-Body or Organ Donation.* You may wish to consider donating a particular organ or organs of your body—eyes, kidneys, heart—or your entire body for research or educational purposes. Donating a particular organ or organs of your body can help someone who may be in desperate need. Such a donation is probably the most meaningful gift you can make to promote life and happiness for someone else.

Making this donation through a properly signed and witnessed document is legally binding on the heirs of the deceased. Often, however, some of the survivors object, and medical schools, research foundations, and hospitals are reluctant to go to court to enforce such a gift because the delays of a court case make the organ useless for transplantation. If you desire to donate your body or any part of it, you should discuss your wishes with your family to obtain their agreement. Be sure that they understand the procedure to be followed after your death. A free Uniform Donor Card can be ordered from the United Network for Organ Sharing (UNOS), P.O. Box 28010, Richmond, Virginia 23228. 1-800-446-2726.

■ *Direct Disposition.* In direct disposition, the body is transferred from the place of death to the place of disposition, either a cemetery or a crematory. Direct disposition is less expensive than a traditional funeral, because it involves no embalming, no viewing, and no need for an expensive casket.

The two least expensive options are wholebody donation and direct disposition.

ARRANGING A FUNERAL

Time is limited in arranging a funeral, but crucial decisions must be made regarding disposal of the body, selection of a casket, the type of funeral service, and other details.

A funeral ceremony offers an opportunity to commemorate the life of the deceased and to recognize the loss that has occurred. The type of funeral ceremony is determined by personal preferences and religious beliefs. If you wish to plan your own funeral, you should write your preferences as part of your supplemental letter of instructions. Traditional religious funerals vary among different religious groups. Whether you are planning your own funeral or a funeral for a relative or friend, the best guidance you can obtain is your local minister, priest, or rabbi.

A memorial service, at which the body is not present, is becoming increasingly popular. The memorial service is generally held after a burial or cremation and is conducted in a church, a synagogue, a funeral home, a private home, or any other meeting place. The service is very flexible and is designed to meet the preferences of the deceased or the family. Other types of services include fraternal ceremonies, such as those conducted by the Masons or Knights of Columbus. These services are supplementary to a regular funeral service.

If you are planning a funeral ceremony, consider whether you desire a religious or a nonreligious service; the type of readings and/or music to be included; the number and names of the participants; whether the body will be present or not, and if it is present, whether the casket will be open or closed.

The *Final Report* of the Federal Trade Commission on the Funeral Industry Regulation Rule reveals that 66 percent of funerals held are open casket service with ground burial; 20 percent are closed casket service with ground burial; 12 percent involve cremation either before or after a service; and 2 percent entail above-ground burial.

Funeral Costs

In 1995, the charges billed through a funeral home for the funeral ceremony and burial average $5,000 and confirm the high cost of dying. For many consumers, this is one of the most expensive purchases of a lifetime. The cost of direct cremation is significantly less than a ground burial, averaging between $1,000 and $2,000. Since these are averages, there is considerable variation in cost in different parts of the country. The United States funeral industry consists of about 22,000 funeral homes with an annual volume of $10 to $12 billion in merchandise and services.

The economics of the funeral industry requires high costs. With about two million people dying each year, the 22,000 funeral homes handle an average of 100 funerals each per year. At least half of the nation's funeral homes, particularly in rural areas, do fewer than 25 cases a year, while those in urban areas may average well over 1,000 a year. This number of customers must generate enough income to keep the facility attractive, to maintain a year-round staff, and to provide for new hearses and limousines. The funeral director must generate maximum income out of every funeral in order to meet overhead costs.

Critics of the funeral industry state that some funeral directors take advantage of grief-stricken and ill-prepared customers who, under the pressures of bereavement, make poor decisions that prove to be very costly. These critics argue that more government regulation is needed to protect the public. They advise consumers to learn well in advance about the choices that are available.

The Federal Trade Commission established a rule on funeral trade practices, effective April 30, 1984, requiring the nation's funeral directors to:

■ Provide purchasers with full disclosure of prices on caskets, burial vaults, and other elements of a funeral, including an itemized list before the funeral is scheduled.

■ Refrain from misleading advertising and deceptive practices such as advising a prospective customer that embalming is required and that this process will preserve a body indefinitely.

■ Provide price information over the telephone to customers who request it.

■ Refrain from the "bundling" of services into packages that force the consumer to buy unwanted services.

■ Refrain from unfair and deceptive practices such as requiring a casket for cremations.

The funeral rule was renewed and toughened by the Federal Trade Commission in 1994. It expanded the funeral rule by banning casket handling fees, which some funeral directors had charged customers who bought caskets from another source.

A Complete Funeral

The price of a *complete funeral* includes certain standard items, extra items, and burial or cremation costs.

■ *Standard Items.* Undertakers generally include the following standard items in the price of a complete funeral: removal of the body to the funeral establishment; use of funeral home facilities; embalming and restoration; dressing of remains; cost of casket; use of hearse and one limousine; staff services; arranging for religious services, burial permit, death benefits, and newspaper death notices; providing pallbearers; arranging and care of flowers; providing guest register and acknowledgment cards; obtaining copies of the death certificate; and in some cases, extension of credit.

■ *Extra Items.* Extra items that may be purchased include a vault, which is very costly; extra limousines; music; an honorarium for clergy, which may be handled directly by a survivor; flowers; and burial clothing. The tax on these items will also be an added cost.

■ *Burial Costs.* Burial costs—charges for opening and closing a grave—also add to the cost of a funeral. The undertaker may be called upon to assist survivors with the purchase of a cemetery plot, and will arrange with the cemetery for preparation of the grave. These burial costs are often paid for by the undertaker and then reimbursed by the survivors.

Price itemization makes it easier to reject

those goods and services that are not wanted. In some instances, the funeral director may increase other prices to compensate for the items rejected. The FTC notes in one study that unscrupulous funeral directors put higher price tags on caskets before prosperous-looking survivors enter the selection room. Another fraudulent tactic is the substitution of a less expensive casket for the more expensive one selected by the survivors.

Even when prices are itemized, however, you have no way of knowing whether you are being charged the same prices as everyone else. The FTC notes that documents obtained from a large California mortuary revealed a compensation system for salespersons that penalized them for low-priced sales and rewarded them for high-priced ones.

Pre-Paid Funerals

Pre-paid funerals have been promoted very heavily in some areas of the country. The complete funeral is usually pre-paid in full, and the price that is quoted is a guaranteed amount that cannot change. However, the most widely used pre-payment plan is known as a *pre-needs arrangement* in which the final cost of the funeral will depend upon costs at the time of death. Each state has legislation that spells out individual variations of the plan. The legislation also specifies how the money paid into the plan is handled. These rulings are known as *Pre-Need Funeral Laws*.

New York State has recently revised its 1994 law so that the money advanced in planning a funeral must be placed in an escrow account. All interest earned on the deposit must be retained in the account until the time of need or until cancellation of the plan. In some states, the money is placed in an irrevocable trust. Some states do not require that 100 percent of the deposit be placed in an escrow account and often permit deductions of fees and commissions from the account.

Some states allow burial insurance that is earmarked for the final costs of a funeral. Burial insurance policies are sold through a funeral home in some states or by an insurance company in others.

Caskets

Caskets are made of a variety of materials, including wood; metals such as steel, copper, and bronze; and fiberglass. Prices for caskets vary according to manufacturing costs in different areas of the country, ranging from less than $500 to as much as $50,000. The cost variation is affected by the material used as well as by the interior trimming. Part of the cost of the casket is the shipping charge from the factory to the ultimate destination.

Death Announcements

An *obituary* is a news article about the deceased individual that appears on the obituary page. It is printed by the newspaper at the editor's discretion and is free of charge.

A *death announcement* is a paid announcement, and the cost varies from newspaper to newspaper. A prominent East Coast paper, for example, charges $22 per line for papers printed from Monday through Saturday and $26 per line for the Sunday paper, probably the highest rate in the country.

Embalming

Second to the coffin in the price of a funeral is embalming, which makes possible the viewing of the body in an open casket. If survivors reject embalming, then the funeral home will add a charge for *preservation*, which is simply refrigeration, and this service may cost as much as embalming.

Vault

A vault is a container that encloses the casket when it is placed in the ground and can be one of the most costly components of a funeral. No evidence is available to prove that a vault prolongs protection for a body. Indeed, the airtight vault may hasten the decomposition of the corpse. Some cemeteries require a vault to keep the ground from collapsing as the casket gradually disintegrates. Some cemeteries sell their own concrete boxes, which are less expensive than the steel or concrete vaults sold by funeral homes. It is estimated that almost three-fourths of all burials include a vault.

Monument

The manufacture and sale of a marker or monument for a gravesite is a separate industry. Markers or monuments are usually granite, marble, or bronze and account for a major expense associated with interment. The monument is selected by the survivors and must then be inscribed, moved to the cemetery, and erected on a concrete foundation on the gravesite. A considerable amount of time elapses after burial before a monument is erected.

Memorial Societies

Memorial societies are nonprofit, cooperative-type organizations created by consumers and designed to help people get the kind of funeral they want at a reasonable price. Over 200 memorial societies have been organized in the United States, with about 1,000,000 members. They are usually affiliated with churches, senior citizen centers, unions, or civic groups, and are staffed primarily by volunteers. They pro-

vide information about low-cost funerals, cremation, bequeathal of the body or organs of the body, and other information on death arrangements. You can join a memorial society by making a one-time membership payment of $10 to $20.

Since the memorial society is operated by volunteers, it has no incentive to earn a profit and it does not provide or sell any funeral merchandise or funeral service. It serves as liaison with funeral directors to fulfill the needs of its membership. Generally, the price for a funeral arranged by a memorial society is lower than that of a funeral home because the memorial society is a large purchaser of funeral services. While memorial societies are geared specifically to assist their members, most societies will assist nonmembers in obtaining low-cost funerals. The society may even furnish comparative cost data for your area.

To locate your nearest memorial society, you can contact the Continental Association of Funeral and Memorial Societies, 2001 S Street, N.W., Suite 630, Washington, D.C. 20009. The phone number is 202-462-8888.

Cemetery Plots

As indicated previously, state law requires that a human body be buried in an officially designated cemetery or graveyard. If you plan to continue to live where you are now living, and if you wish an earth burial, you should buy a burial plot or graves. This will spare your survivors the unpleasant and painful task of having to buy a gravesite quickly after your demise.

All cemeteries are regulated and supervised by agencies of the federal, state, or local governments. Depending upon their ownership, cemeteries may be classified into three categories:

1. Those owned and operated by religious, fra-

ternal, and philanthropic groups with private funds.

2. Those owned and operated by private corporations for profit.

3. Those owned and operated by a public authority and supported by tax funds.

When buying a cemetery plot, the factors to consider are:

■ *Location.* You must decide whether you wish to be buried where you grew up or spent your adult life or where you are living in retirement. You should also find out whether you have the right to resell your plot if you decide to buy one elsewhere or whether the cemetery will buy it back from you and at what price.

■ *Size.* Cemetery plots are usually sold as single graves (one for yourself), or two gravesites (a plot for you and for your spouse), or a cemetery plot for the entire family. Some cemeteries allow double depth graves, where one casket can be buried on top of another. This is a cost-saving factor that should be considered.

■ *Maintenance Costs.* Determine what the annual upkeep costs are as compared to the costs of perpetual care of the grave or graves.

If you buy a cemetery plot before it is needed, you have the opportunity to look around and to compare prices. You can ascertain the reputation of a cemetery by checking with the local Better Business Bureau or a member of the local clergy.

BENEFITS TO DEFRAY FUNERAL EXPENSES

The two most important benefits generally available to survivors are the Social Security death benefit and the Department of Veterans Affairs death benefit. Many people do not realize that they are entitled to one or both of these and often money is lost because the time limit for application expires.

Social Security Survivor Benefit

The benefit is a lump-sum payment to a survivor(s), in an amount up to $255. The application for death benefits must be submitted within two years from the date of death, using Form SSA8.

If the deceased left no surviving spouse, the death benefit may be paid to any survivor responsible for the expenses of the funeral. If the survivor wishes, Social Security will send the payment directly to the funeral home. If a body is donated to a medical facility, the cost of transporting the body is an expense that Social Security will reimburse, not exceeding the maximum of $255. (See Chapter 7, Social Security.)

Veterans' Survivor Benefits

The Department of Veterans Affairs will pay a $300 burial and funeral allowance for deceased veterans who had been receiving a pension or compensation at the time of death. This department will also assume responsibility for the burial of those veterans whose deaths occurred while in a hospital facility or nursing home of the department. If specified eligibility requirements are met, the department will pay an additional $150 plot or interment allowance. This benefit, however, is payable only if the veteran is interred in a private cemetery. Grave space in a national cemetery is free for a veteran who served honorably in the armed forces. All veterans are entitled to a United States flag with which to drape the coffin.

If the veteran's death is service-related, the government will pay an allowance of more than $1,000. Veterans Form 21-530 must be filed within two years after the death whether the death is service-related or non-service-related.

The payment will be made to the individual who paid for the funeral. Contact your local Department of Veterans Affairs office for further details.

Documents Required
for Collecting Funeral Benefits

Survivors will need copies of the following documents when applying for the various funeral allowances:

■ *Death Certificate.* A copy of the death certificate, certified by the issuing agency.

■ *Birth Certificate.* A certified copy of the birth certificate of both surviving spouse and minor children for Social Security and Department of Veterans Affairs benefits.

■ *Marriage Certificate.* A certified copy of the marriage certificate.

■ *W-2 Form.* A copy of the W-2 form or the federal income tax return for the most recent year as proof of the decedent's recent employment record for the Social Security benefit.

■ *Veteran's Discharge.* A copy of the veteran's discharge papers for Department of Veterans Affairs benefits.

■ *Receipted Bill.* A copy of the receipted bill from the funeral home for Department of Veterans Affairs benefits and for Social Security benefits.

■ *Social Security Number.* Survivors should have available the Social Security number of the deceased to claim Social Security benefits.

DEALING WITH LOSS OF A LOVED ONE

Most individuals prefer to avoid the topic of death and dying. The subject is ignored or spoken about only in private. Actually, it cannot be brushed aside and must be confronted honestly.

Death does occur. It is a reality you must face because it is the ultimate human experience.

Discussion of death has increased significantly over the last several years. A large number of books and articles have been published on the subject, and colleges and universities around the country are offering courses about death and dying. Psychologists are dealing with the complex problems of survivors and their adjustment after the loss of a loved one. Some of the major aspects of dealing with loss are discussed below.

The Crisis of Bereavement

The loss of a loved one creates a deep wound. The healing process is often slow and painful. While the wound may never heal completely, an adjustment to living is ultimately effected. It is natural to think that you cannot live without the deceased, and you feel lost. You function and do what has to be done, arranging the funeral, and finally giving away the deceased's clothing and other items. You are in shock.

As the shock of the event wears away, the pain becomes more evident. It is difficult to shake off and seems to persist over the weeks and months. You need the support of relatives, friends, and clergy to help you get a grip on yourself once again and come to terms with reality. Eventually, you begin to emerge from this phase of grief and begin to take note of the world around you. The experience helps you grow. An understanding of the feelings and needs of others emerges. You become wiser and warmer in your relationships.

Living Alone

Now you are alone. The daily chores of running a household persist. Food must be bought and stored; a meal for one must be prepared; the house must be cleaned; laundry must be taken care of; and you may have to report back to work to do your job. And then, every night you must come home to an empty house which is silent and dark. Living alone may be a fearful experience. It is important to feel secure in your surroundings, and you worry about locking the door and windows at night. The slightest sound may awaken you. The reality of your aloneness is devastating.

As a widow or widower, you must now become active in the handling of the details of the will, of probate proceedings, of distributions to children and possibly grandchildren, and of a variety of other financial matters with which you may be unfamiliar. Questions that will arise require solutions. A change in housing arrangements may be in order. You may wish to pursue a second career or a new career. This may require training and career counseling. Other problems will arise: dating, sexuality, and remarriage. You may wish to develop new friendships, continue your education, or enjoy new leisure activities. *But do not make any changes until at least one year has elapsed.*

Self-Study
Basic Information About Yourself

Collect basic information for your obituary and/or eulogy. It will be very helpful for your survivors.

	(Name of husband or individual)	(Name of wife or individual)
1. Full name		
2. Place of birth		
3. Date of birth		
4. Schools and colleges attended		
5. Degrees		
6. Honors		
7. Father's name		
8. Father's birthplace		
9. Father's occupation		
10. Mother's maiden name		
11. Mother's birthplace		
12. Mother's occupation		
13. Your occupation		
14. Your place of work		
15. Years in your occupation		
16. Armed services record		
17. Memberships in clubs and/or fraternal organizations		
18. Your children's names and addresses		
19. Number and names of grandchildren		

Self-Study
Instructions for Your Survivors

The following is a sample list of instructions that you should prepare for your survivors. When it is completed, make it available to your spouse, relative, or close friend.

Instructions for Funeral and Burial

	(Name of husband or individual)	(Name of wife or individual)
1. Name, address, and phone number of funeral home selected	_____	_____
2. Type of service preferred: a. At funeral facility?	_____	_____
b. Church or synagogue?	_____	_____
Name and address	_____	_____
c. Gravesite? Name and address	_____	_____
	_____	_____
d. Religious or nonreligious service	_____	_____
e. Type: Private? Public? Memorial service later?	_____	_____
	_____	_____
f. Name of person to conduct service	_____	_____
Phone number	_____	_____
g. Names of speakers	_____	_____
Phone numbers	_____	_____
h. Music? Flowers?	_____	_____
i. Casket flag for a veteran	_____	_____
3. Casket: a. Type and price range	_____	_____
b. Open for viewing or closed	_____	_____

	(Name of husband or individual)	(Name of wife or individual)

4. Disposition of body:
   a. Burial. Specify:
      Earth burial or above ground
      in a mausoleum

   b. Cremation. Specify:
      Earth burial of urn;
      Niche in columbarium;
      Delivered to survivors;
      Scattered: land or sea

   c. Donation of body or parts.
      Specify: Entire body;
      List parts

      Name, address, and phone number
      of recipient organization.
      (Attach authorization)

5. Name and location of cemetery:

   a. Individual grave or plot?

   b. Location of cemetery deed

6. Memorial contributions:
   Name and address of charity or
   organization to receive memorial
   donations.

7. Organizations to be notified:
   a. Name of organization

   b. Person to be contacted

   c. Address and phone number

8. Membership in memorial society:
   a. Society name

   b. Person to be contacted

   c. Address and phone number

Self-Study
Your Thoughts on Surviving a Loss

1. From your personal experience, what problems have you observed in the life of an individual who has suffered a loss?

_____

_____

_____

_____

_____

2. If you had the opportunity, what suggestions would you make to this grieving individual in order to alleviate the problems?

_____

_____

_____

_____

_____

3. What plans do you have for dealing with a loss if you should suffer one?

_____

_____

_____

_____

Glossary

Burial. *See* Cremation; Earth Burial; Entombment.

Burial society. An organization of individuals that assumes responsibility for all the details of burial and/or cremation.

Burial vault. An outer receptacle used to enclose a casket or similar container in a grave.

Casket. A coffin or rigid container that encases a body. May be ornamented and lined with fabric. (*See also* Minimal Container.)

Cemetery. A burial ground or tract of land set aside for graves or tombs.

Cemetery Plot. A burial site for one or more graves owned by an individual, family, or organization.

Columbarium. A building in which cremation urns are stored.

Cremation. The act of incinerating a body. The residue of ashes consists of small bone fragments. (*See also* Earth burial, Entombment.)

Crematory. An establishment that incinerates a body as the means of disposal.

Crypt. A room or cell that serves as an alternative to earth burial. May be located underground. (*See also* Mausoleum.)

Death benefit. The two most important benefits generally available to survivors are the Social Security death benefit and the Department of Veterans Affairs' death benefit.

Death certificate. A document, signed by a doctor, medical examiner, or coroner, giving pertinent information about a deceased person, such as name; age; date, time, place, and cause of death.

Direct disposition. The act of burying or cremating a body without a ceremony or viewing.

Earth burial. The act or ceremony of burying the remains of a deceased person in the ground. It is the most widely used form of disposition in the United States and Canada.

Embalming. The process of treating a dead body using chemicals and drugs so as to preserve it to make viewing possible in an open casket. (*See also* Preservation.)

Entombment. The placing of a casket with the remains in a *mausoleum,* an above-ground tomb. (*See also* Cremation, Earth burial.)

Eulogy. A speech or writing in honor or praise of a deceased person.

Family plot. A burial site for one or more graves owned by a family.

Funeral director. A mortician or undertaker who is in charge of arrangements for a funeral and burial or cremation.

Funeral home. An establishment specifically intended as a place where the body of the deceased may repose before the funeral and where those who knew the deceased may pay last respects. Also known as *funeral chapel, funeral parlor, mortuary.*

Funeral service. A ceremony that is usually held with the body present.

Funeral Trade Practices Rule. Sets forth rules of operation for the nation's funeral homes. It was approved by the United States Federal Trade Commission and became effective April 30, 1984.

Grave liner. *See* Burial vault.

Grave marker. *See* Monument, Tombstone.

Immediate disposal. *See* Direct Disposition.

Lot. *See* Plot.

Mausoleum. An above-ground building where crypts are located. (*See also* Crypt.)

Memorial service. A ceremony usually held after a body has been buried or cremated.

Memorial society. A non-profit cooperative designed to help people arrange for the funeral services they want at a reasonable price.

Minimal container. A nonmetal, alternative container to hold a body, possibly a nonrigid pouch made of canvas that is simple and much cheaper than a casket. (*See also* Casket.)

Monument. A tombstone or structure erected as a marker for a grave. (*See also* Tombstone.)

Mortuary. (*See* Funeral Home.)

Obituary. A notice of the death of a person, generally in a newspaper, and often containing a brief biographical sketch.

Plot. The cemetery land purchased by an individual for burial in a grave.

Preservation. Refrigeration of the dead body to make viewing possible in an open casket. (*See* Embalming.)

Supplemental letter of instructions. A memorandum of personal details that should be attached to your will with a copy to your executor and one for you and your spouse so that it may be kept up-to-date. The supplemental letter of instructions should include such information as location of vital documents, location of assets, employment or business information, funeral and burial instructions, and disposition of personal valuables.

Tombstone. A stone marker, usually inscribed, on a grave or tomb.

Uniform donor card. A card prepared in advance of death, indicating the decedent's wishes for disposal of the body, including possible donation of the body or specific organs for medical purposes, and prepared in accordance with the Uniform Anatomical Gifts Act.

Urn. An ornamental container used to hold cremated remains.

Will. A legal document, almost always in writing and properly executed, which describes how a person wants his or her property distributed after death. May include funeral and burial instructions.

Conclusion

Congratulations! Those of you who have read through the entire book and have reviewed the self-study sections, personalizing the material and applying the relevant information to your situations, are well on the road to a future relatively free of financial anxiety. You stand on the threshold, ready to join millions of other Americans who are enjoying a comfortable retirement.

For them and for you, a sound financial base is the heart of the golden years ahead. This base relies on three fundamental sources of income: Social Security, a pension, and savings and investments. It is important to stay alert and aware of changes that may occur in any of these three areas.

First, consider Social Security. The generous benefits currently paid by this system may be reduced to some extent over the next decade or two. However, you can be assured that Social Security, already part of the American social and economic fabric, will be there for you when you retire and will be continued for generations to come.

Similarly, current levels of pensions may be curtailed. Employers may move more and more from the traditional, predominantly employer-paid, defined benefit pension plans to defined contribution plans that require employee contributions. Future benefits will be determined by the amount contributed over one's working years and by the success of the investments made with the funds contributed.

With the uncertainty of the amount of Social Security and pension benefits in the future, you, as a retirement planner, will have to rely more heavily on your own personal savings and investments. To plan for a successful retirement today, you must take a greater responsibility for your own future by becoming a regular saver and a prudent investor. To guarantee a comfortable retirement, you must start your savings and investment program as early as possible to enable your money to grow through the magic of compounding.

By working with this book, you have learned the basics of Social Security, pensions, savings, and investments. You have taken the first important step toward a comfortable future by coming to grips with the basic considerations in financial planning. Along the way, you studied all the other components of a complete retirement plan: life and health insurance including Medicare and medigap, budgeting, taxes and tax shelters, estate planning including wills and trusts, other legal considerations, retirement housing, work and leisure plans. Finally, you've looked at coping with life's inevitable losses.

You are now well prepared to begin the retirement lifestyle. Very few people are as well prepared, but the time and effort you have expended will return significant dividends in the years ahead. You are well on the way toward a secure retirement because you have touched base with all the key elements of a retirement plan.

Having said all of this, my final advice is to be prepared for retirement's change of pace. If possible, retirement should not be a complete break with your working lifestyle. Try to ease into the transition. Before you stop working, give more time to interests you want to pursue in retirement. And along the way, keep updating and revising your retirement plan as developed in the self-study sections of the book. Move forward with confidence in all you have discovered and with a positive approach to the years ahead.

Looking Ahead
to the Next Edition

Anyone wishing to submit suggestions, additions, or corrections for the next edition of this book should send them directly to the publisher:

Retiring Right
c/o Avery Publishing Group
120 Old Broadway
Garden City Park, NY 11040

Appendix A
Inventory of Personal and Financial Data

Most people are careful about maintaining bits of information and records concerning their personal and financial status. Too often, however, the material is scattered in files or drawers, recorded in places that may be forgotten, or jotted down on scraps of paper that have become outdated and yellowed with age. When the person or the person's family is suddenly confronted with the need for basic information that is necessary to resolve the myriad of physical and financial situations that inevitably occur, the material is often difficult to locate.

The following Inventory of Personal and Financial Data will preclude the possibility of loss or delay when time is of the essence and information must be supplied. If you take the time to fill in all the blanks, you will have everything in one place and you will be in a better position to review and evaluate your own personal and financial position. Also, if ever you are temporarily incapacitated or unable to handle matters because of illness, your family will be able to keep things flowing smoothly.

The time that you spend on the inventory now will certainly be worth the effort. Remember also to check the information from time to time to be certain the inventory is current, and kept with your important papers.

PERSONAL AND FAMILY INFORMATION

	(Date)
	(Name of husband or individual)	(Name of wife or individual)

Full legal name	_____	_____
Address: Number and Street	_____	_____
City, State, Zip Code	_____	_____
Birth date	_____	_____
Place of birth	_____	_____
Father's name	_____	_____
Mother's name	_____	_____
Social Security number	_____	_____
Marital status (Single, married, widowed, separated)	_____	_____
Most recent marriage: Date of marriage	_____	_____
Place of marriage	_____	_____
Date of termination (Death or divorce)	_____	_____
Divorce: Name of previous spouse	_____	_____
Date of divorce	_____	_____
State of jurisdiction	_____	_____
Military service: Branch	_____	_____
Serial number	_____	_____
Date of entry	_____	_____
Date discharged	_____	_____
Place discharged	_____	_____
Disability (Service connected)	_____	_____

Children (including those legally adopted)

Full name	Full address	Birth date	Place of birth	Relationship
_____	_____	_____	_____	_____
	_____			
_____	_____	_____	_____	_____
	_____			
_____	_____	_____	_____	_____
	_____			
_____	_____	_____	_____	_____

Current or Last Employer

	Name	**Address**
	_____	_____
(Dates: From_____		_____
To _____)		_____

Location of Personal and Family Documents

	_____	_____
	(Name of husband or individual)	(Name of wife or individual)

Item(s)	**Location of document**	
Birth certificate	_____	_____
Marriage certificate(s)	_____	_____
Divorce papers	_____	_____
Adoption papers	_____	_____
Naturalization papers	_____	_____

Location of Personal and Family Documents

	(Name of husband or individual)	(Name of wife or individual)
Item(s)	**Location of document**	
Social Security card	_____	_____
Passport	_____	_____
Military records	_____	_____
Will: Original	_____	_____
First copy	_____	_____
Second copy	_____	_____
Paid bills	_____	_____
Past tax returns	_____	_____
Cancelled checks	_____	_____
Stock and bond certificates	_____	_____
Insurance policies: Life	_____	_____
Automobile	_____	_____
Residential	_____	_____
Health	_____	_____
Other _____ (specify)	_____	_____
Pension documents	_____	_____
Bank books	_____	_____
Real property documents	_____	_____
Deed to cemetery plot	_____	_____

PROFESSIONAL CONSULTANTS

Consultant	Name	Address	Phone
Accountant	_____	_____	_____
		_____	
Lawyer	_____	_____	_____
		_____	
Broker	_____	_____	_____
		_____	
Banker or trust officer	_____	_____	_____
		_____	
Insurance agent	_____	_____	_____
_____ (Type of coverage)		_____	
Doctor (Internist)	_____	_____	_____
		_____	
Doctor _____ (Specialty)	_____	_____	_____
		_____	
Doctor _____ (Specialty)	_____	_____	_____
		_____	
Dentist (General)	_____	_____	_____
		_____	
Dentist _____ (Specialty)	_____	_____	_____
		_____	
Minister or rabbi	_____	_____	_____
		_____	

SAVINGS AND CHECKING ACCOUNTS

	Savings Account	Savings Account	Savings Account	Checking Account
Name of bank	_____	_____	_____	_____
Address of bank	_____	_____	_____	_____
	_____	_____	_____	_____
Account number	_____	_____	_____	_____
Individual or joint account? (Name[s])	_____	_____	_____	_____
Location of passbook or check book	_____	_____	_____	_____
Balance as of _____ (Date)	_____	_____	_____	_____

U.S. SAVINGS BONDS

Type (Series E,H, EE, HH)	Serial number	Denom- ination	Owner(s)	Location
_____	_____	_____	_____	_____
_____	_____	_____	_____	_____
_____	_____	_____	_____	_____
_____	_____	_____	_____	_____
_____	_____	_____	_____	_____
_____	_____	_____	_____	_____
_____	_____	_____	_____	_____

RETIREMENT PLANS

	(Name of husband or individual)	(Name of wife or individual)
Are you a member of a retirement plan? (Yes, No)	_____	_____
If yes, name of company or plan	_____	_____
Address	_____	_____
	_____	_____
Telephone number	_____	_____
My pension number	_____	_____
I am currently receiving pension benefits from the following company or plan	_____	_____
Address	_____	_____
	_____	_____
Telephone number	_____	_____
My pension number	_____	_____

INDIVIDUAL RETIREMENT ACCOUNTS (IRAS) & CERTIFICATES OF DEPOSIT (CDS)

	(Name of husband or individual)	(Name of wife or individual)

Individual Retirement Account (IRA):

Name of bank or institution

Address of bank or institution

Account number

Location of passbook or receipt

Balance as of _____
              (Date)

Certificate of Deposit (CD):

Name of bank or institution

Address of bank or institution

Account number

Amount and maturity date

LIFE INSURANCE POLICY(IES) INVENTORY

	Policy		
	1	2	3
Name of insured	_____	_____	_____
Name of company	_____	_____	_____
Policy number	_____	_____	_____
Type: term, cash value, endowment, specialized	_____	_____	_____
Face amount	_____	_____	_____
Beneficiary(ies)	_____	_____	_____
	_____	_____	_____
Current loan, if any	_____	_____	_____
Current cash value, if any	_____	_____	_____
Premium amount	_____	_____	_____
Premium due date(s)	_____	_____	_____
Name of insurance agent	_____	_____	_____
Address of agent	_____	_____	_____
	_____	_____	_____
Telephone number of agent	_____	_____	_____
Location of policy(ies)	_____	_____	_____

ANNUITY(IES) INVENTORY

	Annuity		
	1	2	3
Name of annuity owner	_____	_____	_____
Name of company	_____	_____	_____
Address of company	_____	_____	_____
	_____	_____	_____
Premium amount	_____	_____	_____
Premium due date(s)	_____	_____	_____
Payout Plan	_____	_____	_____
	_____	_____	_____
Income per month	_____	_____	_____
Beneficiary(ies)	_____	_____	_____
	_____	_____	_____
Survivor's rights	_____	_____	_____
Name of agent	_____	_____	_____
Address of agent	_____	_____	_____
	_____	_____	_____
Telephone number of agent	_____	_____	_____
Location of policy(ies)	_____	_____	_____

STOCK INVESTMENTS
AND/OR MUTUAL FUND SHARES

Name of Company or Fund	Number of shares owned	Serial numbers	Date acquired	Cost per share	Total cost	Owner(s)
____	____	____	____	____	____	____
____	____	____	____	____	____	____
____	____	____	____	____	____	____
____	____	____	____	____	____	____
____	____	____	____	____	____	____
____	____	____	____	____	____	____
____	____	____	____	____	____	____

(Continue on a separate sheet)

CORPORATE AND GOVERNMENT BOND HOLDINGS, U.S. TREASURY BILLS, AND NOTES

Issuer	Type	Interest rate	Number owned	Serial numbers	Purchase price	Date bought	Maturity date	Owner(s)
____	____	____	____	____	____	____	____	____
____	____	____	____	____	____	____	____	____
____	____	____	____	____	____	____	____	____
____	____	____	____	____	____	____	____	____
____	____	____	____	____	____	____	____	____
____	____	____	____	____	____	____	____	____
____	____	____	____	____	____	____	____	____

(Continue on a separate sheet)

REAL ESTATE HOLDINGS (INCLUDING YOUR HOME(S))

	Property			
	1	2	3	4
Description of property and address	_____	_____	_____	_____
Form of ownership (solely or jointly owned)	_____	_____	_____	_____
Location of property	_____	_____	_____	_____
Date acquired	_____	_____	_____	_____
Original cost	_____	_____	_____	_____
Down payment	_____	_____	_____	_____
Current market value	_____	_____	_____	_____
Original amount of mortgage	_____	_____	_____	_____
Term of mortgage	_____	_____	_____	_____
Monthly payment	_____	_____	_____	_____
Maturity date of mortgage	_____	_____	_____	_____
Name of mortgagee (lender)	_____	_____	_____	_____
Name(s) of owner(s)	_____	_____	_____	_____

SAFE-DEPOSIT BOX

Every household should rent at least one safe-deposit box for storing important documents and valuable jewelry. Items to be kept in your safe-deposit box include certificates of birth, marriage, divorce, and death; military discharge papers; stock and bond certificates; naturalization papers; copyrights and patents; adoption papers; deeds; mortgages; and jewelry. Your will should be kept in a box rented in your spouse's name and your spouse's will should be kept in a box rented in your name. Usually, a bank seals a box as soon as it learns that the owner has passed away. It is important to note that the contents of a safe-deposit box are not insured. If you wish to insure the contents of your box, you can purchase a separate policy or a rider to one of your other policies. Enter below the information pertaining to your safe-deposit box(es).

Information About Safe-Deposit Box	Box 1	Box 2
Name of bank where it is located	_____	_____
Address of bank	_____	_____
	_____	_____
Box number	_____	_____
Name of deputy who has access to box	_____	_____
Address of deputy	_____	_____
Location of key	_____	_____
Inventory of contents	_____	_____
	_____	_____
	_____	_____
	_____	_____
	_____	_____
	_____	_____

CAPITAL IMPROVEMENTS IN YOUR HOME

Keeping a permanent record of the capital improvements you have made in your home will help to minimize the amount of capital gains subject to tax when you sell your home.

Date	Capital Improvement	Cost

COLLECTIBLES AND VALUABLE POSSESSIONS

	Item			
	1	2	3	4
Description of item				
Original value				
Current value				
Date acquired				
How acquired: purchase, gift, or inheritance				
Location				

CREDIT CARDS

Issuer's name	Account number	Issuer's address	Issuer's phone
_____	_____	_____	_____
		_____	
_____	_____	_____	_____
		_____	
_____	_____	_____	_____
		_____	
_____	_____	_____	_____
		_____	
_____	_____	_____	_____
		_____	
_____	_____	_____	_____
		_____	
_____	_____	_____	_____
		_____	
_____	_____	_____	_____
		_____	
_____	_____	_____	_____
		_____	
_____	_____	_____	_____
		_____	

HEALTH INSURANCE INVENTORY

	(Name of husband or individual)	(Name of wife or individual)

Medicare

Claim number

Hospital insurance (Part A):

Effective date   Effective date

Medical insurance (Part B):

Effective date   Effective date

Medigap insurance

Name(s) of insured

Name of company

Address of company

Policy number

Coverage dates: From—To

Risks covered and amount of each

Premium amount

Premium due date(s)

Name of insurance agent

Address of agent

Telephone number of agent

Other health coverage	Company	Policy number	Premium amount
Basic hospitalization	_____	_____	_____
Basic medical/surgical	_____	_____	_____
Supplementary hospi- talization	_____	_____	_____
Comprehensive major medical	_____	_____	_____
Catastrophe major medical	_____	_____	_____
Disability income insurance	_____	_____	_____
Dental insurance	_____	_____	_____
Optical expense benefits	_____	_____	_____
Hearing aids	_____	_____	_____
Prescription drug plan	_____	_____	_____
Blood program	_____	_____	_____

RESIDENTIAL INSURANCE

Name of company   _____

Address of company   _____

                                         _____

Policy number   _____

Dwelling coverage $ _____

Deductible $ _____

Other structures $ _____

Personal belongings

   a. _____ $ _____

   b. _____ $ _____

   c. _____ $ _____

Valuable items floater

   a. Jewelry $ _____

   b. Fur coats $ _____

   c. Other $ _____

Personal liability $ _____

Medical expenses $ _____

Other

   a. _____ $ _____

   b. _____ $ _____

Coverage dates: From—To   _____

Premium amount $ _____

Premium due date(s)   _____

Residential Insurance

Name of insurance agent _____

Address of agent _____

_____

Telephone number of agent _____

AUTOMOBILE INSURANCE

Car or cars insured _____

Name of company _____

Address of company _____

_____

Policy number _____

Coverage dates: From—To _____

Risks covered and amount of each _____ $ _____

_____ $ _____

_____ $ _____

_____ $ _____

_____ $ _____

Premium amount $ _____

Premium due date(s) _____

Name of insurance agent _____

Address of agent _____

Telephone number of agent _____

INVENTORY OF THE CONTENTS OF YOUR HOME

An updated inventory of the contents of your home should be maintained for insurance purposes as well as for estate planning. Using the format suggested below for the living room, prepare a worksheet for a detailed listing. A similar listing should be prepared for the dining room, master bedroom, second bedroom, third bedroom, bathrooms, den or library, kitchen, basement, and garage. It is also recommended that photographs showing the contents of each area be available. You should also prepare a list for each of the following: jewelry, furs, silverware, dishes, stemware, table and bed linens, personal belongings, and any other valuable possessions, such as art, antiques, and cameras.

Area	Contents	Date acquired	Cost	Current value
Living room	_____	_____	_____	_____
	_____	_____	_____	_____
	_____	_____	_____	_____
	_____	_____	_____	_____
	_____	_____	_____	_____
	_____	_____	_____	_____
Master bedroom	_____	_____	_____	_____
	_____	_____	_____	_____
	_____	_____	_____	_____
	_____	_____	_____	_____
	_____	_____	_____	_____
	_____	_____	_____	_____

(Continue on a separate sheet)

INVENTORY: YOUR WILLS

	(Name of husband or individual)	(Name of wife or individual)
Have you made a will? (Yes, No)		
If yes, date of will		
Executor: Name		
Address		
Telephone number		
Alternate Executor: Name		
Address		
Telephone number		
Have you prepared a supplemental letter of instructions? (Yes, No)		
If yes, note location of the supplemental letter*: Original		
First copy		
Second copy		

*Should be attached to original, first copy, and second copy of your wills.

INVENTORY: TRUSTS

	(Name of husband or individual)	(Name of wife or individual)
Have you created a trust? (Yes, No)	_____	_____
If yes, type (living, testamentary)	_____	_____
Date created	_____	_____
Name of attorney	_____	_____
Address of attorney	_____	_____
	_____	_____
Telephone number of attorney	_____	_____
I am beneficiary of the following trust	_____	_____
Name of Trustee	_____	_____
Address of Trustee	_____	_____
	_____	_____
Telephone number of Trustee	_____	_____

LOCAL OFFICES: SOCIAL SECURITY AND INTERNAL REVENUE SERVICE

Social Security Office*

Enter here the address and phone number of your local Social Security office. If you are in doubt, check your phone book under *Social Security Administration.*

_____

Number and Street

_____

City   State   Zip Code

_____

Phone Number

Internal Revenue Service Office

Enter here the address and phone number of your local Internal Revenue Service office. If you are in doubt, check your phone book under *U.S. Government, Internal Revenue Service.*

_____

Number and Street

_____

City   State   Zip Code

_____

Phone Number

*It is suggested that you phone the Social Security office before you go there. You may be helped on the phone. Even if you must appear in person, your individual circumstances may require specific information that you will then be prepared to provide.

Appendix B
Resources

Now that you have considered all the elements of a retirement plan, you may wish to utilize the variety of resources that are available. For example, you might join a membership organization, such as the American Association of Retired Persons (AARP). Other organizations, listed below with their addresses, can provide you with leads in the areas of education, health, legal services, paid employment, travel, and volunteer work.

MEMBERSHIP ORGANIZATIONS

Action for Independent Maturity (AIM)
1909 K Street, N.W.
Washington, D.C. 20049
(202) 872-4850

AIM offers actively employed people between the ages of 50 and 65 a wealth of useful information about money management, health matters, leisure possibilities, and other issues, the successful management of which can make life more enjoyable and satisfying. AIM is a division of AARP.

**American Association
of Retired Persons (AARP)**
1909 K Street, N.W.
Washington, D.C. 20049
(202) 872-4700

AARP is the nation's largest and most experienced organization of older persons. More than 2,400 chapters work for local community welfare, and provide educational and social programs for members. Persons who are 50 years of age or older, and actively employed, semi-retired, or retired are eligible to join AARP.

American Society on Aging (ASA)
833 Market Street, Room 516
San Francisco, CA 94103
(415) 543-2617

ASA is a nonprofit organization that strives to improve the well-being of senior citizens and to promote unity among those working with and for older Americans. The society monitors legislation affecting the elderly and issues policy recommendations for consideration at all levels of government. It operates ASA Answers, an information service that provides access to aging resources. The ASA newsletter, *ASA Connection*, is distributed free to members and is available to nonmembers by subscription. There are no local chapters. Inquiries should be directed to headquarters in San Francisco.

Gray Panthers
311 South Juniper Street
Philadelphia, PA 19107
(213) 438-0276

Founded for the purpose of fighting "ageism," discrimination against people on the basis of chronological age, it advises and organizes 70,000 members of all ages in more than 80 local chapters nationwide. Members advocate for better housing, the rights of the disabled, and the expansion of health care programs. The group conducts seminars and research on issues affecting older Americans. Its publications include *Health Watch* and a newspaper, *Gray Panther Network*. For membership information and the location of the chapter nearest you, contact headquarters in Philadelphia.

Institute for Puerto Rican/Hispanic Elderly
105 East 22 Street, Room 401
New York, N.Y. 10010

Founded in 1979, the institute is a nonprofit organization whose mission is the improvement of the quality of life for Puetro Rican and Hispanic elderly. It provides direct services and referral through its bilingual staff. It also offers access to government entitlements and benefits, and provides its clients with advocacy, training, and information.

**National Caucus and Center
on the Black Aged, Inc.**
1424 K Street, N.W.
Washington, D.C. 20005
(202) 637-8400

This group seeks to improve the standard of living for all older Americans and especially for blacks. It supports changes to raise economic, health, and social status of lower-income senior citizens; provides consultation to members; sponsors employment programs in eleven states; publishes *Golden Pages*, available to members

only. Contact headquarters in Washington, D.C. for membership information.

National Council of Senior Citizens
925 15th Street, N.W.
Washington, D.C. 20005
(202) 347-8800

An advocacy group dedicated to fighting for the interests and concerns of its members, the council supports increased Social Security benefits, better housing for older Americans, improved education and health programs, and Medicare. It offers advice and assistance to help members resolve specific problems; sponsors rallies and educational workshops. All members automatically receive *Senior Citizen News*; nonmembers may request a free sample copy. For information about state and local affiliates, contact headquarters in Washington, D.C.

**National Retired Teachers
Association (NRTA)**
1909 K Street, N.W.
Washington, D.C. 20049
(202) 872-4700

A division of AARP, NRTA is open to all retired (and active) teachers and educators. Services offered include group hospital insurance, tax assistance, consumer and health education, consultation/information services, and preretirement planning. Members are also eligible for discounts at certain hotel and motel chains and from rental car companies. Distributes the same publications as AARP.

Older Women's League
666 11th Street, N.W.
Washington, D.C. 20001
(202) 783-6686

Membership consists of middle-aged and older women plus those who share the league's concerns. Through educational materials and speakers bureaus, the league brings to public attention the need for reform in such areas as job and pension availability for older women, long-term care and health insurance for the uninsured, and support for family caregivers. The league's publication, *OWL Observer*, is distributed free to members.

EDUCATION

**Adult Education Association
of the U.S.A.**
810 18th Street, N.W.
Washington, D.C. 20006

**College Level Examination
Program (CLEP)**
Educational Testing Service
Princeton, New Jersey 08540

**National Association for Public Continuing
& Adult Education**
1201 16th Street, N.W.
Washington, D.C. 20036

National Home Study Council
1601 18th Street, N.W.
Washington, D.C. 20009

**University of Kentucky Writing Workshop
for People Over 57**
Council on Aging
University of Kentucky
Lexington, KY 40506

U.S. Department of Education
Bureau of Adult, Vocational & Library
Programs
Seventh and D Streets, S.W.
Washington, D.C. 20202

HEALTH

**Alzheimer's Disease and Related Disorders
Association, Inc.**
360 North Michigan Avenue
Chicago, Illinois 60601

American Association of Homes for the Aging
1050 17th Street, N.W.
Washington, D.C. 20036

American Cancer Society, Inc.
777 Third Avenue
New York, N.Y. 10017

American Dental Association
211 E. Chicago Avenue
Chicago, IL 60611

American Dietetic Association
430 N. Michigan Avenue
Chicago, IL 60611

American Foundation for the Blind
15 W. 16th Street
New York, N.Y. 10011

American Heart Association
44 East 23rd Street
New York, N.Y. 10010

**American Health Care Association
(Nursing Homes)**
1200 15th Street, N.W.
Washington, D.C. 20005

American Optometric Association
7000 Chippewa Street
St. Louis, MO 63119

American Podiatry Association
20 Chevy Chase Circle, N.W.
Washington, D.C. 20015

American Speech and Hearing Association
9030 Old Georgetown Road, N.W.
Washington, D.C. 20014

Arthritis Foundation
221 Park Avenue South
New York, N.Y. 10003

National Association of Jewish Homes
for the Aged
2525 Centerville Road
Dallas, Texas 75228

National Cancer Institute
Office of Cancer Communications
Bethesda, MD 20205

LEGAL SERVICES

American Bar Association
1155 East 60th Street
Chicago, Illinois 60637

National Legal Aid
and Defenders Association
2100 M Street, N.W.
Washington, D.C. 20037

National Senior Citizens Law Center
1709 W. Eighth Street
Los Angeles, CA 90017

PAID EMPLOYMENT

Green Thumb, Inc.
1012 14th Street, N.W.
Washington, D.C. 20005

Mature Temps
Exxon Building
1251 Avenue of the Americas
New York, N.Y. 10020

National Council of Senior Citizens
925 15th Street, N.W.
Washington, D.C. 20005

National Council on the Aging
1828 L Street, N.W.
Washington, D.C. 20036

U.S. Small Business Administration
409 Third Street, S.W.
Washington, D.C. 20416

TRAVEL

BritRail Travel International Inc.
630 Third Avenue
New York, N.Y. 10017

Elderhostel
100 Boyleston Street, Suite 200
Boston, MA 02116

Eurail Pass
c/o French National Railroad
610 Fifth Avenue
New York, N.Y. 10020

Farm and Ranch Vacations, Inc.
36 East 57 Street
New York, N.Y. 10022

Floating Through Europe
271 Madison Avenue
New York, N.Y. 10016

RECREATION

National Recreation and Park
Association (NRPA)
2775 S. Quincy Street
Arlington, VA 22206-2204
(703) 820-4940

Founded in 1965, NRPA is a public interest organization dedicated to improving the human environment through improved park, recreation, and leisure opportunities. Activities include programs for the development and upgrading of professional and citizen leadership in the park, recreation, and leisure field; dissemination of innovations and research results; technical assistance to affiliated organizations, local communities, and members; information on public policy and public education. Has an annual conference, always in October.

U.S. Department of the Interior
National Park Service
18th and C Streets, N.W.
Washington, D.C. 20240

Anyone 62 or over can obtain a *Golden Age Passport*—a free lifetime entrance pass to national parks, monuments, historic sites, and recreation areas administered by the federal government. The pass also provides for a 50 percent discount on fees charged for use of facilities and services (parking, boating, and camping). It does not cover fees levied by private concessionaires. The passport can be obtained from the office above or from most federally operated recreation areas or National Park Service Regional Offices. Applicants must appear in person with proof of age (driver's license, birth certificate, or Medicare card). Contact the Information Office at the Washington office for the address of the office nearest you.

Anyone who has been medically determined to be blind or permanently disabled and is eligible to received federal benefits can obtain a *Golden Access Passport*. This is a free lifetime entrance pass that provides the same privileges as the Golden Age Passport. Applicants must apply in person and provide proof of disability.

VOLUNTEER WORK

ACTION
1100 Vermont Avenue, N.W.
Washington, D.C. 20525
(202) 393-3111

ACTION is the principal Federal agency for sponsorship of volunteer programs. It administers several programs in which older volunteers may participate. Among them are the following:

Retired Senior Volunteer Program (RSVP). The goal of this program is to establish a recognized role in the community and a meaningful life in retirement by developing a wide variety of community volunteer-service opportunities for persons 60 years of age or over. It provides grants to public and private nonprofit organizations.

Foster Grandparent Program. The goal of this program is to provide part-time volunteer opportunities for those age 60 and over and to render supportive person-to-person services in health, education, welfare, and related residential settings to children with special needs.

Service Corps of Retired Executives (SCORE), and Active Corps of Executives (ACE). The goal of these programs is to provide advisory and counseling services for the benefit of new and existing small businesses, as well as nonprofit community organizations, by utilizing the management experience of retired and semi-retired (SCORE) and active (ACE) business executives.

Volunteers in Service to America (VISTA). The goal of this program is to provide specialized services, training, advisory services, and counsel to supplement efforts of community organizations working to eliminate poverty. VISTA enables individuals from all walks of life and all age groups to perform meaningful and constructive service as volunteers in situations where they help to overcome the handicaps of poverty and secure opportunities for self-advancement.

Senior Companion Program. The goal of this program is to provide part-time volunteer opportunities for persons age 60 and over and to provide supportive person-to-person services to persons (other than children) with special needs, especially older persons living in their own homes, and in nursing homes and other institutions.

If any of the foregoing programs interests you, contact ACTION for further information.

National Council of Senior Citizens
925 15th Street, N.W.
Washington, D.C. 20005

Offers part-time work in community service agencies involved in activities ranging from child care and adult education to home health and homemaker services.

National Council on the Aging
1828 L Street, N.W.
Washington, D.C. 20036

Provides part-time work in Social Security and state employment service offices, public housing, libraries, hospitals, schools, and food and nutrition programs. Also provides escort, homemaker, and home-repair services.

National School Volunteer Program
300 N. Washington Street
Alexandria, VA 22314

Offers information on how to start or join a school volunteer program.

Appendix C
Suggested Readings

This appendix presents suggested readings relevant to each chapter of the book. The publications enumerated in each subject area were carefully selected to provide the reader with the most informative and up-to-date knowledge. If you wish to delve more deeply into a particular topic, any of the sources suggested would be valuable. The use of this bibliography will help you to expand your knowledge in specialized areas of retirement planning.

First Facts

Butler, Robert N. *Why Survive? Being Old in America.* New York: Harper and Row, 1975.

Schultz, James H. *The Economics of Aging.* 2nd ed. Belmont, CA: Wadsworth Publishing Co., Inc., 1980.

U.S. Department of Commerce, Bureau of the Census, Suitland, MD. Periodic research reports on population characteristics.

U.S. Department of Health and Human Services, National Center for Health Statistics, Hyattsville, MD. Life expectancy statistics.

U.S. Senate, Special Committee on Aging. *Aging America: Trends and Projections.* Washington, DC: 1992.

Chapter 1
Working in Retirement

Hoffman, Ray. *Extra Dollars: Easy Money-Making Ideas for Retired People.* New York: Stein and Day, 1977.

Kleiman, Carol. *The 100 Best Jobs for the 1990s*
and Beyond. Chicago: Dearborn Financial Publishing, 1992.

Marsh, DeLoss L. ed. by Susan Williamson and Roger Griffith. *Retirement Careers: Combining the Best of Work and Leisure.* Charlotte, VT: Williamson Publishing Co., 1991.

May, Bess Ritter. *Starting and Operating a Business After You Retire: What You Need to Know to Succeed.* Garden City Park, NY: Avery Publishing Group, Inc., 1993.

Chapter 2
Playing in Retirement

Allison, Maria. *Play, Leisure and Quality of Life.* Dubuque, IA: Kendall Hunt, 1992.

Flatten, Kate, et al. *Recreation Activities for the Elderly.* New York: Springer, 1988.

Gault, Jan. *Free Time: Making Your Leisure Count.* New York: John Wiley and Sons, 1983.

Heise, Jon O. and Julia R. Rinehart. *Travel*

Book: Guide to the Travel Guides. Pawtucket, RI: Scarecrow, 1993.

St. Clair, Allison. *Travel and Older Adults.* Santa Barbara, CA: ABC-CLIO, 1991.

Chapter 3
Retirement Housing

American Association of Retired Persons. *Home-Made Money: Consumer's Guide to Home Equity Conversion.* Washington, DC: 1991.

American Business Directories Staff. *Retirement Communities and Homes, 1993.* Omaha, NE: American Business Directories, 1993.

Golant, Stephen M. *Housing America's Elderly: Many Possibilities, Few Choices.* Thousand Oaks, CA: Sage, 1992.

Katsura, Harold M., et al. *Housing for the Elderly in 2010: Projections and Policy Options.* Washington, DC: Urban Institute, 1989.

Lewis, Evelyn L. *Housing Decisions.* South Holland, IL: Goodheart-Willcox Co., 1993.

U.S. Department of Housing and Urban Development. *Options for Elderly Homeowners: A Guide to Reverse Mortgages and Their Alternatives.* Washington, DC: 1989.

Valins, Martin. *Housing for Elderly People.* New York: Van Nostrand Reinhold, 1988.

Chapter 4
Care Facilities

American Business Directories Staff. *Nursing Homes 1993.* Rev. ed. Omaha, NE: American Business Directory, 1993.

Health Care Financing Administration. *Medicare/Medicaid Nursing Home Information.* 75 volumes. Washington, DC: U.S. Government Printing Office, 1988.

Innis, Pauline. *Nursing Home Companion.* Arlington, VA: Seven Locks Press, 1993.

Joiner, Charles M. *Nursing Home Adjustment and Satisfaction.* New York: Garland, 1991.

Manning, Doug. *Nursing Home Dilemma: How to Make One of Love's Toughest Decisions.* New York: Harper and Row, 1986.

Chapter 5
Legal Affairs

American Bar Association. *Your Rights Over Age 50.* Chicago: American Bar Association Press, 1981. Pamphlet.

Curry, Hadyn and Denis Clifford. *Legal Guide for Lesbian and Gay Couples.* Berkeley, CA: Nolo Press, 1992.

Josephson-Millman, Linda and Sallie C. Birket. *Legal Issues and Older Adults.* Santa Barbara, CA: ABC-Clio, Inc., 1992.

Lane, Marc J. *Legal Handbook for Small Business.* New York: Amacom, 1989.

Reader's Digest Family Legal Guide: A Complete Encyclopedia of Law for the Layman. Pleasantville, NY: The Reader's Digest Association, Inc., 1981.

Very, Donald and Eugene F. Keefe. *Legal Guide for the Family.* Chicago: Ferguson, 1993.

Chapter 6
Savings and Investments

Bodie, Zvi, et al. *Essentials of Investments.* Homewood, IL: Irwin, 1992.

Breitbard, Stanley H. and Donna Sammons Carpenter. *The Price Waterhouse Book of Personal Financial Planning.* New York: Henry Holt and Co., 1988.

Case, Samuel. *The First Book of Investing: The Absolute Beginner's Guide to Building Wealth Safely.* Rocklin, CA: Prima Publishing, 1994.

Fredman, Albert J. and Russ Wiles. *How Mutual Funds Work.* New York: Institute of Finance, 1993.

Gup, Benton E. *Basics of Investing.* 5th ed. New York: John Wiley and Sons, 1992.

Hogan, Linda. *Savings*. Minneapolis, MN: Coffee Hse., 1988.

Kapoor, Jack H., Les R. Dlabay, and Robert J. Hughes. *Personal Finance*. 2nd ed. Homewood, IL: Irwin, 1991.

Klott, Gary L. *Complete Guide to Personal Investing*. New York: Times Books, 1987.

Levitt, J. Stanley. *A Beginner's Guide to Investing in No-Load Mutual Funds*. Chicago: International Publishing Corp., 1993.

Martin, J. Michael. *Life After CDs: How to Double the Return on Your Savings With Government-Backed Safety*. Ellicott City, MD: Financial Advantage, Inc., 1993.

McInerney, Ralph. *Savings and Loan*. Thorndike, ME: Thorndike Press, 1990.

Tucker, David M. *The Decline of Thrift in America: Our Cultural Shift From Saving to Spending*. Westport, CT: Praeger, 1990.

Tucker, James F. *Buying Treasury Securities at Federal Reserve Banks*. Federal Reserve Bank of Richmond, P.O. Box 27622, Richmond, VA 23261. Free.

Chapter 7
Social Security

Aaron, Henry J. *Economic Effects of Social Security*. Washington, DC: The Brookings Institution, 1982.

Bernstein, Merton C. and Joan Brodshaug Bernstein. *Social Security: The System That Works*. New York: Basic Books, 1988.

Brain, Charles M. *Social Security at the Crossroads: Public Opinion & Public Policy*. New York: Garland, 1991.

Hardy, Dorcas and C. Colburn Hardy. *Social Insecurity: The Crisis in America's Social Security System and How to Plan Now For Your Own Financial Survival*. New York: Villard Books, 1991.

Light, Paul H. *Artful Work: The Politics of Social Security Reform*. New York: Random House, 1985.

Matthews, Joseph and Dorothy M. Berman. *Social Security, Medicare and Pensions: A Sourcebook for Older Americans*. Berkeley, CA: Nolo Press, 1990.

Steuerle, C. Eugene and Jon M. Bakija. *Retooling Social Security for the Twenty-First Century: Right and Wrong Approaches to Reform*. Washington, DC: Urban Institute, 1994.

U.S. Department of Health and Human Services, Social Security Administration, Washington, DC. *Thinking About Retiring?* Periodical.

————*What You Have to Know About SSI*. Periodical.

————*Your Social Security*. Periodical.

Chapter 8
Pensions

Allen, Everett T. Jr., et al. *Pension Planning: Pensions, Profit-Sharing, and Other Deferred Compensation Plans*. 7th ed. Homewood, IL: Business One Irwin, 1992.

Andrews, Emily S. *The Changing Profile of Pensions in America*. Washington, DC: Employee Benefit Research Institute, 1985.

Burkhauser, Richard V. *Pensions in a Changing Economy*. Washington, DC: Employee Benefit Research Institute, 1993.

Internal Revenue Service. *Pension and Annuity Income*. Publication #575. Washington, DC: Annual.

Kotlikoff, Laurence J. and Daniel E. Smith. *Pensions in the American Economy*. New York: National Bureau of Economic Research, 1983.

Mansfield, Clay B. and Timothy W. Cunningham. *Pension Funds: A Commonsense Guide to a Common Goal*. Homewood, IL: Business One Irwin, 1992.

U.S. Department of Labor, Pension and Welfare

Benefits Administration. *What You Should Know About the Pension Law.* Washington, DC: 1988.

Chapter 9
Annuities

Institute of Financial Education Staff. *Annuities, Mutual Funds and Life Insurance.* Chicago: Institute of Financial Education, 1988.

Internal Revenue Service. *Pension and Annuity Income.* Publication #575. Washington, DC: Annual.

Shapiro, David and Thomas F. Streiff. *Annuities.* Chicago: Dearborn Financial Publishing, Inc., 1992.

U.S. Department of Agriculture. *Building Your Future With Annuities: A Consumer's Guide.* Washington, DC: 1991.

Chapter 10
Budgeting

Kapoor, Jack H., Les R. Dlabay and Robert J. Hughes. *Personal Finance.* 2nd ed. Homewood, IL: Irwin, 1991.

Lawrence, Judy. *The Budget Kit.* Chicago: Dearborn Financial Publishing, 1993.

McVey & Associates Staff. *Budgeting.* Englewood Cliffs, NJ: Cambridge, 1988.

Quinn, Jane Bryant. *Making the Most of Your Money.* New York: Simon & Schuster, 1991.

U.S. Department of Labor, Bureau of Labor Statistics. *Budget for Retired Couples.* Washington, DC: Periodic.

Chapter 11
Credit

Board of Governors, Federal Reserve System. *Consumer Handbook on Credit Protection Laws.* Washington, DC: 1992.

Kimmel, Jay. *Credit, Bankruptcy and Living*

Will. Portland, OR: Corey-Stevens Pub., 1993.

Parker, Allan A. *Credit, Debt & Bankruptcy.* 8th ed. Bellingham, WA: ISC Pr., 1990.

Strong, Howard. *Credit Cards: How You Can Have All You Deserve!* Beverly Hills, CA: Boswell, 1994.

Williams, John J. ed. by Laurie Williams. *Credit Card Scams.* Alamogordo, NM: Consumertronics, 1992.

Chapter 12
Inflation

Beckerman, Paul. *The Economics of Inflation.* New York: St. Martin, 1992.

Galarza, Vicente D. *Inflation and Decision Making.* New York: Vantage, 1992.

Hahn, Frank. *Money and Inflation.* Cambridge, MA: The Massachusetts Institute of Technology Press, 1984.

Hall, Robert E., ed. *Inflation: Causes and Effects.* Chicago: University of Chicago Press, 1982.

McNabb, Robert and Chris McKenna. *Inflation in Modern Economies.* New York: St. Martin, 1990.

Smith, Michael R. *Power, Norms and Inflation: A Skeptical Treatment.* Hawthorne, NY: Aldine de Gruyter, 1992.

Chapter 13
Taxes and Tax Shelters

Taxes

American Association for Retired Persons. *Relocation Tax Guide: State Tax Information for Relocation Decisions.* Washington, DC: 1991.

Internal Revenue Service. Washington, DC. *Investment Income and Expenses.* Pub. #558. Annual.

————*Tax Information for Older Americans.* Pub. #554. Annual.

Rogers, Glenn F. *Taxes Made Easy: A Simple Step by Step Guide to Income Tax Preparation.* Redlands, CA: Simpson & Brooks, 1992.

Tax Shelters

Andersen, Arthur Inc. *Tax Shelters: The Basics.* Chicago: Andersen, 1985.

Law & Business Inc. *Tax Shelter Controversies.* San Diego, CA: Harcourt Brace Jovanovich, 1983.

Westin, R. *Tax Shelters for the Middle Class.* New York: McGraw-Hill, 1982.

Chapter 14
Life Insurance

Baldwin, Ben G. and Maureen M. Baldwin. *Insurance as an Investment: Getting the Most for Your Money.* Chicago: Probus Publishing Co., 1991.

Black, Kenneth, Jr. and Harold Skipper. *Life Insurance.* 12th ed. Englewood Cliffs, NJ: Prentice-Hall, 1993.

D'Amico, Raymond A. and Harold Luckstone, Jr. *Life Insurance Primer.* Hauppauge, NY: Werbel Publishing, 1992.

Dorfman, Mark and Saul Adelman. *Life Insurance: A Financial Planning Approach.* 2nd ed. Chicago: Dearborn Financial Publishing, 1991.

Lieberman, Trudy and Consumer Reports Book Editors. *Life Insurance.* Yonkers, NY: Consumer Reports, 1988.

Liner, John, ed. *Insurance Buyer's Handbook.* Saint Paul, MN: Standard Publishing Co., 1992.

O'Donnell, Jeffrey P. *Insurance Smart: How to Buy the Right Insurance at the Right Price.* New York: John Wiley and Sons, 1991.

Chapter 15
Health Insurance

Chasen, Nancy H. *Policy Wise: The Practical Guide to Insurance Decisions for Older Consumers.* Glenview, IL: Scott, Foresman and Company, 1983.

Enteen, Robert. *Health Insurance: How to Get It, Keep It, or Improve What You've Got.* New York: Paragon Hse, 1992.

Lynch, Margaret, ed. *Health Insurance Terminology: A Glossary of Health Insurance Terms.* Washington, DC: Health Insurance Association of America, 1992.

Mayer, Thomas R. and Gloria G. Mayer. *Health Insurance Alternative: A Guide to Health Maintenance Organizations.* New York: Putnam Publishing Group, 1984.

Mills, Miriam K. and Robert H. Blank. *Health Insurance and Public Policy: Risk, Allocation and Equity.* Westport, CT: Greenwood Press, 1992.

Thomas, Larry. *Health Insurance: What You Don't Know About It Can Hurt You!* Newtown, CT: Quest Communications, 1993.

Chapter 16
Medicare and Medicaid

Budish, Armond D. "Medicaid: Middle Class Need Not Apply," *Modern Maturity*, June 1994.

"How a Spenddown Works," *Consumer Reports*, June 1991.

Inlander, Charles B. *Medicare Made Easy* 3rd ed. Redding, MA: Addison-Wesley, 1992.

Lemov, Penelope. "States and Medicaid: Ahead of the Feds," *Governing*, July 1993.

"Medicare Under Siege," *Consumer Reports*, September 1994.

U.S. Department of Health and Human Services. *The Medicare Handbook*, Washington, DC: U.S. Government Printing Office, 1994.

Chapter 17
Medigap and Long-Term Care Insurance

Evensky, Harold and Deena Katz. *Planning for*

Long-Term Health Care. Port Washington, NY: Lee Simmons Associates, 1994.

Hellman, Susan and Leonard H. Hellman. *Medicare and Medigaps: A Guide to Retirement Health Insurance.* Thousand Oaks, CA: Sage, 1991.

National Association of Insurance Commissioners. *A Shopper's Guide to Long-Term Care Insurance.* Kansas City, MO, 1993.

National Committee to Preserve Social Security and Medicare. *Buying Your Medigap Policy.* Washington, DC, 1992.

Wilcox, Melynda Dovel. "Smart Shopping for Medigap Coverage," *Kiplinger's Personal Finance Magazine,* April 1994.

Chapter 18
Estate Planning

Clifford, Denis. *Plan Your Estate: Wills, Probate Avoidance, Trusts & Taxes.* Berkeley, CA: Nolo Press, 1989.

Kahn, Arnold D. *Family Security Through Estate Planning.* 2nd ed. New York: McGraw-Hill, 1983.

Koren, E.F. *Estate and Personal Financial Planning.* Deerfield, IL: Calaghan & Co., 1992.

Leimberg, Stephan R., et. al. *The Tools and Techniques of Estate Planning.* 5th ed. Cincinnati, OH: The National Underwriter Co., 1985.

Moy, Doug H. *Estate Planning: Simplified Coursebook.* New York: John Wiley and Sons, 1992.

Whitney, Victor P. *Estate Planning in the Nineties.* Glendale, CA: Fiduciary FL, 1989.

Chapter 19
Minimizing Estate Taxes

Clifford, Denis. *Plan Your Estate: Wills, Pro-bate Avoidance, Trusts & Taxes.* Berkeley, CA: Nolo Press, 1989.

Dunlap, Susan. *Death and Taxes.* New York: Delacorte, 1992.

Hughes, Theodore and David Klein. *How to Use the Various Forms of Ownership to Reduce Your Taxes, Preserve Your Assets, and Protect Your Survivors.* New York: Charles Scribner's Sons, 1984.

Internal Revenue Service. *Federal Estate and Gift Taxes.* Publication 448. Washington, DC: Annual.

Nigito, D. *Avoiding the Estate Tax Trap.* Chicago: Contemporary Books, 1991.

Pennsylvania Bar Institute. *Taxes Affecting Decedents' Estates.* Harrisburg, PA: Pennsylvania Bar Institute, 1989.

Chapter 20
Trusts

Crouch, Holmes F. *Trusts & Trustees: Tax Guide 305.* Saratoga, CA: Allyear Tax Guides, 1993.

Evans, Michael. *Trusts.* Salem, NH: Butterworth Legal Publications, 1989.

HALT, Inc. (An Organization of Americans for Legal Reform). *Trusts: A Guide to Trust Options for Avoiding Probate and Taxes.* Washington, DC: 1991.

Insall, Howard K. *Trusts.* 2nd ed. Holmes Beach, FL: W.W. Gaunt, 1991.

MacLean, D.M. *Trusts and Powers.* Holmes Beach, FL: W.W. Gaunt, 1989.

Chapter 21
Probate

American Association of Retired Persons. *A Consumer's Guide to Probate.* Washington, DC: 1989.

Dacey, Norman F. *How to Avoid Probate:*

Updated. New York: Crown Publishers, 1990.

Donnelly, K. *Probate Procedure Notes.* New York: Macmillan, 1988.

HALT, Inc. (An Organization of Americans for Legal Reform). *Probate: A Practical Guide for Settling an Estate.* Washington, DC: 1986.

National Association of Legal Secretaries. *Probate Handbook.* Saint Paul, MN: West Publishing Co., 1993.

Schumacher, Vickie and Jim Schumacher. *Understanding Living Trusts: How to Avoid Probate, Save Taxes & More.* Los Angeles, CA: Schumacher Co., 1990.

Chapter 22
Preparing for the Inevitable

Backer, Barbara A. et al. *Death and Dying: Understanding and Care.* 2nd ed. Albany, NY: Delmar, 1993.

Clignet, Remi. *Death, Deeds, and Descendants: Inheritance in Modern America.* Hawthorne, NY: Aldine de Gruyter, 1992.

Dickenson, Donna and Malcolm Johnson. *Death, Dying and Bereavement.* Thousand Oaks, CA: Sage, 1993.

Nelson, Thomas C. *It's Your Choice: The Practical Guide to Planning a Funeral.* Glenview, IL: Scott, Foresman and Co., 1983.

Index